CONTENTS

D1294323

FIGURES

TABLES

PREFACE

Whitechapel has not fared well with history. Stereotyped if not neglected, it has stayed a shadowy and myth-ridden place. In this book Derek Morris sets about shedding some historical light. Through systematic, thorough and, above all, indefatigable documentary research he takes hold of a broad range of material from two centuries of the recent past of a complex, variegated and mutating district, peoples it with communities and individuals, and organizes its affairs into intelligible categories.

His sources, both primary and secondary, are numerous, but, as in his earlier work on other parts of east London, he makes especially enlightening use of Land Tax returns, wills and inventories. The subjects of investigation range from servants to freemasons, silk throwsters to butchers, bell foundries to bagnios, sugar refining to gun making, the Hay Market to the Rag Fair, and the London Hospital to the Tower Hamlets Militia. Merchants, their careers and networks, and industries are strong elements in the story.

Whitechapel, it is clear, has long been cosmopolitan. This book helps to give Whitechapel a stronger historical identity, and has wider value for all those interested in London and early-modern urban history more generally.

Peter Guillery
The Survey of London

AUTHOR'S NOTE

This is the third book in a series which later will include Ratcliff and Shadwell. By using a wide variety of archival material a new picture is emerging which is challenging many of the well-established stereotypes that purport to describe London's eastern parishes in the eighteenth century. By using the land tax and other records it is now possible to understand these eastern suburbs on a street by street basis and Chapter 14 summarises many of our initial conclusions.

As with the earlier books my objective is to explore the lives of the people living in Whitechapel and closely adjoining areas with the emphasis on the period between 1700 and 1800. Professor John Marriott is the latest historian to provide "a history of East London since its emergence as a distinct area of the metropolis in the eighteenth century to its postwar decline". There has been no detailed investigation of Whitechapel though there is a specialist literature on gun-making, glass-making, silk-weaving, sugar refining and aspects of the Poor Law. Indeed the only hamlets and parishes east of London that have received detailed studies in the past thirty years are seventeenth-century Shadwell, Mile End Old Town and Wapping in the eighteenth century, several studies of Spitalfields and the Isle of Dogs, and a detailed study of family structure in seventeenth-century Aldgate.

Whitechapel cannot be understood without a deep appreciation of the importance in the eighteenth century of family based groups of merchants. We now know they were supplying Londoners with meat, cheese, beer, hay, soap and other essentials; were trading with suppliers in the Home Counties, and on a world-wide basis in sugar, timber, rum and slaves. Equally importantly they were taking the large victualling contracts for the army and Royal Navy.

After many names, dates appear in two forms; either as [1727-63], which records the birth and death of the person named, or as (1754-63), which records the dates that they paid the land tax. Not all persons in the Tables have been indexed. A detailed glossary is included. Generally "Stepney" is used as shorthand for the area between the Tower and the river Lea and between the Whitechapel Road and the north bank of the Thames.

The National Archives web site has a currency calculator which indicates that £1 in 1750 is worth £85.16 in 2011. Broadly the pound in 1700 is now worth £78.09 and the pound in 1800 is now worth £32.17.

The main abbreviations used are BL British Library, London, C18 for eighteenth century, CMH for the Centre for Metropolitan History, DNB for the Dictionary of National Biography, EICo for the East India Company, HAC for the Honourable Artillery Company, HBC for the Hudson's Bay Company, MEOT for Mile End Old Town, OBIN for the Oxford Biography Index, PCC for the Prerogative Court of Canterbury, RSA for the Royal Society of Arts, Manufactures and Commerce, SPCK for Society for Promoting Christian Knowledge, THM for Tower Hamlets Militia, TNA for The National Archives at Kew, and VCH for the Victoria County History of Middlesex.

Additions and comment on any aspect of our research of these fascinating inner London suburbs are welcome and we hope it will encourage similar studies of other London parishes.

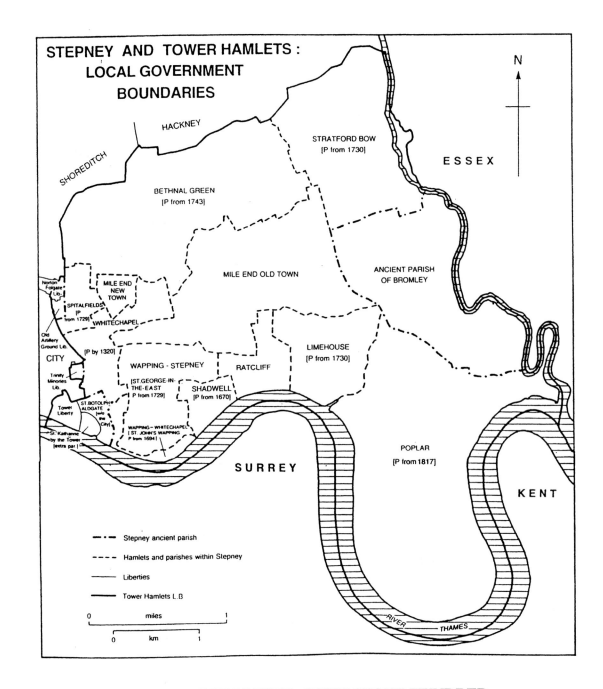

Figure 1   MIDDLESEX: OSSULSTONE HUNDRED

1. INTRODUCTION

Introduction – early views

In the eighteenth century (C18), Whitechapel had a population of about 25,000, double the size of Hull and about the same size as Glasgow and Liverpool.[1] In spite of its size, and the importance of its industries and service facilities to the economy of London, it has been neglected by historians. Modern perceptions of eighteenth-century Whitechapel rarely mention the people who lived there; millionaires such as Samuel Perry, Fellows of the Royal Society such as Samuel Jackson, the authors of text books and dictionaries, or the entrepreneurial merchants. Instead, judging by the success of tourist guides in the area, modern views are dominated by its association with Dick Turpin, Jack the Ripper, and more recently the Kray brothers. For academics the unrivalled Old Bailey records have provided additional material to explore London's criminal underclass. However, many other extensive archives need to be examined, such as the land tax, which was created in 1692, lists of victuallers and freeholders, insurance records and newspapers, to provide a more rounded picture of life in Whitechapel.

In 1777 John Noorthouck, wrote of the parishes to the east of the Tower that they were *chiefly inhabited by seafaring persons, and those whose business depends upon shipping in various capacities, are in general close and ill-built: therefore afford very little worthy [of] observation, except the parish churches.* Noorthouck ideas were still prevalent two hundred years later for Guillery relates that "Classically, early modern suburbs housed the poor and transient; to reach the suburbs was always to take a step downwards".[2]

But what was the area really like in the eighteenth century? This book attempts to answer this and similar questions with its emphasis on the people who lived and worked in Whitechapel, their origins, education, occupations, social and commercial networks, and religious interests. The success of this research depends on the methodology described later.

From 1320 to 1600

The parish of Whitechapel was created in 1320, when an area of 211 acres was taken from the great mediaeval parish of Stepney; and its early history is well described in the VCH, *History of the County of Middlesex*, vol. XI. As now, the dominant feature was the High Street, which led east from Aldgate towards Mile End Old Town, Stratford, and the east coast port of Harwich.

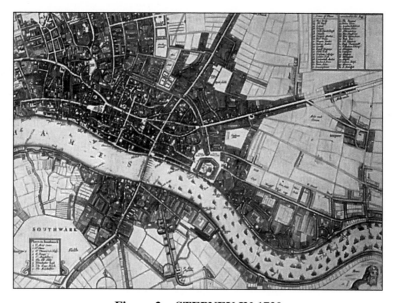

Figure 2   STEPNEY IN 1720

In 1572 Braun and Hogenberg's map of London showed that to the east of Aldgate there were a few houses scattered along the Great Essex Road, surrounded to the north and south by open fields.

Not shown on the map were the many taverns and a theatre. It was a common practice at this time for bands of actors to perform in the central yards of the larger inns such as the Boar's Head tavern in Whitechapel. This was one of the first two inns recorded as being used as a playhouse; the other was in Islington. The Boar's Head from 1557 until at least 1608 offered its patrons theatrical performances. Roaming actors would build a temporary platform in the yard and then drape curtains from the gallery above; thus creating space for a changing room. In 1597 the stage at the Boar's Head "occupied much of the former inn yard and was surrounded with new galleries on three sides, with the existing inn gallery on the fourth. The galleries and stage were roofed." Clearly, a significant attraction to Londoners and visitors.

Stephen Porter in his scintillating book *Shakespeare's London*, states that "The first purpose-built playhouse [in London] was the Red Lion, erected on the south side of Whitechapel High Street in 1567. Described as a 'messuage or farme house', the building had a turret 30 feet high and tiers of galleries. The builder was John Brayne, a grocer and brother-in-law of the actor and impresario James Burbage". So the theatre in Whitechapel preceded the much vaunted Globe Theatre built in 1598-9.[3]

John Stow, an early historian of London, writing in the last year of reign of Queen Elizabeth, has left a valuable description of many aspects of the City and the suburbs in 1603. He clearly identified the inns providing hospitality to travellers along the Whitechapel Road and *Bowling Allyes* in the fields to the east of Hog Lane; the northerly extension of Petticoat Lane. He also noted that since 1535 water had been brought down by pipes from Hackney. Stow sympathised with the anxiety of Elizabeth's government about the unwanted growth of the capital. In 1580 a royal proclamation had forbidden any new buildings within the three miles of the gates of the City. Three years later commentators [the Privy Council] directed attention to the great increase in building *to the danger of pestilence and riot*, and to the practice of dividing single tenements.[4]

In 1593 a statute was passed, declaring:

> *great mischiefs daily grow and increase by reason of pestering the houses with*
> *diverse families, harbouring of inmates, and converting great houses into several*
> *tenements, and the erecting of new buildings in London and Westminster.*

Stow wrote as follows:

> *From Aldegate east, againe lieth a large street, replenished with buildings, to wit on*
> *the north side, the parish church of S. Botolph, and so other buildings to Hog Lane,*
> *and to the barres on both sides.*

> *Also without the barres, both sides of the street be pestered with cottages, and allies,*
> *even up to Whitechapel church: and almost half a mile beyond it, into the common field:*
> *all which ought to to lye open and free for all men. But this common field, I say,*
> *being sometime the beauty of this City on that part, is so encroached upon by building*
> *of filthy cottages, and with other purprestures, inclosures and Lay –stalles*
> *(notwithstanding all proclamations and Acts of Parliament made to the contrary) that*
> *in some places it scarce remaineth a sufficient high way for the meeting of Carriages*
> *and droves of Cattell, much less is there any faire, pleasant or wholesome way for*
> *people to walk on foot: which is no small blemish to so famous a city, to have so*
> *unsavoury and unseemly an entry or passage thereunto.*

> *On the south side of the high way from Aldgate, were some few tenements thinly*
> *scattered, here and there, with many void spaces between them, up to the Bars, but*
> *now that street is not only fully replenished with buildings outward, & also*
> *pestered with diverse Allyes, on either side to the Barres, but to white Chapel and beyond.*

With regard to victualling, Stow mentions that east from St Botolph's church in Aldgate were *certain faire Innes for receipt of travellers repairing to the City, up towards Hog lane End, somewhat within the Barres, a mark showing how far the liberties of the City do extend*.[5]

The most comprehensive review of the eastern parishes for the period 1550 to 1700 has been provided by Dr Michael Power. This period saw the first great expansion eastward from the City of London, with a population of less than 5,000 in the parishes of Stepney and Whitechapel growing to one approaching 90,000. To house such large numbers of people considerable building was undertaken, especially along the riverside east of the Tower and in the inner suburban districts of Spitalfields and Whitechapel. Most construction was carried out by small builders, and during the first half of the period development was haphazard and unplanned. Later, the large scale developer left his mark in the grid-pattern streets in such areas as Spitalfields and the development of squares such as Well Close Square late in C17.

The rapid urbanization of the area created problems of administration, law enforcement and health which seem always to have kept ahead of attempts to solve them. Considering the increasing unhealthiness of the area as the period advanced, it seems that the green fields of mediaeval East London gave way to dense streets and industrial advance at the expense of the quality of the life of the people living there.

The parish registers for Whitechapel reveal that the totals of births and deaths between 1600 and 1610 were 2,724 and 2,729 respectively and by the 1690s 5,711 and 8,370. These suggest a doubling of the population over the century, but the burials in any plague year would effect such estimates. For Whitechapel there were three years when plague appears to have had a continuous presence - 1636, 1637 and 1638 – but it was also prevalent in 1603, 1609, 1624, 1625, 1630, and 1665.

After a detailed discussion of the different methods of estimating the population Power concluded that in the 1600s there were 21,834 people in Stepney, Whitechapel Shadwell and Whitechapel, which increased to 84,953 in the 1690s - a four-fold increase. These totals do not include estimates of the number of immigrants, especially of young men and women, who may not appear in the parish records.

Power's analysis of baptismal records for the riverside parishes shows an increase between 1550 and the 1640s, followed by twenty years of falling birth rates, probably coupled with under-reporting, before the increase that lasted from the 1660s until the end of the century. Whitechapel showed rapid growth in the 1670s and 1680s, a period which also showed increasing Huguenot immigration, especially in Spitalfields.[6]

Professor Vanessa Harding and others have explored families, households and housing in early modern London and from the records for Aldgate reached the following conclusions. In the 1690s Aldgate householders "answered for an average of 4.8 persons" compared to 6.6 persons in Cheapside; the latter area having more apprentices and servants. Aldgate also had "a slightly higher proportion of single adults in the population", and "only 16 per cent of households had female servants in 1695". However, their research did not extend to merchants and their networks.

Whitechapel, 1664 - 1675

The Hearth tax returns from the seventeenth century have received a great deal of recent attention, which has attempted to unravel the complexities revealed by these returns. Peter Guillery and Michael Power have found that in 1664 there were 2,482 households and 5,897 hearths in Whitechapel, which means about 2,100 houses, of which some "18% were multiply occupied". Guillery concluded that the Middlesex survey of Michaelmas 1674 and Lady Day 1675 indicated that the assessors "were recording houses rather than households". This has led to the conclusion that in 1674/5 there were 2,304 houses, an increase of about ten per cent. The "overwhelming majority of houses in Whitechapel, ... had three or fewer heated rooms".[7]

The one-room layout of from 12ft to 17ft square was "widespread in small two-storey speculations" in East London. These "were built in pairs and in short rows, of timber or brick, sometimes with chimney stacks that suggest two hearths and unheated garrets, sometimes as what appear to have been three-hearth houses with heated garrets." Houses with front staircases were suitable for multiple occupation.

There were, of course, some larger houses and in 1674/5 some 580 houses (25 per cent) had four or more hearths, and these would have housed the more prosperous merchants and skilled artisans. William Meggs [1616-1678] had a "Mansion House" with fifteen hearths in Whitechapel, a counting house and adjoining tenements, in the 1664/5 returns. His will reveals considerable wealth and he was "the principal benefactor" of St Mary, Whitechapel. His nephew William Goulston esquire was left £1,000 and his investments in the East India Company, "But must repay his debts before receiving this bequest". Meggs is best remembered today because he left money to purchase and fund Almshouses for twelve poor men and women. They had to be over 50 years of age and were not already to be in receipt of a parish pension.[8]

In 2000 Craig Spence in his invaluable *Atlas of London in the 1690s* showed that in 1693-4 Whitechapel had an area of 68.8 hectares (170 acres) with 1,957 households. The household density of 28.8 households per hectare reflects the existence of more open ground in the nearby tenter's fields and nursery gardens that were gradually built over during the C18. The housing density was much higher in the City of London with 80.1 households per hectare. In the riverside parishes of Wapping-Whitechapel the density was 92.5 households/hectare and in Shadwell 43.8 households/hectare.

Spence recognised that "in most areas of London there was a wide range of household rental values. Furthermore, it was common for substantial residences to be found in close proximity to smaller ones."

This is confirmed by the rents in Whitechapel which ranged from £1 to £300. This wide range continued into the C18. This is particularly true for the Whitechapel High Street, which as will be shown later, had many large properties with rents of £20 or more per year, whilst the adjacent alleys conformed to Stow's descriptions of 1603.

Spence recognised four classes of "nested mean values" of rent across London. On the east side of the City, he recorded a district centred on Aldgate and Whitechapel High Street and inside the City Wall, with mean household rental values of £15-18s.-00d. whilst outside the City Wall the rents were £12-7s.-00d.. He also noted "Low value rents within the area from the eastern riverside to the north of Whitechapel High Street stood at 68.3%".[9]

John Rocque's map of London in the 1740s shows the built-up area extended eastwards as far as the parish church, but then more open fields occur out towards Mile End Old Town. However, the map does not record individual houses. Given the wide variations in household rents across the parish it is best to use the land tax and insurance policies to allow a clearer description of the main streets. A separate section in Chapter 8 describes Richard Johnson's businesses which were centred on Goodman's Yard and Leman Street.[10]

East London from 1700 to 1800

Long before the C18, London "had been the indisputable centre of national wealth and the hub of the professions" and we need to understand the role of the eastern parishes in these activities. The Pevsner guide provides an excellent review of the development of London's eastern parishes between the 1650s and 1800 and generally agrees with the thesis of Dr. Power. The increasing population placed pressure on the existing chapels and churches.

One result was the New Churches Act of 1711, which allowed the building of three significant churches by Nicholas Hawksmoor, Christ Church in Spitalfields, St George-in-the-East and St Anne, Limehouse. With regard to residential development the Pevsner guide notes "Many streets in Spitalfields and Whitechapel were laid out haphazardly, their siting conditioned by tenter grounds, brick yards and an artillery ground." In 1698 Nicholas Barbon was gradually developing Well Close Square. Mansell Street was laid out in 1680s and then re-developed in the 1720s with more substantial houses as will be described later.

Elizabeth McKellar noted that Daniel Defoe [c1651-1731] DNB had been one of many writers who observed the growth of London, and wrote:

> *It is the disaster of London, as to the beauty of its figure, that it is thus stretched*
> *out in buildings, just at the pleasure of every builder, or undertaker of buildings*
> *... and this has spread the face of it in a most straggling, confused manner, out*
> *of all shape.*

McKellar has provided the most recent and authorative examination of the importance of the period 1660-1720 in the development of London. She concluded that "the modern city, although undeniably radically different and new, developed out of existing housing types and traditional layouts and maintained links with the countryside and older patterns and associations of land usage. The creation of modern London was an evolutionary not a revolutionary process." She also emphasises that, throughout the Georgian period, buildings were put up as speculative developments within a free-market economy. Within the area covered by this book McKellar regards Barbon's 1680s development of Well Close Square as a "brave attempt to introduce fashionable architecture to the East End with limited success".[11]

In Chapter 3 these issues are explored in greater detail with the emphasis on the wide variety of housing and the long-standing elements of the road system in Whitechapel within which local building developers such as Edward and Samuel Hawkins operated.

Probably the most frequently repeated quotation about the development of eighteenth-century East London is that of Dr Dorothy George. Basing her views on the *Customs and Privileges of the Manors of Stepney and Hackney*, she wrote "East London grew obscurely, its development apparently influenced by the custom (confirmed by statute) of the great liberty of Stepney and Hackney, by which copy-holders were empowered to grant leases of thirty-one years without fine to the Lord of the Manor, under penalty of forfeiture of the copyhold if a longer lease was granted".

This quotation has appeared in many books and articles; most recently in Professor John Marriott's history. However, local researchers have known for many years that, while this may have been the original intention of the Lord of the Manor, the actual practice was very different. Leases were granted of 66, 99 or 500 years in order to obtain the fines. This practice was followed by the Wentworth family, lords of the manor of Stepney until 1695, to reduce their large and long-standing debts, and also by their successors. It is, however, certainly possible that some developers took advantage of the manorial custom.[12]

Methodology

Introduction

The research for this book, and its companion volumes covering Mile End Old Town and Wapping, is based on ten years of detailed analysis of hundreds of documents in the archives of London and elsewhere. The success of this research depended upon the order in which records were examined and then linked together. The final optimal sequence proved to be:

> Land tax, sewer taxes, hearth tax and rate books
> Licensed victuallers records
> Lists of freeholders
> Insurance records
> Directories, newspapers
> Freemasons
> Livery companies and apprenticeship records
> Middlesex Deeds Register
> Stepney manorial records
> Parish registers
> IGI
> TNA wills, probates, carriage and silver duties of 1754-1762
> TNA 1780 male servants tax
> Internet searches

The web sites of the Guildhall, LMA, TNA and THLHL provide information sheets describing their records and the following comments provide additional information.

Land Tax

Studies of eighteenth-century London have been made at a variety of scales, from individual buildings to streets, estates and parishes, and have utilised a wide range of sources such as maps, deeds, wills, and insurance records, but rarely the land tax assessments. Hugh Phillips made use of the rate books in his study of Mid-Georgian London. Francis Sheppard in his article on the methods used by the Survey of London commented on the difficulty of interpreting the parish rate books correctly. Whilst this generalisation may apply to some parts of London, the land tax registers for London's eastern parishes are nearly 95% complete for the period 1740-1790 and, with care, individual properties can be traced for over forty years. One problem after 1790 is that in 1798 the land tax became a perpetual charge which could be redeemed by payment of a lump sum. When this was done individual houses "disappear" from the records.[13]

Gibson recognised the usefulness of the land tax in urban studies and Chapter 2 provides further information on the collection of the land tax. The LMA's information sheet No. 9 describes some of the problems that might be encountered when using these records. On a more positive note, Baigent's study of eighteenth-century Bristol concluded "The Land Tax returns, in which one would initially have the least confidence and which are almost uniformly discarded as useless, proved in fact very useful".

Until 1765 the land tax assessments were based on the "rent" and thereafter on the "rack rent", which was about fifty per cent higher. This confirms Dr. Johnson's definition of "rack rent" as being the "Annual rent raised to the utmost". The land tax covered land, property and *stock* and the smallest category for assessment was a room with a rent of £2. As an example of the information available when the land tax is combined with other records, including the IGI and victualler's records, we have for the *Carpenters Arms*, near the Turnpike in MEOT, the following changes between 1750 and 1769:-

DATE	TAXPAYER	COMMENT
1750	Charles Woodall	For *Carpenters Arms*
1756	Ann Woodall	Widow of Charles
1759	William Smith	Married Ann Woodall
1762-70	Ann Smith	Widow of William

In 1771 Ann Smith, by now twice-widowed, moved away from her home of twenty years to a house in Stepney Green.

The land tax registers for Whitechapel have been used to identify everyone whose rent was £10 per year or more in 1740, 1750, 1760 and 1770. All the men paying rents of £10 or more per year were deemed by statute throughout the C18 to be worthy of filling the many unpaid jobs that were required to keep the local administration working. They were also eligible to serve as jurors at the Old Bailey, trustees for overseeing the 'relief of the poor' and as voters in parliamentary elections. The lists of freeholders for the Ossulstone Hundred provide a valuable view of thousands of men who met this requirement. Subsequently they can be frequently traced in other records such as those of the manorial courts and the insurance companies.

My detailed studies of the merchants living in London's eastern parishes have shown that a "personal estate" of £100 or more represented a man of considerable wealth. Such a man was Laurence Sulivan who returned from India in 1753. In 1755 he chose to settle in one of the best houses in MEOT at 37 Stepney Green. Sulivan used his fortune to establish himself as one of the leaders of the *shipping interest*, and to become the accepted leader of the EIC, the largest and most powerful private company in the world at that time.

It must be remembered that the levels of "personal estate", sometimes recorded as "stock", were not an attempt to exactly identify a person's total wealth. They were a device used to assist in the raising of a precise sum of money every year, as demanded by the land tax Commissioners. For the tax collectors it was sufficient to place a person's "personal estate" into categories such as £25, £50, £75, £100 up to £200, and these amounts were taxed at £1 in £100. So in 1770 the *Quota* for Whitechapel was the very precise sum of £3,172-7s.-3½d. and the collection amounted to £3,279-13s.-0d.[14]

Insurance policies 1710-1839

In recent years there have been two major improvements to the indexing of the extensive Sun Fire Office insurance policies at the Guildhall, London, now held at the LMA. The most important on-line project is *A Place in the Sun*, which is available on the TNA web site. Indexing started in 2003 and this finding aid for Ms 11936 currently covers 1790 to 1839 and is being extended backwards towards 1787. It already contains over 400,000 names plus trades and addresses. Probably ninety per cent of the entries relate to families and property (including ships and pictures) in London. Lodgers and labourers can also be found insuring their modest "household goods" and sometimes other property.[15]

In 1986 a team from NADFAS began indexing some selected trades in the Sun policies. The work was continued by non-NADFAS volunteers with broader interests, who, between 1986 and the end of their project in 2010, indexed over 600 trades between 1710 and 1780 in Ms 11936. Their interests included artists, brewers and distillers, furniture, instrument makers, metal workers, the shipping industry, textiles, and covers England, Scotland and Wales. They have also indexed these trades between 1780 and 1810 in the London area together with all the trades outside London between 1793 and 1816 in Ms

11937. These indexes are on cards, copies of which are now held at the V and A, Museum of London, the National Maritime Museum and the Royal Armouries Museum, Leeds.

The task of compiling an on-line index to the insurance policies of London before 1775 has yet to be started.

Licensed victuallers records

In the C18 there were over 120 licensed premises in Whitechapel and about 40 in nearby Mile End Old Town. Many of the pub names have persisted to the present day such as The Grave Maurice, which can be traced back to 1723. At the beginning of the C18 probably one building in twenty was a licensed premise.

Although the population of Whitechapel doubled between 1740 and 1780 the number of licensed premises remained constant, curbed by magistrates' attempts to restrict the Englishman's propensity to like a drink or three. Probably as a result of this policy there were many more unlicensed premises, particularly in the alley ways off the main street. It was very easy in those simpler times for a house owner to put a trestle table and some chairs in his basement, get a barrel or two of porter or ale on credit from one of local breweries and open up a small bar for his neighbours.[16]

Wills and Probates

The importance of wills and probate records in local and social history are well-known. Jane Cox in her lively book *Hatred Pursued Beyond the Grave* provides a general introductory approach to wills. For Whitechapel over 1,000 PCC wills between 1740 and 1790 have been examined, so this is a large, robust sample in statistical terms. In particular, wills allow the identification of the links between the will-maker and his family, neighbours, friends and business associates. One result of such study was the identification of the Scandinavian timber merchants living in Well Close Square described by Morris and Cozens.[17] If a will was disputed then it was necessary to draw up an inventory of the deceased's estate together with lists of debtors and creditors. The resulting probate records have allowed descriptions to be made of the contents of several houses and workshops in Whitechapel.

The Streets of Whitechapel

It is not always clear to the modern reader or visitor exactly where the boundaries of Whitechapel are located. Probably the most misleading aspect for the modern visitor is the vast sprawl of Aldgate East station which extends eastwards into the parish of Whitechapel. Another problem is that the parish of Aldgate lies within the City boundary, whilst the Portsoken Ward lies outside the City wall in the parish of Whitechapel.

Essential to an understanding of Whitechapel in the mid-eighteenth century is John Rocque's map published in the 1740s and now available as *The A to Z of Georgian London*. For subsequent developments *The A to Z of Regency London* based on Richard Horwood's [1757/8-1803] DNB maps of 1799-1819 should be consulted. Rocque's maps appear to be accurate in surveying terms, even if not all individual houses are shown. Rocque was aware of the possibility of errors arising in the placement of street names and invited the *Curious* to point out *Inaccuracies and Omissions*. Even so, a number of the street and house names were mispositioned on the map or their spelling or location have changed over time, and this makes comparisons with later maps more difficult. Buckley Street referred to in deeds of 1707 appears to have been recorded by Rocque's surveyors as Buckle Street.

Some streets such as Lemon/Leman Street, Prescot Street and the Whitechapel Road have retained their names for over 250 years, but war-time bombing and slum clearance and development since 1945 have created many changes. The main street layout of the C18 is still visible today, and to assist the reader Appendix 1 traces street names across 250 years.[18]

FURTHER READING

M. Ball and D. Sunderland	*An Economic History of London, 1800-1904*, 2001
B. Cherry et al	*London 5: East*, 2007, Pevsner Architectural Guides to Greater London
J. Cox	*Hatred Pursued Beyond the Grave: Tales of our Ancestors from the London Church Courts*, 1995
D. Defoe	A *Tour through the whole Island of Great Britain*, 1734-36
East London History Group	The Population of Stepney in the early 17th century, *East London Papers*, vol. XI, No. 2, 1968, pp. 75-84
J. Gascoyne	*Survey of Stepney, 1703*, L. T. S.
M. D. George	*London life in the Eighteenth Century*, 1965
M. A. Gliddon	*Material collected towards a history of Stepney*, 1844 THLHL
P. Guillery	*The Small House in eighteenth-century London, A Social and Architectural History*, 2004
P. Guillery	Houses in London, C. Ferguson and W. Wareham, *London and Middlesex Hearth Tax*, 2011
P. Guillery	London's Suburbs, House Size and the Hearth Tax, P. S. Barnwell and M. Airs eds, *Houses and the Hearth Tax: the later Stuart house and society*, 2006
V. Harding and P. Baker	*People in Place: families, households and housing in early modern London*, 2008
D. Hey	*The Oxford Companion to Local and Family History*, 2010
C. Kerrigan	*A history of Tower Hamlets*, 1982
LMA	*Stepney Manorial Records*, Ref. M/93
	W. Robinson *A history of Stepney and neighbourhood*, c. 1843 Ms 78, O, Rob, [8 volumes of material]
W. Maitland	*The history of London from its foundation ... a new edition, continued to the year 1772, by J. Entick*, 1775
J. Marriott	*Beyond the Tower: A History of East London*, 2011
E. McKellar	*The birth of modern London: The development and design of the city, 1660-1720*, 1999
G. E. Mingay	The Land Tax Assessments and the Small Landowner, *Economic History Review*, 2nd Series, vol. XVII, 1964
D. Morris	*Mile End Old Town 1740-1780: A social history of an early modern London Suburb*, 2007
D. Morris and K. Cozens	*Wapping 1600-1800, A social history of an Early Modern London Maritime Suburb*, 2009
J. Noorthouck	*A new history of London including Westminster and Southwark*, 1773
S. Porter	*Shakespeare's London: Everyday Life in London, 1580-1616*, 2009
M. J. Power	The East and West in early modern London in *Wealth and power, Tudor England*, ed. I. W. Ives and others, 1978, pp. 167-185
J. Rocque	*The A to Z of Georgian London*, 1981 Introduction by R. Hyde
L. D. Schwarz	Social class and social topography: The middle classes in London at the end of the eighteenth century, *The Eighteenth Century Town, A Reader in English Urban History, 1688-1820*, ed. P. Borsay, 1990
L. D. Schwarz	London 1700-1840, *The Cambridge Urban History of Britain, vol. II, 1540-1840*, 2000
C. Spence	*London in the 1690s: A Social Atlas*, 2000
J. Stow	*A Survey of London*, 1603 reprinted 1971
VCH	*History of the County of Middlesex*, vol. XI, Early Stepney and Bethnal Green, ed. T. F. T. Baker, 1998, Stepney, P. E. C. Croot

Web Sites

http://www.british-history.ac.uk	Whitechapel 'Four Shillings in the Pound Aid, 1693-94'
http://www.eastlondonhistory.org.uk	East London History Society
http://www.history.ac.uk/projects/ life-in-the-suburbs	CMH Life in the Suburbs
http://www.londonlives.org/static/Project	London Lives 1690 to 1800
http://www.royalarmouries.org	The Royal Armouries Museum, Leeds

2. GOVERNING WHITECHAPEL

Governance

The great East London parish of St Mary Matfelon or Whitechapel was established in 1320; formed from the older parish of Stepney. Its governance before 1700, the gradual development of the land on either side of the Whitechapel Road before 1600 and very briefly the industries before 1550, are fully described by the VCH. One important development occurred in 1551 when King Edward VI by his letters patent dated the 16th of April "granted to Lord Thomas Wentworth, Lord Chamberlain of the kings household, for and in consideration of his good and faithful service before done, part of the late received gift, to wit, the Lordships of Stepney and Hackney" which covered Whitechapel and much of the land as far east as the river Lea. The Wentworths were to be lords of the manor until 1695.[1]

The problems of the poor, water supply, road maintenance, lighting, victualling, policing, and the collection of stray animals, constantly exercised the inhabitants of Whitechapel and the adjoining parishes. In the C18 the funding and maintenance of these services was the source of many disputes between the poorer residents of the riverside parishes and the wealthier residents of Whitechapel and MEOT. This was not surprising because, as noted many years ago by Beatrice and Sidney Webb, and summarised by Professor Penelope Corfield[2]:

> "The parishes outside the City were governed in the eighteenth century by over 300 bodies, all with differing authorities and constitutions."

Dr Joanna Innes has more recently re-examined in great detail these London-wide problems of governance. She notes that "Much innovation in local government in this period involved the supersession of systems that obliged households to provide services in kind – for example, by taking a turn at the watch, or by lighting or paving the street – with an obligation to contribute in the form of rates to fund the co-ordinated provision of services".[3]

Figure 3   ST MARY, WHITECHAPEL

In addition to the vestry, local governance relied on the actions of Meetings of Inhabitants, the Lord of Stepney and Hackney Manor, the trustees of the Whitechapel to Shenfield Turnpike Trust, Justices of the Peace, the commissioners of sewers and paving, and the private enterprise water companies. However, many of the leading citizens found themselves serving in several of these groups over a long period of time, and the degree of complexity was less than Corfield implied. In Whitechapel one man who held several positions was William Quarrill, a "prominent oil man", who was a Justice of the Peace, a commissioner of paving, and a governor of the London Hospital. His father Thomas Quarrill had been in 1755 one of the Honourable Deputy Lieutenants of Tower Hamlets.

The Whitechapel Vestry

In the C18 local affairs were governed by the actions of the vestry. The role of churchwardens, in addition to their church duties, included the management of parish property, the moral state of parishioners and the provision of schools and almshouses. Fortunately, there always appeared to be men of wealth and status in Whitechapel willing to undertake these tasks. Whitechapel was governed by an "Open" Vestry, and all those who paid the rate had a right to vote in the Vestry meetings. As there were over 1,300 ratepayers in the 1730s this led on occasion to very crowded and excited meetings at which there was *such Cursing and Swearing and Noise, at the choosing of Parish Officers and making the Rates*. Indeed Sir Clifford William Phillips claimed to have been struck at such a meeting, and Nathaniel Fowler, a churchwarden, reported being *hissed and spit upon*.[4]

Clearly these conditions were not acceptable to the "principal inhabitants". They, together with the churchwardens and the overseer of the poor, submitted in 1733 a Petition to the House of Commons. This stated, amongst other things, the *clamorous proceedings and irregular behaviour ... discouraged the principal inhabitants from attending and obstructed the business of the Parish*. Their solution was that the *Right of voting in the Vestry be confined to such persons as either contribute the greatest share of the public expense, or have served the Office of Churchwarden or Overseer of the Poor*. A committee of the House of Commons examined the petitioners and objectors to the proposed change, but eventually in 1733 rejected the proposed act by 107 votes to 57 votes.

Generally, at the beginning of each legal year about the middle of April, each hamlet held an election for churchwardens. There were also elections for the posts of constable, the overseer of the poor, the surveyor of the highways, the headboroughs, beadle, bellman, and vestrymen. Broadly, there was an established sequence, which might last twenty years or more, by which a man would start by being elected a headborough and then progress to more important positions, such as overseer of the poor and churchwarden. Unlike MEOT it was said that the churchwardens of Whitechapel only came from the "Third Class" of "tradesmen of lower degree such as artificers, carpenters bricklayers, glaziers and painters".

Whilst we do not have good records for all of the vestry's activities there are three important aspects of the work of the vestry which can be studied - the workhouse, support for the poor and the Committee for Paving.

The Poor

Help for the poor came from two sources. Chapter 10 discusses the help provided by individuals and charities. In this Chapter the emphasis is on the workings of the vestry and its attempts to implement the Poor Law. As today, it was difficult to define the poor or poverty. Thus arose the concept of the *deserving poor*, usually widows, orphan children and those who had fallen on hard times due to causes outside their control. In contrast there were the *undeserving poor, wastrels and ne'er-do-wells*.

For Whitechapel there is a major problem in that few records concerned with poor relief have survived; compared with other local parishes such as Poplar, Bromley and Bow, and other London parishes such as St George, Hanover Square and Marylebone.

Throughout the eighteenth and nineteenth centuries poverty was widespread in London. Charles Dickens's novels and Charles Booth's *Life and Labour of the People of London* have conveyed a vivid picture of the life of the poor in Victorian London.

The primary task of Dr. Dorothy George in her *London Life in the Eighteenth Century*, was to give "a picture of the conditions of life and work of the poorer classes in London". Very recently David Green has provided an excellent review of the operation of the English Poor Law in London between the late C18 and the late C19. His work provides the basis for the following brief summary. None of these authors has attempted to describe the conditions of the poor in Whitechapel, and how, if at all, they differed from those in other parts of London.

James Boswell reported Dr Samuel Johnson as saying that '*the poor in England were better provided for, than in any other country of the same extent*". More recently Tom Hitchcock has remarked that "The system of poor relief in eighteenth-century London was extensive, expensive and remarkably comprehensive." But David Green also emphasised that "significant differences in poor law practices existed between parishes that were sometimes in close proximity".[5]

In 1997 David Green examined the "processes and impacts of economic and social change in London" in the late C18 and the C19. He followed this in his 2010 book by delineating "the changing ideologies of economic justice, which involved a shift from a moral economy, based around the concept of a just price for labour and goods, to a political economy in which the market ruled, had a profound effect on attitudes towards the poor and policies relating to relief."[6]

In the C18 vestries were responsible for the administration of relief and were guided by numerous Acts of Parliament. Their ability to implement such relief depended on a variety of local factors; such as the effectiveness and attitudes of the unpaid and over-worked officers and the ability of the tax collectors to collect the poor rate. From the 1661 Act of Settlement onwards, every English and Welsh person had a legal settlement in the parish of their birth or by apprenticeship, through marriage, domestic service or "by virtue of renting property worth £10 per year for a period of 40 days, equivalent to about four shillings a week". As the eastern parishes had many houses with rents of £10 they naturally attracted large numbers of the poor, which increased the pressures on the vestries, especially as the wealthier residents moved elsewhere.

Professor David Hey described the duties and responsibilities of the overseer of the poor as follows:

> "The overseer received no payment for his work, nor any recompense for loss of earnings. He had to submit his accounts at the end of the year of office for the approval of the vestry meeting and was himself expected to pay for anything that was not allowed by the meeting. … The overseer had the face-to-face responsibility of deciding the merits of appeals for poor relief. He had to temper mercy with the knowledge that the ratepayers of the parish would demand an explanation of his expenditure."[7]

If the Surveyor of the Poor accepted such evidence of settlement, then he had a variety of policies to choose from described as either 'indoor' or 'outdoor' relief. Indoor relief comprised workhouses and pauper farms and was the preferred action in many London parishes. Indeed in 1803 in Whitechapel, Bethnal Green and Shadwell between 85 and 92 per cent of poor law expenditure went on indoor relief.

The Workhouse

Knatchbull's Act of 1723 was the major piece of legislation that enabled many parishes across England and Wales to build a workhouse. The Whitechapel vestry was quick to take advantage of the Act; and on the 1st August 1724 it was reported that *the inhabitants of Whitechapel have bought a piece of ground near Goodman's Fields to make a workhouse to employ their able poor according to a late Act of Parliament.* This was soon followed in November 1724 when an advertisement appealed for *All persons who are willing to serve the Workhouse lately erected in Whitechapel with Beds and Bedding also with Sheeting and Towelling ... may bring in their proposals to the Vestry on the 27th November at 2 pm.* By May 1725 the vestry was advertising *For any persons who are able to provide Work, or who will in any way employ the Poor in the Workhouse in Whitechapel* were to deliver their proposals to Mr William Chadsey at the Seven Stars in Whitechapel High Street before the 9th June.[8]

In 1732 *An Account of Several Workhouses* from the SPCK reported that:

> *A Workhouse was set up in Ayliffe Street near Goodman's Fields in the Year 1724, which for some time promised to answer the Expectation of the Projectors of it, but since then the Officers of the Parish have thought fit to turn it into a House for Lodging only such Poor as are not otherwise provided, who go out daily for Work where they can get it, and return in the Evening. There are now about 60 men, Women and Children so lodged under the Care of a Mistress, who takes Care to keep the House clean, and have beds made ready for those that lodge there.*[9]

In 1767 Richard Whiteshead, a prominent coach maker, insured *the Poor House of the parish of Whitechapel*, which was next to the Charity School in the Whitechapel Road. There were three buildings under construction and the insurance values indicate a sizeable institution[10]:

The Front Building	£1,200
The Middle Building	£700
The Back Building	£1,100

The principal method for paying for the workhouse and other support for the deserving was the poor rate. This was paid by persons with incomes above £40 or £50 a year, in other words the "middling sort". How many in Whitechapel paid the poor rate we do not know, but elsewhere in England it was thought that between a quarter and a third of the housekeepers were so rated. The problem for everyone was that the "poor-rate might rise or fall suddenly in response to harvest, disease or any number of trivial local accidents".[11]

John Marshall in *Mortality of the Metropolis*, recorded the expenditure for the relief of the poor in London parishes and for the year ending Easter 1776 the following were noted:

St Mary, Whitechapel	£4,000
St Andrew Holborn & St George	£4,551
Marylebone	£4,914
St Giles & St George, Bloomsbury	£5,156

Professor Tim Hitchcock has explored in great detail the "beggars and the beggarly poor of the eighteenth-century London" and states that "Despite their porous and occasionally homely character, workhouses were frequently loathed by the poorer population of London, particularly by householders. When a parish first opened a workhouse the number of paupers willing to enter its doors was regularly a third to a half of the number who had previously received pensions."

"For elderly housekeepers the offer of a workhouse place could be heart-breaking, but for the beggarly poor, for the homeless and the truly desperate, workhouses formed a surprisingly flexible and useful resource. For the street beggars of London, for the whores, chimney-sweeps and link-boys, a workhouse place was something to be valued and sought after rather than disdained. As much as workhouses provided a bed, a meal and a warm fire, they were also the gateway for a wide range of medical and social services. Once inside a workhouse a beggar, even one who did not have a legal settlement, could be assured of some medical care, even if they found themselves removed to another parish in due course."

"In fact, the vast majority of adult workhouse inmates were there precisely because they were disabled, or ill, or pregnant" and so it became necessary to provide an infirmary, which had not been part of the original design of many workhouses.

"Gaining admittance to a workhouse as an accident victim, in labour or after spending a night in a watch-house was commonplace. Watch-houses were a particularly important avenue through which the poor could gain admission. Many watchmen sent the obviously ill and desperate to the workhouse door, a note in hand, rather than marching them before a justice, as the law directed. But more common still was a direct appeal to the overseer, the churchwarden, or simply the workhouse master or mistress." "Like domestic service, time spent in a workhouse ensured that a pauper would have clean linen, changed once a week, and a robust, if plain set of clothes."[12]

For the workhouse in Whitechapel in 1795 the menu was as follows:

DAY	BREAKFAST	DINNER	SUPPER
Sunday	Small beer and bread	Boiled beef	Broth
Monday	Milk porridge	Rice milk	Bread, butter, beer
Tuesday	Milk porridge	Boiled beef	Broth
Wednesday	Milk porridge	Dumplings	Broth and butter or cheese
Thursday	Milk porridge	Boiled mutton	Broth
Friday	Milk porridge with 5 oz. of butter or 10 oz. of cheese to serve till Sunday		
Saturday	Milk porridge with 5 oz. of butter or 10 oz. of cheese to serve till Sunday		

The demand for workhouses increased during the C18 and by 1776 there were at least 80 workhouses in London with space for 16,000 poor. There was a large workhouse in St George-in-the-East and that in Whitechapel, which had moved to the north side of the Whitechapel Road, housed up to 600 inmates, "making it one of the largest in the country". Writing about 1800 J. P. Malcolm said the workhouse contained 380 persons on average of which ninety were children. The children, exclusive of the infant poor, were sent to nurses in the country at 2s/6d. per week. This was a common solution to a particular problem at this time.[13]

What happened when the time came for the poor to be discharged from a workhouse? The archives of the workhouse in nearby Redman Row, MEOT, that belonged to the parish of All Hallows, Barking, the famous church on Tower Hill, provide a background. This workhouse was established in 1738 and the Master was responsible for assisting the boys and women who left the workhouse. William Stanley was apprenticed to the local chair-maker, Henry Hollely, for seven years for the sum of £3. Eliza Withers was placed out as an apprentice *to Elizabeth Turner to learn the Art of Slapp making*, and given fifty shillings. When Mary Fowler, a forty-one year old poor woman, was discharged for misbehaviour, it was agreed that the Master would allow her 5d. or 6d. for a gown. One wonders how she survived on the streets with such a small sum. When Ann Cox was discharged, she was treated rather better, as it was agreed that she would be clothed *and provided for at the discretion of the Church Wardens*, and she was given *one pair of shoes, one shift, one cap and one pair of stockings*. In some cases women would be *paid ten shillings to Buy something to sell about the Streets*, thus adding to the number of poor street-sellers, as described by Dr. Dorothy George.[14]

Supporting the Poor

Records are sparse for Whitechapel, but from the Minutes of the trustees for St George-in-the-East for 1790 we can gather some idea of the problems raised by managing the local poor. There were twenty-one trustees including the Rector Dr Mayo, Henry Wardle from St George-in-the-East and John Camden, a prominent ship owner in Wapping. The Clerk to the trustees was William Finlay on a salary of £100 on account of the poor rate and another £30 on account of the Conjunct Rate.

It was in the preamble to one Act that the collection of the Poor Rate was said to be attended by much difficulty. There were many houses in the parish that were let at small rents or to weekly and monthly tenants or were entirely let out in Lodgings or separate apartments or let ready furnished.

In 1790 the trustees invited bids for the maintenance of the poor and received five proposals based on a price per head per week:

Richard Goldthorp	3s.-4d.	John Evans	2s.-9d.
Ralph Venables	2s.-9d.	Thomas Miller	2s.-10d.

The bid of William Reid of 2s-10d. was accepted even though it was not the lowest.[15]

At least once a week a group of trustees would meet to review applications for help, decide on aspects of running the work house, and especially decide on who should be given help and those who should be returned to their parishes of settlement. Basically, applicants for the workhouse had to produce proper vouchers to prove their settlement in the parish. On 3 May 1790 it was ordered that, Martha

Simpson was to go by sea to South Shields and half a guinea was paid to the Beadle for that purpose, and that Joseph Burgess was to be passed as a Vagrant to Liverpool. Both were unable to prove their settlement in the parish in order to obtain support.

For those who did receive support it was quite varied in scope, if not very generous, for the parish considered itself to be poor. For Sarah Bowles it was one shilling and a half peck loaf a week. For Elizabeth Bell an infant was given *a gown, a Shift and a pair of Shoes and Stockings*, while Mary Mars with three children was *allowed 3/6d and a half peck of loaf per week.*

They were particularly keen to obtain security to indemnify the Parish from erring husbands and the fathers of illegitimate children. Thus in 1790 they ordered that a Warrant be applied against James Mentz for deserting his four children and leaving them chargeable to the Parish. Sarah Pearce was examined concerning the *Father of the Child* she has lately been delivered of.

Mr Elijah Goff provided the coals, and Mr Arnold the beer to the workhouse. The beer allowance was a pint on each meat day and a quart on meagre days. Beef was seven ounces a day for the healthy with the apothecary deciding what should be given to the infirm.

In December 1739 and January 1740 very cold weather affected the whole of Europe. Vienna reported the coldest winter since 1709; *There were so many Tents upon the frozen Tyne for the entertainment of the people ... that it looked more like a country fair*, and in Northern Ireland it was possible to walk across the ice from one side of Lough Neagh to the other, a distance of some eight miles. In London a Countess living near Grosvenor Square sent a clergyman out to discover *poor people distressed by the cold weather*. He came back with a list of a great number of families so was sent back by the Countess with money to relieve some of their suffering. The streets of London were clogged up by the snow and ice and the newspapers fulmigated against the *Great neglect of those whose Duty it is to clear the streets*, and with another modern touch remarked that housekeepers *pay enough already* for street cleaning.[16]

In Whitechapel and adjoining parishes the winters of the early 1740s created many problems for the overseers of the poor. The Thames was frozen over and the collier ships had difficulty unloading in Wapping; so the price of coal was very high. Building work and other labouring jobs were also curtailed. Directly affected by these conditions were the poor and their possibility of making a living. For members of the livery companies there were often small payments or deliveries of coals to assist them in such conditions. On 15th January 1740 the Court of the Distillers' Company decided that in *Consideration of the present Rigorous Season Do Order that Ten shillings be paid to each of their Pensioners this Day for Coals.*[17]

An additional and common method for raising money for the poor was through the preaching of Charity Sermons. As early as February 1723 the *Daily Post* announced that on Sunday the 24th *there will be two Charity Sermons preached at the parish church of St Mary Whitechapel for the Benefit of One Hundred poor children belonging to the parish*. We do not know how much money was collected, but further sermons took place in 1725. In 1733 one of the sermons was preached by John Harris, Bishop of Llandaff, which implies some high-level church connections with the Whitechapel clergy.[18]

Outdoor and casual relief provided several options to the Overseers. For some of the poor it was sufficient to provide "shelter for a night or a small handout". Jonas Hanway's Act of 1767 permitted all metropolitan parishes to send their pauper children aged below six at least three miles away into the country. Until 1816 older pauper children could be apprenticed not only locally, but also as far away as the cotton mills and factories in the Midlands and the north.[19]

"The most difficult group of paupers to assess are the casual poor who sought some form of temporary help. In many cases, these paupers did not possess a settlement and in this situation overseers had a choice. They could hold firm and refuse to offer relief, and instead seek an order of removal. It would appear that most London parishes tried to avoid the high cost of removing the non-settled poor to their settlement parishes compared to the rest of the country."

"It is becoming clear that the poor were well aware of their rights to claim relief. A few realised the opportunities for claiming relief in several parishes simultaneously; as communications between parishes were minimal compared to the scale of the problem". Indeed in 1829 "a man called Paxton had managed to get money, shoes and clothing from Bishopsgate under a false name, as well as receiving regular relief over a period of years from Holborn, St George Southwark and from Mile End Old Town".[20]

Pavements and Sewers

In Whitechapel in 1690 *a greater part of Church Lane was paved* but by 1692 it needed *to be repaired at parish charge*. The cost of the repairs was £53-3s.-9d. and the rate to collect this sum was *not to exceed 4d. in the pound for tenements and 8d. in every £20 of personal estate*. The first "improvement" Act for London was as early as 1701 but it was not until the 1760s that there was a rapid growth across the country in those Acts which allowed towns and parishes to tackle the problems of paving, lighting watching and other improvements.[21]

Until 1762 there was an obligation for every householder in London to pave and keep in repair the street in front of his front door. This was not a very satisfactory state of affairs. Sheds and penthouses encroached on to the streets. Piles of rubbish and dung accumulated on the pavements which were often uneven and seldom repaired. The change in 1762 was due to the passing of the first Westminster Paving Act, which allowed the appointment of commissioners, with powers to raise a rate, which was to be spent on the laying of new pavements to much higher standards, together with a variety of other services, including cleaning.

The result of the many Acts passed in subsequent years was a great improvement to the look and sanitation of London's streets, and it was with great enthusiasm that Whitechapel residents tackled the task of improving their own environment; when their Paving Act was passed in 1771. The new commissioners were worthy men, several of whom lived in Whitechapel, such as Luke Alder an oilman and Thomas Price a cheesemonger, both of whom were voters in 1768. The Whitechapel Act led to the formation of committees to oversee the workings of the Act in different parts of the parish. The Minute books have fortunately survived for both the Goodman's Fields and High Street committees and provide an insight into their workings and the problems that arose. At the first meeting on 11th March 1771 the committee responsible for the High Street met in the Vestry Room at St. Mary church under the chairmanship of the Rector, the Rev'd Dr. Robert Markham. There were twenty-one trustees present at this first meeting, of whom nine had been voters in 1768. Also present were two of the local sugar refiners, John Christian Suhring and Frederick Ryder.[22]

There were many important decisions to be made quickly. John Scutt was appointed clerk at £20 per annum; Mr. Wyatt was appointed surveyor and William Hamilton became the treasurer. The latter was an important post as several hundred pounds were going to be raised every year by the rates on property. In 1778 the rate amounted to £294–13s.–1d.. Thomas Burton, who was already the *receiver or collector of the toll on Hay*, was given the additional task of collecting the rate, and received over sixty pounds per year for all his work, which continued until his resignation in 1791. The rate, which was set at one shilling and sixpence in the pound, was to fund the paving work, as no money would be forthcoming from the government. For householders, on the south side of the High Street, who suffered from the presence of the Hay Market in front of their houses, the rate was reduced to one shilling and three pence in the pound. A minor appointment was that of Evan Jones as a messenger, at a salary of £15 per year, but by 1781 he was said to be "very infirm". Jones died in 1782 and William Carter was appointed "Street Keeper and Messenger".

The next problem was to identify local men of wealth, who would be prepared to quickly lend money to the committee, against the security of the rates. Charles Digby, esquire, a well-known local ship chandler, who lived in Mile End Old Town, was prepared to lend £1,000 at 4½ per cent, but the committee rejected this offer. Eventually they accepted offers from James Waller for £1,000, Edward Bangham for £500 and William Spencer for £1,400. Within a few weeks the committee had invited bids for undertaking the paving work, and quickly decided to award contracts to Robert Campbell from Northumberland Avenue, and to Richard Barwise, a well-known local stone mason, from Mile End Old Town. Barwise was to continue to work for the committee until his death in 1796.

The minutes for the Goodman's Field's paving commissioners contain the following specification for the pavement:

> *The footways with Purbeck or Yorkshire Ealing Hedge Stone at two and a half inches thick, and a Moore Stone curb one foot by seven inches, and from the curb to the channel with old stones or pebbles Sized, Sorted, Squared, and between the channels with Granite or Guernsey squared stones not less than six inches deep.*

In the High Street it appears that the contracts required the granite stones to be at least nine inches thick. However, is was soon realised that before work could commence it was necessary to ensure that the old pavements were cleared of *Porter stands*, old sheds and rubbish. This led to contracts with local carpenters, builders, and smiths, who made the iron covers for drains. The *Porter stands* or *Pitching Places* were to be moved to new positions in the High Street and the carpenters were to construct new stands for them.

Eventually it was decided to place the *Pitching Places* at the end of Petticoat Lane before Bilbies, the Bulls Head Alehouse and before Holdsworths, the Whittington and Cat Alehouse, and before the Seven Stars Alehouse.

It was also decided to use the opportunity to number the houses in the High Street and after some discussion it was resolved that No. 1 would be Mr. Soame's house at the sign of the Three Tuns. It was also decided that *the names of several Streets, alleys and courts ... be painted on Boards and affixed to up at the entrances of such*. To speed the numbering, contracts were given to Thomas Hodgson and William Long, one to work along the north side of the High Street and the other on the south side. For some reason the street names chosen by the commissioners did not meet with the approval of the local residents, who began to put up their preferred signs. The response of the commissioners in 1778 was to demand that *all Fictitious or New Names affixed at the ends of Alleys and Yards, etc in the High Street be erased and the Original Names painted in their Room.*

Once the paving contractors started work a number of new problems arose. First it was felt necessary to employ a watchman to *Watch and Light the High Street, whilst the Sewer or Drain is making therein.* Perhaps someone had fallen into a sewer and was threatening to sue? It also became clear that Robert Campbell's contract was not being performed to expectations. His workmen were not proceeding as fast as expected and there were doubts about whether the stones he laid were nine inches thick or not. So by September 1771 counsel was being asked for his opinion on how to deal with the situation. The counsel suggested advertising the contract again, and this threat seemed to be sufficient to bring Campbell under control for he was later awarded a ten-year contract to maintain the pavements.

As the work progressed the committee was quickly advised at its weekly meetings of new difficulties, usually related to sewers. These raised a problem as the main sewers were the responsibility of the Commissioners for Sewers. The difficulty seemed to be with unofficial sewers from houses to the main sewers. There were frequent reports of sewers being blocked and over flowing, which *injured several persons* or led to damage to houses. So who should pay for their repair? Sometimes it was found that the new pavement had been laid too high which caused flooding, and this led to more complaints.

In July 1771 a spring was found when they took up the old pavement *before the house of Mrs Stockdell and Mr. Clayton.* The commissioners ordered that a new pump be installed in the old well and announced with great satisfaction that *the Spring of water therein being found to be good and wholesome.*

It is very noticeable how very quickly problems were identified and action taken to remedy the situation. When the problem involved another authority then a sub-committee would be appointed; and the clerk instructed to write to the other party with details of the dispute. A typical problem was how to raise the rate on houses which stood on a corner in Red Lion Street. The pavement on one side of the house was the responsibility of the High Street commissioners, whilst on the other side it was the responsibility of the Goodman's Fields committee.

After about eight months of work by the two main contractors and half a dozen sub-contractors, it was only necessary for the commissioners to meet every two or three weeks, to review progress, settle disputes and authorise payments. Not unexpectedly fewer men attended the later committee meetings and often these were cancelled as being non-quorate. It then became necessary to have a *Public Notice affixed to the Church Door* to keep the committee members informed of the date of the next meeting.

Following the practice elsewhere the commissioners advertised in 1772 a contract for the long-term maintenance of the carriage-way. After due consideration it was awarded to Campbell at the rate of two shillings and two pence per square yard per year. The initial contract was for ten years, but in 1773 Campbell proposed that he be given a twenty-year contract at the increased rate of three pence per sq. yard per year. The commissioners were too experienced in the commercial world to accept such a submission, and told Campbell he would be held to his original contract.

It was noticeable that small contracts for *keeping the foot pavement in repair* were still being given to Richard Barwise, a contractor against whom no complaints had been made. He would have been known to many of the commissioners as his mason's yard was at the junction of the Great Essex Road with Dog Row; which led north to Bethnal Green and Cambridge, and he was there from 1769 until at least 1790.

Disputes sometimes arose between contractors and in 1781 a Mr Harrison, a successful contractor complained that Mr Staines, the unsuccessful bidder, was *monopolising the Guernsey pebbles and refusing to supply him with a sufficient Quantity*. Again the commissioners showed their commercial sense and told Harrison to find an alternative supplier and that they would not hold him to the completion dates for the repairs.

After three years it was clear that the commissioners had been very successful at collecting the rate from housekeepers and controlling the costs of their sub-contractors. Bad debts were only a few pounds a year and together these factors led to the treasurer reporting that he had over £500 on account, and it was resolved to begin repaying some of the loans.

Watering the Pavements

In 1777 the commissioners advertised a contract for the watering of the pavements in the High Street between 1st May and 1st September. Again the commercial sense of the commissioners came forth and it was agreed that they should provide *two proper Barrows with Tubs and to employ men to water the street*. In 1778 a contract was awarded to Abraham Lilley who proposed to water the High Street at the rate of six shillings per week *to be paid weekly*. The street was to be watered twice a day and more often when necessary *to keep the dust down*.

From 1788 the commissioners began to receive complaints that John Marshall, the Street Keeper was greatly neglecting his duties. This was partly due to his old age and infirmity so it was decided to appoint Joseph Levy as his assistant; and Marshall was put on half pay. Levy died within a year and the commissioners magnanimously allowed Quarrill to buy some clothes for Levy's son, which suggests they were a poor family.

Complaints against the Street Keeper continued and clearly he was not coping with the situation in spite of warnings. Then he was accused of using *very unbecoming language* and insulting members of the public. Marshall's reply was to accuse the *Inhabitants of placing their goods and wares on the pavements before their respective houses*. He also said he was prevented from doing his duties by the persons that sell hay and straw and would not place their carts in the assigned positions. Again the response of the commissioners to this continuing saga was to find more help to assist Marshall and in 1790 they asked the Peace Officers, John Fann and Benjamin Nash, to attend to the regulation of the Hay Market.

By 1792 the residents who lived along the High Street were still complaining about *the obstructions and Nuisances in the Street by suffering Fish Stalls, Apple Stalls and Ballad singers, etc on the pavement*. These complaints gives some idea of the bustle that surrounded the Hay Market. Finally, it was agreed that Marshall was no longer a fit and proper person to be a Street Keeper, but generously he was allowed a pension of ten pounds per year.

His replacements, Richard Lanoeman and Benjamin Constable, were already the Night Beadles and each was paid five shillings a week for their extra duties. But when were they expected to sleep? These decisions only partially dealt with the complaints, and in 1793 handbills were printed to remind housekeepers that they were to sweep before their houses every morning and that market-traders' barrows were not be driven on to the pavements.

Relations with Parliament

Dr Innes reminds us that parliament "served as an important forum for the discussion of metropolitan issues, and indeed, as a metropolitan regulatory body in its own right. Almost all MPs were, of necessity, resident in the metropolis during a substantial part of the year. Some were alderman of the London, a few were active Middlesex justices, some were active in parish affairs. Clearly, these élite metropolitan residents had ready access to parliament". It is for these reasons that Sir William Curtis and John Wilkes, both MPs, had such great influence in London's eastern parishes. The diaries of John Wilkes record an endless succession of lunches and dinners in the City and Westminster, and occasionally in East London. His brother-in-law George Hayley, MP, who lived in Great Alie Street, near Goodman's Fields in a house with a rent of £25, was the most frequently visited person and enabled Wilkes to be up-to-date with Whitechapel affairs. There were also dinners at the Ship in Ratcliffe with the forty-shilling freeholders, at the Denmark Tavern in Aldgate with Serjeant Glynn, a leading lawyer of the times, and at the Vine in Wapping with Messrs. Glover and Joseph Hill.[23]

As an example of parliamentary action we have "the pressures of war in 1710 prompted the imposition of what was intended to be a revenue-yielding system of licensing and regulating hackney coaches throughout London, Westminster and all parishes within the weekly bills of mortality."[24]

For improvements to roads, paving, lighting and policing it was necessary in the C18 to petition parliament. Sometimes the parishes found it necessary to share the costs of such petitions between them. This did not necessarily lead to harmony and there was no guarantee that an Act would not in turn lead to more controversy. A typical petition was presented to parliament in 1696 from the *Inhabitants of St John Wapping*, which read:

> *That by an Act, made in the last Parliament, the said Parish was made a distinct Parish from the Parish of Whitechapel; but is obliged to contribute towards the Repairs of the Highways of the Parish of Whitechapel, which lie near a mile from the new Parish: That the Act does not determine which Part of the Highways the Petitioners are to repair, by reason of which Uncertainty, many Differences have arose between the Two Parishes; and the Petioners are liable to many indictments, which might be prevented, if they were at a Certainty: And praying, That the House will appoint certain Persons to set out what part of the Highways the Petioners shall keep in repair.*

It was ordered that the petition *shall lie upon the Table*, but this problem was to continue to return for many years, because the people of Wapping could not see why they should pay towards the maintenance of the turnpike from Whitechapel to Shenfield, as it did not go through their parish.[25]

The Whitechapel to Shenfield Turnpike

The first Turnpike Trust Act was passed in 1663 for the Wadesmill-Stilton road, north of Hertford, but it was not until 1696 that an Act was passed for the Shenfield-Harwich Trust. On the 5th June 1721 parliament received a Petition from:

> *Several Deputy Lieutenants, Justices of the Peace of Middlesex and Essex and other Gentry living in or near the several towns and parishes lying on the highways leading from Stones End, Whitechapel to Shenfield, Essex, that by reason of the many heavy carriages, great number of Stage and Hackney coaches, Passengers and Drovers of Cattle, daily passing through the said Highways, are becoming ruinous, and in many Parts thereof so bad, that in the winter Season, the same are very dangerous to all Persons ... and the Inhabitants of the said Towns have been at great expense in Repairing and Amending thereof ... that they are almost impassable.*

Such a petition, although formulaic in expression, was very important to the residents. Amongst the local gentry who were petitioners were Captain Thomas Heath MP and Captain Stephen Martin Leake. By early July 1721 a committee of parliament had established that a yearly levy of £400 was raised by the Trustees of the Turnpike on Stepney on a *discretionary basis* for the road from Whitechapel to Bow, but *statements could not be checked due to the lack of books showing the amounts collected and spent*. Messrs Wykes and Coker had surveyed the road from Stones End to Bow, a distance of two miles and eighteen rods. They estimated that if gravel was laid three-feet deep and thirty-feet wide it would cost £3,000 to repair the road and almost £600 per year to keep it in good repair. There were no petitions against the proposed turnpike, and an Act was finally passed in 1722.

The *Daily Courant* 21th February 1724 announced a General Meeting of the trustees for repairing the highway from Stones End, Whitechapel, to Shenfield. The meeting at the Court House in Whitechapel was to choose officers for the coming year. Typical of the problems they tackled was the complaint of the *Inhabitants of Mile End Old Town* that the other hamlets were refusing to repair the road from *the Watch house in Mile End Road to Stepney [church]*. Finally the problem was passed to Sir Thomas Roberts and other eminent residents, but how they resolved it was unclear.

Certainly this dispute reveals the tensions between the residents of Whitechapel and Mile End Old Town and their poorer neighbours. There was also a gradual change taking place between the old system that relied on statute labour supervised by the surveyors of the highway, and the new system that relied on the creation of efficient and well-funded turnpike trusts. Statute labour was the requirement by law that parishioners perform in person certain tasks for the parish each year in turn. There were many problems associated with statute labour; not least the reluctance of a labourer or farmer with only one cart to lose several days earnings, whilst working on the highway.

The election of surveyors of the highways took place every year until 1749 at vestry meetings, and all the prominent residents were liable to perform this unpaid role, whether they had an engineering mind or not. In early 1737 the Trustees of the Turnpike petitioned parliament requesting an enlargement to the terms and powers of the Act. The reason for this request, typically fifteen years after the original Act was passed, was that in 1722 the trustees had been:

> *Obliged to borrow a considerable sum of money on the Credit of the tolls [£2,560] ... but there still remains due the sum of £1,500 ... and that parts of the road are very bad in the winter season and the rest will soon be in a ruinous condition.*

Mr. Thomas Donne, Clerk to the Trustees, believed they would *collect upwards of £3,000 per year from the Turnpike Gates*, and spend a similar sum on the repairs to the road; this activity led to the passing of another Act. At the same time the churchwardens, constable and other inhabitants of Bethnal Green petitioned parliament for the road from *the turnpike at the end of Dog Row, Mile End, unto Shoreditch* to be turnpiked. This very *large road* was described as:

> *Being the most commodious way to Smithfield's Market from Essex ... by the vast Numbers of Cattle of all Sorts perpetually passing to and from the said Market besides many heavy carriages that pass that way.*

The petition went on to describe the hamlet of Bethnal Green as now *being very poor, the greatest part of the inhabitants consisting of journeymen weavers and are not in a capacity any longer to support the [road] ... in necessary repairs*. The Act was passed in 1738. At the same time parliament received a petition from the inhabitants of the hamlet of Poplar and Blackwall requesting provision to be made to repair their road, which was the only one from Essex and Middlesex into Kent by the ferry at the Isle of Dogs. The number of inhabitants had for several years *greatly decreased* inasmuch that many of the houses were uninhabited, and *the said Hamlet, though so very poor continue to pay a large Share of the composition paid by the parish of St Dunstan's Stepney, to the Trustees of the Turnpike*.

Whilst these petitions emphasise the poor quality of the roads it is now generally accepted that both the roads, and the vehicles travelling on them, were constantly being improved, with a subsequent reduction in travel times throughout the C18. Trustees and commissioners were given authority by the Acts to raise rates on property, but even in the wealthier parish of Whitechapel the collection of the rate for the turnpike was not without its problems as revealed in the evidence provided to parliament in 1733. Henry Goodwin described how as churchwarden he had to collect £100 a year for the turnpike rate. When he had collected £60 or so he sent for the constable to collect the remainder from reluctant ratepayers, and *that with much trouble he collected £80 and would not go any more.* In 1770 the Commissioners for Paving the City of London announced that they intended to borrow a sum of money *on the Credit of the Sundry Tolls ... at the Turnpikes at Mile End, Bethnal Green and Goswell Street.*[26]

Voters from Whitechapel in 1768

The poll book for the 1768 election noted about 370 men from the eastern parishes who were qualified to vote. The full list is in Appendix 2 and a selection of the more prosperous voters is in Table 1.

Table 1   SOME VOTERS FROM WHITECHAPEL IN 1768

NAME	ADDRESS	NOTES	LIVERY COMPANY	PERSONAL ESTATE £	Rent £
John Adams	High Street	Cooper	Coopers'	33	25
Luke Alder	High Street	Oil and colourman	Farriers'	50	30
Eugene Allen	High Street	SUN	Innholders'	75	36
William Bond	High Street		Grocers'	75	32
Isaac Collnett	High Street	Blacksmith	Blacksmiths'		32
John Coope	Rupert Street		Salters'		30
George Crosby	Buckle Street	Sugar refiner	Fishmongers'	90	25
Joshua Crowden	High Street		Cordwainers'	50	18
William Denman	Mansell Street		Joiners'		15
Thomas Denning	High Street	Cooper, will.	Coopers'		25
William Draper	High Street	Cheesemonger, Victualler	Vintners'		60
John Everard	Goodman's Fields		Skinners'		15
William Fillingham	Tongue's Yard	Livery keeper	Ironmongers'	50	70
Joseph Fisher	Prescot Street		Tallow Chandlers'	75	15
William Hamilton jnr	High Street	Upholsterer, undertaker	Clothworkers'	50	25
Thomas Hawes	High Street	Probate	Grocers'		21
Samuel Hawkins	Leman Street	Builder	Carpenters'	25	30
Humphery Haydon	High Street	Sailmaker	Blacksmiths'	75	22
Charles Holdsworth	High Street		Patten-makers'	25	25
William Hollamby, jnr	Leman Street		Innholders'		20
Joel Johnson	Church Lane	Carter	Carpenters'		25
William Lindus	High Street	Gentleman	Butchers'		28
Robert Newcombe	Mansell Street		Glass-sellers'		15
Allens Parsons	High Street	Hay salesman	Tallow Chandlers'	25	12
Joseph Pettitt	High Street	? James	Coachmakers'		22
Thomas Price	High Street	Cheesemonger	Clothworkers'		30
William Read	High Street	Distiller	Embroiderers'	75	22
John Rex	High Street	Distiller	Distillers'	45	25
William Scott	High Street		Barbers'		30
William Scullard	Goodman's Fields	Broker	Vintners'	100	18
James Spalding	High Street	Grocer	Grocers'	75	45
William Thoytes			Armourers' and Brasiers'	300	50
Redman Tomkins	High Street	Butcher, governor L. H.	Butchers'	75	16
Cecil Waring	Great Alie Street		Skinners'	25	12
Richard Whiteshead	Tongue's Yard	Coach maker	Coachmakers'		30

It has been possible to identify the occupations, livery companies and the rental values for nearly fifty of these men. One problem, of course, as noted in the London Poll Book; was that *the spelling of names is arbitrary*, to which can be added the lack of the precision in the "Place of Abode". The voters belonged to 49 livery companies, of which the most popular were the Innholders', the Joiners', and the Butchers'. A few of the local voters belonged to the Grand Twelve livery companies, such as the Drapers' and Ironmongers.

It is clear from the land tax that only a few of the men meeting the requirement to have a house with a rental value of £10 or more were on the list of voters for 1768. Generally, it is thought that only 18% of those eligible to vote appeared on the lists of voters.[27]

Many of these voters would have been involved in the famous election of 1768. In parallel with the campaign in support of the Radical MP John Wilkes [1725-1797] DNB; many other groups in London took part in protests, demonstrations and riots. These included tailors, Thames watermen, sailors, silk weavers from Spitalfields and Bethnal Green, and coal-heavers from Shadwell and Wapping, as described by Colm Kerrigan and George Rudé. This culminated on the 26th July 1768 in executions in Sun Tavern Fields in Shadwell, when a crowd of 50,000 is said to have attended. Undoubtedly political tensions would have been high in East London.

One of Wilkes's supporters was Mr. Serjeant Glynn, a leading lawyer and Recorder of London. In November 1768 an advertisement appeared in the *Daily Advertiser*, announcing that *The Friends of Mr. Serjeant Glynn, residing in or near the Tower Hamlets intend celebrating the Anniversary of King William III's Landing in England* [in November 1688] *on Friday next, the 4th inst. at the Mile End Assembly Room; the Company of any of the Gentlemen Freeholders that are in the interest of Mr. Serjeant Glynn will be esteemed as a Favour. Dinner to be on the Table at Half past Three.*

In 1770 Wilkes languished in the King's Bench prison in St. George's Fields and a further example of the support he enjoyed was the announcement in February 1770 that his release from prison *is to be celebrated in a manner not altogether dissimilar from the twelfth of November. There will be bonfires, illuminations and every testimony of public joy exhibited on this occasion.* There was also going to be *a procession in which the effigies of Mr Wilkes persecutors, together with those of the conspirators to violate the privileges and immunities of Englishmen will be carried and afterwards burnt in triumph.* Typically, these processions would wend their way down through the crowds lining the Whitechapel Road towards the Mile End Assembly Rooms; probably led by a band, followed by the coaches of the leading citizens, and crowds of supporters wearing blue cockades, and shouting *Wilkes and Liberty* or even *Wilkes, Liberty and coal-heavers for ever.*[28]

The Land Tax

The land tax has been mentioned in Chapter 1 and provides another example of the way in which the government's needs were handled at the local level. The allocation and subsequent collection of the land tax basically involved a hierarchy of officials. The *London Journal* for 20th July 1734 announced that the Lords Commissioners of the Treasury had appointed William Selwin esquire of Paternoster Row as the Receiver General for that year's land tax for the cities of London and Westminster. A similar appointment was made for Middlesex and in turn receivers were appointed for each parish and their signatures can be found at the end of each year's tax collection. The Receiver General was instructed on the sum of money to be raised in the area under his jurisdiction. He in turn informed each parish of the amount to be collected. So it was a tax to raise a specific sum of money and not a tax on the value of land and property.[29]

The *London Gazette* for 12th September 1724 contained notice of a General Meeting of the Commissioners of the land tax for Middlesex at the White Lion tavern in Whitechapel. The meeting was to arrange the sale of the property and personal estate of Richard Newton, one of the collectors of the tax in Wapping for 1723. The reason for the sale is not clear, but perhaps he had failed to collect the taxes in an adequate manner? The evidence from the land tax for nearby MEOT was that the vestry were very quick to identify a newcomer, who was eligible to be elected as headborough; that is someone in a house with a rental value of £10 or more. The ten-pound qualification held throughout most of the C18 defining *freeholders* who could be considered for various parish duties as well as serving on juries. In addition we have information on the collectors of the land tax such as Thomas Bowrey, merchant and shop keeper in the Minories. He was summoned to the White Lyon in Whitechapel on the 26th of February 1712 *to meet the rest of the commissioners acting for the Tower Division ... to examine the collectors deficiencies on the land tax.*[30]

Such summonses were constantly received by the leading members of East London society and their names can be found signing off the land tax registers. Typically, in 1764 men such as Edward Hawkins, William Quarrill and Redman Tomkins signed off the Whitechapel land tax.[31]

FURTHER READING

D. Andrew	*Philanthropy and Police: London Charity in the Eighteenth Century*, 1989
G. Boyer	*An Economic History of the English Poor Law, 1750-1850*, 1990
P. J. Corfield	*The Impact of English Towns, 1700-1800*, 1989
J. H. Curtis-Dolby and N. Brazil	*Billy Biscuit: A Colourful Life and Times of Sir William Curtis*, 2010
M. Daunton, ed.	*Charity, Self Interest and Welfare in the English Past*, 1996
M. D. George	*London life in the eighteenth century*, 1951
D. R. Green	*From Artisan to Paupers: Economic Change and Poverty in London, 1790-1870*, 1995
D. R. Green	*Pauper Capital: London and the Poor Law, 1790-1870*, 2010
D. T. Hawkins	*Fire Insurance Records for family and local historians, 1696 to 1929*, 2003
D. Hey	*Oxford Encyclopaedia of Local History*, 2010
T. Hitchcock	*Down and Out in Eighteenth-Century London*, 2007
T. Hitchcock et al eds.	*Chronicling Poverty - The Voices and Strategies of the English Poor, 1640-1840*, 1997
J. Innes	Managing the Metropolis: London's Social Problems and their Control, *c.*1660-1830, *Two Capitals: London and Dublin: 1500-1840*, ed. P. Clark & R. Gillespie, 2001, pp. 53-79
J. Marriott	*Beyond the Tower: A History of East London*, 2011
J. Marshall	*Mortality of the Metropolis*, 1832
R. Porter	*London: A Social History*, 1994
M. Rose, ed.	*The Poor and the City: The English Poor Law in its Urban Context*, 1985
G. F. E. Rudé	*Wilkes and Liberty: a social study of 1763-74*, 1962
F. H. W. Sheppard	*Local Government in St Marylebone, 1688-1835: A Study of the Vestry and Turnpike Trust*, 1958
P. Slack	*The English Poor Law, 1531-1782*, 1990
J. Stow	*A Survey of London*, 1603 reprinted 1971
VCH	*Middlesex*, vol. XI, *Early Stepney and Bethnal Green*, 1998, ed. C. R. J. Currie, pp. 63-70, P. E. C. Croot

Web Sites

http://www.british-history.ac.uk
http://www.lma.gov.uk
http://www.oldbaileyonline.org.uk
http://www.workhouses.org.uk

3. LIVING IN WHITECHAPEL

A Walk through Whitechapel

The Hoop and Grapes, on the south side of Aldgate High Street, is a good place to start a walk eastward into Whitechapel to search for the street scene as it may have appeared in the seventeenth and eighteenth centuries. It is one of a pair of timber-framed houses, which the Pevsner Guide thinks might post-date the Great Fire of 1666, in spite of the new building regulations of the 1670s that tried to reduce the use of timber. The narrow frontage is typical of many of the buildings that in the eighteenth century (C18) could be found to the east along the Whitechapel High Street and Peter Guillery noted that "tall but shallow timber houses of the seventeenth-century lined the larger roads" in Whitechapel.[1]

Continuing eastward past St Botolph church into Whitechapel High Street reveals that few buildings from the C18 have survived until you reach Davenant's School on the north side and the Bell Foundry on the south side. Both are well-built and demonstrate how the street scene may have looked in earlier years.

Until the late C20 buildings on the High Street, and its continuation Whitechapel Road, remained predominately three and four-storeyed. There was a plentiful supply of inns, a mixture of narrow C18 and C19 frontages, and narrow alleys leading off, typical of an ancient street pattern. War damage and indifferent redevelopment have left only scrappy remains and the gradual creep of the City further threatens the intimate scale. A typical narrow-fronted house can be seen at No. 129, but this is late C19, with stucco trim, two bays, and four storeys. The White Hart is only one bay wide and has a C19 front with a tripartite window, grandly flanked by giant Corinthian pilasters.[2]

You then arrive at the Davenant Centre, formerly the Davenant Foundation School. Robert Schnebbellie's drawing of 1815 shows a seven-bay house of two storeys with a front garden behind a high brick wall. It now has a five-bay stucco frontage to the road and is dated 1818, with two storeys above a basement with the three central bays projecting and "Whitechapel School" in the frieze above.[3]

Altab Ali Park, named in 1989 in memory of a local Bangladeshi youth murdered in 1978, was developed on the former churchyard of St Mary Matfelon. The church was demolished in 1952 after war damage. Its outline is traced by stones laid out in the grass and in the south-east corner of the park is a "a fine tapered sarcophagus to the Maddock family (†1770s-†1801)".

Figure 4   66 LEMAN STREET

Housing

Introduction

For a detailed analysis of the smaller and middling housing in C18 London there is no better starting point than Peter Guillery's well-illustrated book on small houses.[4] Of the many points that he makes the most relevant to this study are:

- There were not large houses and small houses, but houses of all sizes along a continuum, on the whole thoroughly jumbled together, the humble and the grand often cheek by jowl.

- A house with a frontage of 20ft or more is not considered to be "small".

- There can be no simple equation of house size with status. Clearly people lived only in houses they could afford, but it should not be assumed that people always lived in the largest house that they may have done.

- House occupancy, single or multiple, is a highly problematic area. This subject is discussed in later chapters.

To these points can be added the fact that probably only 20% of householders owned their house. Many tenements were built specifically for multiple occupation. Renting was widespread and contributed to the flexibility and movement of London's population at this time. Indeed, examples are known of families moving into the next house to gain a few additional rooms. Dr Dorothy George commented that "A large proportion of the poorer classes in London lived in ready-furnished rooms, paying a weekly rent … there were furnished lodgings for all classes and the letting of lodgings was a great industry."[5]

Guillery and his co-workers relied on detailed studies of the houses that survived from the C18 together with plans, drawings and photographs and other resources. The following section contributes to this discussion by making great use of the land tax and insurance records to provide descriptions of the housing available in the area, and to look at the surviving houses in nearby MEOT. Inventories are then used to gain an insight into how these houses were furnished.[6]

Whitechapel in the mid-eighteenth century still had a wide range of houses available, but without extensive gardens and orchards, thus continuing the pattern of the 1690s noted by Spence. The residents did not have as wide a choice of property as was available to the house-holders in MEOT. There it was possible to choose the location, size, scope, and facilities best suited to their family and business needs, with the added advantage over the City of London and Whitechapel that land was available for gardens, paddocks and orchards. In a few cases summerhouses were built in the gardens and orchards.[7]

Extensive insurance records have survived for London from 1696. Those of the Hand-in-Hand Company are particularly valuable as they provide details of the size of the house, the numbers of rooms with wainscoting and marble or Portland stone mantelpieces. They also show the proportion of the house consisting of brick and the proportion consisting of timber – all details relevant to the evaluation of the fire risk. Insurance policies often refer to the linking together of two adjacent houses; a practice that enabled a merchant to quickly enlarge his living space and stay close to his workshops.[8]

The land tax registers have been examined for the period 1740 to 1770. Broadly, the land tax assessment was based on two pounds per room. So a two-up – two-down house of four rooms would be assessed on a "rent" of £8; to which might be added a rent of £2 for *land*, or a *garden, or a workshop, or a stable*. Similarly, £3 might cover a *coal shed* or a *workshop*. Many houses had a timber washroom equipped with a boiler; and a kitchen in the back yard with dimensions of approximately 10ft by 10ft, but there is no specific mention of a "bathroom" in the insurance policies or inventories.

Larger houses with a rack rent of £25 can still be seen in Ireland Row, Mile End Road, and are illustrated in Guillery's book. They were built in 1717, and were refurbished in the 1990s by the Spitalfields Trust. Of these No. 111, a listed Grade II house, has two rooms in the basement, a ground-floor reception room and dining room, a first-floor drawing room and a bedroom and finally two bedrooms on the top floor. The reception room, 14ft by 13ft 4ins was fully panelled with a full box cornice, and the dining room, 14ft by 11ft 3ins still has the original stone chimney-piece.

In 1779 the occupier was Admiral Abraham North, who had lived in MEOT from 1765. He had married into one of the prominent land-owning families and in 1780 was taxed for one manservant. North has a minor role in maritime history for he was one of the two Admiralty men who signed Captain James Cook's passing certificate, before he set out on his first voyage of exploration of the Pacific.[9]

Bearing in mind Guillery's comment about houses ranging along a continuum, the following sections look at three broad categories – large, middle and small houses - remembering that very little is known about the very smallest houses and hovels.

The Large Houses

It is not surprising to discover that three of the largest houses in Whitechapel belonged to prominent sugar refiners - Frederick Rider, Henry Lear and Christopher Phillipson, - but unfortunately no sign of their houses has survived.

Frederick Rider lived in Angel Alley and had taken out the largest insurance in Whitechapel for £1,350 in 1767 on his house and other buildings. The two-storey house had four rooms wainscotted and three rooms with marble mantelpieces. The house was 34 ft by 19 ft and included a *Great Parlour*. There was also a three-storey timber building for *servants rooms* plus a large coach house and stable.[10]

On the west side of Catharine Wheel Alley, south of Wentworth Street, Henry Lear, sugar refiner, insured for £900 two houses which had been joined together. One house was 24 ft by 18 ft and the other 15 ft by 17 ft. The linking together of two adjacent houses was a common practice at this time.[11]

Christopher Phillipson, another sugar refiner, insured for £1,000 his house on the west side of Leman Street, which had three-storeys and a garret and was 36 ft by 35 ft. There was also a washhouse 16 ft by 9 ft. Five rooms were wainscotted and there were two marble chimney-pieces. Phillipson's rent of £24 and his personal estate of £150, are indicative of his wealth and status.[12]

However, none of these houses was as large or as grand as that of Mary Fitzhugh, a few hundred yards to the east in Mile End Old Town. On the 7th August 1738 Mary Fitzhugh insured with the Hand-in-Hand Insurance Company *a brick house on the south side of the Road a little beyond the turnpike at Mile End ... standing clear of all other Building, her Dwelling House*. The house was 41ft by 51ft and had three-storeys, a pediment, leaded windows, eight rooms wainscotted with *right wainscot* and two rooms with deal. There were seven marble chimney-pieces, and five made of Portland stone, which was also used for the staircase.

The significance of this house was shown by the insurance value of £1,800; more than double that of any other house in MEOT, including the famed houses on the east side of Stepney Green. Later the insurance value was increased to £2,000. Other houses in London, which by virtue of similar insurance values confirm the significance of the Fitzhugh house, were those of Sir William Heathcote, on the north side of St James's Square, insured for £1,300, and of Sampson Gideon, the famous Jewish financier, in Lincoln's Inn Field, insured for £1,500.[13]

The Middling Houses

In 1750 there were about 500 houses with rents between £10 and £19 and several probates have survived to indicate the number of rooms, out-houses and shops within this range of rents.

The *true inventory* of John Creed, a draper, in 1762 describes the contents of a house in Rosemary Lane with an annual rent of £16. In addition to the garret there were:

Second floor	A front room with a four-posted bed and *crimson harrateen furniture*
	A back room with an old stove grate and one bed
First floor	A back room with a stove, six chairs and a mahogany square table
	[The front room was probably rented out]
Ground floor	A kitchen and a back room together with a cellar, a shop, a counting house and a lumber room backwards

Outside there was a *Sign and a Sign Iron as fixt at the Door*. His estate was valued at £278-2s.-1½d. and there was a very long list of his stock in trade:

4 pieces of dyed fustian	£3-12s.-00d.
17 yards of Black lasting	£0-10s.-00d.
36 yards of Shalloon	£5-13s.-4d.
11 yards of Worsted Shagg	£0-16s.-6d.
8 Coats	£2-12s.-6d.
26 pairs of Boy's Yarn stockings	£0-8s.-8d.
16 pairs of new breeches	£4-0s.-00d.

As was common at this time John Creed had to provide extended credit to his clients. Surely his widow Sarah must have been concerned that Thomas Price, a local cheesemonger, owed the significant sum of £199-12s.-7d., which was recorded as a *desperate debt*.[14]

As an example of a slightly smaller house we have that of Thomas Sibley (II), a blacksmith, with a personal estate of £75. He had a house in the High Street with a rent of £13 per year, which in addition to a garret consisted of:

First floor	A dining room and a bed chamber
Ground floor	A kitchen and a back room together with a cellar and a lumber room backwards.

In the dining room there were a stove, eight cherry tree chairs with leather seats, an eight-day clock, tables, a chimney glass and a tea chest. In the kitchen were a range, a crane, 2 pair of brass candlesticks, some Delft plate and four old chairs. Amongst his books, in addition to two bibles, were Birckett's *On The New Testament*, and *A History of Prince Eugene*.

This quite modest house was complemented by a house at Clay Hill in Essex, which provided an escape to the country for the family. When his widow Elizabeth died in 1759 the probate reveals that amongst her belongings were *A History of the World*, a book of maps, a bible and Rapier's *History*.[15]

The Small Houses

There were at the lowest end of the market thousands of small houses in dilapidated courts and alleys. The crumbling tenements and the "dangerous" districts were chiefly in the belt which had grown up round the City between the reign of Elizabeth and the end of the seventeenth century. As Dr George explained "There were however, in densely populated districts, courts within courts and alleys behind alleys forming perfect labyrinths". She thought that this complex network of alleys would present challenges to the surveyors working on Rocque's maps in the 1740s. However, the land tax collectors were perhaps more persistent for they went into the uniquely named *Shall I go Naked Street*.[16]

Some of these smaller houses were owned by Robert Slater, gent, from nearby MEOT. In 1756 he insured for £250 six timber tenements and sheds on the south side of the High Street just west of the Turnpike. They were all 11 ft 6 ins by 12 ft, so probably consisted of a single room, which might easily take lodgers, a single family, or be turned into a shop or workshop, depending on economic conditions.[17]

Guillery provides an illustration of Angel Court in New Gravel Lane, where twelve modest early C18 brick houses, each about 15 ft square on plan, were given an elegant classical finish that suggests concern for amenity. This he considered typical of East London. In 1780 each of these small houses had an annual rent of £7.[18]

The Streets of Whitechapel

To indicate the variation that occurred from one street to another in the C18 the following section describes the High Street, Ayliff Street, Leman Street, Prescot Street and Tongue's Yard.

High Street

The High Street has for hundreds of years been the centre for the victualling and support of the thousands of travellers coming up from Essex, Suffolk and Norfolk to visit London for a variety of reasons. Travellers from the Continent were making their way from Harwich to the City. The wealthy came up in October for the season, whilst on a daily basis drovers and carriers brought their stock and other goods for sale in the wholesale markets and elsewhere. The High Street was the first part of a line of shops that by the end of the C18 stretched through Aldgate, Cheapside and past St Paul's cathedral to the Strand.

Visitors new to London would no doubt be impressed by the large number of imposing buildings stretching for half a mile on either side of the High Street from Aldgate eastwards to the *Barrs*. These reflected the locally available retail trades, industrial businesses and support services. In 1694 there were at least forty merchants in the High Street whose stock was valued at £100 or more including Sir James Etheridge at £600 and Edward Parris at £900.[19]

In 1750 there were sixty-one properties with an annual rental of £20 or more. These were occupied by the most important traders and merchants, who were involved in the victualling and carrying trades. In addition there were men employed in professional occupations. The largest retail traders found along the High Street were bakers, butchers, carriers, cheesemongers, chemists, drapers, grocers, and an upholsterer. Vital professional services were available from John Coverly, a scrivener, whose rent was £18, and Charles Boone, a surgeon, whose rent was £30.[20]

The largest industrial enterprises along the High Street were typical of the wider area and included Sir James Creed's White Lead Factory, several sugar refiners, together with oil and colourmen, coopers, a coppersmith, distillers, a line-spinner, a miller, a sailcloth maker, and many silk throwsters. The properties with rentals above £20 on the north side of the High Street are shown in Table 2.

Table 2   TAX PAYERS ON THE NORTH SIDE OF WHITECHAPEL HIGH STREET

NAME	RENT £	PERSONAL £	NOTES
John Dawson	30	50	The Bulls Head, victualler
Thomas Massa	25		Miller and baker, supplier to the London Hospital. 1774 life governor London Hospital.
Luke Alder	30		Oil and colourman
Charles Boone	30		Surgeon
John Lander	22		The Coach and Horses, victualler
Anthony Wall	80	75	The Angel and Crown Tavern, victualler
Eugene Allen	26	75	Grocer
John Fearnley	22		The Horseshoe and Magpye, victualler
Job Mathews	32	100	Grocer, The Rising Sun and Fig Tree
Joseph Wood	30	75	Cheesemonger
John Adams	33		Cooper. Supplier to London Hospital.
Henry Vernon	36		The Seven Stars, victualler
Jonathan Fuller	34		Silk throwster
Richard Newman	24		The Tewkesbury Church, victualler
Esther Thompson	72	50	The Red Lyon, victualler
Stephen Leach	22	75	Chemist, druggist
William Thoytes	30	150	Copper smith
James Reed	22		Distiller
Benjamin Goodwin	22		Gentleman, Endowed Magg's Almshouses
Walter Archer	35	75	Nags Head and Woolpack, victualler
Robert Jones	20		The Green Dragon, victualler, carrier, stabling
William Forster	22	150	Distiller
Mathew Bateman	20	150	Esquire, estate Essex
Humphery Hayden	22	75	Sail cloth maker, supplier to Royal Navy

The Grave Maurice, refers to Graf [Count] Maurice of the Rhine born in 1620. At 22 he fought as a general for King Charles I against the Roundheads. Later he led the life of a pirate and drowned in the West Indies. Perhaps in view of its name the tavern was a centre for local Jacobites to meet?

The full list of those traders whose rents were £20 or more and whose occupations have been clearly identified can be seen in Tables 2 and 3. It should be noted that the identification of an occupation was only possible for about one-third of the 1750 sample, using wills, lists of licensed victuallers and insurance policies.

Occupations whose rents were £18 or £19 included:

William Carpenter, brewer	John Coverly, a scrivener
Richard Cross, The Angel, victualler,	Joshua Crowden, a cordwainer
George Hubbard, a baker	William Judd, victualler
William Ratcliffe, an ironmonger	Samuel Shepherd, a butcher
Joseph Swaffield, a stationer	William Winstanley, a Barber-Surgeon

The offices of the Manor of Stepney were just east of the Bell Foundry, and clearly benefited the King family. Thomas King was taxed in 1750 and was followed by his widow Ann in 1760 and 1770, but neither lived locally. The Stewards of the Manor were John Wielder in 1740, George Wielder in 1750 and John Langmore in 1760 and 1770, and their names can be found on many Manorial documents.

The south side of the High Street had fewer of the wealthier businesses as shown in Table 3.

Table 3   TAX PAYERS ON THE SOUTH SIDE OF WHITECHAPEL HIGH STREET

NAME	RENT £	PERSONAL £	NOTES
Thomas King	20		For the profits of the Court
George Wielder	30		Steward at the Manor of Stepney for his income and profits
John Rowland	30		Chief Bailiff
William Newman	20	150	The Rose and Crown, chemist, victualler
William Quick	50		Brewer
Thomas Lester	25	75	Bell founder
Jane Taylor	50	75	The George, victualler and livery keeper
Lambert Fielding	22		The Man in the Moon victualler
William Hamilton	27	50	Upholsterer, undertaker. Supplier London Hospital.
Sir James Creed	60	500	Merchant, owner of the White Lead Factory
William Sharp	22		The Whittington Cat, victualler
James Crisp	40	75	Grocer

Ayliff Street

Ayliff Street was laid out in the 1680s and had several reasonable size houses suitable for the "middling sort" of person, which included a variety of merchants, who appreciated its closeness to the City. In 1694 there were sixteen merchants with a stock of £100 or more including Lady Loyd with £1,200 for her four daughters. Samuel Barons was a merchant, whose house on the south side of Ayliffe Street was insured in 1748 for £600. The house had three-storeys and garrets and ten of the rooms were wainscotted, indicative of his wealth.[21]

Nearby, Susanna Massa, a wealthy spinster, in 1758 insured her house on the south side of Ayliffe Street for £800. The house of 36 ft by 26 ft plus an outside kitchen 20 ft by 13 ft 6 ins had three storeys with a garret, six rooms were wainscotted and four rooms were half-way wainscotted, and there were eight marble and two Portland stone chimney-pieces.[22]

On the north side of Ayliff Street was a Meeting House with galleries and pews, part-slated, part-lead insured by the Reverend Joseph Denham for £1,000. He also insured his house and summer house on the south side of Ayliffe Street for £600. This large house was 40 ft by 27 ft and had three-storeys and garrets; six rooms were wainscotted, and there were two marble chimney-pieces and one Portland chimney-piece.[23]

Leman Street

Leman Street, also known as Lemon Street, was the principal street in the development laid out in the 1680s by William Leman, the great-nephew of Sir John Leman, the Lord Mayor of London in 1616-17. As elsewhere in London the streets, Mansell Street, Prescot Street and Ayliff Street, were named after family members. In 1694 there were seven merchants in the street with a stock of £100 or more, including Samuel Butt and James Clarke, both with £500 of stock.

"Strype described these *fair streets of good brick houses* in 1717, but most were replaced by Richard Leman and his builder, Edward Hawkins, in the late C18, when the area was still fashionable. Its social decline was promoted by the noxious sugar refining industry." Leman Street was the most important street in Whitechapel after the High Street, but also had a certain notoriety due to The Bagnio, more fully described in Chapter 8. On the east side can still be seen the Eastern Dispensary, founded in 1782 by City doctors, and which was amongst the first to provide free health care to the poor of East London. On the west side of the street is No. 66 "a genuine 1760s town house of a type once common in the area. It stands slightly back from the railed basement area." It has a big pedimented doorcase with Ionic columns and there is a bracketed cornice to the third floor. It had "a grand panelled interior and staircase, with thin carved balusters".[24] Figure 4.

Samuel Hawkins, a local building developer, insured for £7,100 several houses in Leman Street. One individual house insured for £700 was that of the widow Jennings, whose rent was £25. From insurance records we have a brief description of the dwelling house of Frederick Schumacker in Leman Street, which he insured for £600. It was the fifth house south of Prescot Street and consisted of four-storeys, with five rooms wainscotted, three rooms half-way wainscotted, and three marble chimney-pieces and one Portland chimney-piece.[25] Also in Leman Street was Simon Youd who paid the land tax on his rent of £17. Later in 1760 four houses were advertised for sale by the executors of Mrs Elizabeth Youd.[26] Each of these four leasehold houses consisted of:

2 Garrets	3 Bed chambers
Dining Room	2 Parlours
Kitchen, cellar, pantry	Pleasant garden with palisades before the houses

Tongue's Yard

Tongue's Yard on the south side of the High Street, close to the junction with Field Gate Street and east of the church, has a long history of industrial activity. In 1694 there were six merchants with stock of £100 or more. In the middle of the C18 a great variety of enterprises could still be found in this small yard as shown in Table 4:

Table 4   TAXPAPERS IN TONGUE'S YARD, 1750

NAME	RENT £	PERSONAL £	NOTES
William Quick	50		Brewhouse
Thomas Lester	27		Bell founder
John Brissault	40	150	Sugar refiner
Arthur Granger	16	50	Carpenter, timber yard
Richard Whiteshead	10		Coach maker
Jane Taylor	50	75	Victualler, livery keeper
William Newman	15		Silk throwster

In 1754 Richard Whiteshead insured for £300 his timber workshops described as the *7th building east from church*.[27]

The business of stable keepers with livery stables is worthy of note, as it demonstrates the continuity of one family's interest for over thirty years. Being well-situated on the High Street ensured that their business would be clearly visible to the passing travellers and perhaps can be traced back to the seventeenth-century?

The succession of land tax payers was as follows:

> Avery Taylor and John Avery in 1740 were stable keepers with a rent of £32
> Jane Taylor followed and in 1750 her rent was £50 and she had a personal estate of £75

Avery Taylor's sister was Susannah Fillingham and her son, William was under the conditions of Taylor's will *to go into partnership with his wife in business of a stable keeper.*[28] William Fillingham succeeded to the business and appears in the land tax in 1760 and 1770 with a rent of £50 and a personal estate of £50. He insured in 1762 for £1,550 *stabling and coaching* on the south side of the Whitechapel Road. This covered ten stables, the largest 60 ft by 36 ft, which together indicate the importance of this livery business.[29]

Similarly, the sugar refining business can also be traced from 1736 and is to be found under Field Gate Street in Mawer's excellent book on the sugar industry.

1736	Brissault
1742-45	Brissault and Turquand
1758-74	Leonard Turquand
1760-63	J. Brissault junior
1771-74	James Lewis Brissault

Household Contents

Introduction

Given the traditional emphasis of historians on the poor of London's eastern parishes it may come as a shock to some to discover the wealth revealed by wills and probate records. However, this should be of no surprise given that earlier paragraphs have revealed the large houses lived in by men and women of considerable wealth. To this can be added our knowledge of those who owned silver in the late 1750s described below.

Professor Carole Shammas, now at the University of Southern California, made a detailed study of inventories contained in probates between 1550 and 1774. She compared inventories from North America with three areas of England; Oxfordshire, Worcestershire together with:

> 129 inventories from the East End of London for 1661-64
> 177 inventories from the East End of London for 1720-9

These inventories were taken from the Commissary Court records at the LMA and inventories at the TNA and came from the parishes of Stepney, Whitechapel, Stratford-le-Bow and St Leonard Bromley. Perhaps to her surprise the mean wealth of £1,239 for East London in the period 1720-9 was the largest in the samples; compared with the South Worcestershire mean of £305 for 1720-1721 and a mean of £299 in Virginia for 1724-9. Her impression of the area was of one that lay "around the docks, and contained a lot of paid labourers, seamen and foreign artisans. As might be expected the probate coverage was very limited, only about 16% of adult male decedents left an inventory." She also commented that:

"Because wealth was so distorted in London and because the probate coverage of the ordinary East End inhabitants was so incomplete, this sample is the most unreliable of all those I collected. Wealthy decedents dominate the means and percentages, and give the area a more affluent cast than it should have." Her analysis was very statistical and interestingly showed that these wealthy East Enders held 5.6% of their wealth in consumer goods, which was a "much lower percentage than in the other samples". Quite why she thought in the first place that these inventories represented the entire community in East London is not clear.[30]

As one example of the wealth to be found in Whitechapel we have the will and inventory for a merchant Samuel Perry. The Perry family originated near Rodborough close to Stroud, in Gloucestershire. The most famous member was Captain John Perry (1), [1669/70-1733] DNB, a hydraulic engineer who worked on a plan to link the Caspian with the Black Sea for the tsar of Russia. He was also involved in stopping "the Great Break at Dagenham", when it was overwhelmed by the Thames flooding.

In 1694 John's brother Samuel was probably living in the Portsoken Ward near Aldgate; and was assessed on a house with £30 rent and stock of £100, an early indication of his wealth. Subsequently, Samuel lived in Goodman's Fields where he died in 1723. Samuel Perry held several senior positions in local society; a Justice of the Peace, one of the Deputy Lieutenants of Middlesex, a Commissioner of Sewers for Tower Hamlets and one of the Commissioners of the Lieutenancy of the City of London. The inventory shows that he was worth £11,472, which in today's terms is nearly £1,000,000. His house had two-storeys plus garrets and cellars, together with a yard and a stable. Some of the rooms had tapestry hangings, pictures and prints. He owned 200 bound books and 300 ounces of plate valued at five shillings per ounce. His investments included lottery tickets, property, bonds of the Bank of England, the EICo and the South Sea Company.[31]

Dr Lorna Weatherill has also studied inventories and the main question underlying her book was "whether people's material lives reflected their social position?". The framework of the book was a comprehensive collection of 3,000 probate inventories from eight parts of England (Kent, Hampshire, Cambridgeshire, the north-east, the north-west, Staffordshire, Cumbria and London) in the middle of each decade from 1675 to 1725. There were also 300 inventories for the same years taken from the London Court of Orphans in the City of London, in order to include a wealthy group of consumers not covered in the main sample.

"There were three patterns of change in the frequencies with which items were recorded in both series of inventories. A few goods were representative of basic furniture and utensils (pewter, tables and cooking pots), many associated with 'backstage activities'. These also represent well-established aspects of the economy. Secondly, some goods were already in use in 1675, but were not common; these include books, silver, table linen, pewter dishes, pewter plates, looking glasses, and earthernware. They were mostly associated with 'frontstage' activities. Change here was often rapid."

"Lastly, there were some important new goods, some of which were virtually unknown in 1675, such as china and various equipment for the new hot drinks, tea, coffee, and chocolate. Others were extremely rare in 1675, including clocks, pictures, window curtains, and knives and forks. These too were 'frontstage' goods and were either decorative or associated with new mealtime behaviour. Ownership of all of them expanded very rapidly."

Weatherill demonstrated how the ownership of clocks and other items varied with types of occupation in England between 1675 and 1725.

Table 5   A CONSUMPTION HIERARCHY:
FREQUENCIES OF OWNERSHIP OF GOODS IN ENGLAND, 1675 - 1725

OCCUPATION	CLOCKS %	PICTURES %	SILVER %	WINDOW CURTAINS %	BOOKS %
Dealing Trades	27	33	43	28	27
Gentry	51	33	61	26	39
Craft trades	17	15	22	13	17
Yeomen	19	4	13	5	18
Husbandmen	4	0	2	2	4

The group of "yeomen" includes farmers with total estates valued at over £60, whilst "husbandmen" includes farmers with estates of less than £60.[32]

The results of Dr Shammas and Dr Weatherill can be compared with the details of the contents and values of household property in Whitechapel found in Old Bailey Proceedings and probate records. Seventy-four probates have been found for men and women in Whitechapel between 1723 and 1800; they lived in houses with rents of between £14 and £50. From the inventories we discover the wide range of furniture and household goods; and note the popularity of four-poster beds, silverware, card tables and birdcages, the last reflecting a popular East London pastime. Indeed, William Bezer in St George-in-the-East had 27 bird cages and three *Nightingale Traps*, and perhaps was supplying a local need to the residents in dark and dingy alleys?[33]

The probates range from wealthy men like Thomas Jarvis and Samuel Perry to the more modest possessions of Henry Cooley. The very long probate in 1778 of Thomas Jarvis, reveals that he was a watchmaker, jeweller and silversmith with a considerable stock of silver candlesticks, clocks, eleven *new silver waiters* and nineteen pairs of silver salts. A silver quart mug weighing 24 ounces and 15 pennyweights was valued at £7-6s.-5d. His assets were valued at nearly £2,000, which would be over £130,000 in today's money. He had *36 volumes of old books*, a mahogany settee with *crimson furniture*, and four walnut chairs and a mahogany dining table. His clothing included a green suit of superfine cloth, one new hat and four old hats and sixteen pocket handkerchiefs.

For the men responsible for conducting the probate of Thomas Jarvis their first important duty was to provide a guard *day and night to watch the deceased's body until the funeral and for guarding his stock*. They recruited Benjamin Roberts and Robert Eustace for this work, who were paid ten guineas; clearly his stock was considered to be very valuable. Thomas Jarvis was at 128 Whitechapel and held numerous watches by makers; Jarvis Nos. 835, 1032, 1033, 1044, Pepills, Nos. 793 and Jones, Nos. 765, 775 and 773.[34]

As befitted a man of some considerable wealth his probate contains a list of many tradesmen, which included Henry Somes, a vintner who provided the wine at the funeral. J. J. Gorsuch, a surgeon had attended him to treat his *Fistula in Ano* and Lewis Tomlinson supplied newspapers. A small bequest was also left to William and Elizabeth Honeychurch, Captain James Cook's neighbours in MEOT.[35]

In addition the probate refers to:[36]

Messrs Phipps and Co., undertakers	Robert Brownson, coal dealer
Thomas Hodgson, painter	William Brown, guilder
H. Bateman, goldsmith	John Smith (1), tailor
Jonathan Wathen, surgeon	John Faux, silversmith
George Lee, broker	John Gilson, apothecary

Among the possessions of George Mussell of Ayliff Street, the father of Ebenezer Mussell, the property developer from Bethnal Green, were a *Coach lined with blue cloth, two pairs of harness and three bogies valued at £30, one musket and two pistols*.[37] There were also:

Two pieces of tapestry hangings	Nine family pictures, 26 prints and pictures
£13,250 South Sea annuities	11 gold rings and three snuff boxes

Henry Cooley, a member of the Merchant Taylors' Company, a watchmaker, had a house with a rent of £15 in the High Street.[38]

Garrets	The two rooms in the garret contained vices, odd tools and *thirteen old clocks damaged by fire*
Second floor	Forward room with a four-post bed and a walnut double chest of drawers
	Back room, 2 old feather beds
First floor	A dining room with a large oval dining table and card tables
	A bed chamber with a four-post bed and a walnut double chest of drawers
Ground floor	A kitchen with a yard and wash house
	A shop and a cellar

Charles Povey, an elderly and infirm gentleman, left to the parish of Newington Butts his organ together with 15 guineas to pay for the move[39]:-

My Great Organ being 5 feet in depth and 6 feet in breadth and 9½ feet high, with three sets of keys. Mr Aaron Davis, an organ maker having agreed with me to cause the organ to play six several Psalm tunes and four voluntaries and to perform the same from time to time without any persons playing upon the keys thereof as also the Bellows to move the same, being made so to perform by clockwork."

Silver

Governments have always shown great imagination in finding ways of taxing the community. The lists of men and women paying tax on their silver in the late 1750s and on their male servants in 1780 provide valuable insights into the distribution of wealth in London's eastern parishes.

In the reign of George II an Act was passed which enabled the government to raise *Rates and Duties* on all persons and corporate bodies *having certain Quantities of Silver Plate*. The Act covered Great Britain and was put into effect on 5th July 1756. The Act relates amongst other things that:

> *For and upon one hundred Ounces Troy Weight ... the Sum of five Shillings* and
> *For and upon four hundred Ounces Troy ... the Sum of twenty Shillings*.

In England and Wales there were about 34,000 payers of these duties and of these approximately 13,000 lived in or close to London. Clearly, the ownership of silver was widespread and hundreds of men and women living in London's eastern parishes also paid these duties.[40]

In Whitechapel the wills of the following included silver in their bequests and their rents and personal estates also confirm their wealth. The duty collected between 1757 and 1762 clearly demonstrates that the ownership of silver was very widespread in London.

Table 6   SOME SILVER BEQUESTS IN WHITECHAPEL WILLS, 1755-1762

NAME	OUNCES T 47/5	YEARS	OCCUPATION	LAND TAX £	WILL PROB 11
Henry Balchen	100 oz.	1757	Gent	18	1063
Mathew Bateman	300 oz.	1757	Esquire	20	869
Samuel Bayley	100 oz.	1757-58	Carpenter	16	1039
Robert Brooke	200 oz.	1757-58	Gent	10	878
George Caffey		1755	Schoolmaster		819
John Coverly	200 oz.	1757-62	Scrivener	18	909
William Dawson	300 oz.	1757-60	Gent	—	856
Anthony Denew		1755	Gent		818
John E. Dodsworth		1759	Merchant		846
William Fillingham	200 oz.	1757-59	Stable keeper	56	993
Benjamin Goodwin	400 oz.	1757-62	Gentleman	—	930
Sir Samuel Gower	100 oz.	1757	Merchant	60	832
John Hill	100 oz.	1765	Esquire	25	905
Mary Kerby		1759	Spinster		843
Richard Manning		1759	Victualler		845
William Sims		1759	Distiller		848

Dr Weatherill found that "Silver was more common in the London sample than elsewhere; in 1675, 48% in London owned silver, but only 8% in Carlisle and 9% in the Cambridgeshire samples, while virtually all the Orphans' Court inventories recorded it. Influences on the ownership of silver were probably different from those on any other item here, because it has an intrinsic value and fluctuations in ownership could have varied with family needs and prosperity. It could have represented the 'traditional' attitude of investing in things of known value rather than spending money on other goods of a more useful or decorative nature".[41]

Thomas Daniell was a well-known silversmith at The Silver Lion in Foster Lane, and possibly supplied silver to the wealthier merchants of Whitechapel. For *Sensible to the power of advertising*, Daniell stated in a handbill of about 1789 that he always had on hand, *Twenty Thousand Ounces of every species of Silver Goods ... finished in the highest elegance of patterns, and particularly excellent workmanship, and embellishments from the best and latest designs*.

Naturally, criminals were very keen to add silver to their collections. *The Public Advertiser* on Saturday 30th October 1762 records that Peter Laprimaudaye had been *relieved of certain silverware including a tea kettle, a large coffee pot, a large waiter and Four Salts with three Feet, 23 oz. 17 dwt*. The reward for finding this silverware was twenty guineas.

The probate of Sarah Sparke, who lived in a good house in Leman Street with a rent of £30, provides an indication of what one hundred ounces of silver might consist of[42]:

> *Fourteen silver tea spoons, a sugar dish, one pair of candlesticks, mugs and six*
> *tea spoons were valued at 5 shillings and 4 pence per ounce which amounted to*
> *£26-8s.-00d.*

The ownership of silver was widespread throughout all the parishes in East London and at least 550 men and women were assessed between 1757 and 1762. This list includes prominent men such as Sir Benjamin Truman, the brewer of Brick Lane who had 400 ounces. Also listed was Stephen Martin Leake, the Garter King of Arms who lived in MEOT and had 500 ounces. He was also a well-known collector of coins. The returns of duty paid on silver show, that in addition to the above there were thirty-one men and women who paid duty on holdings of 300 ounces or more, Appendix 3.

Clearly there would be people who were suspected of not paying the duties. In 1776 the tax commissioners rather belatedly began to search for those people who evaded the tax since the 1760s. The searches revealed that Elizabeth Stockdale hadn't paid for her 100 ounces since 1773, and William Thoytes hadn't paid for 500 ounces since 1762, both of Whitechapel.[43]

Servants

"The employment of domestic servants was virtually universal amongst the middle class and indeed went down into fairly lowly strata of the artisan population of Augustan London." The operation of even the most modest households in the C18 relied on a wide variety of servants. Basic essentials such as coal and firewood were delivered into the cellars. So there was a need for someone to carry these heavy items to the higher floors, and subsequently to carry the ashes and rubbish downstairs. Another problem which required healthy young servants was that of water supply.

For some properties in Whitechapel water was obtained from shallow wells which required more work to carry the water indoors. Water from Shadwell came from a cistern at the top of a tower and, could provided there were no leaks at the joints (an unlikely situation), return to the cistern level or just below. The Shadwell Waterworks Company, the New River Company, and after 1743 the West Ham Waterworks, all delivered water through elm pipes laid along the streets. Elm was a good material for the water mains as it remained tight for many years as long as it remained wet. It was also much cheaper and stronger than lead pipes. Water was delivered intermittently from the mains by gravity through elm or lead pipes into lead cisterns in the cellars and if there was sufficient "head" water might be supplied to an upper floor. In poorer areas the water might be piped to a standpipe in the yard serving a group of houses. It was only early in the C19 that it became economic to use cast iron pipes that had the capacity to regularly deliver piped water to the upper floors of a house or hospital.[44]

Clearly, a hot bath on the first or second floor of a house was a major exercise in domestic logistics.

There was then the problem of keeping houses and clothing clean in smoky London; indeed it was reported that "well-kept houses were washed twice a week". Wash rooms were normally either in the cellar or in the back yard and were equipped with coppers and ironing boards. There was still a residual requirement for householders to keep clear and clean the pavement in front of their houses. For those houses with silver cutlery, mugs and salts there was more cleaning to be done. With a "maid of all work" employed to carry out these basic chores the master and mistress of a house would then consider whether their budget would allow the employment of a chambermaid, a cook, or a gardener.

For the wealthier families a coachman, a butler and a footman, suitably clothed to establish the social position of their master, might be thought essential. It was certainly useful to have at least one male servant in a household as he could accompany his master at night, lighting the way with a link, and acting as a deterrent to footpads.

Households also had a need for items to be collected from shops, and for messages and packages to be delivered to friends and business associates. Whilst these trips would provide a welcome change for a house-bound maid it was likely that one of the trusted street urchins lurking near the back door might be rewarded with a sixpence for carrying out the task to the satisfaction of the master. Of course, if the urchin failed to deliver the salmon and oysters being sent to a friend or return with the lamb chops from the chop house he would be in great trouble with the headboroughs and beadles.

The presence of servants in a house did not necessarily lead to domestic harmony as the strictures of Daniel Defoe revealed[45]:

> *Maid servants...are an exceeding tax upon house-keepers; those who were formerly hired*
> *at three pounds to four pounds a-year wages, now demand five, six and eight pounds*
> *a-year; nor do they double anything upon us but their wages and their pride; for,*
> *instead of doing more work for their advance of wages, they do less: and the ordinary*
> *work of families cannot now be performed by the same number of maids, which, in*
> *short, is a tax upon the upper sort of tradesmen, and contributes very often to their*
> *disasters, by the extravagant keeping three or four maid-servants in a house, ...*
> *where two formerly were thought sufficient.*

Peter Earle's analysis of two wealthy City parishes showed that over half the households had only one servant and about 10% had four or more servants. So it is no surprise that John Fielding in 1733 speaks of the amazing number of women servants wanting places. Later, Colquhoun estimated in 1800 that there were seldom less than 10,000 domestic servants of both sexes looking for work in London.

Clearly, many were employed as domestic servants in London, even if their numbers and duties are imprecisely known.[46] Modern reviews of the role of servants in early modern households can be found in Earle and Richardson.[47] Definitions of the services to be performed by servants differed between urban and rural environments. In the latter case a servant might be a farm worker, and we have the words of Scrub in George Farquhar's 1707 comedy *The Beaux' Stratagem* to illustrate the situation he found himself in. When asked if he was a butler, Scrub replied:

> *Monday, I drive the Coach*
> *of a Tuesday I drive the Plough;*
> *on Wednesday I follow the hounds;*
> *a Thursday I dun the Tenants;*
> *on Friday I go to Market;*
> *on Saturday I draw Warrants;*
> *and a Sunday I draw Porter.*

Earle noted that "Much the commonest employment of girls before marriage was domestic service, good experience for a future housekeeper but not of much value for the junior partner of a businessman." As Dr. Schwarz observed "For a young woman, especially a young woman newly arrived in London, it was best to become a domestic servant. This provided some security and an opportunity for saving; historians have also suggested that it provided an opportunity to learn some arts of looking after a household that a potential suitor might value" and "When servants reached their late twenties and early thirties they tended to marry and leave service altogether."[48]

In 1780 over 2,800 men and women in Middlesex were taxed on male servants, and Schwarz noted that there were 25 towns or townships in the county which had at least thirty employers of servants. This statistic reflects the great wealth in and around the City of London. In Whitechapel and Well Close Square there were at least forty-six families taxed on male servants and they included the Rector, attorneys, sugar refiners, merchants, bell founders and a victualler. In the nearby "middling sort" hamlet of Mile End Old Town there were twenty-five or so households with a manservant. A household would in addition to its male servants also contain several female servants.

The wealthiest widow in MEOT was Susannah Jones (1777-86); her husband Samuel having been a director of the Hudson's Bay Company. She maintained a large household as follows:

House keeper	Ann Spratley	£50	Cook	Jane Webster	£35
Footman	John Tate	£35	Housemaid	Jane Caigo	£30
Gardener	James Nairn	£30	Watchman	Philip Salt	£30

The bequests are considerable and would easily be regarded as equivalent to two or more years' wages. They reflect both her generosity and possibly her appreciation of the loyalty and support she had received from these servants over many years. Equally, her servants would have been aware of their status compared to other servants in the area by working in the Jones family home in Worcester House, near Stepney Green.[49] Appendix 4 and Table 7 present information on households with male servants.

Table 7   1780 WHITECHAPEL HOUSEHOLDS WITH 2 OR 3 MALE SERVANTS

NAME	STREET	NUMBER OF SERVANTS	OCCUPATION
John Baker	Mansell Street	3	
Charles Bowles	Glasshouse Yard	3	Glass manufacturer
Thomas Bullock	High Street	3	? Brewer
De Daniel Castroo	Great Ayliffe Street	2	
Samuel Charlett	Brick Lane	2	
John Coope	Rupert Street	2	Sugar refiner
George Crosby	Road side	2	Sugar refiner
Edward Hawkins	Great Ayliff Street	2	Building developer
George Hayley	Great Ayliff Street	3	Alderman, MP
Dudley Hyatt	Great Ayliff Street	2	
Thomas Jordan	Great Ayliff Street	3	Brewer
Dr George Lenner	Mansell Street	2	? spelling
Claude Scott	Great Ayliff Street	2	Merchant
William Scullard	Mansell Street	2	Merchant
Robert Wilson	Great Ayliff Street	2	Corn factor
George Wolff	Well Close Square	2	Sugar refiner

William Scullard, merchant of Mansell Street, in his 1792 will made many charitable bequests and typically he left £10 to each of his male servants, and an annuity of £20 to his maid Ann Blowfield as long as she stayed in service for his wife.[50]

Leisure and Entertainment

The coronation of George III in September 1761 was celebrated in a variety of ways that attracted the crowds. Major displays of fireworks took place in London, but not on Tower Hill, where they were banned in case of an accident; an early example of the application of Health and Safety regulations. George III then embarked on a series of processions and in December 1761 *their Majesties attended by a party of Light Horse went over Westminster and London Bridges and through the streets to Whitechapel Turnpike, from where they returned by the New Road to Islington and returning to St James's*. Not mentioned, but probably guarding the route with other militia regiments would have been the Tower Hamlets Militia.[51]

There are not many records of life in Whitechapel by those who lived there in the C18. We have newspaper reports together with the diaries of Adam Williamson, the Deputy Lieutenant of the Tower of London from 1722 until 1747, another for few months in 1777 kept by John Allen [1757-1808] a young Quaker brewer, and that of Elijah Goff, a leading coal merchant. The letters of Eliza Rhode provide an insight into the life of a young lady from a wealthy background in Whitechapel. She married Edward Hawkins (II) [1770-1867] DNB, Keeper of Antiquities at the British Museum.[52]

Broadly speaking, the residents of Whitechapel had a choice between local entertainments in their homes or at the local taverns, and at various times at the theatres around Goodman's Fields. The number of households that had tea pots, *china* cups and saucers, and sugar bowls, supports the notion that the better off households were enjoying the elaborate rituals of tea drinking. In their homes were also to be found card tables, games of draughts, coffee and chocolate pots, guns and possibly musical instruments although these are rarely recorded.

At this time "a host of venues often combined the functions of public house and music hall, putting on dramatic shows, pageants, plays, music and circus performances." In the taverns of Whitechapel billiard tables could be found, for example, at the Horse and Magpye. There was a bowling green at the Ship and Castle in Goodman's Fields which was opened every April between 1730 and 1738; a place *where all Gentlemen will find suitable Entertainment.* Nearby was a ninepin green and a shuffle board room at the Cock Inn in Lambert Street. Others undoubtedly would be attracted by the delights to be found at The Bagnio in Leman Street described in Chapter 8.[53]

For those wishing to dance, an Academy near the Golden Lion in Leman Street under the direction of Mr Hart (1) advertised in 1754 that:

> *Grown persons are taught to dance a Minuet and Country Dances in a genteel Manner and with as much Privacy and Expedition as can be wished for ... there are a set of Gentleman and Ladies meet of an evening to practise Set and Country Dances, where no Strangers are admitted.*

The Academy was open on Mondays and Thursdays from 8am to 11pm and on Tuesdays and Fridays from 8am until noon. Mr Hart also conducted a Dance Academy in Essex Street in the Strand.[54]

On long summer days many would make their way down the Whitechapel Road to the more rural taverns in MEOT or down into the fields behind the London Hospital. Others went further out to the meadows, rivers and marshes of nearby Essex, where they could enjoy walking, riding, swimming, rowing, fishing and shooting. In winter there was the possibility of skating, especially in the very cold winters of 1715-16, 1739-40 and 1788-9 when the Thames froze over and Frost Fairs were held on the ice.

William Roper was a keen local fisherman, a pattern maker and last maker, who lived opposite the Field Gate at 32 Whitechapel Road. In 1779 he insured on behalf of the Lea Bridge Amicable Society of Anglers their house and fishing tackle on Hackney Marsh for £200.[55]

In 1720 cock fights were organised at the Ship Tavern in Prescot Street and on the 9th February *A Great Cock Match ... was held between the Gentleman of London and the Gentleman of Herefordshire.* There were prizes of six guineas on most *battles,* but £100 on one battle. These wagers illustrate the popularity of gambling at this time and many succumbed to the fun of the three-card trick.[56]

Horse racing and road races were very popular and the *Daily Journal* 15th June 1730 described the race between Thomas Oliphant and John Dawson, two boys of about 15 years. The race from Whitechapel to Romford was won by the former who ran it in one hour four minutes As this is a distance of about ten miles there is possibly something of an exaggeration in the time! Similarly the *Daily Courant* 18th July 1734 reported that yesterday morning at four of the clock a *Match was run between Mr Pye's mare and Mr Smithergill's horse from Whitechapel church to the Turnpike at Romford for twenty guineas, which was won by the former.*

The Taverns

With over one hundred taverns and inns licensed in the 1750s there was no shortage of suitable locations for entertainments, and in East Smithfield could be found the brothels and houses of low repute. Dr Dorothy George devoted many pages to describing "the orgy of spirit-drinking which was at its worst between 1720 and 1751, due to the very cheap and very intoxicating liquors, which were retailed indiscriminately and in the most brutalizing and demoralizing conditions".

"The cheapness of British spirits caused a new demand and altered the tastes and habits of the people. Brandy-shops and Geneva [gin] shops multiplied in the poorer parts of London." However, recent research indicates "that contrary to the views of some eighteenth-century moralists and earlier twentieth-century historians, the taste for gin drinking that was accused of sweeping over London during the earlier C18 was not only limited but had little effect upon mortality."[57]

In the 1768 election John Wilkes wanted his supporters to meet at the Crown and Magpye in Whitechapel, which was run by Benjamin Kenton [1719-1800] DNB. However, they found that the tavern had already been booked by candidates in the Essex election and Wilkes's men met instead at the Crown tavern in Leadenhall to find the coaches that would take them to the poll booths in Brentford.[58]

At the Crown and Magpye in 1762 an *elegant entertainment* was given to Captain William Hamilton, commander of the *Melvin* by sixty commanders of the June Fleet from the Leeward Islands. This was the time of the Seven Years War with the French. The fleet had been led by Captain Ovry, commander of H. M. frigate *Acteon*. It appeared that Captain Ovry had deserted the fleet. This led Hamilton to assume responsibility for the fleet and he nursed them safely back to Britain. As another mark of their appreciation the commanders subscribed towards a *genteel sword* for Captain Hamilton.[59]

The Angel and Crown was frequently the scene of meetings of the Commissioners for the Highways, the Justices of the Peace, the Vestry, livery companies, the Lord of the Manor and his customary tenants. It was also possible to buy tickets there for the Lincoln's Inn Fields theatre, so it provided a focus for a range of local activities; reflecting the local absence of a Town Hall or Assembly Rooms.

The tavern was also the meeting point for electors wishing to travel from London in order to vote in Essex. So in August 1727 the *Daily Post* carried an advertisement concerning an election in Essex which stated that supporters of Lord Castlemaine would find carriages awaiting them at the Angel and Crown to take them to the polling station.[60]

In 1769 Jonathan Blands, Valentine Brown and Isaac Graham, Snr, and several others could have been found drinking at the Angel and Crown in Whitechapel. Indeed, every month or so for over two-hundred years a group of men would meet in one of the taverns in Stepney; they were the customary tenants summoned to a meeting with the representatives of the Lord of the Manor. In winter they favoured the Angel and Crown in Whitechapel, but in the summer the meetings usually moved out to taverns such as the Crown in Mile End, the Green Man in Bethnal Green, and the India House in Blackwall. To this list was added on the 29th December 1766 the new Assembly Rooms in Mile End Old Town.[61]

The Justices of the Peace for Middlesex chose in 1753 to meet at the Angel and Crown on *Mondays, Wednesday and Fridays, from Ten in the Morning to One in the Afternoon ... in order to receive complaints against Felons or others guilty of misdemeanours, within the [Tower Hamlets] Division, for the more easy and speedy bringing such offenders to justice.*

Freemasons in Whitechapel

Dr Johnson defined freemasons as "one of a society bearing the epithet of free and accepted". Nineteenth-century encyclopaedists echoed his definition and described freemasonry as "the system observed by the secret associations of "free and accepted masons". Modern freemasonry in England dates from the foundation of the Grand Lodge of England in 1717.

Fortunately for local historians the freemasons have in recent years opened up their archives. In particular the membership lists of British Freemasonry lodges provide us with some scintillating insights into the social networks of early modern Britain. The membership lists of the London lodges contain a wide cross-section of merchants and tradesmen wishing to network and improve their social station in life. The records of the growth of freemasonry from 1717 onwards show that many Lodges were based on taverns.

One of the oldest "Modern" lodges in the world, known as The Dundee Arms Lodge No. 9, was established in Wapping about 1733 and can be traced to 1835. Since that date it was known as "The Old Dundee Lodge" No. 18, (England). The Dundee Arms Lodge was therefore operating in maritime Wapping during the C18 and its membership included many local merchants and mariners who either resided or operated in the local area.[62]

The following Lodges were formed in Whitechapel in the 1730s:[63]

Table 8   FREEMASON LODGES IN WHITECHAPEL IN THE 1730s

FIRST DATE	NAME	SERIAL NUMBER	LOCATION	COMMENT
29/05/1733	Theatre Tavern	SN 140	Goodman's Fields	Whitechapel land tax
31/03/1735	King and Queen	SN 122	Rosemary Lane	Whitechapel land tax
11/12/1735	Duke of Marlborough's Head	SN 157	Petticoat Lane	Whitechapel land tax
13/04/1737	Angel and Crown	SN 69	High Street	Whitechapel land tax
25/01/1738	Court House	SN 191 City Lodge	High Street	Whitechapel land tax
25/01/1738	Three Tuns and Half Moon	SN 192	Probably High Street	Whitechapel land tax

There is a major gap in the membership records for Masonic lodges between the early 1730s and c. 1768.

We then find, amongst others, the Lodge of Unity No. 376 D in Whitechapel, whose many members between 1781 and 1812 (with the dates they were made masons) included:

> William Daniel, a hatter from Leman Street, 1782
>
> William Loft, a dancing master, Little Alie Street, 1781
>
> Thomas Moore, an auctioneer, Whitechapel, 1783
>
> Thomas Ryrwood, a victualler, Red Lyon Street, 1783
>
> Charles Taylor, a shoemaker, White Lyon Street, 1784

The Lodge of Unity attracted men from a variety of trades from Cheapside, Ratcliff, Rotherhithe, Shoreditch and Wapping. From further afield were a Captain Alexander Ide from Woodbridge in Suffolk and Daniel Hurd a mariner from Southend.

In addition to fellowship and the opportunity to strengthen business contacts the Freemasons could also receive charity when in deserving conditions.

Three boys who benefited from this were Peter, Daniel and Timothy Folger, who were living with their grandmother in St George-in-the-East. Their father, an American captain, had died after four years in a French prison, and the grandmother was dependent on the support of the parish. Many local merchants supported this charity including Samuel Foulger in Old Gravel Lane, J. Walton in Well Close Square and T. McKenzie in the Whitechapel Road.[64]

FURTHER READING

S. Bradley & N. Pevsner — *London 1: The City of London*, 1997

B. Cherry, C. O'Brien and N. Pevsner — *London 5: East* in *The Buildings of England* series, 2005

J. Cox — *London's East End: Life and Traditions*, 1994

D. Defoe — *The Complete English Tradesman*, 1726, 1987

H. W. Dickinson — *Water Supply of Greater London*, 1954

P. Earle — *The Making of the English Middle Class*, 1989

P. Earle — *A City Full of People: Men and Women in London, 1650-1750*, 1994

M. D. George — *London life in the Eighteenth Century*, 1965

P. Guillery — *The Small House in eighteenth-century London, A Social and Architectural History*, 2004

J. P. Malcolm — *Londinium Redivivum or an ancient history and modern description of London*, 1803-7

B. Mawer — *Sugarbakers – From sweat to sweetness*, 2007, 2011

D. Morris — *Mile End Old Town, 1740–1780; A social history of an Early Modern London Suburb*, 2007

D. Morris and K. Cozens — *Wapping 1600-1800, A social history of an Early Modern London Maritime Suburb*, 2009

R. C. Richardson — *Household servants in early modern England*, 2010

L. D. Schwarz — London 1700-1840, *The Cambridge Urban History of Britain, vol. II, 1540-1840*, 2000

C. Shammas — *The Pre-Industrial Consumer in England and America*, 1990

C. Spence — *Atlas of London in the 1690s*, 2000

J. Stow — *A Survey of London*, 1603 reprinted 1971

L. Weatherill — *Consumer behaviour and social status in England, 1660-1760*, 1988

Web Sites

http://www.british-history.ac.uk — Whitechapel 'Four Shillings in the Pound Aid, 1693-94'

http://www.freemasonry.london.museum — Library and Museum of Freemasonry

http://www.hrionline.ac.uk/lane — Lane's Masonic Records on line

http://www.shef.ac.uk/ccr — The Centre for Research into Freemasonry and Fraternities, University of Sheffield

4. THE SERVICE INDUSTRIES

Introduction

For its residents, visitors and for the thousands of passing travellers, the merchants of Whitechapel had developed over the centuries a full range of services. Close to the Great Essex Road were to be found dozens of taverns, a bagnio, scriveners and saddlers, butchers and bakers, blacksmiths, coach makers and stable keepers, cheesemongers and grocers, and theatres. There was also from 1501, and perhaps earlier, until at least 1685 a long tradition of market gardening in Whitechapel and the famous Hay Market continued until 1928.

There were also merchants and brokers living in the area who traded internationally, such as Henry Blommart, an eminent Dutch merchant of Goodman's Fields, and the wealthy John Spieker with links to Sweden and Finland.[1]

For the broader context Leonard Schwarz has explored "the enormous manufacturing sector that made eighteenth-century London the largest manufacturing town in the Western Hemisphere." In addition to looking at Westminster which "was, by definition, as near as being a service town as was possible for a central part of a large multifunctional city during the eighteenth century", he also addressed the issues of age and migration into London.[2]

Victualling

John Stow's remarks in 1603 illustrate the long history of victualling along the Whitechapel Road that extends east from St Botolph church in Aldgate:

> *certain faire Innes for receipt of travellers repairing to the City, up towards*
> *Hog lane End, somewhat within the Barres, a mark showing how far the*
> *liberties of the City do extend.*[3]

In 1750 a dusty traveller arriving from Harwich or Colchester or a thirsty labourer emerging from one of the sugar refineries in Whitechapel had no shortage of places in which to find a drink. There were over 120 licensed premises in Whitechapel and about forty in MEOT, and many of the pub names have persisted to the present day such as The Grave Maurice, which can be traced back to 1723.

Figure 5   THE HOOP AND GRAPES

Licensed premises varied greatly in size, and the services they provided. Essentially inns, taverns and alehouses all supplied a variety of drinks such as brandy, cider, porter, Shrub and Spanish wines. In addition, an inn would supply overnight accommodation for passing travellers; and could send out to a local pie shop or arrange for food brought in by a traveller to be cooked. Some inns were important in proving support for the stage coaches and post-chaises between London and East Anglia; they were also places where livery companies would sometimes take their dinners and auctioneers ply their trade. A tavern was more specialised and sold wine and food. Alehouses, which greatly exceeded in numbers both inns and taverns, were "the basic everyday drinking place of the lower orders".[4]

Though there were many stables in Whitechapel it is possible that many travellers would prefer to leave their horses and ponies in the fields attached to the main taverns in MEOT, such as The White Horse. Their owners then going into London on a coach, for which the charge was sixpence.

The language of brewing and of places in which to drink is large and complex, and definitions have changed with time and place. Brewing was not confined to the main breweries as there was a well established tradition of brewing in domestic houses. Indeed John Nixon, formerly of the Bank of England, and living in Redman Row, MEOT, had a set of brewing utensils in his cellar *which were very old and almost worn out not having been used for seventeen* years.[5]

The main brews at this time were porter, beer and ale. India Pale Ale was developed under the auspices of the East India Company because of the need for a beer that could be safely shipped to India without going off. At this time a sailor in the Royal Navy had a ration of one gallon of beer per day; and probably hoped that he would have the ability and the cash to carry on drinking at the same rate on land![6]

Although the population of Whitechapel doubled between 1740 and 1780, the number of licensed premises remained constant; and probably as a result of this policy there were many more unlicensed premises, particularly in the alleyways off the main street. It was very easy in those simpler times for a house owner to put a trestle table and some chairs in his basement or front room, get a barrel or two of porter or ale on credit from one of the local breweries, and open up a small bar. Indeed, in 1735 there was concern at *the vast number of Brandy and Geneva shops, sheds and cellars in Tower Hamlets* and elsewhere in London, and specific mention *was made of ninety weavers in Bethnal Green, who sold these liquors.*

Table 9   THE MAIN TAVERNS AND INNS, WHITECHAPEL HIGH STREET

NAME	RENT £	PERSONAL £	NOTES
Walter Archer	35	75	Nags Head and Woolpack, victualler
John Dawson	30	50	The Bulls Head, victualler
John Fearnley	22		The Horseshoe and Magpye, victualler
Lambert Fielding	22		The Man in the Moon, victualler
Robert Jones	20		The Green Dragon, victualler, carrier, stables
John Lander	22		The Coach and Horses, victualler
Job Mathews	32	100	The Rising Sun and Fig Tree, grocer
Richard Newman	24		The Tewkesbury Church, victualler
William Newman	20	150	The Rose and Crown, chemist, victualler
William Sharp	22		The Whittington Cat, victualler
Jane Taylor	50	75	The George, victualler and livery keeper
Esther Thompson	72	50	The Red Lyon, victualler
Henry Vernon	36		The Seven Stars, victualler
Anthony Wall	80	75	The Angel and Crown Tavern, victualler

We do not have descriptions of the larger taverns in Whitechapel, but Richard Winpenny a victualler in Church Lane, insured the Cherry Tree House in 1767 for £300. It was of brick and timber construction and the main two-storey building was 50 ft 6 ins by 16 ft and there were four wainscotted rooms and some outbuildings.[7]

With regard to the value of household goods, utensils and stock to be found in licensed properties several policies have been found in the archives of the Sun Fire Office. Abraham Chitty was a wine merchant at the Bunch of Grapes in Little Alie Street, Goodman's Fields, which he insured for £1,200 plus another £1,000 for stock. Another indication of insurance values in taverns comes from Robert Ellis, a victualler and distiller, at the Coach and Horses, who insured his property, goods and *stock in trade in the still house* for £700 in 1743 and £1,100 in 1748. Similarly, Sarah Thompson, widow and innholder at the Red Lyon in the High Street, insured her goods and stock for £900; so both were considerable establishments.[8]

Some idea of the contents of the taverns can be gained from the probate inventories at The National Archives. When someone died, and there was a dispute over the will, a detailed inventory would be made down to the last bent spoon and broken glass. Typical features of the contents were the games such as draughts and backgammon. Singing was a popular pastime, but no mention has been found of any musical instruments in taverns in the period up to 1780.

The inventory of John Barney in 1725 includes four gallons of old wine, eight gallons of Canary wine, 15 gallons of White port. Another inventory exists for Joseph Prick, who was the innkeeper at the Why Not Beat Dragon in nearby MEOT from 1747 until his death in 1750. In the *closets* were found *One Gallon of brandy, Five gallon of rum, One gallon of Shrub, Five gallon of gin, 48 glass bottles and 9 pairs of small glasses*. In the cellars were twenty-five *bottles of Cider, sixteen Bottles of ale and sixteen Barrels of beer*. Finally, for entertainment there were *One skittle, stone bowls and skittles*, and amongst his animals, were *one horse with harness, one sow, twelve pigs, seven fowls and two ducks*.[9]

One danger of visiting a great coaching inn on the main roads into London was mentioned by Daniel Defoe, that master of observation, when describing one of Moll Flander's areas of expertise. Dressed in her best finery she had gone to Whitechapel *just by the corner of Petticoat Lane, where the coaches stand that go out to Stratford and Bow, and that side of the country*. So when a lady descended from her coach, and needed help with her parcels it was Moll that was ever alert. He did not record her pickings in Whitechapel, but on another such venture she acquired a *very good suit of Indian damask, a gown and a petticoat, a laced-head and ruffles of very good Flanders lace and some other things, such as I very knew well the value of*.[10]

Market Gardens, 1501-1685

Stephanie Hovland has written "London and its suburbs in the fourteenth and fifteenth centuries were green with gardens that served a variety of purposes for medieval Londoners". Some, indeed were already market gardens or nursery gardens, where professional gardeners made contributions to the commercial and trading life of London, and to the diet and health of Londoners. She identified three gardeners in Whitechapel, Cornell Kelly in 1501 followed by Peter Doffe in 1504 and Thomas Lockey in 1566. What is not yet known is precisely where their gardens were, but one possibility is that their land was on the north side of the Whitechapel Road that was eventually held by Leonard Gurle.[11]

In 1643 Edward Montague esquire of Boughton in Northamptonshire and others purchased an estate, which covered parts of Spitalfields and the yet to be built Mile End New Town. The site of some 43 acres included a *nursery and garden plot*. In 1717 the land was leased to John Ward esquire and William Mason. It was on this land that during the 1660s and 1670s was developed the largest nursery in London. This could be found between Brick Lane and Greatorex Street north of Old Montague Street. This large open area still existed in the 1740s. The nursery had been established in the early 1640s when Leonard Gurle [c. 1621-1685] DNB moved there from Southwark. In 1656 Gurle had a lease from the Hon. George Montague for a term of 65 years at a rent of £58 per annum. He recouped himself by subletting parcels of land and by building six houses before he died in 1685.

Much information is available on both the wide range of his stock and their prices. An apple tree cost one shilling and a peach tree was five shillings. Ornamental plants were quite dear: the limes cost three shillings each, barberries [Pipparidge] two shillings and laurustinas [an evergreen bush] one shilling.

Gurle's specialised in fruit trees and he also supplied ornamental trees, shrubs and seeds. Leonard Meager in *The English Gardener* (1670) printed a catalogue of divers sorts of fruit, *which I had of my very Loving friend Captain Garrle*, containing over 300 varieties, many of them from France. By 1661 Gurle had raised the hardy nectarine 'Elruge', and given it his own name reversed, with an extra 'e' for euphony. One bill from Gurle listed *twelve varieties of peach, two of nectarine, eight of plum, eight of pear, three of cherry, three of apple, two of apricot and one quince*.[12]

In 1672 Gurle sold pear and other fruit trees, cypresses, spruces, and other forest trees, jasmine, and honeysuckles. He sold a box of seeds to Sir Roger Pratt, for his garden at Ryston Hall, near Downham, Norfolk. Late in 1674 he supplied fruit trees to Sir Richard Temple at Stowe, and to William Russell, first duke of Bedford, at Woburn Abbey. The Woburn order included dwarf plums and cherries, French pears, an Elruge nectarine, and other fruit, with more young trees *to make good those that died last year* in accordance with Gurle's guarantee to supply *the best of every sort in case any fail or die.*[13]

In 1677, Gurle was appointed the king's gardener at St James's Palace, with £320 a year to maintain the garden and another £240 a year as his own salary. Gurle died in the spring of 1685 in Woodham Walter, near Maldon, Essex.

Gurle also had a nursery in Hackney and in his Whitechapel garden could be found:

299 beds of Asparagus   179 young Walnut trees
55 young Chestnut trees   127 Mulberry trees and a heap of white Mulberry
11,600 of plum, cherry and pear stocks

According to Jane Cox this large block of land in Whitechapel "stayed in the family until the eighteenth century", and Harvey relates that in 1719 part of the land was occupied by Martin Girle.[14]

Scriveners and Attorneys

By far the most important scriveners in Whitechapel were the John Coverlys, senior and junior, who were involved with will making and other legal business for nearly forty years from 1735. So far eighteen wills have been discovered in which they are noted as executors or witnesses. With a house on the High Street they were easily available to potential clients. John Coverly senior was buried at Bunhill Fields in June 1765. His son moved to Prescot Street and by 1767 he was described as an attorney; and was a member of the Royal Society of Arts in 1767 and 1768, reflecting his wider interests.

Major Wright was a clerk to John Coverly junior and went on to to become very successful in his own right. He became the leading attorney in Wapping and prospered greatly for, as his will reveals, he was living in Wanstead where he kept his carriage, horses, cows, carts and stocks of hay, and had property in Sandgate, Kent, and Upton Place, Essex. His benefactions included £20 p.a. to the London Hospital and £25 p.a. to St George-in-the-East for the purchase of bread and beef for the poor. His will reveals links with Elsinore in Denmark where his brother Henry was a merchant. More surprising was that his executor was Joseph Merceron [c. 1764-1839] DNB the notorious trading justice from Bethnal Green. His other executor was the sugar refiner Carsten Dirs (I) formerly of St George-in-the-East who also moved to Wanstead, and was another member of the Scandinavian community.[15]

A more notorious attorney was James Fisher, who in 1778 had joined the Protestant Association, which was the leading organisation behind the Gordon Riots in 1780. Fisher was "a lawyer with a mainly criminal practice in Whitechapel", but was much disliked by Lord George Gordon as "a very fluent orator, specious and crouching and submissive with a plentiful supply of crying and whining about religion in his speeches; and no lack of buffoonery and low jesting". For these and other reasons Lord George and the Reverend Erasmus Middleton of the Association reposed no confidence in Fisher.[16]

Butchers

London with a population of about 550,000 in 1700 required great quantities of meat and Forshaw has described the long history of the cattle market established in Smithfield. As early as 1174 it was described as a "smooth field where every Friday there is a celebrated rendezvous of fine horses to be sold, and in another quarter are placed vendibles of the peasant, swine with their deep flanks, and cows and oxen of immense bulk".

By 1722 Londoners were "consuming 60,000 cattle, 70,0000 sheep and 239,000 pigs every year". These animals were being driven to London from as far away as Scotland, Yorkshire and Wales along well-established drovers roads. The journey from Scotland might take three weeks and the animals then needed fattening up in areas such as Norfolk and the Isle of Dogs before reaching the market. The Whitechapel butchers would buy their meat in the wholesale markets unless they had gone out into Essex and bought in Romford Market in an attempt to obtain meat at lower prices. Spence noted the slaughter-houses sited behind butchers' houses in Aldgate High Street in the 1690s.[17]

Whitechapel had many butchers who from time to time were subjected to *Searches* by officials from the Butchers' Company in the City of London. On 4 November 1762 it was reported that:

> *several pieces of Beef having been seized last Night at the House of Thomas Swan*
> *in Church Lane, Whitechapel, and the same now being Viewed and Inspected it*
> *appears to be Casually and Unwholesome Meat and are not fit for Human Food*

These were therefore:

> *Condemned And it is Ordered that the same be Carried tomorrow morning before*
> *Mr. Justice Quarrill for his Directions [about] what should be done and if*
> *he declines interfering therewith that the same be Burnt as near the place where*
> *the same was seized as possible.*

Three weeks later the Court of the Butchers' Company were told that on the 5th November Mr Orton and Mr Maynard had *applied to Mr Justice Quarrill, who ordered that the Beef seized at the house of Thomas Swan to be burnt near the place the same was seized and [he] directed a Number of Constables to Attend, which they did and the same was burnt.* Thomas Swan appeared before the Court and pleaded that they *did not commence any prosecution against him.* The Court agreed to his request as long as he immediately paid a fine of forty shillings, which he did.[18]

Transport

London was central to the nation's transport system for both people and for goods; and London Directories in the middle of the C18 list the hundreds of available coach services. The late Professor Roy Porter noted that the "capital's carriers trebled between 1637 and 1715. Passenger facilities improved too, with scheduled stagecoaches appearing after 1650. By 1681 London was linked to 88 towns, and by 1705 to 180. 'Flying coaches' clipped times and by 1670 a stage coach would get you from Oxford to London in a day."[19]

Coaching became big business, with specialist coaching inns, such as the Bull and Mouth at St Martin's-le-Grand, and the Spread Eagle in Gracechurch Street. The coaching inns provided much of the office, stabling and storage facilities required by the long-distance carrying trade and many innkeepers "were able to supply the traveller with a complete service, supplying refreshment and accommodation should it be required". They were also a centre for the distribution of letters between lawyers and their clients. Dr Spence noted that "By the 1730s London's carriers served more than 200 routes, with over 300 services a week departing from some seventy-five inns." His map shows that there were seven inns east of Aldgate providing both coach and carrier services.[20]

Each large coaching inn was the centre for a number of routes. From the Blue Boar Inn in Whitechapel coaches left every Wednesday and Friday for Maldon in Essex. From the White Swan John Morris ran the East Ham Stage Coach in 1755 and the *stand* for coaches to Stratford and Bromley was by the Angel and Crown. In 1746 advertisements appeared announcing the opening of *A Coffee and Punch Room which will be very convenient to Gentleman who are obliged to wait their going off. Fresh Jellies every day at 3d per glass.* In addition, the proprietor Anthony Wall proudly added *the Daily Papers are regularly taken and Punches sold in small Quantities at reduced rates.*[21]

The *stand* for the coaches to Cambridge was The Bull at 25 Aldgate High Street, the tavern from which Dicken's Mr Pickwick set out for Ipswich. For many years at the end of the C18 and early C19 it was run by the Nelson family, a noted race of inn and coach keepers. It was Mrs Ann Nelson, who was the presiding genius until her death in 1812, for her husband was a "good, easy going man ... and had no head for business". In addition to the *Ipswich Blue* she ran a Southend "Opposition" every afternoon by Romford, Brentwood, Billericay, Wickford, Raleigh and Rochford. The Bull provided sleeping accommodation for 150 travellers and Mrs Nelson insisted that there were no damp sheets and neither did she permit drunken brawlers.[22]

A Problem on the Highways

In the 1760s the innholder at the Cock and Bell, Romford, began taking out advertisements complaining at various actions taken by his competitors in the supply of stage coaches for gentlemen travelling into

Essex. It would appear that unwary gentlemen would be taken to a selected tavern, but on arrival would find that there were no coaches available. They were thus forced to stay over-night, thus increasing the cost of the journey. It would also appear from Mr Mellor's strictures that he was resisting the pressure to pay protection money to some nefarious villains.[23]

Long distance travel

For longer journeys it was necessary to go into the City. Travellers from London to Whitby in the 1740s made their way to the Bear Inn in Basinghall Street, and those for Warminster to the Kings Arms in Holborn. As noted by James P. Bowen, "With the improvement of roads in the second half of the sixteenth century, and the general growth in trade, the operations of a complex network of scheduled public carrying services using waggons, and pack horses emerged. As trade continued to grow and the economy to expand in the seventeenth century, they began to operate over greater distances."[24]

To support this massive transport system with thousands of horses, mules and donkeys, there were two large haymarkets around the City. To the west in the C18 there was a large market in the area still known today as the Haymarket. In the east was Whitechapel, which was the centre for one of the largest markets until it finally closed in 1928. Chapter 7 describes more fully the Hay Market and the extent of coach ownership in England and Wales based on the duties paid between 1757 and 1762.

The Costs of Coaching

A TNA document conveniently separates the "hirers" of carriages in London from "private" owners. In the eastern parishes those who only wished to hire a carriage or a chair would make their way to a livery stable based at one of the local taverns. One such person was Stephen Martin Leake, the Garter King of Arms, who lived in MEOT. His account books recorded every detail of his expenditure for a period of nearly forty years; and cover his expenses on his annual visits to his estate near Thorpe-le-Soken and Kirby-le-Soken in north-east Essex and on business for the College of Arms.[25]

In 1736 his expenses to St James's Palace *to attend on His Majesty* were three shillings. On a more domestic note the carriage of a *Barrel of Oysters* was one shilling and sixpence and porterage of some trout from Canterbury cost three shillings. In 1762 carriage of *wild fowl* from Mr Shearcroft at Thorpe-le-Soken was one shilling and sixpence. In 1751 his expenses for a seventeen-day journey in August to Thorpe-le-Soken, near Walton-on-the Naze were:

To the coachman	£0-10s.-00d. per day
Expenses on the road	£2-0s.-7d.
Expenses on the road up	£1-18s.-0d.

The road expenses would have included payments to the Whitechapel-Shenfield Turnpike and the costs of staying at inns and tips to sundry servants and porters. On 26th May 1760 he *Paid Mr Borrill's Bill for coaching £9-10s.-00d*; confirming the importance of this Whitechapel carrier, and Leake's reliance on others, to cope with the varied nature of his excursions on behalf of the College of Arms.

Suppliers to the Coaching Trade

In the *London Gazette* 25th August 1744 appeared an advertisement for the General Post Office:

> *This is to acquaint the Public That the several Post Masters on the Road between London and Norwich, London and Cambridge are ready to furnish gentlemen or others with Post-Chaises, safe, cosy and well secured from the weather, upon as short a Warning as for Post Horses, at any hour, either of the day or night,. Gentleman who have Occasion to go Post on the above roads are desired to apply to Mr Roberts at the Black Bull in Whitechapel.*

There was a Bull's Head tavern in Whitechapel High Street and Mr Roberts had responsibility for the coaching and mail post from London to East Anglia.[26]

For those who only wished to hire a carriage or a chair would make their way to one of the local taverns.

The two main suppliers in Whitechapel were:

> Lucy Biggs, victualler at the Black Horse on the west side of Leman Street, who had five coaches, one landau and one chariot.

> Richard Borrill, victualler at the Yorkshire Gray and Kings Head in Whitechapel High Street, who in 1756 had a coach, four chaises, a chariot and a landau.

In addition William Goodall at the Red Lyon in the High Street, kept seven two-wheel chaises, Robert Jones at the Green Dragon in the High Street kept six chaises and two chairs and John Wynn, a member of a family of coach makers and carpenters, kept seven chairs and a chariot.

A few years later a major supplier of *carroons* was Richard Boston, a carman, who in his will proved in 1782 left his fourteen carroons as follows:[27]

Nos.	43, 95, 118, 132 and 320 in trust for the benefit of his sister Hannah
Nos.	285 and 288 to Thomas Cooper, a carman from St George-in-the-East
No.	190 to Richard Spooner, a carman in the Borough
No.	289 to his kinsman John Boston, a Fellowship Porter
No.	329 to Robert May of Goodman's Fields, a tobacco warehouse keeper
Nos.	163 and 174 to his nephew Thomas Boston of Bethnal Green
No.	213 to Joseph Boston a pensioner in the Greenwich Hospital
No.	402 to Thomas Boston a blacksmith in Shoreditch

Blacksmiths, Saddlers and Stable Keepers

To support the carriage trade there were blacksmiths, coach-makers especially Richard Whiteshead and James Exeter, Isaac Colnett, a tyresmith, and John Fothergill, a saddler.

Thomas Sibley and his son, also Thomas, were blacksmiths in Whitechapel for over 15 years; and in his will Thomas the son expressed the hope that his wife Elizabeth would follow his business as a blacksmith. The subsequent probate contains detailed lists of his stock, which included:

Spanish iron	7 cwts one quarter and 12½ lbs
Spanish wrought iron	2 cwt 1 quarter 21 lbs
New iron	17 cwts and 2 quarters
Old furnace iron	11 cwt 2 quarters 14 lb

Clearly, he had a wider trade than just supplying horseshoes to farriers. In Chapter 3 can be found details of the household possessions of Thomas Sibley II.[28]

John Fothergill, a saddler, lived near The Nags Head in Whitechapel and his stock, in addition to 28 whips and 5 pair of womens' stirrups, included:

3	Shagg saddles	2	Leather saddles
9	Buck saddles	24	Hunting saddles
1	Old side saddle	13	Best snaffle bridles
72	Assorted lashes	19	Pair of iron stirrups

Amongst his debtors was a Mr Thompson a victualler at the Red Lyon in the High Street, who owed £4-0s.-8d.[29]

Goddard Williams, a saddler, appears in London about 1754 and with his brother Henry, immediately upset the Saddlers' Company by publicising prices that were 30 to 60% lower than those prevailing in the market. The Saddlers' Company reacted by searching his warehouse and taking away samples of his work to check if they met their standards. This did not stop the growth of his business for in September 1760 Goddard Williams and Co. announced that they were opening a new warehouse for their saddlery goods near Red Lion Street in Whitechapel. He already had warehouses in Holborn and on the Oxford Road. This was an easterly extension of his enterprise *for the convenience of the Merchants in the City of London and the Gentry of Essex*. An additional attraction was that they were selling *every kind of Saddlery and Coach Harness* and these were to be sold at the same prices they had held for seven years. In 1767 he was "Saddler to the Queen", but by June 1773 the *Lloyd's Evening Post* recorded his bankruptcy.[30]

Richard Whiteshead, a coach maker, insured in 1754 three warehouses – the seventh building east from the church. The timber workshops were quite large being two storeys high, 60 ft by 20 ft, 59 ft by 22 ft and 50 ft by 16 ft.[31]

An important stable keeper in Whitechapel was William Tillingham who in 1762 insured for £1,550 stabling and coaching on the south side of the Whitechapel Road. This covered ten stables the largest 60 ft by 36 ft.[32]

FURTHER READING

W. Albert	*The turnpike road system in England, 1663-1840*, 1972
T. Barker and D. Gerhold	*The Rise and Rise of Road Transport, 1700-1900*, 1993
K. J. Bonser	*The drovers, who they were and how they went, an epic of the English countryside*, 1970
J. P. Bowen	The Carriers of Lancaster, 1824-1912, *The Local Historian*, August 2010, vol. 43, 3, pp. 178-190
B. Cherry, et al	*The Buildings of England, London, 5, East*, 2005, pp. 456-476
P. Clark	*The English Alehouse: A social history 1200-1830*, 1983
P. J. Corfield	*The impact of English Towns, 1700-1800*, 1989, p. 81
J. Cox	*London's East End: Life and Traditions*, 1994
Daniel Defoe	*Moll Flanders*, 1722 reprinted 1965
H. W. Dickinson	*Water Supply of Greater London*, 1954
C. Driver & M. Berriedale-Johnson	*Pepys at Table*, 1984
A. Forshaw & T. Bergström	*Smithfield, Past and Present*, 1990
D. Gerhold	The growth of the London carrying trade, 1681-1838, *Econ. Hist. Rev.*, 2nd. Series XLI, 1988, pp. 392-410
C. G. Harper	*The Norwich Road*, 1903
J. H. Harvey	Leonard Gurle's Nurseries and some others, *Garden History*, vol. 3, 3, Summer 1975
P. Haydon	*The English Pub: A History*, 1994
C. Hibbert	*King Mob: The story of Lord George Gordon and the Riots of 1780*, 2004
S. R. Hovland	The Gardens of Later Medieval London, *The London Gardener*, 2006-7, Appendix
P. Mathias	*The Brewing Industry in England, 1700 -1830*, 1959
D. Morris	Silver and Carriage Duties; 1757-1766, *Genealogists' Magazine*, vol. 30, no. 5, March 2011, pp. 147-151
D. Morris	Drinking in Mile End, 1750, *East London Record*, vol. XIX, pp. 37-40, 1998
R. Porter	*London: A Social History*, 1994
L. D. Schwarz	Hanovarian London: The Making of a Service Town, *Two Capitals: London and Dublin: 1500-1840*, ed. P. Clark & R. Gillespie, 2001, pp. 93-110
C. Spence	*London in the 1690s: A Social Atlas*, 2000
Survey of London	*Spitalfields*, vol. XXVII, 1957, pp. 278-80
S. Ville	Transport, *The Cambridge Economic History of Modern Britain, vol. 1: Industrialisation*, ed. R. Floud and P. Johnson, 2004

Web Site

http://www.thersa.org/about-us/history-and-archive   Royal Society of Arts

5. THE MANUFACTURING INDUSTRIES

Introduction

Dr Leonard Schwarz, Dr Peter Earle and Dr David Barnett have examined many aspects of London's industries in the eighteenth century (C18); the VCH provides an overall summary of industry in Middlesex and Dr Craig Spence provides an overview of London in the 1690s. The late Dr Roy Porter briefly summarised the situation by stating that it is well-known that "Prominent among East End industries were distilling, sugar-refining and brewing", and that "In Whitechapel stood the long-established bell foundry, which was sending bells as far afield as Cologne and Carolina."

London's "dirty trades" were scattered throughout the East End and the poorer Surrey suburbs. Here were to be found bone-boilers, grease-makers, glue-makers, and paint-makers. Trades such as tallow-making consumed the offal of Smithfield, poisoning the atmosphere, and starch-works were to be found in East Smithfield, Whitechapel and Poplar. Whilst Porter followed a long tradition in describing these industries as "dirty"; he and many other historians failed to explore the technical and financial skills involved in these industries, and avoided important questions about the men and organisations that made them so successful in their chosen markets. A better appreciation can be found in the research of David Barnett and Leonard Schwarz. Morris and Cozens summarised the glass-making in Goodman's Fields in their Wapping book, and we await with interest Michael Noble's forthcoming book *Eighteenth-Century English Glass and its antecedents*.

Between 1750 and 1825 London not only more than doubled in size it also became the largest single business and industrial centre and market of the world's first modern industrial economy. It is estimated that almost thirty per cent of all businesses in London were engaged in manufacturing by 1826.[1]

This Chapter provides new information on the manufacturing industries based in Whitechapel and St George-in-the-East.

Figure 6   WHITECHAPEL BELL FOUNDRY, c. 1928

Barnett shows that many of these industries were spread across the entire city, and were thus able to take advantage of its economic infrastructure. As early as 1747 over three-hundred trades had been identified in London; many of these were to be found in Whitechapel, in addition to its speciality trades of bell and gun making, glass making, brewing, distilling and sugar refining. It is a well-established characteristic that throughout London in the C18 a wide range of services could be found within a few hundred yards of even the most exclusive residential areas. This was certainly true of Whitechapel, especially along the High Street and in Well Close Square.

The London Trade Directories of 1760 and 1770 provide a broad outline of the distribution and the variety of trades to be found in the eastern suburbs, but they do not include all merchants and traders and the criteria for selection are not known. In the eastern suburbs there were apparently no hay salesmen, attorneys or booksellers; but it is now known that these trades could be found in Whitechapel; and that there were many other merchants who were not listed in the Directories.

Approximately six per cent of the 1770 directory entries relate to the eastern suburbs. Out of a total of 361 entries nearly forty per cent (144) relate to Whitechapel and another twenty-two per cent (82) relate to Wapping, reflecting the long history of the concentration of trades in these two parishes. Further east in MEOT was a more residential area with brewing and ropemaking the main industries.

Industries in the eastern parishes did not have available a ready-source of water-power, and the only raw materials were brick, clay and gravel. There was however a large supply of both the male and female labour needed to bring raw materials into the refineries from the Port of London, and to work in the factories and workshops. There was always a need for gardeners, builders, carpenters and for men with experience of working with horses and carts.

Artificial and Coade Stone

For a few years Whitechapel was one centre of the specialised industry making *artificial stone*. Architects and the developers of fine Georgian houses sought a covering that could be applied to outer walls and withstand London's sooty and acidic atmosphere. The first Letters Patent for *artificial stone* was granted in 1722 to a Richard Holt in Lambeth whose factory was near the Kings Arms Stairs, and production continued there for some years. A second Royal Letters Patent was granted in 1737 to Alexander Emerton; and he was followed by his widow, Elizabeth, who in 1742 was at the Bell *over against Arundel Street in the Strand* and was advertising:

> *An invention which makes Timber, plaisters and other materials used in Building, much more durable than any covering of Lead, Slate or Tiling, ... and is likewise very ornamental being an exact imitation of stone, and by its strong cement, may be justly deemed an Artificial Stone.*

Elizabeth was followed in turn by her son, also Alexander, and by May 1746 he added to the advertisement that the covering would only cost two pence a yard. So far this business has been traced to 1758.

The patents expired in the 1760s and about 1763 the "Original artificial stone manufactory" was established near Cold Bath Fields in Clerkenwell. It is not clear who set this up, but it may have been Daniel Pincot. In 1767 Daniel Pincot set up a *manufactory* for the production of artificial stone in Goulston Square, Whitechapel. Being remote from the clients he wished to attract, Pincot organised auctions of hundreds of his factory's products; first at James Christie's New Auction Rooms in Pall Mall in 1767; and subsequently in 1768 at Mr. Moreings at the Great Sale Room, Maiden Lane, Covent Garden. The wide range of products included *near one hundred different subjects in antique busts, figures, vases, tablets, friezes, medallions, chimney pieces, both antique and modern.*[2]

In October 1767 the Whitechapel business in Goulston Square passed to a Mr Davy. His entire stock of the Manufactory of Artificial Stone consisted of *an elegant Variety of large and small Statuary Figures, Busts and Basrelievos, ornamental Vases, etc. many of them taken from the finest Antiques, elegant Chimney Pieces, Tablets, Friezes, Masks, Brackets, Capitals in the several orders, etc.* He recommended his goods to the Nobility especially *because its durable Nature has appeared on the severest Trial and Proof of three successive Winters.* This appeared to be a business in decline for in June 1770 Davy announced that he had sold off all his stock of ready-made goods *and does not intend to make any more, but by particular orders.* He reserved a room to display specimens of all 120 different subjects in his house in Boar's Head Yard, Petticoat Lane, but it seems doubtful if the gentry from the West End would venture beyond Aldgate in preference to a visit to the more rural Lambeth.[3]

Daniel Pincot established himself in Lambeth in 1767 and in 1769 was joined by Miss Eleanor Coade [1733-1821] DNB. This partnership did not last long for in September 1771 Eleanor announced that she had *thought proper to dismiss Pincot from any further employ in her manufactory at King Arms Stairs, Lambeth.*[4]

Coade Stone is a remarkable 18th century invention which modern tests have shown to be a ceramic material that was sold to builders and sculptors for its ability to withstand the severe weathering experienced by natural stone in London's acidic environment. Coade stone is a form of stoneware and was a mixture of "grog" (finely crushed pre-fired items such as wasters, which had already been fired once), and soda lime silica glass (also already fired once). The formula used was 10% grog, 5-10% of crushed flint, 5-10% fine sand to reduce shrinkage and 10% crushed soda lime. These were then added to 60–70% Ball clay from Dorset and Devon. Ball clay is a fine-grained clay comprising up to 70% kaolinite plus illite, quartz and other minor components, which is still quarried because of its importance to the ceramics industry. It was the careful control and skill of the kiln firer which ensured success.

The materials used made it impossible to make a one off by hand to fire because of the lack of plasticity. This is why a model and then a mould were made. This was an expensive way to produce the first sample, but a mould could be kept carefully for years. The use of certain moulds also facilitated basic items being "customised" before firing with odd bits of handles or swags being added or taken away. The site of the Coade works was very close to the subsequent site of the Festival of Britain on the south bank of the Thames. In front of the Festival Hall can be found the bed of the horse mill from Coade's works discovered during excavations in 1949.

The production of Coade Stone expanded greatly and Summerson noted that:

> "most of the architectural ornaments in the West End of 1774 onwards came from
> Lambeth. From Buckingham Palace to Twinings tea warehouse in the Strand …
> Coade Stone was triumphant".

Hundreds of examples have survived in pristine condition to the present day. The Coade Lion, formerly placed over the entrance of the Lion Brewery near Hungerford Bridge, stood for a time at the entrance to Waterloo Station and is now at the south end of Westminster Bridge. A frieze of Coade Stone can also be seen on the Royal Opera House, Covent Garden, and the large Coade Lion is now at the England Rugby Union ground in Twickenham.[5]

Brewing and Distilling

There is a long history of successful brewing in London's eastern parishes. In the 1590s Jacob Wittewrongle, the son of a Ghent merchant, was in partnership with other *alien* brewers and involved with several breweries including a third share in the Katharine Wheel in East Smithfield. By the time of his death in 1621 Wittewrongle was extremely wealthy with bequests totalling more than £8,000. Subsequently the family established itself on a large estate at Harpenden in Hertfordshire, which is now the home of the famous Rothamsted agricultural research station.

In 1693-4 the most valuable brewing establishment in London was the Red Lion brewery located in the vicinity of St Catharine's Lane, Wapping, in the ownership of Sir John Parsons and his partner with a rent value of £120. Parsons lived in Well Close Square and his rent of £117 and his stock of £3,200 indicate the extent of his investment. Sir John Parsons became Lord Mayor of London in 1703.[6]

By the middle of the C18 the three largest brewers in the eastern suburbs were Sir Benjamin Trueman at the Black Eagle brewery in Brick Lane; John Charrington at the Anchor brewery in Mile End, and the Trinder and Green families at the White Swan brewhouse also in Mile End. Later in the century the Albion brewery was established on the corner of the High Street and Cambridge Heath Road. However, within Whitechapel the largest business was that of the distiller Samuel Davy Liptrap.

Distillers

The Liptraps first appear in Whitechapel in 1767 at the back of Whitechapel Court House, on the north side of Whitechapel Road. Samuel Davy Liptrap was a liveryman of the Distillers' Company and took as apprentices his two sons John and Samuel. It is possible that they had taken over the still houses of one of the earlier distillers in Whitechapel:

Table 10   DISTILLERS IN WHITECHAPEL

NAME	DATES	NOTES	SOURCE	INSURANCE £
Nathaniel Clarkson	1757		PROB 11/827	
William Foster	1752	Angel and Still	Sun 99/132546	£500
Elizabeth Monckfield	1749	The Mermaid	Sun 85/115152	£300
John Rex	1768		Hand 107/86020	£1,000

Rex insured four still houses 23 ft 6 ins. by 42 ft. and Monckfield's still house was *distant from her dwelling house*; an important point for the insurers.

The Liptraps were initially in business as starch makers. This was already a prosperous line of business for they insured their *household goods* in their works, workshop and a dwelling house for £1,000. Within three years the utensils and stock in Whitechapel were insured for £3,000 and by 1781 the stock was valued at £10,000. The 1767 insurance policy refers to a 14 foot windmill and in 1770 they had *hog pens*. Hogs were an important aspect of the profitably of distilling, for they could be fed on the remaining husks and then sold to local butchers or at Smithfield Market. In 1776 Samuel and David Liptrap contracted with the Navy Board to supply 2,000 Hogs at forty-four shillings per hog. The eventual contract price was over £8,200. This appears to have been their only direct contract with the Victualling Office up to 1785, but they may have been a sub-contractor to others. They also held stock in John Milward's water corn mills at Four Mills, Bromley, which was insured for £500. Milward was involved in the subsequent decisions to move into distilling.[7]

The partners then decided to broaden their commercial interests to include distilling, and in September 1780 Samuel Davy Liptrap entered into a co-partnership agreement with John Milward and William Cotterall, a timber merchant in Whitechapel. Cotterall appears in the records of the Butchers' Company in 1776 when he is described as a *salesman of Mile End*. John Milward was a miller in Bromley, Middlesex. Liptrap contributed £15,000 to the £30,000 capital of this group, [over £2,000,000 in today's money] which was established to run the malt distillery in Whitechapel on the southern side of the main road. Both Liptrap and Cotterall were entitled to a salary of £300 per annum together with a house on the distillery site, and their coals, candles, beer, horses and a coach. Liptrap was responsible for the purchase and grinding of corn and grain, the selling of spirits and bacon, keeping the books of accounts and collecting the monies due to the group. Cotterall was responsible for *managing the Brewery … and also the buying and selling of Hogs, inspecting the Bacon house, ordering and directing the workmen and horses.*[8]

Liptrap owned the Upper and Lower Spring Fields near Woodford, and these were another asset taken into the new malt distilling partnership. The initial agreement was for seven years and in 1785 the partnership dissolved when Cotterall left. Milward died in 1786 and his estate was entitled to a payment of nearly £13,000 from Liptrap. In the event Liptrap paid about £3,000 in cash and retained the balance as a loan on which he paid interest at 5% pa. The original agreement allowed Liptrap to take his son John, as an apprentice, and entitled him to join as a partner after seven years. Looking at the agreement it is difficult to find a commercial issue that was not covered.

In 1785 Liptrap was Chairman of the London Hospital. His increasing wealth and prestige are shown by his election as Master of the prestigious Distillers' Company in 1788. He then made a short move down the Whitechapel Road to the very large Fitzhugh House in MEOT, described in Chapter 3, with a rack rent of £80, where he died within a year.

Brewers

The history and development of brewing, both at the national and the local level, have been explored in many publications including P. Mathias and L. A. G. Strong; consequently this section concentrates on aspects of the trade not covered by these books or the publications of the Brewery History Society.[9]

Drinking was widespread in the local inns, taverns, homes, schools and at the London Hospital; for it was widely recognised that beer was safer to drink than water. In the 1760s the Raine's Foundation School was allowed a barrel of beer per week, to be shared between staff and the children, but this amount could be increased at the discretion of the Steward. One supplier of *small beer at 6s 6d per barrel* was Joseph Asquith, and in 1777 the suppliers were Messrs Wilson and Price at 6s 9d per barrel.[10]

At the London Hospital the victualler was John Cholsey who died in 1762, and Clark-Kennedy noted that:

> "Small beer was the standard drink, and the fact that every quarter about thirty shillings
> (derived from the sale of yeast) was handed over by each matron to the steward
> suggests that much of it was brewed on the premises. It seems to have been liberally
> supplied, and before long it became clear that the consumption of it, and indeed of all
> the hospital victuals, must be more carefully watched. 'Ordered that Mrs Broad remove
> the small beer into another Cellar, and that the Door be made wider for the more
> conveniently carrying in the Barrels, and that the Door be kept Locked, and that in
> Future no person whatsoever shall have any Victuals at the Hospital except the
> Servants or Patients of it' ".[11]

In 1790 Richard Ivory acquired the lease of the tavern, a small brewhouse and surrounding land, at the corner of the High Street and Cambridge Heath Road, next to the Blind Beggar of Bethnal Green. He evidently wished to exploit the potential of this valuable site and in 1807 an advertisement appeared inviting subscribers for a new brewery to be built in the Mile End Road. It was planned that the brewery should be capable of producing 10,000 barrels per annum, and a sixty-year lease was offered. The initial interest did not meet Ivory's expectations and it was not until September 1807 that the first tenant John Hoffman appeared. The link with the well-known brewers Mann, Cross and Paulin developed after 1808.[12]

There were also several smaller brewers in Whitechapel and St George-in-the-East, and of these John Phillips was very successful for he had a house in Chigwell, Essex, and left his wife £18,000. Thomas Jordan had a brewery in Chislehurst Green, in south-east London.

Table 11   THE SMALLER BREWERS AND DISTILLERS

NAME	OCCUPATION	ABODE	NOTES
Timothy Biscon	Distiller	Whitechapel	PROB 11/811
Edward Brewer	Brewer	Whitechapel	Sun 176/24940, 41767
George Setcole Healey	Brewer	St George-in-the-East	PROB 11/1188
Thomas Jordon	Brewer	Whitechapel	Hand 100/82710
John Phillips	Brewer	St George-in-the-East	PROB 11/1147
Hugh Roberts	Brewer	St George in-the-East	PROB 11/973
Thomas Stubbs	Brewer	Whitechapel	PROB 11/717

A Day in a Brewery

The diary of John Allen, a Quaker brewer in Wapping, describes some of the day-to-day activities and incidents experienced by a young twenty-year old man. In June 1777 he was left in sole charge of the family brewery in Bett's Street, whilst his father visited relatives in Yorkshire.[13]

3 June	Brewing as before. Orders pour in uncommonly fast, can hardly supply them.
6 June	Drays and men returned not the last time until near 9 o'clock.
6 June	Brewing again … as we find the quantity not nearly sufficient for the Orders we expect.
7 June	Prepared Casks to put the beer in that was brewed yesterday.
15 June	His parents left for Yorkshire leaving him in sole command.
17 June	Having cooled the first liquor too much for Mashing had like to thrown me out of sorts, but

	recovered it well in to third Liquors, after which everything went well and pleasant; the Men finished by about seven and had the Worts down under eleven o'clock.
18 June	Called before 6am but did not rise until after the Excise and took the Length before I came down; the drays out at half past seven. Pleased with appearance of the beer in the Tunns, which afterwards came a rather too forward.
19 June	Brewing all day
22 June	A remarkably wet week – sales down.
28 June	Set the Drays off, carried out and delivered some Bills.
30 June	Brewing, which went easily, the Men done very soon, the Zeal of going to a Club Feast animated them.
2 July	To Excise Office to pay a Malt Bill. Cleansed all the Guile.

The Bell Foundry

Still prominent on the Whitechapel Road stands the long-established bell foundry, which in addition to supplying churches throughout the British Isles, in the C18 sent bells as far afield as Russia and America.

The history of the bell foundry has been described by the company, the VCH and A. D. Tyssen, but problems arise in understanding the business in the C18 as the records of the Bell Foundry have not survived. Fortunately it is possible to identify bells made in Whitechapel in the publications describing the bells to be found in many counties. An early publication on church bells was that of William Jones and John Reeves. Their *Clavis Campanalogia and a Key to the Art of Ringing* was published in 1788; and William Mears at the Whitechapel Bell Foundry bought 20 copies and John Lyford also of Whitechapel bought one copy.[14]

The Bell Founders

The earliest London bell founders are met with towards the end of the thirteenth-century. The trade was located near the City's eastern boundary being chiefly connected with the parishes of St. Andrew, Cornhill (now Undershaft), and St. Botolph Aldgate. From Aldgate the trade extended to Whitechapel where in 1570 Richard Mot established a business on the north side of the High Street in Essex Street, where Tewkesbury Court survived for over three-hundred and fifty years.

The earliest known bell from this foundry bearing Mot's name has the date of 1575, and was formerly at Danbury, Essex. There are also four bells out of six at St. Andrew Undershaft, three of which dated from 1597 and the fourth from 1600. In 1738 the foundry moved from Essex Street to the Artichoke Inn, which is its present site on the south side of Whitechapel High Street.

The VCH describes the history of bell founding in Whitechapel before 1700, and emphasises the importance of the Bartlett family, who were the proprietors from 1619 until January 1701. Thomas Bartlett cast the curfew bell at Charterhouse in 1731, and the VCH comments that the family "worthily maintained its reputation", throughout the C17.

Throughout the C18 there were a number of Master founders and partnerships including:

> Richard Phelps from 1701 until about 1735
> Thomas Lester, Phelp's foreman, who became the principal from about 1738 until his death
> in 1769. During this time bells were sent York Minster, the Elector of Cologne and seven
> bells were sent to St Petersburg in Russia.

Lester formed a partnership with Thomas Pack in 1752 and in 1761 they supplied bells to the London Hospital. This was a period of prosperity and as they had few competitors in their field they consequently grew "a large business". The treble bell supplied to Newport Pagnall, Bucks, cast by Lester in 1749, bears the verse:-

> At proper times my voice I'll raise
> And sound to my subscribers praise

In the 1750s Hugh Boyd built Holy Trinity church in Ballycastle, Northern Ireland, as part of his development of the Georgian town. Only one of the original bells supplied by Lester and Pack of Whitechapel in 1760 remains. A clock mechanism of 1854 is still in the tower, though not the original works from 1756.[15]

Thomas Lester in his will, proved in 1769, devised the foundry to John Exeter, then of Hornchurch and probably related to James Exeter, a prominent coach maker and neighbour in Whitechapel. The foundry was *for the sole use and benefit* of the testator's granddaughter Sarah Oliver. The will also requested that Thomas Pack took into partnership on equal terms the testator's nephew William Chapman. William had formerly been foreman to Lester and Pack, so had the necessary technical expertise for this specialist profession. The will of Thomas Pack reveals he had two maid servants and his clerk Samuel Bromfield was left £15. His executor was James Exeter a well-known coach maker.[16]

In the 1770s Chapman invited William Mears to learn the trade of a bell founder. Thus began the family's association with the foundry which lasted nearly a century. William Chapman's will shows that he left £100 to his wife Hannah, but disappointingly reveals nothing about the foundry.[17]

For some years there were disputes about the ownership of the foundry led by Robert Patrick, who had married Sarah Oliver. Patrick's attempted sharp practice proved a failure, and William Mears had returned to the foundry by 1789. He then took into partnership his brother Thomas Mears, who was acting alone by 1790.

Another problem is revealed by a letter from William Tolham in 1791 from Thomas Mear's bell foundry in Whitechapel to the churchwardens of the parish of Ashdon, near Saffron Walden in Essex. Following the bankruptcy of Thomas Mears, Tolham, who had been granted a power of attorney, was trying to collect what appeared to be outstanding debts. In the case of Ashdon they totalled £59-19s.-3½d.. Much to his embarrassment it became clear that the bill had been paid sometime previously. At the end of 1791 Tolham had to write an apology explaining that if *Myers [sic] had not left the country, but staid in town and given his assistance I might not have written to you.* He went on to reassure them that "Mr W. Mears was not entirely out of the business and the trade goes on very promisingly by Mr John Myers alone". Reportedly the Thomas Mears, father and son, were extremely wealthy in the early C19.[18]

Soap Manufacturers

Professor Peter Razzell has explored the role of hygiene in shaping mortality patterns, and noted that in an earlier age "Henry VIII's practice of bathing was similar to that of his daughter Elizabeth, who used her portable bath 'twice a year for medicinal purposes'". Standards of hygiene were slowly improving in the C18, and there were local men meeting the need for soap, such as Joseph Crosby in Seven Star Alley, Ratcliff Highway. In 1770 Neave and Rawson Aislabie, soap makers in East Smithfield, insured their stock for £2,000. The production of soap in Britain rose from 17,000 tons in 1785 to 35,000 tons in 1814. One of the main London suppliers was the Russell family whose factory was in Goodman's Fields, and whose success allowed them to later make their home in Walthamstow.[19]

The Russell family originated in Newcastle-under-Lyme and John Russell and his wife Martha (Shepherd) had six sons of whom Jesse Russell [1743-1820] was the youngest. It is not yet clear when they moved to London, but in 1762 George Russell (one of Jesse's older brothers) and one George Wyatt leased premises in Goodman's Fields; which till then had been a glass works, and took up the manufacture of soap. Jesse seems to have been a partner in this business.[20]

A large soap boiling house contained numerous soap pans; in addition there would normally be a frame room, warehouses, laboratories, carpenter's and blacksmith's shops for making boxes, crates and equipment, sheds, stables, a yard and a counting house.

An important development in this industry was that in the C18 imports of tallow more than quadrupled and by 1796-8 the quantities retained for use in Britain had reached 37.5 million lb, but we have no way of knowing what proportion was used in the manufacture of candles.[21]

One problem in the soap works was that of theft for Jesse Russell informed the Old Bailey in 1791 that he had *lost soap many times from the manufactory ... in Goodman's Yard, Minories*. Another aspect of their business was the need to import tallow as Jesse Russell revealed in another case at the Old Bailey in 1796. The imported tallow was landed at Mr Mashiter's wharf near the Tower of London. The tallow was stolen on the wharf so Russell knew nothing about it until Stephen Tew, his clerk, identified the tallow and a cask of pearl ash, which *was marked with an R in a triangle*. The theft was detected by the alertness of an officer and two constables as they walked through East Smithfield.[22]

In 1777, differences between the two brothers led to a break up of the partnership. Jesse continued the trade of soap-maker, at which he was clearly very successful, becoming one of the leading manufacturers and being asked to advise the Customs and Excise authorities on the bonding system for the taxing of soap-making. Jesse held the lease until shortly before his death, when in 1820 he assigned the lease to his son-in-law, Peter Kendall. During that period, he prospered mightily; and like other successful local merchants he increased his fortune by a wide variety of speculations and property deals. In 1790 he was a governor of Magdalen Hospital and a governor of the London Hospital in 1796.

The house attached to the soap factory was a substantial one, with an Elizabethan ceiling to bear witness to its age. He seems to have purchased Clock House, Wood Street, Walthamstow by 1778, another sign of a successful merchant.[23]

It was thought that in the 1760s between £2,000 and £5,000 was needed to establish a soap boiler. The importance of the business of George and Jesse Russell in a London context is shown by their insuring their property and stock for £11,010 in 1771 and £16,800 in 1819, a rise of 53 per cent. The following year Peter Kendall and Company insured their counting house, soap house and warehouse in Goodman's Yard for £2,000 and their stock and utensils for £10,000.[24]

The White Lead Works

Amongst the local "dirty trades" was the White Lead Works, of which Professor John Rule has written that "in the works for manufacturing white and red lead for paint, which were situated in the Whitechapel area, the life destroying process of manufacture was carried out by engines, horses and labourers".[25]

The early history of the White Lead Works has yet to be fully researched, but a major figure in its development was Richard Lindsey, a London merchant. He had begun as early as 1706 to purchase the leases on land and property in the area of Buckle Street, Colchester Street and Church Lane. One lease was obtained from Edward Buckley, a brewer, in 1713, and Lindsey continued these investments until at least 1723. The documents refer to Buckley Street, though this does not appear on the maps of the 1740s; suggesting that Rocque's surveyors miscalled it Buckle Street.

In 1720 a notice appeared concerning a new business venture in which *Several Persons, both traders and consumers of that useful commodity White Lead have agreed a co-partnership ... with a Capital Share of £120,000*, that would be over £10,000,000 in today's money. It is probable that Richard Lindsey was involved in this venture. It is not clear where this new venture was to be located, but one possibility is Whitechapel.[26]

Later an indenture of 1727 refers to land around Buckley Street on which were found starch mills, a brewhouse, warehouses, a Vinegar House, and *all such Coppers, Casks, Mill work and other utensils and implements necessary or or used in the business of White Lead making now carried on in the above mentioned premises*.[27] It would appear that by 1727 Lindsey was running into financial problems; because he mortgaged for £4,000 much of his property in Whitechapel. The mortgage provided by Robert Jackson esq, of Alie Street, with interest at 5%, was due to be repaid by Lindsey on 24 June 1728. Even this mortgage did not save Lindsey for the *London Gazette* in October 1728, records a Commission of Bankruptcy against Richard Lindsey, and offered for sale his interest in the White Lead Works in or near Buckley Street, Whitechapel. Also affected by his problems was Elizabeth Lindsey, who in March 1728 was involved in case concerning a loan of £8,000; the subject of a legal judgement in June 1728.[28]

The earliest link between James Creed and the lead industry appears to be in the General Ledgers of the East India Company in October 1725 when he was paid £1,705-10s.-00d. for lead. He continued in this business and during 1740 Stainbank and Creed received over £15,000 for lead, which was being exported to India.[29]

The Creed family have their origins in Kent. James married Mary Hankey at Clapham on 13 July 1725 and in 1731 Creed bought at Greenwich "a most handsome house, of three and a half storeys, seven bays wide, with a double flight of curved steps to the main entrance hall", and this was still his home in the 1750s. Creed was clearly a merchant of substance and status for he was Master of the Haberdashers' Company in 1744 and was followed in that post the next year by his brother-in-law Sir Thomas Hankey.

Creed was knighted in 1744, was a director of the East India Company 1755-58, and MP for Canterbury 1754-62. The RSA Membership lists show that he became a member in 1756 and was introduced by Sir Thomas Hankey. He died on 7th Feb 1762 aged 57 and Lady Creed died on 14th October in the same year; their monumental inscription can be found at Greenwich. Creed's will, proved in 1762, shows that he had a house in Mansell Street, Goodman's Fields, another in Greenwich and at least two farms in Sussex and Hampshire. The town house was to be kept for his wife and their house in Greenwich was to be sold. His brothers-in-law were Sir Joseph Hankey, Alderman, and another Honourable Deputy Lieutenant of Tower Hamlets, and Sir Thomas Hankey of Clapham. One of his senior clerks and mentioned in Creed's will was Flower Freeman, who lived in MEOT from 1765 to 1777 and was also a prosperous merchant in his own right.[30]

George Creed appears in Leman Street in 1739 and continues until 1741 in the land tax. James Creed of East Greenwich appears in the land tax in 1740. In June 1741 he petitioned for a Letters Patent for his invention of three machines: a) for cutting lead pipes to any required width; b) for making water pipes of any diameter; c) for raising water. These give an indication of the products being created in Whitechapel. One wonders whether given the large number of gun-makers in the area they also produced gun shot? Lead pipes were used to connect the water mains to houses and hospitals, but were too expensive and weak to be used elsewhere. The records of the Shadwell Waterworks Company mention the order in 1753 of iron pipes to lay over the bridge in Stepney Causeway. This suggests that the rope walk, which reached as far west as the later Devonport Street ran under Stepney Causeway. Generally, iron pipes were used when a very strong water main was needed.[31]

Creed paid an important part in the development of the lead industry with his Letters Patent (No. 651) in 1749 which outlined the basic principles of the "chamber process"; broadly a controlled stack process that was not satisfactorily developed until the late C19 by German technologists.

From the lead mines in Derbyshire pig lead was sent to London via Hull. From Flintshire the pig lead was carried as ballast in "cheese boats" to London. In Whitechapel, Creed required a good supply of vinegar, which was made on site and could also be obtained locally, plus coal. Lead was smelted in pots at low temperatures (325°C) in the presence of vinegar. Hundreds of pots were placed in layers within a stack and covered with spent tan or dung. After several weeks of heating the vinegar and the carbon dioxide evolved from the decaying tan would lead to the oxidisation of the lead. Depending on the precise process the end result was one of the oxides of lead, white lead, red lead or yellow lead; each having different physical and chemical characteristics and a variety of industrial uses.[32]

In 1751 Creed insured his White Lead yard at the east end of Buckley Street, Whitechapel for £2,500. On the site were melting houses, a hot house and a vinegar house built in brick and timber. In 1760 Sir James Creed was assessed in the Whitechapel land tax for property in Gower's Garden with a rent of £60 and his personal estate was £500, which places him amongst the wealthiest of local merchants. This was confirmed by his appointment as one of the Honourable Deputy Lieutenants of Tower Hamlets in 1745. By 1770 the land tax was paid by Ann Creed Farr and the 1780 tax on male servants refers to Creed, Farr and Company.[33]

Captain James Cook in his log for the 26th May 1769 on the *Endeavour*, whilst recording the Transit of Venus in the Pacific, and before the Navy found that sheathing hulls with copper was more effective, wrote[34]

> *This morning we hauled the Pinnace a Shore to examine her bottom and had the satisfaction to find that not one worm had touched it, ... this must be owing to the white Lead with which her bottom is painted.*

Wax Chandlers, Oilmen and Colourmen

Dr Barnett records that in 1770 there were at least 229 retailers of oils, candles and paints in London, for clearly they supplied essential items to the majority of houses and workshops. Most firms were of middling size; 69 per cent insuring for between £100 and £500 in 1770, which agrees with the 1760s estimate that a capital of £200 was needed to establish a tallow chandlers.[35] In Whitechapel the most prominent men in this trade were the Luke Alders (father and son) and Thomas and William Quarrill (father and son), who can be traced from the 1740s to the 1790s. Elsewhere could be found starch makers and turpentine makers. Another important tallow chandler was Joseph Langer in Leman Street, who insured his utensils, stock and warehouse for the large sum of £2,300.[36]

By 1740 Thomas Quarrill was established on the south side of the High Street, just west of Red Lyon Street. His increasing business is revealed by the land tax for 1750 when his tax had nearly doubled from £28 in 1740 for two adjacent buildings to £54. Typically for a growing business he began to purchase or lease and then insure a number of buildings and warehouses in the area. He experienced a fire in a warehouse next to the White Hart in 1755 which killed three men. In 1761 Thomas Quarrill insured for £450 his Mill House known as the "Land of Promise" on the east side of Catharine Wheel Alley. A year later Thomas and William Quarrill insured stock in their warehouses in Leman Street for £2,200. This value places them amongst the top ten per cent of London's colourmen. They also supplied soap, Fullers Earth and lamps to the London Hospital from 1757 to at least 1778.

William Quarrill is listed in the Directories up to at least 1791 as a colourman. From 1774 he lived at 37 Whitechapel Road in a house with a rent of £25. He was clearly a man of local status for he was a Justice of the Peace in 1788. He married Jane, the daughter of John Jones, a Whitechapel distiller, so was living close to his father-in-law.[37]

In 1758 Luke Alder, an oil and colour man, was living in Irish Court, Whitechapel, just west of the Quarrills, and insured his stock in a timber warehouse for £500. By 1775 the firm was known as Luke Alder and Son at 11 Whitechapel Road. They were at 133 Whitechapel Road by 1785. In 1775 Luke Alder was on the Middlesex Jury at the Old Bailey, and in 1776 he was appointed a Commissioner of Paving, but died in the same year. It was his son, also Luke, who took over the Quarrill premises about 1778. He was evidently successful, for many years later he left £1,000 to Davenant's School.[38]

The Sugar Industry

The development and history of the sugar industry is very well documented. A good starting point is Bryan Mawer's excellent book *Sugarbakers – From sweat to sweetness*, followed by the books of N. Deerr and P. J. Marshall and the articles of R. B. Pares. Mawer's comprehensive web site, complete with maps, shows the locations of the refineries. Selected information can be found in Appendix 5. As summarised by Bryan Mawer:

> "By 1725, sugar houses had begun to spring up to the east and north-east of the Tower, in the parishes of Whitechapel and St George-in-the-East, slowly at first, in Angel Alley, Buckle Street and Salt Petre Bank. … Businesses spread throughout both parishes towards the almost rural Mile End, and along the river's edge to Wapping, Shadwell and Limehouse … So many streets in Whitechapel and St George's had refineries, but a few deserve special mention. Alie Street, just south of the Whitechapel High Street, and right in the heart of the trade, was where St George's German Lutheran Church was built along with its school." Leman Street was important to the sugar industry and "was busy with refineries throughout the 18th century and most of the 19th, important names like Tielhen, Shum, Constantien, Rhode, Harbusch, Martineau, Gadsden and Goodhart all worked there."

The development of the sugar industry depended on a number of factors and the industry in Whitechapel required three elements to be successful:

- Large amounts of finance, mainly raised in the City
- Technical expertise in sugar refining, which came mainly from Germany
- An increasing public demand for sugar

Sugar Refining

In 1706 Thomas Twining, at the age of thirty-one, decided to open a shop to sell tea at Tom's Coffee House in Devereaux Court in the Strand, and so founded the House of Twining, which has survived to this day. In addition to eighteen types of tea, including Bohea and Pekoe, and many types of coffee, he also sold sugar for about a shilling a pound. Sugar was sold by the loaf, the smallest loaf being 4½ lb, and the largest over 7lb. Twining's perception of the need for a specialist shop was very prescient for between 1740 and 1769 the annual demand for sugar in England doubled to the massive amount of over 70,000 tons. It was said in 1753 that even the meanest people *now use hardly any other but improved sugar*. The poorer classes bought "brown lumps", which were also in demand overseas.

Over the centuries the importation of raw sugar into Europe had begun with the Portuguese and in succession was dominated by the French, then the Dutch and the Germans. The British became increasingly involved at the end of the C17. By 1748 the sugar consumption in the UK per head of the population was ten pounds and this had to increased twenty pounds by 1800. Coffee houses appeared in Whitechapel in the 1720s and in MEOT in the 1730s, and tea, coffee and sugar were available from many shops in the area.[39]

From the 1750s until the 1820s sugar from the West Indies was Britain's largest single import until it was overtaken by cotton. "Prior to the nineteenth century the plantation islands of the Caribbean were the most valued possession in the overseas Imperial World". Most of this West Indian sugar came into the London market, which dominated the price. The most important buyers of sugar in the London market were grocers, such as Twining, and the refiners. Each group demanded different qualities. For grocers colour was important, whilst the refiners wanted a strong grain, *and the better they have been cleaned the brighter they will appear to be, and sell the better*.

It was very noticeable that the trade in sugar and tobacco became concentrated in fewer firms as the C18 progressed. One reason for this was that heavy import duties on sugar and tobacco were imposed in 1685 and meant that only wealthy merchants could get substantial people to sign their bonds with Customs and Excise. The duty on sugar lapsed in 1693, but continued on tobacco.

Generally, sugar prices halved between 1717 and 1732, to the distress of the merchants and plantation owners. Thereafter the industry was more stable and by the middle of the century there was a "silver age of relative prosperity". Even so John Barrel, a sugar refiner of Well Close Square, was declared bankrupt in 1750. In the 1780s the London sugar refiners petioned Parliament because of a collapse in their trade caused by the high price of molasses. Several Whitechapel men were called before the Parliamentary committee to give evidence and one of these was William Davis, who lived in Well Close Square.[40]

Davis had been employed for sixteen or seventeen years as a clerk to Carsten Rhode, a prominent sugar baker; but he also carried on *a considerable Business of my own, chiefly in Molasses*. Davis recalled that the price of molasses had doubled between 1778 and 1781 and that Mr Rhode had lost money in 1780. It was also stated that the number of sugar refineries had dropped from about 159 in 1766 to about 100 in 1781.

Many Stepney merchants were able to take advantage of this rapidly growing sugar market, and were involved in all aspects of the trade including the provision of shipping and credit, owning plantations, and acting as sugar brokers. Those in Whitechapel and St George-in-the-East specialised in sugar refining. There were also opportunities for local carriers, coal merchants, potters, coopers, copper smiths and iron founders to support the industry.

In MEOT lived several families that owned plantations in the Caribbean. One such family was that of Nathaniel Phillips senior and his son, also called Nathaniel. Phillips senior owned estates in Jamaica and returned to London in 1749 and rented a house in MEOT until his death in 1765. His son was in Jamaica from 1759 and when he finally returned to London in 1789 he was very wealthy and invested in the Slebech estate, Pembrokeshire, for which he paid £38,000. He was also a sleeping partner in the Milford Bank. In London, where he had a town house, he was a member of the powerful West India Committee, which led the campaign for the building of the West India Docks. He unsuccessfully contested the 1812 election in Haverfordwest.[41]

One of the earliest Stepney merchants to be involved with the sugar industry was Arthur Bailey, who bought land in MEOT in 1677 and died a wealthy man in 1712. He owned land in Virginia and was reputed to import over 100,000 pounds of sugar a year, as well as having a significant trade in tobacco. He was also a witness in 1706 when he gave evidence to the Commissioners for Trade and Plantations, on the need for the Navy to guard convoys to and from Virginia.

Also in Stepney there were many men who owned ships that were involved in the triangular trade that took slaves from West Africa to the Caribbean and brought sugar, rum and timber back to England.[42]

Financing the Sugar Industry

Each refinery represented a considerable investment and in 1761 it was estimated that between £1,000 and £5,000 was need to start up as a sugar baker. In 1781 a Parliamentary committee learnt that in times of Peace, i.e. before the American War of Independence (1775-81), the investment in each *pan* was about £3,000, but it had risen to £4,500 by 1781. In addition there were rents to be paid of about £200 a year plus the wages of the many labourers. Typically refineries were described in insurance policies as *one pan* or *two pan*. In 1749 George Crosby insured his sugar house for £1,000 and on a larger scale Spalding, Slack and Hawes of Gravel Lane, Whitechapel, insured their sugar house in 1777 for £22,000. James Spalding lived in the High Street and had a personal stock of £75 in the land tax, indicative of his wealth. In 1774 he was a life governor of the London Hospital.[43]

Confirmation of the large capital sums invested in the industry is found in the co-partnership agreement of 1722 between Sir John Fellows, Richard Houlditch and Thomas Emerson, sugar baker. They raised £40,000 to finance their purchase of eight sugar refineries in and around London. In modern terms that is over £3 million. In addition to Mortlake and Battersea they also leased sugar refineries in Leman Street and Lambert Street near Goodman's Fields. The two largest lenders were a Sir William Scawden £20,000 and a Miss Ann Carleton £10,000, both based in Carshalton.[44]

The Work of a Sugar Refinery

From the Legal Quays the hogsheads of raw sugar were taken by horse and cart to the East London sugar refineries, easily distinguished by their eighty-foot high towers and tall brick chimneys.

In the refineries the men worked six days a week and ten or eleven months in a year until trade dropped by twenty to thirty per cent in the late 1770s. The refiners were then making 5 per cent on their money; the same rate as could be found by investing in bonds, but without the commercial risks. Several refineries had been forced to close down, including some in Whitechapel and St George-in-the-East, and others were forced to work only two or three days a week. Another cost was coal, for a *two pan house in full work consumes between 200 and 300 chaldron of coal a year*. [A London chaldron was about 36 bushels].

Another problem was that because of their unique construction the tall refineries could not be easily turned to other uses, leaving the refiners to continue to pay the rent even in lean times. It was also said that the refiners had to continue to buy raw sugar, regardless of cost, as *their syrups would spoil for lack of proper sugar to be used with them.*

Hogsheads of raw sugar or the bags of sugar were emptied on to the upper floor of the sugar house and then discharged in shoots to a lower floor to be melted in *blow-ups*. These were cast iron tanks fitted with mechanical stirrers and steam pipes for heating the water. The solution called the *liquor* was brought to a certain degree of gravity (25 to 33 degree Baumé) and then filtered through twilled cotton bags, encased in a meshing of hemp. The syrup was then decolourised by being passed through beds of animal charcoal, inclosed in cisterns to a depth from 30 to 50 ft. The sugar was then discharged into tanks where it was boiled and subjected to various finishing treatments before being sent to the wholesalers.[45]

Insurance policies reveal that a typical sugar house was seven-storeys high, with a base of 40 ft by 36 ft, and there might also be a two-storey mill house, warehouses, a yard, a brick boiling house and *arched stoves with iron doors*. By the 1870s the inside of the sugar houses were described as being "coated with a thick preserve of sugar and grime. The floor was black and all corrugate and hard ... the roof was black, and pendant from the great supporting posts and bulks of timber were sooty, glistening icicles and exuding like those of the gum-trees".[46]

Because of the large amounts of inflammable material, the conditions were hazardous for workers. Stock and utensils in the refineries were originally insured with the Hand-in-Hand and the Sun insurance companies. However, because of the increase in their premiums, a consortium of local sugar refiners set up the competing Phoenix Assurance Company in 1782.[47]

The value of the sugar in stock varied considerably between refiners. In 1754 Richard Hayer and Henry Riners insured their stock for only £500. Other refiners such as John Camden, George Lear and Peter Thellusson insured their sugar house and stock on the east side of Meeting House Lane, Old Gravel Lane for £6,000. Thomas Slack and his associates insured their stock in their sugar house in Goodman's Yard for £9,900 in 1767, and in 1763 Samuel Touchet and Company in Billiter Lane, off Leadenhall Street in the City, insured their stock for £17,000.[48] Because of the highly fluctuating nature of the sugar business the refiners were constantly re-assessing the value of their stock. Thus Paul Turquand, a sugar refiner in Great Garden Street, took out ten policies between 1749 and 1772, but reportedly by 1781 had closed down his refinery because of the collapse of the market.

Germans in the Sugar Refineries

In 1747, Campbell in *The London Tradesman* concluded:

> *The Dutch are better Boilers than we and we have a number of working boilers from thence and Hamburg. I do not find that they take Apprentices ... The Boiler is the chief workman in a Sugar house and earns from thirty to fifty pounds a year; the rest are only labourers.*

His conclusions are confirmed by the many records of the 18th century that reveal that in St George-in-the-East and Whitechapel there were dozens of sugar bakers, many with German names, such as Beckman, Dirs, Gotcke, Gramlitch, Lehman, Mackerbath, Neuman, Scheinz, and Wackerworth.

From their naturalisation records we know that John Christian Suhring, a sugar refiner in Angel Alley between 1750 and 1769 had been born in Hamburg, and John Henry Suhring was born at Altone in Denmark. John was a governor of the London Hospital in 1774, as were other sugar refiners such as Jens Pedersen, James Turquand, Carsten Rhode, Major Rhode, and Theophilus Pritzler.

Carsten Rhode [sometimes spelt Rohde] was a sugar refiner and Director of the Phoenix Fire Office, and there were several connections between his family and the wealthy Hawkins family. Edward Hawkins (I) of Leman Street married Ann Schumaker in 1778 and the Settlement involved Major Rhode, a prominent local attorney, another Director of the Phoenix Fire Office.

Carsten Dirs (I) was a prominent sugar refiner who lived in Well Close Square until his death in 1777. His will reveals that his brother Court Dirs, was also a sugar refiner, whose son was Carsten Dirs (II). Other local sugar refiners in the area were Carsten Holthouse and Christopher Ludekin in Ratcliff Highway. The will also reveals his continuing links with family members in Germany, the town of Warp and the County of Heya. The surprising thing is that in spite of running a large business Carsten Dirs (I) could only make his mark on his will.

In addition to the entrepreneurial merchants there were also many German labourers recruited from the Hamburg area. These men were said to be prepared to work harder in the hot and dangerous conditions than Englishmen; though there were always bound to be young strong local boys willing to work there. The refiners were looking for *stout and able men from the age of eighteen to thirty*, and in 1794 they were offering £12 p. a. plus board and lodging. Dr Rössler has studied the origins of the young German labourers, especially those who came from the area between the Elbe and Weser rivers. In the C18 this was an area with an increasing population, but with insufficient agricultural work for all the young men. As a result there was a long tradition of migrating to work either in the sugar refineries in Hamburg and Bremen or further away in Holland and England.

With so many German sugar refiners in St George-in-the-East and Whitechapel it was natural that they should also recruit labourers from the region where they had family and possibly commercial connections. For the young men the move to England was less traumatic and permanent than emigrating to America, though probably some used their time in London to save up for the voyage across the Atlantic. When they arrived in England they would find lodgings locally with German families, who would also speak 'low German'. They also lived in hostels run by the sugar refiners, such as Frederick Rider who had a *Men's Lodging House* which he insured for £200. For those so minded there was a German Lutheran chapel nearby in Little Alie Street and after 1818 the St Paul's German Reformed church in Hooper Square. Generally, these young Germans preferred to marry young women from the same area of Germany, but gradually were assimilated into English society within two or three generations.[49]

Ropeworks and Sailcloth Manufacturers

Suppliers of sails and rope to the shipping industry were to be found in Whitechapel, but not as many as in the river-side parishes. The latter having the commercial advantages of being closer to their clients, the river, and with a wider range of supporting industries and skills. There was a demand for rope and twine from the sugar refineries and other local industries together with the Merchant Navy. The Royal Navy would also have been a major client in spite of its poor payment record.

John Rocque's surveyors in the 1740s mapped four ropeworks in East London. One was just east of St. Mary Church, Whitechapel, running south from Field Gate. It was about 550 feet long and existed until at least 1765. The ropeworks were actually in MEOT. Paul Johnson insured for £800 in 1766 a variety of buildings which included *Six houses adjacent at the head of Ropeworks for labourers,* and *a range of Timber Wash Houses and offices [toilets] at the bottom of the garden.* By 1770 there were only two Whitechapel ropemakers; Catharine Johnson who followed her husband Paul, and John Trapp. Trapp a ropemaker in Fieldgate Street insured three timber sheds for £100 and lived in MEOT from 1777 to 1790. There was another ropeworks, which ran north from Cable Street and Knock Fergus that persisted until 1821.[50]

The important sailcloth makers in Whitechapel were Humphery Haydon, Sir Samuel Gower, Captain John Gower, John Hammond and William Jones.

In 1748 Gower insured a sailcloth manufactory in Church Lane, a furlong south of St. Mary Church, Whitechapel, for £525. There were a variety of brick and timber buildings; the largest 112 ft by 19 ft. Gower died in 1755 and his will refers to his foreman John Hammond. He was succeeded by Captain John Gower and John Hammond. In a 1770 Directory the partnership was referred to as Gower, Hammond and Jones, sailcloth manufacturers, Gower's Garden, just east of Lambeth Street.[51]

Hammond's 1799 will shows that he was a wealthy sailcloth manufacturer. His partner was William Jones; and there was a link to Philip Splidt, a ropemaker in St George-in-the-East. Humphery Haydon insured in 1757 his stock in Chappel's warehouse in Sheppard's Yard in the Minories for £1,000 and appears in a 1770 Directory. He was a contractor to the Royal Navy in September 1770; and supplied a variety of canvases to the Deptford Dockyard, such as 100 bolts of No. 1 at £0-1s-4½d. A bolt was about 38.65 yards. His contracts in 1771 totalled £603 but the Navy Board always delayed payment for six months after the date of the invoice.[52]

Gunmakers in Whitechapel, 1700-1800

On the 8th November 1663 Samuel Pepys visited the armourer's stores in the Tower of London and pronounced them a "noble sight". Well into the C19 gunmaking was an important industry in the area to the east of the Tower, and especially in Whitechapel. The works of Howard Blackmore provide an essential background to guns and gunmakers, and Stan Cook is a major source of information.[53]

By the end of the fifteenth century London was the largest gunmaking centre in the kingdom and at the centre of the trade were the King's armourers based in the Tower of London. The Board of Ordnance was the government office responsible for the supply of weapons to the Army, and in the 1550s this attracted Dutch gunmakers to settle in St. Katharine's and East Smithfield. In 1562-63 the Board began a period of re-organisation and expansion, when it took over buildings near the Minories for use as additional magazines, store houses and workshops.

Gun making required skills in both metalwork and woodwork and this led to many years of conflict between the Blacksmiths' Company and the Armourers' Company, as each tried to establish control over this important industry. Eventually the charter of the Gunmakers' Company was granted in 1638, and of the 125 gunmakers named in the charter, many came from streets close to the Tower in the parishes of Aldgate, Wapping, Whitechapel, such men as John Bedford, John Freezer and William Graves.

In 1693-4 there was a large gunpowder house in Hangman's Acre off Ratcliff Highway, and the residents of Wapping frequently complained about the gunpowder stored in their midst.[54]

By the middle of the C18 there were hundreds of gunmakers in this area of London, and many local tradesmen became Masters of the Gunmakers' Company such as[55]:

Henry Bleamire	1686	Charles Kipling	1709
Richard Loder	1714	John Hawkins (2)	1711, 1722
Thomas Phillips	1731	John Hawkins (4)	1734, 1745
George Halfhide	1736	William Wilson (1)	1760, 69, 72, 1774
Richard Wright	1783	Joseph Loader	1784
Robert Barnett (2)	1785	John Pratt	1787, 1791
William Wilson (2)	1794, 96, 1817, 30	Charles Chambers	1798
Samuel Pritchett	1800, 1812	Henry Nock	1802

From its establishment in 1414 until 1855, the Office of Ordnance has been a major department of state. Basically, it was responsible for ensuring that the King's armies were supplied with everything from guns and rifles to gunpowder, rope and tents. This work involved a gun foundry on Tower Wharf, a variety of workshops in the Minories and firing grounds in the Old Artillery Grounds. As it was unable to manufacture all the armaments that were needed an extensive number of sub-contractors established themselves in the adjoining parishes of Aldgate, Whitechapel and St. George-in-the-East.

Shotguns have to withstand very high breach pressures (up to 3 tons per sq. in.), and in earlier times this led to many accidents. So, in 1637, the London Proof House was established by charter and all sporting arms had to be submitted for examination and a firing test. The government Proof House was built on the side of the wharf at Tower Hill. In 1757 a new Proof House was built by the Gunmakers' Company at what is now 48 - 50 Commercial Road, where it can still be seen. The company still tests and marks small arms gun barrels.

The trade continued to grow and by 1851 over fifty per cent of gunsmiths in London were in the three parishes of St. George-in-the-East, Stepney and Whitechapel. A total of 547 out of 1048 were to be found throughout the eastern suburbs and gunmakers could be found in every street in Whitechapel during the C18.

For the most part these were small enterprises with workshops and storehouses. There was a great deal of sub-contracting of specialist skills to gun-stock cleaners, gunmakers, gun-lock makers, gun-barrel borer, gunpowder flash makers, gun engravers, gun case makers, and setting up contractors. Some of the local firms did manage to grow and John Hirst employed thirty-four workers in 1755. Women were to be found in the gun making trades and Mary Payne, a gun ramrod manufacturer, was living in Whitechapel area between 1832 and 1841; probably the widow of John Payne.

The most famous Whitechapel born gunmaker was John Purdey, who was born in 1784, and christened at St. Mary. His sister Martha had married a well-known gunmaker Thomas Keck Hutchinson and the young Purdey was apprenticed to him in 1798, and worked at various workshops around Moorfields, the Minories and Southwark. When Purdey completed his apprenticeship in 1805 he went to work with the great English gunmaker Joseph Manton, who had his shop and workshop at 314-315 Oxford Street. Some nine years later Purdey opened his own shop off Leicester Square and was known for his single and double flint lock guns. The company developed throughout the nineteenth and twentieth centuries to the present day.[56]

One of the leading local families of gunmakers was that founded by Henry Nock, whose workshop was in Castle Alley, Whitechapel in 1779, with factories in Moses and Aaron Alley, at 27 Goulston Street, and at 9 Castle Alley. His brother Richard was a gunsmith at 15 Fieldgate Street, Mile End Old Town, from 1793 until his death in 1800.

The royal family always showed a great interest in the guns that they used and several of their suppliers were men from Whitechapel. Samuel Nock, nephew of Henry, became gunmaker in Ordinary to George III, George IV, William IV and Queen Victoria.

George Mellor of Grayhound Lane, Whitechapel, made a shotgun for the Prince of Wales in 1789 and Ezekial Bailey, a gunmaker who lived in Little Alie Street 1791-1804, became gunmaker in ordinary to George IV, and had worked with Henry Nock.

There was a strong demand for guns from the Hudson's Bay Company and the East India Company and many of the tradesmen in Whitechapel and the adjoining hamlets worked for these important companies. John Hawkins was proof master to the HBC, 1717-1721, and Alexander McCorest was an armourer at Fort York in 1779 but was described as a "good man but shifty" while William Horton, a gunmaker from MENT had sailed on the East India ship the *Pigot*.

Amongst the wealthy gunmakers was James Waller, who lived in Mansel Street for he left £4,000 of stock to his nephews Richard and Thomas Waller. He also left £4,000 of stock and all his household goods, plate and furniture to his housekeeper Mrs. Jane Ward, who lived with him. Richard Waller also lived in Mansel Street and in 1768 rented a house at £28 and his personnel estate was valued at £100.[57]

Of intermediate wealth James Reynolds of Little Prescot Street who had just £600 of Bank of England 3% stock to leave to his wife.[58] Less well off was William Pursell, a gunmaker in Glass House Yard, Goodman's Yard, who ensured that each of his daughters inherited "one feather bed and a bolster".[59]

It is possible to trace many links between gun making families through their wills. So Thomas Sherwood chose as his executors Michael Memory, gunmaker, and William Brooks, of Tower Hill. Similarly William Debenham selected as his executor William Brooks, a gunmaker of George Street.[60] Joseph Knock's will refers to his brother Henry Knock, Ludgate Hill, gunmaker, and Joseph Knock was in turn witness to the will of William King, Tower of London.[61] Within families there was some continuity from one generation to another but perhaps Joseph Green was more optimistic than most when he hoped that his wife and son Samuel Green would continue the business "in full reliance that perfect harmony will subsist between them".[62]

FURTHER READING

D. Barnett	*London, Hub of the Industrial Revolution: A Revisionary History, 1775-1825*, 1998
R. Beaumont	*Purdey's: The guns and their makers*, 1984
H. L. Blackmore	*British Military Firearms, 1650-1850*, 1961
H. L. Blackmore	*A dictionary of London gunmakers, 1350-1850*, 1986 and its supplements
R. Campbell	*The London Tradesman*, 1747
N. Deerr	*History of Sugar*, 1949-50
P. Earle	*The Making of the English Middle Class*, 1989
J. Havill	*Eleanor Coade*, 1986
A. Kelly	*Mrs Coade's Stone*, 1990
P. J. Marshall	*The Oxford History of the British Empire; The Eighteenth Century*, 1998. Has extensive background to the sugar industry
B. Mawer	*Sugarbakers – From sweat to sweetness*, 2007, 2011
D. Morris	Fitzhugh House, Mile End Old Town, Stepney, 1738 - 1849, *Newsletter*, No. 48, May 1999, London Topographical Society
R. Porter	*London: A Social History*, 1994
H. Rössler	Die Zuckerbäcker waren vornehmlich Hannoveraner, *Jahrbuch* der Männer vom Morgenstern, Bd 81, 2002
L. D. Schwarz	*London in the age of industrialisation: entrepreneurs, labour force and living conditions, 1700-1850*, 1993
C. Spence	*London in the 1690s: A Social Atlas*, 2000
W. M. Stern	London Sugar Refiners around 1800, *Guildhall Miscellany*, No. 7, 1954
VCH	*Middlesex*, vol. 2, 1970, ed. W. Page, Industries, C. Welch

Web Sites

http://www.genuki.org.uk for details of Cook's *Gunmakers and Allied Trades Index*.

http://www.mawer.clara.net Contains much information on sugar refiners and sugarbakers, their origins, lives and works.

6.   THE TEXTILE INDUSTRIES

Introduction

The textile industry in Great Britain in the C17 and C18 had two important aspects that strongly affected Whitechapel; the increasing European demand for raw silk and textiles imported from Asia, and the long established domestic industry.

As noted in 2004 by Professor Tony Wrigley:

> "It is no coincidence that textile and clothing employment was so often the largest single employment category in towns before the industrial revolution. As with other products, the raw materials of the textile industry came from the country, but urban clothmakers and tailors could produce a better product, and might even produce a cheaper product, than was commonly available from village weavers and textiles. Textiles and clothing offered the best opportunity for the urban sector to solve its balance of payments problems with the countryside."[1]

The earlier emphasis on fustian weaving in London was replaced by silk weaving, which was established by the Huguenots in the eastern suburbs, particularly in Spitalfields, MENT and Bethnal Green but rarely in Whitechapel.

The development of silk weaving is traditionally ascribed to the Huguenots arriving in Spitalfields after the Revocation of the Edict of Nantes in 1685. But it may have originated earlier, possibly in Jacobean mulberry-growing at Bishop's Hall in Bethnal Green, although government attempts to encourage mulberry growing in England in the time of James I were unsuccessful. The nursery established in Whitechapel in the early 1640s by Leonard Gurle [c. 1621-1685] DNB, had at one stage 127 Mulberry trees and a heap of white Mulberry, which suggests he was meeting a local demand before the Huguenots arrived.

Figure 7   EAST INDIA HOUSE, LONDON

The Huguenots were mainly silkworkers, weavers, throwsters, and dyers from Normandy and Picardy, and in the 1740s names such as Desormeaux, Godin, Lemaistre and Ogier dominated the Weavers' Company's records. By 1793 the Huguenots were under 9 per cent of the Weavers' Company. "They were, however, 14.28 per cent of the Court and nearly 17 per cent of the Livery".[2]

However, only one aspect of this complex industry, that of the silk throwsters, was to be found in Whitechapel. There is little evidence of master weavers, silk merchants or dyers, who were prominent in nearby Spitalfields.

Dr Johnson's Dictionary defined a throwster as "One whose business is to prepare the materials for the weaver", and details for over twenty such men and women have survived for Whitechapel. Appendix 6.

The establishment of weaving and the silk industries in Spitalfields, Bethnal Green and Mile End New Town, all to the north of the Whitechapel High Street, is well-known, as is the history of George Courtauld, who started his business in Spitalfields in about 1782.[3]

Professor Margaret Cox, in her wonderful book on the Spitalfield burials wrote:

> "London's silk industry established itself on the eastern outskirts of the city from the late 16th century. It increased in size and range as a direct result of settlement by Huguenot immigrants with silk manufacturing expertise assisted by a growing export market to America and the proximity of the main demand for quality clothing."[4]

Sources of Raw Silk

In the early part of the C17 James I [1566-1625] DNB made vigorous efforts to develop a silk industry at Greenwich and encouraged the aristocracy to plant mulberry trees. However, black mulberries were planted instead of white and the venture failed leaving the weavers to import yarn.

Mulberry trees can still be found in Bethnal Green, but in the C18 the London weaver was able to use ready-thrown or organzined silk imported from Italy through individual merchants. Other silk men imported raw silk from Turkey through the Levant Company, possibly using the services of two young men from MEOT, William and Valentine Fitzhugh, who established themselves in the 1740s in the Middle East as merchants with the Levant Company.[5]

Most of the silk imported by the East India Company from India and China was reeled silk, though it was the custom at that time to call it spun silk. The company's instructions to the factors purchasing silk in China was they must look for:[6]

> *evenness and cleanness ... the thread must be free from gouty thick places, knots etc both inside and outside the bundle ... The best silk is generally very white, clear and glossy.*

Nick Robins has succinctly described the growth of the Company and noted that its prospects improved after the return of Charles II in 1660. In 1664, "it imported a quarter of a million pieces of cloth" and "by the end of the decade cotton and silk textiles made up 56 per cent of Company imports". Catalogues of forthcoming EIC auctions were to be had from the Warehouse Keeper in Seething Lane.

The selling price in the auctions in 1698 revealed a mark up of over four-hundred per cent, and as noted by Nick Robins "For the Company, the textile craze in Europe created immense wealth for its traders and shareholders".[7]

Georgina Green has examined the EIC's *Commercial Journal*, between 1735 and 1742, and has kindly provided me with examples of goods imported from India on the *Wager*. The commander was Captain Charles Raymond, [1713-1788] the nephew of Sir Hugh Raymond, [1674-1737]. Hugh Raymond retired from the sea in 1712 and began a new career investing in shipbuilding and managing voyages for the EICo. For a long time Hugh Raymond had a house in Well Close Square, which subsequently was the home for a time of Charles. In 1754 Charles Raymond purchased Valentine House in Ilford, Essex.

The mixed cargo on the *Wager* included cotton yarn and raw silk as well as redwood and saltpetre, which was used as ballast. In June 1737 the cargo included raw silk valued at £1,253-1s.-7d. and in March 1740 raw silk valued at £650-18s.-3d.; values that indicate the great investment being made in silk imports by London's merchants.[8]

From the C17 the EIC imported raw silk from China, but were limited as the combined rate of duty and impost on China silk was double that on Italian and Bengal silk. When this policy was finally rescinded there was "a great leap in the Company's imports of raw silk from China from 1752 onwards and soon exceeded that imported from Bengal, which was politically unstable". The importance of this change was that only Chinese raw silk was fine enough for the manufacture of organsin in addition to Italian raw silk. Raw silk remained a valuable item in the Company's trade, though there were a number of years when the total quantities record a severe shortfall.[9]

The General Ledgers of the EICo contain hundreds of references to the prices paid for silk and other imports but only provide a merchant's name, not his abode. Two names have been found in both the Ledgers and Whitechapel records. Samuel Spragg, Citizen and Leatherseller, paid £263-0s.-4d. for *Silk* in 1700 and Jonathan Fuller paid £611-18s.-4d. for three bales of *Raw Silk* in 1701. The amounts indicating the cash that was needed to purchase silk at the auctions.[10]

Silk was also available from time to time at auctions in London when a merchant died or was declared bankrupt. When Samuel Sidebothom, a merchant and warehouseman of Birchin Lane, was declared bankrupt in 1742 the auction included *900 lb of mohair, thrown silk, raw silk, silk and mohair and stuff twill.*[11]

Lewis Chevalier, a weaver of Gun Street, Spitalfields, died in 1751 and the subsequent auction included *300 lb of raw silk, 103 lb of dyed silk, and 900 dozen Scotch handkerchiefs.* The value of this silk can be estimated from the EICo sales in September 1751 when bales of silk from the 400 ton *Portfield* sold at about 18 shillings per pound.[12]

Silk Twisting

Dr Schwarz follows Dr Dorothy George in stating that:

> "Silk twisting was an early stage of the production process, the product was undifferentiated, the work was not skilled, the transport costs for silk were not high and it was notoriously a job for the poorest women. ... Silk twisting accordingly left London".

Dr George observed "by the beginning of the nineteenth century silk-winding for the weavers and the throwsters as a domestic and largely casual occupation in London had disappeared."[13]

The making of silk goes through half a dozen processes. Silk, which had already gone through the process of *reeling*, would be delivered to the silk throwsters of Whitechapel in the form of *books* or *bales*. The first process they applied was that of *winding*. The skeins of silk were put on to large reels known as *swifts*, and wound off on to bobbins. The silk was then cleaned by being drawn through cleaning devices on a drawing engine where it was wound on to a further set of bobbins ready for throwing.

In a throwing mill, "two sets of bobbins revolved at separate, carefully adjusted speeds. The bobbin containing the silk to be thrown was attached to a spindle to the top of which was fastened a flyer. The silk was drawn off the bobbin through the eye of the spindle and the rotating action of the latter inserted twist into the yarn. The amount of the twist depended on the relative speeds of the two bobbins."

A description of a mill survives:

> …were of the most primeval and barbarous type…A drum, round about a strap passes, embraced in its course two or three dozen clumsy bobbins, and returns round a small roller at the end of the mill to which a blind old man, fit for no better work, than this, groaningly turns the drum round…[14]

As an indication of the size of the larger mills, Thomas Pearson, a silk throwster of Goodman's Fields, said in 1755 that he employed about 800 people; some of whom worked on his mill, which had 160 bobbins and some at home. Perhaps this was the same Mill described ten years later at the Old Bailey when John Sharrard a silk throwster said, *he carried on a very large manufactory in Goodman's Fields where I employ 1000 people*. His problem was that he was loosing £1,000 worth of silk a year.[15]

The Whitechapel throwsters lived mainly in Goodman's Fields, Leman Street and Ayliffe Street and many throwsters had workshops and dormitories adjoining their homes. The probate of Daniel Cook in Black Lyon Yard reveals a modest house with a rent of £10. There was a *Long Room with nine bedsteads, with 8 flock beds bolsters covers and blankets*, which were presumably for his workers, and heating came from two grates.

In the adjacent two-storey house was a shop, a spinning room, and six looms, 20 baskets, a *warping horse*, 7 wheels, 10 stocks and 14 pair of cards. The raw materials included 68lb of "Norwich waste", 77 lb of "Silk waste" and 63 lb of "Quilting Wool". This agrees with the finding of Rothstein that Canterbury weavers always had on hand a wide variety of raw materials, which would enable them to quickly take advantage of any change in the demands of this fashionable industry.[16]

Similarly, John Weld, Citizen and silk throwster, insured for £400 his brick house with *an apartment backwards being part lodging rooms and part silk throwsters shop* on the east side of Church Lane Whitechapel. There were three buildings, one 24 ft by 30 ft, another 37 ft by 18 ft and the third 12 ft by 8 ft.[17]

The provision of such accommodation appears to have been on an ad-hoc basis. There was little to parallel the housing development in Bethnal Green in the 17C, which was mainly small houses for weavers with a few larger houses for masters.[18]

There were many types of silk, but of particular interest in Whitechapel were the so-called "half-silks", which were mixtures of silk and other materials. Combining silk with wool was well practised in Norfolk where "Norwich crepe" was made from silk and worsted. This interest led to the need for good contact between the throwsters of Whitechapel and the woollen clothiers of Wiltshire. This may explain the naming of the Tewkesbury Church tavern in the High Street – a suitable point of call for men and women from the West Country.

We have evidence of the larger retail activities engaged in by George and Thomas Fothergill, silk throwsters of Catharine Wheel Alley, Whitechapel. In 1750 they insured their stock in trade and goods in trust in their silk shop near the Watergate Southampton for £150, and the stock in their shop in St Mary Street, Stamford, Lincolnshire, also for £150. It appears they were moving from being solely silk throwsters into the retail trade and trading across a wide area of southern England.[19]

Weavers

It is well-known that in the C18 thousands of weavers lived in Spitalfields, MENT and Bethnal Green, and there were great differences between the living conditions of the masters and their workers.

The high insurance premiums paid by silk manufacturers and their large estates suggest that substantial profits were to be made. The history of Courtaulds indicates how good were the most industrious merchants in developing both their trade and their wealth. Journeyman weavers, by contrast, were considered among the lowest paid craftsmen of the time.

Their average incomes in 1765 were[20]:

> Children: 2/- to 6/- per week
> Others: 6/- to 10/- per week
> Much the greater part do not exceed 10/- to 16/-
> Others: 16/- to 20/- per week
> Very few: 20/- to 30/- per week

It was the poor wages and working conditions of many in the industry, which led to the area's "tradition of political and religious disaffection, with strong anti-papist sentiment which attracted the Huguenots." Sporadic disturbances arising from the vicissitudes of the silk industry continued until conditions improved after the passing of the first Spitalfields Act in 1773.

Huguenots in Whitechapel

Natalie Rothstein's detailed study of insurance policies reveals few Huguenot silk throwsters in Whitechapel but one of interest is Jonathan Fuller, the father-in-law of James Leman the designer. Fuller was a throwster and his inventory in 1722 adds up to £5,936 -19s.-5d.. In his 1756 will Jonathan Fuller wanted a funeral in *daylight without pomp* with one coach and one hearse but no pall bearers. To his daughter Mary he left £2,000 and to his son Jonathan £1,000. He left his estate in trust to Joseph and Daniel Phillimore, silk throwers in Goodmans Fields, and his wife Mary was to receive all the profits from his investments.[21]

The West Country Links

The impetus to introduce new equipment into the English silk industry arose from the increase "in the cost and irregularities in supply of imported organzine during the wars with the French from 1689 to 1713". However, it was only in 1716 that John Lombe brought back from Italy the designs of the machinery used for silk-throwing; and by 1721 he and his brother Thomas had a mill working in Derby. Typically for pioneers in the use of new technology they were unable to match the quality produced in Italy, and by 1732 John Lombe was petioning Parliament for an extension to his patent. This was not granted, but he received compensation of £14,000 with the strict proviso that a perfect model of his silk-throwing machine was made available to the public.[22]

The Whitechapel silk throwsters would have been watching these developments very carefully. Their mills were becoming increasingly uncompetitive because of their reliance on horse and human power to turn the bobbins; whilst many throwsters, especially in Derbyshire and Cheshire, had since the 1730s been taking advantage of the use of water-power and the new machinery. So from this time there was a move into the country where water power was available. It is also said that an increase in large silk mills took place when the duty on raw silk from China was reduced.

As an indication of the rapid change taking place a Mr Sherrard, in his statement before the Middlesex Sessions in 1765, stated that before 1762 he had employed 500 people in London and 1,000 in Dorset, Cheshire and Gloucester, but now he only had 100 in London.[23]

A Whitechapel man who followed a similar strategy, as Sherrard was John Sharrer, who in the 1768 was paying the rent of £25 on a house in Little Alie Street. It was John Sharrer, a silk throwster, who proposed bringing the silk throwster industry to Sherborne in Wiltshire. This was partly to avoid the "high wages" in London, but more especially to take advantage of a fast flowing river.

In 1752, according to John Toogood, a Sherborne man, who welcomed such proposals for employing the poor, who, he said had been hit by the decline of button manufacturing. In 1753 Sharrer finally acquired the lease of a water mill previously used for grinding corn, together with a dwelling house and three acres in Westbury, from a family named Hart (2), who had leased it from William, Lord Digby, since 1728. Sharrer spent over £2,500 in rebuilding and fitting up the Westbury Mill and in 1764 he took his two nephews George Ward and William Willmott into partnership. By 1765 they were employing some 1,500 people at his various mills including 400 in Dorset. Sharrer died before 1768 and his widow Susanna, appears in a 1770 London directory as a silk throwster. William Willmott [1740-1789] took over the work in Sherborne, Cerne Abbas and Stalbridge and was a governor of Sherborne School.[24]

Wells and Rickards of 23 Ludgate Hill insured their silk mill and its machinery in 1774 for £3,000, which illustrates the capital required to establish a major presence in this trade.[25]

Whitchurch Silk Mill

In Whitchurch, between Newbury and Andover, is one of the few remaining working silk mills in the country; and well illustrates the importance of water power. The current mill dates from the early C18. A sale advertisement of 1816 described "the recently erected buildings lately in the occupation of William Hayter iron founder, brush maker, turner etc., (a bankrupt). … The whole of the machinery worked by water wheel of 9 ft 3 inches diameter." It is thought that William Maddick a Spitalfields silk manufacturer and weaver between 1802 and 1838 developed the Mill, creating three floors.

Producing the warp

The mills received the silk either on cones or hanks; it was then wound by the winding machine on to bobbins. The bobbins were placed on a wooden "creel", which held several hundred bobbins at a time. The warper then threaded three "reeds" with the yarns and attached them to the warping mill. Over 400 yarns were needed per 5 cm (2") of warp. The warping mill revolved pulling the yards off the bobbins for the required length of the order; the creel was then moved along to warp the next section until the required width was achieved. At Whitchurch they can produce warps up to 52" wide. The yarn is then beamed off the warping mill and placed on a wooden beam. The warp beam is then taken to the weaving shed, where the weft threads are introduced between the warp threads by means of a shuttle, which moves backwards and forwards at high speed. With their C19 power looms the weavers at Whitchurch can weave one metre of cloth in an hour.[26]

FURTHER READING

D. Barnett	*London, Hub of the Industrial Revolution: A Revisionary History, 1775-1825*, 1998, pp. 55-7
S. Bush	*The Silk Industry*, 1987
D. C. Coleman	*Courtaulds: an economic and social history*, vol. 1, 1969
M. Cox	*Life and Death in Spitalfields: 1700-1850*, 1996
M. D. George	*London Life in the eighteenth century*, 1992
G. Green	Sir Charles Raymond, *Essex Journal*, 2008, vol. 43, no.1, pp. 38-43
R. D. Gwynne	*Huguenot Heritage*, 1985
A. Hecht	*The Art of the Loom Weaving, Spinning, Dyeing across the World*, 1989
F. Marsden	*A short history of the Sherborne Silk Mill*, 1971
F. Marsden	*Sherborne Mills from silk to glass*, 1980
A. Plummer	*The London Weavers' Company: 1600-1970*, 1972
N. Robins	*The Corporation that changed the World*, 2006
N. Rothstein	Canterbury and London: The silk industry in the late Seventeenth Century, *Textile History*, 1989, vol. 20, 1, pp. 33-47
L. D. Schwarz	*London in the age of industrialisation: entrepreneurs, labour force and living conditions, 1700-1850*, 1992
W. J. Shelton	*English hunger and industrial disorders: a study of social conflict during the first decade of George III's reign*, 1973
J. Stevenson	*Popular Disturbances in England, 1700-1832*, 1992, pp. 88-9, 152-3
F. Warner	*The Silk Industry of the United Kingdom. Its Origins and Development*, 1921

Web Sites

http://www.oldbaileyonline.org
http://www.whitchurchsilkmill.org.uk

7.   THE HAY MARKET, CARTS AND CARRIAGES

Introduction

Before the introduction of the railways in the 1830s, London's transport system was dominated by the use of horses, mules and donkeys; and this had led over hundreds of years to the development of large haymarkets around the City. To the west in the seventeenth and eighteenth centuries there was a market in the area we now know as the Haymarket. In the east was Whitechapel, which since at least 1707, and possibly earlier, was the centre for one of the largest markets in England until it finally closed in 1928.[1]

This Chapter explores various aspects of the Whitechapel Hay Market, including the weather, the prices of hay and straw in 1760. It does not look into the possibility of hay and straw being brought by barges from Hertfordshire down the river Lea or from the Isle of Sheppey. An examination is also made of carts and the ownership of carriages in a broader area of the eastern parishes.

Dr Perren has emphasised the advantage gained by farmers, who were closest to markets, particularly for hay, straw and other fodder crops. Given that a large waggon with eight horses might only be able to travel up to twenty miles per day, most of the hay and straw arriving in Whitechapel came from nearby areas in Essex and Hertfordshire. Generally in the 18th century the waggon horses were becoming stronger, and improved roads meant that larger loads of 7 or 8 tons could be transported.[2]

By the 1750s the Whitechapel market had spread along the south side of the High Street, from Red Lyon Street, at the northern end of Leman Street, to the eastern boundary of the Liberty of the City of London, a distance of several hundred yards. The market was open three days a week. In the spring and summer from Lady Day until Michaelmas, the market was open from 7 am until 3 pm, but closed an hour earlier in the winter months.

In the 1770s there was a charge of four pence on a load of hay plus a charge of two pence for registering the loads of hay and straw. There appear to have been no special buildings or a covered area for the market; so sales were made directly from the haywains parked in the street, or perhaps the larger transactions took place in one of the many nearby taverns. From 1784 the firm of Gardner and Gardner operated from Spreadeagle Yard in the High Street and continued until 1928. They had cart sheds, stables and a cottage for a housekeeper.

Figure 8   THE HIGH STREET

Such a bustling market with buyers and sellers bargaining over prices, and the cart drivers competing for the best locations, often led to complaints about the noise, the rubbish and the obstruction to other users of the highway. As compensation the custom had been established that the householders along the south side of the High Street were given a rebate on their rates of three pence per pound of rent. To prevent the hay carts being parked on pavements the parish employed a street keeper in the 1770s, on a salary of £15 per annum.

The parish employed a Collector of Tolls, and in the 1770s and 1780s he was Thomas Burton. These tolls were used to pay for repairs to the damaged pavements, and the removal of the piles of rubbish and dung. The latter must have been considerable in quantity as hundreds of horse-drawn waggons rolled into the market from the farms of Essex and Hertfordshire. After collection the vast amounts of dung from the lay-stalls would have been distributed to the market gardens in the adjoining hamlet of MEOT and further away in Bow, or taken back in the hay carts to Hertfordshire and Essex.

A significant beneficiary of the tolls on the Hay Market was the Lord of the Manor, Sir George Colebrooke, [1729-1809] DNB who was entitled to one third of all the tolls collected. In the 1770s and 1780s he was being paid about £200 per year, but from this he generously allowed £30 to be paid to the Collector as part of his salary.[3]

The Hay Market in 1760

In 1760 the French lost Canada to the British, and peace was returning to London, but how were the prices in the market reflecting the weather and demand? The newspapers regularly reported the price of hay and straw at the haymarkets at St James in Westminster and in Whitechapel.

The year 1760 has been selected for study as prosperity was returning to England. It was between two periods of dearth, 1756-7 and 1762, so might be regarded as a typical year in the market. In 1760 wheat prices were at a low of 28 shillings per Winchester Quarter, indicating a good harvest that year.[4]

The *Public Advertiser* 25th April 1760 provided useful information on the buying and selling of hay and straw:

> *Old Hay should weigh 36 lb per Truss*   *New Hay should weigh 60 lb per Truss*
>
> *Straw weighs 36 lb per Truss and any sold underweight forfeits 1 shilling per Truss*
>
> *Bad hay or straw put into the middle of a Truss forfeits 20 shillings*
>
> *All Hay and Straw sold in the markets of London and Westminster to be registered in six hours with the Price, [Hay and Straw] sold out of the market in London and Westminster to be registered within 7 days, or forfeits a sum not exceeding 20 shillings and not less than 10 shillings.*

There were penalties for any hay or straw sold underweight at 18d. per truss. It should be noted that definitions of *trusses, loads, sacks* and other units varied from one part of the country to another in the years before weights and measures were standardised. In order to maintain some transparency in the market a Register Book was maintained and could be examined for ½ pence, by which *any gentleman may know the real price that was given for his hay*. In the market prices were based on a load; a *load* of hay being 36 trusses each of 56lb. The larger carts were capable of carrying two *loads* of new hay. A *load* of new hay weighed nearly a ton, whilst a *load* of old hay weighed 18 cwt.[5]

The best hay would come from the traditional water meadows along the river Lea and the rivers Chelmer and Crouch in Essex. A good hay crop required fine, dry weather during the haymaking season beginning in late May or June, when the hay would be cut, turned two or three times to help the drying, and then carted and either taken straight to markets or made into ricks or stored in barns.

In contrast, wheat, barley and oats were grown on the higher areas in the Chilterns where the soil was known as "clay with flints". Because their roots were deeply rooted these crops were less susceptible to weather and could withstand cold winters. Good yields were usually dependent on a long, relatively cool grain-filling period in July and August and the ability to harvest and cart to the barns in dry weather. In C18 wheat had a much longer stalk than in the following centuries.[6]

The Prices of Hay and Straw in Whitechapel in 1760

It is now of interest to examine the changes in the prices *per load* of hay and straw at Whitechapel in 1760 based on newspaper reports. Table 12 demonstrates that the highest prices for hay were fairly constant until June, but then moved above £3 for the rest of the year. There is no discernible pattern in the highest prices for straw, which implies that farmers were able to supply the market on a fairly steady basis throughout the year.

Table 12   HAY AND STRAW PRICES IN WHITECHAPEL IN 1760

DATE	HAY LOW	HAY HIGH	STRAW LOW	STRAW HIGH
16 January	£1-18-00	£2-18-00	£0-15-00	£1-1-00
23 January	£1-18-00	£2-8-00	£0-16-00	£0-19-00
1 February	£1-17-00	£2-8-00	£0-17-00	£1-2-00
22 February	£2-00-00	£2-8-00	£0-18-00	£1-2-00
27 February	£1-18-00	£2-9-00	£0-18-00	£1-4-00
14 March	£1-19-00	£2-8-00	£1-1-00	£1-7-00
21 March	£2-1-00	£2-10-00	£0-18-00	£1-7-00
7 April	£1-15-00	£2-9-00	£1-1-00	£1-6-00
25 April	£1-16-00	£2-8-00	£0-18-00	£1-3-00
30 April	£2-2-00	£2-9-00	£0-14-00	£1-4-00
2 May	£1-18-00	£2-10-00	£0-16-00	£1-3-00
12 May	£2-2-00	£2-8-00	£1-1-00	£1-4-00
14 May	£1-18-00	£2-10-00	£0-16-00	£1-3-00
11 June	£2-00-00	£2-16-00	£1-00-00	£1-5-00
2 July	£2-2-00	£3-00-00	£1-2-00	£1-11-00
14 July	£1-18-00	£3-00-00	£1-2-00	£1-9-00
1 August	£1-16-00	£2-2-00	£0-17-00	£1-4-00
11 August	£2-3-00	£3-00-00	£1-7-00	£1-8-00
17 September	£2-2-00	£3-3-00	£0-10-00	£1-00-00
6 October	£2-2-00	£3-3-00	£0-13-00	£1-00-00
6 November	£2-4-00	£3-4-00	£0-14-00	£1-1-00
3 December	£2-1-00	£3-6-00	£0-14-00	£0-19-6
26 December	£2-00-00	£3-3-00	£0-15-00	£1-1-00

There was an important role in the market for the officials who were on the look out for fraud. As an example, in 1778 a farmer from Essex was fined 36 shillings for selling a *load* of straw in Whitechapel market that was 32 bundles short of that required.[7]

The question is then can the weather of 1759 and 1760 be related to these market prices?

The Weather of 1760

The months of December 1759 and January and February 1760 were very cold in England with a mean temperature of only 2.7°C, at least two degrees below normal. Ice in the Baltic was more widespread than in the previous winter by a factor of nearly four and the port of Riga could not open until very late in April, the latest date since 1740. St Petersburg in December 1759 *had the most excessive cold weather* and Leipzig in January 1760 had eight days of snow which were followed by very cold weather.

In the second half of February 1760 England was swept by widespread storms accompanied by rain, hail and thunder. Ships went aground in Yarmouth, Margate and Brighton and damage to property and loss of life occurred in Liverpool and property was damaged in Bristol, Northampton and Oxford. The losses from one ship were estimated at several thousand pounds. The Admiralty was also informed that Admiral Boscawen had been driven back into Plymouth by the *late strong weather*.

The weather improved in March, April and May with temperatures near the average at 9.2°C, but with much lower rainfall than usual – estimated at only half of the average between 1916 and 1950. The temperature in June, July and August averaged 16°C close to the average for this period. In August an article appeared in the *Royal Magazine and Gentleman's Companion* which discussed the "Terrible Effects of a Thunderstorm in Hertfordshire". Hertfordshire often experienced major thunderstorms in the summer months and later in the C19, when rainfall gauges were in operation, experienced twelve occasions in a period of fifty years when the rainfall exceed 2½ inches in a day – all in June, July and August - reflecting major summer thunderstorms. Then in September *there was the greatest storm of hail, rain, thunder and lightning in Surrey, that had been seen for many years.*[8]

It is thus clear that the winter of 1759/1760 together with the storms in February provided sufficient rain and snow-melt for the rivers of south-east England to be able to supply the water meadows throughout the Spring. Then the drier conditions between May and August guaranteed favourable conditions for drying the hay. The weather also provided good conditions to ensure a good supply of straw, and Hertfordshire farmers were known to be "very attentive to cut [straw] pretty close", to maximise their income.

Thomas Barker FRS [1722-1809] DNB of Oakham was "recognised to be the leading expert on matters meteorological in Britain during the latter part of the eighteenth century". His daily measurements of temperature, rainfall and pressure have revealed much about the weather of his time. In 1760 after a hot summer, water was in very short supply by early September and Barker noted of the period *There has been a remarkable quantity of summer weather and for a year and ¾ past more perhaps than sometimes in three years*. It is perhaps this shortage of water that resulted in the higher prices for hay from July 1760.[9]

Once the hay or straw had been sold the carter or farmer would have been looking for a return load. For many this would have been a load of "night-soil", which Londoners produced in abundance, and was in great demand as manure by the farmers of Essex and Hertfordshire. There were lay-stalls in Whitechapel, from which loads of "night soil" were collected.[10]

Military Contracts

The larger merchants in the Hay Market would have been scanning the newspapers for details of the contracts advertised by the Office of Ordnance in the Tower; for the army required supplies both for men and for horses. On the 15th March 1803 the Office invited tenders to *Supply forage for the Royal Artillery horses stationed at* Woolwich.[11] For Riding Horses the rations were:

12 lbs of Hay	8 lbs of Straw	10 lbs of Oats

For Draft Horses the rations were:

18 lbs of Hay	6 lbs of Straw	8 lbs of Oats

The army also required straw for bedding for their soldiers. For the militia there was an issue of straw for bedding every eight days. Two trusses of 36 lb each were issued for each tent on the first occasion, one truss on the second and one truss on the third, then two on the fourth and so on.[12]

Parking in the Hay Market

By October 1771 the Commissioners of Paving were still struggling with the problem of controlling the competition for space in Whitechapel High Street. Travellers trying to get into or escape from London competed with the hundreds of waggons and carts, heading for the Hay Market. The Commissioners' decision was to require the carts to be placed in the middle of the admittedly very wide High Street. Then in 1782 William Quarrill, J.P., tried to resolve the continuing problems by producing a sketch plan *for the future regulation of the standing of the Hay Carts on the Market Days but the same not being as perfect as he intended*. He detailed how many hay carts could be parked in the High Street and which way they should be facing to minimise problems for other travellers.

This draft plan obviously led to a great deal of discussion and we can imagine groups of Commissioners, hay salesmen and others carefully pacing out in the mucky and muddy High Street the planned locations for the carts. By the next meeting, on 13th December 1782, Quarrill's plan had expanded into a detailed layout for the carts, which began:

> *At the west end of the High Street, at the boundary with the City of London, four Carts or Waggons Loaded with Hay shall be placed and stand with the shafts westward towards Aldgate High Street...*, and *four other Carts or Waggons loaded with Hay shall stand in Reverse Manner with the shafts towards Whitechapel Church.*

The Plan went on to describe the exact location for one hundred and nine carts. They were to be parked along the centre of the High Street in such a way that *the distance of eighteen feet shall be left on each side for Carriages ... to pass and re-pass*. The final layout placed the carts into thirteen groups.

The number of carts in a group varied between six carts and twelve, depending on the width of the High Street which widened to the east. Gaps of twenty-two feet were to be left between the groups and in one case twenty-eight feet.

Clearly, this was an ideal plan and it soon became clear that without control, chaos would soon reign. The reaction of the Commissioners was to order the Clerk to arrange for the printing and distribution of 500 copies of the regulations to be distributed in the Hay Market and to be *on four Boards to be affixed at proper and conspicuous places in the High Street.*

The regulations were in theory quite severe and stated that in the event of an owner or driver of a cart not parking correctly then it was *lawful to seize the Offender ... without any warrant and take them before some Justice of the Peace to be proceeded against for the penalty of forty shillings or fourteen days in the House of Correction.* How often this happened we do not yet know.[13]

A Legal case at the High Court of Justice, 1898

Whilst occurring a hundred years after the period covered in this book, a legal case of 1898 probably illustrates one of the long standing problems in the Hay Market, as it raised questions concerning who had the legal right to impose certain charges and who had rights to enter into contracts for the supply of hay.

The Whitechapel Hay Market was regulated by an Act of parliament, which provided amongst other things that *every common salesman, factor or agent for the sale of hay or straw shall within 7 days next after the sale of every load ... send to the person ... on whose account the same shall have been sold a True and just account ... of the place, time, and the price for which the same was sold.*[14]

The case involved Mary Gingell, executor of William Gingell, Alexander Cruickshank and Thomas Baddely versus Abraham Wackett, a farmer from Berkhamstead. Wackett claimed that there was a customary charge for selling hay at 4 shillings or so per load, whilst Gingell and his associates were charging between five and six shillings per load. After legal discussions the parties agreed that Gingell and partners were entitled to charge 6s. 1d. per load made up as follows:

> 3s. 6d. per load for the salesman's remuneration
>
> 7d. market dues per cart
>
> 1s. per load paid to the buyer's carman

It was also stated that "salesmen were not entitled, if they appropriate sender's hay, etc. to such contracts, to make any deductions for charges at all, they being principals in such cases and not brokers."[15]

Refreshments

With so many waggoners, stall holders, traders and merchants operating in the market there was an obvious demand for refreshments. By the 1750s there were over 100 licensed premises in Whitechapel, plus an unknown number of unlicensed premises. The most important tavern was the Angel and Crown, which was frequently chosen for meetings by the paving commissioners, and sometimes by livery companies. The Grave Maurice is one tavern, whose name has survived to the present day. There were also coffee houses and chop shops nearby.

Carriages and Carts

Governments have always shown great imagination in finding ways of taxing the community - from land to windows and from cider to servants. Horses, donkeys and mules would have been difficult to count and to tax, so in the middle of the C18 they taxed carriages. The National Debt Act of 1746 relates amongst other things:

> "That upon the Payment of the ... respective Rates and Duties" by the owners "their names" and the "Number of the Coaches, Berlins, Landaus, Chariots, Calashes with four Wheels, Chaise Marines, Chaises and Chairs with four Wheels, and Caravans and Calashes, Chaises and Chairs with two Wheels ... shall be entered in Register to be kept at the ... Offices of Excise."

The very full collection of such taxes in England and Wales between 1754 to 1766 has survived and was simply calculated on the number of wheels. A four-wheel coach was taxed at £4 per year and a two-wheel chaise was taxed at £2 per year.[16]

Several types of coaches and carriages are mentioned in the archives and Dr Johnson defined these as follows:

Berlin	*A coach of a particular form.*
Calash	*A small carriage of pleasure with a covering to protect the head of a lady full dressed.*
Chair	*A vehicle born by two men*
Chaise	*A carriage drawn by one or more horses*
Chariot	*A lighter kind of coach with only front seats*
Coach	*A carriage of pleasure, distinguished from a chariot by having seats fronting each other*
Landau	*A coach, of which the top may be occasionally open*

Perhaps the most famous person to be taxed was His Royal Highness the Prince of Wales, the future George III, then living in Leicester Fields, and the keeper of a coach, a landau and a chariot, on which the tax was £12. Similarly Admiral Edward Boscawen kept a coach, a chariot and a chaise.

Carriages in London's Eastern Parishes

In the parishes east of Aldgate and between the Whitechapel Road and the Thames there were about 270 *keepers of coaches* and they, together with the livery and stable keepers, would have taken a great interest in the prices for hay and straw. Many of these men and women were prominent in their localities such as:

Sir Samuel Gower, merchant, Goodman's Fields

William Hamilton, undertaker and upholsterer, Whitechapel

Richard Ricards, glass maker, Goodman's Yard

Samuel Jones, Stepney Green, a director of the Hudson's Bay Company

John Perry (2), ship builder, Blackwall

Nathaniel Phillips, retired West Indies plantation owner, in MEOT

Joseph Bird, sailmaker, Cock Hill, Ratcliff, with links to the East India Company

John Camden, merchant, Wapping

Francis Cockayne, MEOT, and Lord Mayor in 1750

Hugh Roberts, brewer, Old Gravel Lane

John Shakespear, ropemaker and Alderman of London, Stepney Causeway

Elizabeth Tolson, Well Close Square

John Coverly, the Whitechapel scrivener, had a two-man chair in 1755. Clearly, a two-man chair was both cheaper to operate and more suited for manoeuvring through the crowded streets of London. This is shown by the approximately 130 two-wheel chaises kept in these eastern parishes compared with the 100 four-wheel coaches and chariots.

The most exotic keeper of a coach was the Jewish mystic and Cabalist otherwise known as Chayim Samuel Jacob Falk or De Falk or Dr. Falcon. He had escaped from Westphalia, where the authorities, incensed by his pretensions to discover hidden treasures sentenced him to be burnt alive, and he moved to London in 1742. He lived in Whitechapel, where many men of society, including a King of Corsica, visited him. Inside his house were his books of mystery, insured for £3,000, and the chamber in which he carried out his supernatural performances. It was lit by silver candlesticks, and he would sit on a throne wearing a golden turban. He was also said to have buried his gold in Epping Forest, and would drive his coach at high speed down the Mile End Road at midnight wearing a long robe and with his long white hair trailing behind him, while uttering mystic incantations.[17]

T 47/4 conveniently separates the *hirers* of carriages in London from *private* owners. In the eastern parishes those who only wished to hire a carriage or a chair would make their way to a livery stable based at one of the local taverns. One such person was Stephen Martin Leake, the Garter King of Arms, who lived in MEOT. His duties with the College of Arms required him to make extensive journeys and it is clear from T/47 and his account books that he preferred to hire the carriages rather than own them.

Carts

Given the importance of the Hay Market to the local economy it is important to understand some of the problems associated with the large number of carts careering down the High Street, but how big was an 18th century hay cart?

Probably a wide variety of two-wheel and four-wheel carts and waggons brought hay to the market. Some would have wheels with 3-inch rims, whilst 6-inch rims and 9-inch rims were also to be found, particularly by the 1760s. Evidence from the Museum of English Rural Life at Reading University suggests that a four-wheeled hay waggon might be up to 13 ft long without the shafts and an overall width of about 6 ft 6 ins. The Museum of East Anglian Life in Stowmarket similarly remarks that typically an "East Anglian waggon" in the 18th century was 12 ft 1 in to 13 ft 3 ins long and 5 ft 1 in to 6 ft 7 ins wide.[18]

Another approach to the problem is found by examining the various Acts introduced in the middle of the 18th century in the numerous attempts to ensure longer life for the road surfaces of the Turnpikes. In 1768 an Act was passed which gave the trustees of the Turnpikes authority to raise tolls on a wide variety of two and four-wheeled vehicles. The legislators' technical concerns were with the weight of the waggons and the width of the ruts that were created, and the tolls indicate the level of loading that was thought compatible with the Turnpike standards. The largest waggons mentioned in the Acts were allowed to weigh over 8 tons in summer, but only 7 tons in winter, when the road surface was more easily damaged. Summer was defined as the period between the 1st May and the 31st October.[19]

The legislators tried to identify the characteristics of the waggons that might be acceptable and their attention was focussed on the width between the front wheels which was not to exceed 4 ft 6 ins. The distance between the front and back axles was not to exceed 9 ft. Also of concern was the width of the track made by the wheels. The preferred width of the wheel flanges was 9 inches, which ensured the load was spread over as large an area as possible, and may also have rolled the road surface rather than breaking it down. In addition, by clever construction some waggons were made so that the rear wheels were set further apart than the front wheels and thus produced a track of 16 inches in width.

If we allow a two foot wide space around each waggon for access then each waggon would require a space of about 13 ft by 17 ft 3 ins, but did this provide enough space for the hay salesmen, the buyers and the market officials to go about their business?

Typically an eight-ton waggon with 9 inch "fellies" was limited to eight horses when on the Turnpike, but if the gradient exceeded "4 inches in one yard", e. g. a gradient of 1 in 9, then up to ten horses could be used.

One implication is that when over 100 waggons were in the Whitechapel Hay Market there were probably over 600 or 700 horses to be stabled, fed and watered on any one day, thus providing a weekly boost to the local merchants, blacksmiths, farriers and the water company.

The Act exempted from the payment of tolls *carts and carriages employed in carrying Corn or grain in the straw, hay, straw, fodder, dung, lime for the improvement of land, or other manure.*

It was lawful for any five Commissioners to cause the removal of any horses, carts or other obstructions and to charge the owners up to forty shillings to cover their costs; the 18th century equivalent of wheel-clamping and the removal of a vehicle. Horses and carts were taken to the *Green Yard* at the George tavern.

To ensure an orderly market the Commissioners voted that John Marshall should be the *street keeper* following the death of William Carter. But the work was too much for one man and in January 1783 it was decided to pay three Headboroughs *to assist in the regulation of the Hay Market* and to pay each of them two shillings and sixpence per day. Generally, any taxpayer with more than ten pounds of rent could be considered as a headborough, or he could pay for one of his servants or friends to carry out the duties for him. Marshall also thought he was underpaid for the work he carried out in the Market and in 1785 his salary was increased to twenty pounds per annum.

One problem raised by Messrs Darley, Higgs, Woodman and Lee, hay salesmen, was that there were no lines marked out to show where in the street *they were to place the Hay*. Clearly, disputes had arisen between rival drivers competing for the prime positions. The Commissioners, as was their usual practice, agreed that a committee should meet with the salesmen to *settle the manner of dispute between them*.

Not much has been discovered so far about the hay salesmen apart from Allen Parsons and Joseph Auslow. Allen Parsons, was a land taxpayer in 1760, who subsequently moved to Surrey and then to Shoreditch. Joseph Auslow was a hay salesman who lived with Moses Wagg, and though he could not sign his will this was not an obstacle in his chosen occupation, but presumably a clerk was needed to keep a tally on his sales in accordance with the regulations.[20]

FURTHER READING

T. Barker & D. Gerhold   *The Rise and Rise of Road Transport, 1700-1990*, 1993
C. Davies   A haymarket in Whitechapel, *Country Life*, CXLVI, 1969, pp. 1256-8
J. Kington   *The Weather Journals of a Rutland Squire: Thomas Barker of Lyndon Hall*, 1980
H. H. Lamb   *Climate, present, past and future*, 1977
D. Parry   *English Horse Drawn Vehicles*, 1979
R. Perren   Markets and Marketing, *The agrarian history of England and Wales*, vol. 6, 1750-1850, ed. G. E. Mingay, 1989

Web Sites

http://www.reading.ac.uk/merl   Museum of English Rural Life
http://eastanglialife.org.uk   Museum of East Anglia Life

8.   THEATRES, BAGNIOS AND SWIMMING POOLS

Introduction

London's eastern parishes were famed in Victorian times for the vitality and popularity of their music halls, as well described by A. E. Wilson many years ago in *East End Entertainment*. He also noted that the whole history of the East End Theatre is associated with the long-standing battle between the patent theatres, such as Drury Lane, and the so-called minor theatres. The last survivor of the Victorian age is Wilton's Music Hall, in Graces Alley, which opened in 1858 and is now a general performance space. Hopefully it will be eventually restored to its former glory with David Suchet's fund raising campaign.[1]

This Chapter presents the background to the eighteenth-century theatres together with an extended section on Richard Johnson's *Royal Bagnio*; based on the recent detailed research of the Leman Street and Goodman's Fields area by Dr Michael Scott.

The First Goodman's Field Theatre

The sixteenth-century theatres were described in Chapter One, but over 100 years elapsed before new theatres were opened in Whitechapel. The theatrical historian R. D. Hume has commented that it had been difficult to assess how many theatres there were in the area. It was thought there had been three in the 18th century but I think there were four theatres built on three sites. One cause of confusion is that two separate theatres were called *New*.

Dr Dorothy George stated that the Goodman's Fields New Theatre opened in 1703 and Wilson found that in 1702 that "the great playhouse [Drury Lane] has calved a young one in the passage by the Ship Tavern, betwixt Prescot Street and Chamber Street". No advertisements for its performances have yet been discovered and the proprietors are not yet known.[2]

The area was quite lively, not to say infamous, given the number of complaints from the clergy and Justices of the Peace about disorderly crowds, and the number of brothels, bagnios, and other houses of ill fame (distinguished by a sign showing bunches of grapes) that sprang up in the neighbourhood, as described later in this Chapter.

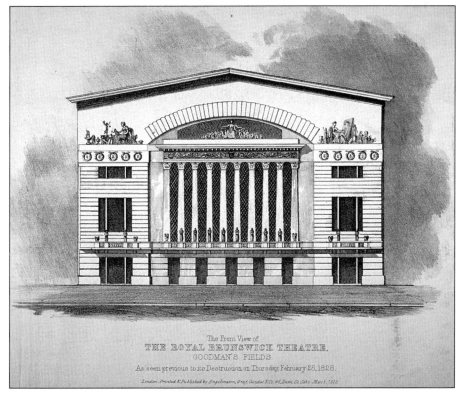

The Front View of
THE ROYAL BRUNSWICK THEATRE.
GOODMAN'S FIELDS
As seen previous to its Destruction on Thursday February 28, 1828.

London Printed & Published by Engelmann, Graf, Coindet & Co. 84, Dean St Soho. March, 1828.

Figure 9   NEW BRUNSWICK THEATRE

The New Wells, Goodman's Fields, Odell's Theatre

Within Whitechapel the most important development took place in 1729 when Thomas Odell, a playwright, [1691-1749] DNB, had the bright idea of converting a silk merchant's premises in Leman Street, Whitechapel, into a theatre. This became known as the New Theatre, Goodman's Fields, supporting the view that there was an earlier theatre in the area. After the passing of the Licensing Act in 1737, Odell was made deputy licenser of plays in the Lord Chamberlain's office.[3]

It was a bold venture because the theatre had no licence and for a time the theatre flourished without interference. Scouten remarks that the opening of a third theatre in London "created a demand for new dramatic authors, it increased the number of plays shown to London audiences, and it provided a school to develop professional actors and actresses. The impact upon the repertory was instant. New types of plays were soon on the boards, notably the satirical, topical comedies and the domestic tragedy". Newspaper advertisements in the 1730s show that *Boxes and Balconies on the Stage* cost five shillings, other Boxes were 4s. 6d, the Pits were 2s. 6d. and the Gallery was 1s. 6d.[4]

A wide number of plays were performed at the New Theatre, Goodman's Fields, and some of those between 1729 and 1736 are presented in Table 13.

Table 13   SOME PROGRAMMES OF THE GOODMAN'S FIELDS THEATRE, 1729-1736

YEAR	PLAY or ENTERTAINMENTS	AUTHOR	SOURCE	NOTES
1729	*The Recruiting Officer*	George Farquhar	*Daily Journal,* 28 October	The part of Captain Plume played by Mr Gifford, late of the Theatre Royal, Dublin
1730	*The Temple Beau*	H. Fielding	DNB	His first play after returning from the Netherlands.
1731	*The Careless Husband*		*Daily Post* 15 January	The Company of Comedians
1732	*King Richard III*	Shakespeare	*Daily Post* 6 March	For benefit of Mr De Lane
1732	*Oroonoko or The Royal Slave*	Thomas Southerne	*Daily Post* 27 November	Mr De Lane After the novel by Aphra Behn. Also on web as Oroonoko: a Tragedy
1732	*The Double Gallant*	Colley Cibber	*Daily Post* 27 November	A comedy at the 'Desire of several Ladies' .
1733	*Timoleon: a Tragedy*	Benjamin Martyn	*Daily Post* 20 February	Mr De Lane
1735	*Harlequin*	Possibly an Anonymous pantomime	*Daily* Post 18 October	With new dances. The King of Spades danced by Mr Richardson
1735	*The [Beaux] Stratagem*	G. Farquhar	*Daily Post* 20 November	Mr Archer played by Mr Gifford
1735	*King Arthur* or *Merlin the British Enchanter*	John Dryden	*Daily Post* 24 December	King Arthur played by Mr Jackson Original music by Mr Purcell.
1736	*Venice preserved* or *Plot Discovered*	Thomas Otway	*Daily Post* 20 March	

Henry Fielding [1707-54] DNB had spent time at the University of Leiden in the Netherlands and returned to England in January 1730. It was arranged for his play, *The Temple Beau* to be produced at the New Theatre, though his biographer in the DNB refers to their "much inferior company of actors". "The comedy was nevertheless well received; Fielding's career as a dramatist next began in earnest".[5]

The theatrical developments around Goodman's Fields were regarded as an affront to the dignity of the Lord Mayor and the City of London, and when Odell opened his theatre there was a clamour of protest as it was thought that it would have very uncomfortable effects upon the health, industry and frugality of local workmen.

> *Gentlemen who have no employment may sleep whole days and riot whole nights ...*
> *Compare the life of a careful honest man who is industrious all day at his trade ...*
> *spends the evenings in innocent mirth with his family .. with a Fine Gentleman who*
> *leaves his work at five at the furtherest ... that he may be dressed and at the playhouse*
> *by six, where he continues till ten and then adjourns to a public house with fellows as*
> *idle as himself.*[6]

Complaints against the non-licensed theatres were probably encouraged by the patent theatres, who petitioned the Crown to suppress the New Theatre in the following manner:

> *That there has been lately erected a play-house in a place call'd Goodman's Fields, near the adjoining to the said City (but not within their jurisdiction) and admits great numbers of Persons concerned in Trade, and particularly Silk, woollen and other Manufactures ... and your petitioners having reason to be apprehensive of very many ill consequences for the continuance of the said play-house.*[7]

Amongst the forecast ill-effects were declining morals, and the losing of time by those employed in said manufactures. No attention was paid to this plea, but the magistrate Sir John Bernard maintained a watch on the theatre. Odell made profits, but was hindered by a lack of a licence; and in the 1730s sold out to Henry Giffard, an Irish actor, who he had employed as his manager.[8]

The Second Goodman's Field Theatre

1732 was a year of significant change in the provision of theatres in London, for it was the year when both the new Covent Garden theatre and the new theatre in Goodman's Fields were built. Both were designed and built under the direction of the architect Edward Shepherd, [c.1692-1747] DNB, who is also remembered as the developer of Shepherd Market in the West End.[9]

In 1732 Giffard built a new theatre, on a subscription basis at a cost of £2,300, on the site of the former Goodman's Fields Theatre, which had been demolished earlier that year. The capital of twenty-three shares and the terms of the agreement re-paid each subscriber with one shilling and sixpence for every performance and a free seat. Whether this was a profitable investment for the shareholders seems rather doubtful for the diary of Lt. General Adam Williamson, Deputy Lieutenant of the Tower of London, recorded in 1747 that he had *A share in Goodman's Fields Playhouse from whence no profit doth or is like to arise.*[10]

The new Goodman's Fields theatre was described as *an entirely new, beautiful convenient theatre.* Indeed, both theatres were amongst the first purpose built theatres with roofs to be built in England. The interior of the theatre was about 47 ft wide by 87 ft deep with a single gallery. There was thought to be a capacity for 750 theatre goers. In July 1732 it was reported that the roof of the new theatre was being completed and *tis thought by Architects it will be as finished as any of the Theatres* and would be *ready to open at the usual Season.*[11]

The Goodman's Fields theatre is famous for two very different reasons. Giffard had seen the text of a play *The Golden Rump*, which was so filled with abuse of the king and his ministers that he sent it to the government. Walpole, the Prime Minister, at once brought in the Licensing Act of 1737, which not only strictly limited the metropolitan theatres to two (Covent Garden and Drury Lane), but also established censorship of the drama as well. This destroyed the legal status of Giffard's own theatre, but he was paid off with £1000.

However, a year later he re-opened the theatre with the legal ruse of offering tickets at prices of one, two and three shillings for a concert, and performed a play gratis between the two parts of the concert. Amongst his productions was the first revival of a *Winter's Tale* for one hundred years.

The second reason for the theatre's importance was the appearance on its stage of the yet to be famous actor-manager and playwright David Garrick [1717-79] DNB. He had been behind the scenes at Goodman's Fields when he was asked to take over the part of Harlequin when the original actor fell suddenly ill. Garrick stayed with the company when it visited Ipswich and made his professional début at Goodman's Fields as Richard the Third on 9th October 1741.[12]

His success was instant and the newspapers declared that his reception was the "greatest and most extraordinary ever known upon such an occasion". After a few nights all fashionable London was journeying east to see the new actor. As a young man of twenty-four years his "excellence dazzled and astounded everyone" said the *Biographica Dramatica*. *Richard the Third* played for 150 consecutive nights and reputedly earned him £300. Four months later he appeared in one of his greatest parts, that of King Lear. The success of the young Garrick led to another attempt by the patent theatres for their rights to be protected. Inevitably with time Garrick left Goodman's Fields for the legitimate theatre and was associated with Drury Lane as an actor and manager from 1747 until 1776. His originality and professionalism completely changed the status and future of the theatre in England and enabled Garrick to become both rich and famous.

William Hallam and his Music House

William Hallam appeared in *Macbeth* at the Theatre Royal, Drury Lane, in 1725; and played in *A Woman's Revenge or a Match in Newgate* at the New Theatre in Goodman's Fields in 1730. Subsequently, he paid the land tax on a *Music House* in Mill Yard just off Leman Street from 1740 until 1749. This had previously been a bowling green and the property belonged to Sir Samuel Gower.[13]

The New Wells Theatre, 1745-1752

The Jacobite Rebellion of 1745 led to a resurgence in the activities of the Tower Hamlets Militia, which perhaps surprisingly involved the theatre. In October 1745 the advertisements for performances of *The Massacre of Paris* at The Late Wells Theatre, Goodman's Fields announced that the Concert would be concluded at 9.30 pm *the Wells being appointed (after the Entertainment is over) for the main Guard of the Militia of the Tower Hamlets.*[14]

Table 14 presents some of the programmes between 1745 and 1751 when the theatre closed down.

Table 14   SOME PROGRAMMES OF THE GOODMAN'S FIELDS THEATRE, 1745-1751

YEAR	PLAY or ENTERTAINMENTS	AUTHOR	SOURCE	NOTES
1745	Dance by Mr Shawford Rope dancing by Mr Morris		*Daily Advertiser* 22 June	
1746	*The Restoration of Harlequin*	Anon	*General Advertiser* 1 July	Pantomime
1747	*Loves make a Man Or The Fop's Fortune*	Colley Cibber	*General Advertiser* 31 March	
1748	*The Jealous Farmer* and *The Temple of Jupiter*	Possibly another Anon?	*General Advertiser* 16 April	Pantomime
1749	Rope dancing by the celebrated Mons. Tartsey		*General Advertiser* 27 March	Tartsey was from Venice and this was his first performance in England
1750	*The Battle of Culloden*		*General Advertiser* 21 July	This battle took place in April 1746 when the Jacobites were decisively beaten
1751	*The Harlequin Collector*	Anon	*General Advertiser* 16 December	Pantomime For the benefit of Mr. Birch. This was the last performance at the Theatre.

From the advertisements we know that amongst the attractions were "An exact representation of Merlin's Cave at the Royal Gardens in Richmond" and "Original music by Mr Henry Purcell".

Tickets for the New Theatre, Goodman's Fields, could be bought at Mr Moors, apothecary, Somerset Street, Whitechapel.

Many complaints linked attendance at the theatres with the local bagnios and it was found:

> *... to the said plays and interludes great numbers of mean, idle, and disorderly people do commonly resort, and after the performance is over from thence go to the bawdy houses ... or to other houses of ill-fame near the the said Wells or Playhouse, which the said justices apprehend are chiefly supported by the concourse of such idle and unwary people as the plays draw together, greatly to the corruption of the morals of his majesty's subjects and the breach of the peace.*[15]

In May 1750 the High Constable reported to the Middlesex Sessions on his visit to the New Wells playhouse in Goodman's Fields. This led to an interesting conflict of interest over this notorious disorderly house for it was owned by Sir Samuel Gower, local dignitary and a Justice of the Peace. The house offered *plays, interludes, and other disorders are often acted, and ... wine punch, ale, and spirituous liquors are constantly sold at exorbitant prices.* Gower insisted on protecting certain keepers of disorderly houses, from whom alehouse licenses had been withdrawn. When his fellow magistrates refused to support his actions, he issued licences on his own signature. This problem did not stop Gower's legal activities as his name appears in Old Bailey records until October 1757.[16]

As shown in Table 14 the theatre tried to survive with jugglers, ropewalkers and circus acts, but it closed down permanently in 1751 and reverted to becoming a warehouse until destroyed by fire in 1802.

The last performance of December 1751 concluded with a *grand collection of Italian Fireworks* and to add to the evening *Those who choose wine may have it for two shillings a bottle.*

Later, Mr Hallam, who had appeared in earlier performances, announced that he was having a Benefit Evening with a *concert of vocal and instrumental music* followed by *King Richard the Third*. It appears that the Wells Theatre had been shut for several months, but re-opened for this one event.[17]

The Royalty and Brunswick Theatres

From 1751 there was no playhouse in Whitechapel until 1787 when the Royalty was erected in Well Street, Well Close Square. The chief promoter of this new project was John Palmer, a Drury Lane actor. Again there was an adverse reaction from local merchants concerned at the corruption of the morals of their workers, and from the patent theatres at un-licensed competition.

One complaint was received from the Reverend T. Thirlwall, a magistrate for the Tower Division, who wrote an indignant pamphlet against the opening of the theatre:

The Royalty Theatre has been the rendezvous of bawds and prostitutes, who as soon as it is opened make it their constant resort ... The consequence is that the the streets are infested with these unhappy wretches, attended by gangs of thieves and prostitutes whom they engage for their bullies.[18]

The Royalty was opened on 2nd June 1787 and was of some size and importance, as the upper gallery held 640 people, the second gallery 1,000, and there was room in the pit for 360 with 198 in the front boxes and 396 in the side boxes. The first play was *As You Like It* with Palmer playing the role of Jacques. In order to get round the law it was announced that the performance would be for the benefit of the London Hospital. The house was crowded for this first performance and coaches were jammed in many of the surrounding streets. In spite of opposition the theatre continued to meet local demand for theatre for the next 29 years under a variety of managers including William Macready, the father of W. C. Macready [1793-1873] DNB, the famous actor. In 1816 it was renamed the East London, and had the added extra benefit of gas lighting. A fire in 1826, due to an escape of gas, led to the complete destruction of the theatre and the loss of work for two hundred workers; including Clarkson Stanfield, R. A., one of the foremost scene painters of all time who had lived in White Horse Lane, Stepney, and in Bow.[19]

The Royalty was succeeded in 1828 by the Brunswick Theatre, a most auspicious and handsome structure that was said to have been modelled on the San Carlo Theatre in Naples. It became infamous for its destruction within a few days by a massive fire.

Captain Richard Johnson and the Royal Bagnio

Michael Scott

Introduction

A striking example of entrepreneurial spirit in eighteenth-century Whitechapel is provided by Richard Johnson. His business interests ranged from property development to the management of a famous bagnio in Leman Street, and thus throws light on an important aspect of life in Whitechapel and adjoining areas with links to royalty.

He first appears on the scene in the mid-1720s, leasing or sub-leasing properties on the Leman estate. The estate, extending principally over the central square of Goodman's Fields and including parts of Rupert and Lambert Street to the east and Goodman's Yard to the west, was undergoing a substantial redevelopment in this period. Ground was leased to builders and developers who modified or new built properties and then sold on the lease or subleased at a better rate. Johnson was a leading participant in this development.

For example, in 1733 he acquired the lease of a parcel of land between Lambert and Rupert Street approximately 40ft by 50ft upon which a sugar house and residential property was built; this was subleased to Christian Schutte, a sugar refiner. In 1736 Johnson acquired a lease to the ground facing Prescot Street approximately 30ft by 100ft that included the gateway to the tenter fields; this was subsequently subleased after two buildings were constructed on it. He additionally held the leases for four properties in Goodman's Yard and, over the course of nearly forty years, numerous tenements and plots of land in the Goodman's Fields area.

Johnson was not only concerned with property development. He held the lease of a tavern, The Yorkshire Grey in Colchester Street, and bought a twentieth share of Henry Giffard's playhouse on Ayliffe Street (paying him 1s 6d per night when any play was aired – although whether he ever received this is doubtful). On a far greater scale, however, was his acquisition of a 99 year lease in 1741 on property situated to the north of Rosemary Lane towards the west end.

He developed this into The Great Exchange, a very substantial shopping centre. It is visible on Rocque's 1746 map, where it shown to be as big as the London Infirmary. It later became widely known as 'Johnson's Change'; in the Horwood map it is called 'Johnson's Buildings'.

According to an advertisement in *The Daily Advertiser* on 18th May 1742:

> *In the Great Exchange lately built in Rosemary Lane, near the Minories, there are now near a hundred Shops open'd, where all manner of Apparel, Table and Bed Linen, new and second-hand, are sold cheaper than any other Place in London; also ready Money given for all manner of cast-off Cloaths.*
> *Note, Swimming-Stays are made by the above Exchange-Keeper to the utmost Perfection.*

The likely explanation for this puzzling concluding comment will become apparent shortly. The advertisement was taken out when the project was only part completed, the land tax records listing *Captain Johnson for The Great Exchange not yet finished* with a rent of £35. By 1746 the land tax records show the rent had increased to £62, implying a near doubling of the size of the buildings.

Johnson's new title of "Captain" was due to his rising position in the ranks of the Tower Hamlets Militia (First Regiment).[20]

In the early 1750s, a tithes dispute brought by the Rector of Whitechapel parish identified Johnson as owing payment on The New Exchange, another shopping centre on the west end of Cable Street; this was part of Rag Fair, a notoriously seedy market for mostly second-hand clothes.

Johnson's most interesting venture, however, was a sublease of a bagnio on Leman Street. Dr Samuel Johnson defined a bagnio as "a house for bathing, sweating, and otherwise cleansing the body". The property was part of a mid-1720s redevelopment of a block of land situated between Rupert Street and Leman Street on the south east side. Three leaseholds from this area were acquired by William Collier, a Citizen and Joiner, on the east side of Leman Street: a residential property, the Goodman's Fields Coffee House, and the bagnio. The bagnio was directly subleased to Richard Johnson and he would be in charge of the running and development of it for the first twenty years of its existence. Collier took out fire insurance on the bagnio (along with the other properties) with Johnson named as the proprietor.[21]

The 1727 marriage settlement between William Collier and Ann Carpenter describes a *new built brick messuages or tenements together with the bathing room and sweating room thereunto belonging situate and being in Leman Street in the parish of Saint Mary Matfellon alias Whitechapel aforesaid commonly called or known by the name of the Princes Bagnio now or late in the tenure or occupation of Richard Johnson, Gentleman.*[22]

In the C18 there was a widespread belief in the effectiveness of the processes variously referred to as "bleeding", "enemas", "blistering" and "cupping". Cupping came in two types - known as "wet" and "dry". The "wet" method meant that blood was withdrawn from the body through a number of incisions. These were made using a glass cup with rounded or roughened edges designed to adhere to the skin. The glass was heated by being warmed in a flame or by burning spirit within it. The glass was applied whilst hot and the subsequent cooling caused a contraction of the contained area which so diminished the surface pressure that blood was quickly drawn from the lower vessels to the skin.

Enemas involved the use of liquid preparations, often water and soap, or oil, which were injected into the rectum through a syringe.

The bagnio business was highly competitive, as shown by the extensive newspaper advertising of the time, and proprietors eagerly sought advantages that distinguished them from rivals and that could be used to publicise their ventures. From the outset, Johnson exploited his royal connections. According to an advertisement in the *Daily Post* 28th December 1724:

> *The Prince's* BAGNIO,
>
> In Leman-Street, Goodman's-fields, near the Tower, is open'd with the best Conveniency for Cupping, Sweating, and Bathing; Mondays, Wednesdays, Thursdays and Saturdays for Men; Tuesdays and Fridays for Women only, at Two Shillings and Six Pence each. Gentlemen or Ladies may be Cup'd at their own Houses, by R. Johnson, Cupper to his Royal Highness; There is also a Woman Cupper to Cup the Ladies, either at the Bagnio, or at their own Houses if requir'd, and Lodgings for Gentlemen. N.B. There is a Cold Bath preparing.

Advertisements from the following year note that the separate cold bath was 20ft in length and was supplied by a natural spring.

Over the first couple of years, the bagnio was a relatively unexceptional affair. Although it was, perhaps, the best bagnio on offer in the area – and it was certainly the best advertised – there was little to distinguish the services it offered from other bagnios in more fashionable regions of London. However, two striking innovations were to follow in the 1720s. The first was to take advantage of the interest in hydrotherapy by redesigning the bath for that purpose. A series of advertisements in *Daily Journal* in 1726 advise readers of the March 7th of the reopening of the bagnio and the new developments therein:

> At the Prince's Royal Bagnio in Leman-Street near the Tower, is open'd the Royal Pleasure Bath, being as hot, and erected after the Manner of the King's Bath in Somersetshire, which is equal to it in Proportion, and doubt not, will be as serviceable in Contraction of the Nerves, and many other Disorders of the Body: it being approved of as such by several eminent Physicians and Surgeons. As there is a continual Discharge and Supply of Water, and every Person's Feet and Legs wash'd by the Water before their Entrance into the Bath; 'twill be impossible any Thing should remain offensive to the Bathers.
>
> A proper Person is continually attending to each Gentlemen to swim, and Women to take care of the Ladies while Bathing: Convenient Apartments to dress and undress in, and proper Habits to be us'd in Bathing; couches and decent Coverings to Repose in after coming out of the Bath: Mondays, Wednesdays, Thursdays, and Saturdays for Men; Tuesdays and Fridays for Women only. There is a large and commodious Cold Bath continually supply'd by a Natural Spring. The Rate of the Pleasure-Bath to Non-Subscribers, is Two Shillings for each Time Bathing therein, and Gentlemen that subscribe, may have Use of the Bagnio Cold Bath, Pleasure Bath, and Cupping, for two Guineas per Year.

Later advertisements in 1729 claimed: *At the same Place is the best Cold Bath in London, as can be made appear, by its relieving a greater Number of People (that have been afflicted with various Disorders) than any other Bath in or about London has done, in the same Space of Time, that it hath been in Use.*

This new departure was no mere gimmick. The London Infirmary was set up in nearby Prescot Street in 1741 by Dr John Andree, [1697/8-1785] DNB, and John Harrison [1718-1753]. "John Harrison was desired to wait on Captain Johnson to ask his Leave to make use of his Cold Bath and, in case of Refusal, to make the best Bargain he could for such of those Patients in the House whose case required such Relief". The London made use of the bagnio's facilities for hydrotherapy until they built baths of their own in 1757. The London's cold bath was in a small room of only about 20 ft by 12 ft and remained in use until 1828.[23]

John Andree was the physician at the London, who took most interest in the advantages of bathing. During his life he was best-known as the physician who extolled the medicinal properties of the alternative water derived from a particular well in the village of West Tilbury, Essex. His account of the benefits of Tilbury water remained in print for half a century; the water was promoted as a 'true specific' for diarrhoeas and all kind of fluxes and was considered to be "fitted by nature to absorb and correct the acrimonious contents of the stomach and bowels".[24]

The Tilbury waters were distributed around London by John Ellison, a Whitechapel druggist and chemist, and were also available from his warehouse in Pall Mall. Ellison can be traced in the London Directories from 1759 until 1772 and his rent of £50 in Whitechapel indicates a property of some size and status.[25]

Johnson's role as royal cupper continued after the coronation of George II in 1727. According to an item in the *Daily Post* for 26th Nov 1727 "Mr. Richard Johnson was Yesterday appointed Cupper to the King, having served his Majesty in the same Capacity when Prince of Wales". Unsurprisingly, the coronation resulted in an upgrade in the bagnio's name to *The King's Bagnio* as well as extensive celebrations.

An item in *The Weekly Journal or the British Gazetteer* 14th Oct 1727 runs:

> We hear that a great Number of Gentlemen met at the King's Bagnio in Leman-street, to celebrate the Coronation, which was done with Fire-works, Bonfires and a Pyramid of 365 Candles: Healths to the King, Queen, Prince of Wales, Prince William, and the rest of the Royal Family were drank, with a Discharge of fifty Pieces to each health: Most of the Gentlemen appear'd in new Cloaths, and Favours in their Hats: A Barrel of Ale was given to the Populace.

The Swimming Pool

The second innovation, already suggested in the advertisement above, was the development of the facilities for swimming. While there were outdoor swimming pools in London, notably the Peerless Pool near Old Street (though this was only developed into a swimming pool in the 1740s), no bagnio could rival the luxury of a warm *indoor* pool large enough to swim in. Advertisements over the late 1720s note the improved warmth of the main pool and place increasing emphasis on the availability of swimming lessons.

Johnson continued to develop the site. The *Daily Journal* in June 1730 advised readers:

> At the KING's BAGNIO *In Leman-Street, Goodman's-Fields, The present Monday will be open'd,* THE LARGE PLEASURE BATH, being 20 Foot Square, for Bathing, Swimming, or for Gentlemen to learn to swim in, Waiters attending daily to instruct and assist Gentlemen therein. It is kept hotter this Year than the last, and filled every Day.

> At the same Place there is a large COLD BATH, supply'd by a Continual Spring.

On 9th May 1732 the bagnio opened with a pool extended to 22 ft in length "much larger than the old one". By June 1743 the pool was "near forty-three Feet long", with a cold bath still available. These developments are reflected in the land tax records, which show that the rent increased from a modest £16 in 1733 to £30 in 1743.

Advertisements for the swimming facilities at the Peerless Pool began in 1743, sometimes appearing in the same newspapers and sometimes the same issues as those for the bagnio. It boasted a pool 170 ft in length and 50 ft broad, waiters on hand to teach gentlemen to swim, and two well-stocked fish ponds for angling were available to subscribers. The annual subscription rate was one guinea, pegged at the same rate (at this time) as the bagnio.

The Later Developments

By the 1740s Johnson's interests were moving beyond Whitechapel to Ratcliffe and Aldgate. He was no longer offering cupping services at the bagnio and "King" was dropped from the bagnio's name (though it is not clear whether this is because of Johnson's increasing distance from the enterprise or because he was no longer cupper to the King). In 1743 Johnson advertised for a new proprietor "the present proprietor intending to leave business", Thomas Barry took on the role and in 1749 he insured his stock for £400.[26]

However, Johnson kept many of his leaseholds in Whitechapel through to the late 1750s, even though there is little evidence of further expansion. He remains listed on the land tax records as co-proprietor of the bagnio with Barry. A 1756 survey of the Leman estate identifies him still holding the leasehold on four buildings on the south side of Goodman's Yard, two on the north side of Prescot Street and four in a passage lying between Lambert Street and Rupert Street.[27]

What kind of business was Johnson's bagnio? Was it, as was true of many bagnios, little more than a brothel? Or did it start with aspirations to be a house for bathing, sweating, and otherwise cleansing the body? Certainly the British were reluctant to take more than a couple of baths a year so a bagnio provided a more pleasant ambience for this essential component of personal hygiene.

This would certainly comport with historical research on the entertainments in Goodman's Fields in the mid-C18, as described by Cruickshank and Dorothy George. An inquiry by the Middlesex Sessions in 1750 into the Turk's Head Bagnio suggests that it was run as a bawdy house.[28]

While this may be the way that the Leman Street bagnio ended up, it seems clear that it did not begin with this intention. Early attempts at segregating men and women, the emphasis on hydrotherapy and swimming lessons, along with the investments in developing the size of the swimming pool, suggest that Johnson was at least initially looking to build a broad and (mostly) reputable customer base. Notably, in the 1740s, it is the Peerless Pool as much as other bagnios that presented itself as the principal competitor to Johnson's business. If Johnson expected that Londoners would prefer a large outdoor swimming pool to a smaller indoor one in an increasingly seamy area, his retreat from the day-to-day running of the bagnio may have been a straightforward commercial decision.

Johnson died in 1769 having already sold off some of his leasehold property in Whitechapel. A newspaper notice from 1758 records the death of "The Lady of Captain Johnson". His short will, proved 20th September, left to his "friend" Mrs Catharine Roberts almost all of his remaining estate. This included The Great Exchange. However, neither Roberts nor any of the subsequent leaseholders or owners appear to have done anything to develop or modernise the property and by the early Victorian period it was in a squalid state.[29]

When Dr. Southwood Smith was asked by the Poor Law commissioners in 1839 to review conditions in Whitechapel, he offered the following grim summary of Johnson's Change:

> *Johnson's-change*, Front and Back. – A cluster of four courts opening into each other; the houses are crowded with inhabitants. Some time ago a cesspool overflowed in one of these courts, and its contents were allowed to remain upon the surface several weeks: after a time fever of a malignant character broke out in the house next the cesspool, and has ever since extended to almost every house in all the courts. There is here no drainage of any kind, there is consequently a great accumulation of filth and the sense of closeness is stifling.[30]

What of the bagnio?

Shortly after Barry's involvement, the name was changed to the unimaginative *Turk's Head*. A cupper was hired from the Royal Bagnio in St James's Street. Swimming and the medical benefits of the bath continued to be advertised; moreover, in the 1750s poor people were given free access to the cold bath "by bringing a Line from any Gentleman, Physician, Surgeon, or Apothecary, that they are real Objects of Charity".

A new proprietor, Benjamin Thornton, took over in the 1760s, but there is no indication of any new facilities or expansion of the existing ones after Johnson's involvement. Several advertisements taken out in *The Daily Advertiser* in 1772 advised readers that the house and baths had been put into *compleat Repair*, suggesting that they had been poorly attended. The business has so far been traced to an advertisement in 1777 for a new waiter, porter, cook and house maid.[31]

One possible reason for the demise of the bagnio was the growing strength through the C18 of the Societies for the Reformation of Manners, which harnessed reason with religion "in order to overcome moral incontinence and immorality".[32]

FURTHER READING

H. Berry	*The Boar's Head Playhouse*, 1986
J. Black	*Eighteenth-Century Britain, 1688-1783*, 2008
J. Coombes	Mr Richardson, Gas Fitter at The Brunswick Theatre, *Cockney Ancestor*, 93, Winter 2001/02, pp. 24-25
J. Cox	*London's East End: Life and Traditions*, 1994
D. Cruickshank	*The Secret History of Georgian London, How the Wages of Sin Shaped the Capital*, 2009
M. Dorothy George	*London Life in the Eighteenth Century*, 1965
T. Hitchcock	*English Sexualities, 1700-1800*, 1997
C. B. Hogan	The New Wells, Goodman's Fields, 1739-1752, *Theatre Notebook*, 3, pp. 67-72, 1949
R. D. Hume	*The London Theatre World, 1660-1800*, 1980
S. Porter	*Shakespeare's London: Everyday Life in London, 1580-1616*, 2009
S. Rosenfeld	Theatres in Goodman's Fields, *Theatre Notebook*, 1, pp. 48-50, 1946
S. Rosenfeld	*The Theatre of London Fairs in the 18th Century*, 1960
A. H. Scouten	*The London Stage 1660-1800*, 1961
C. J. Sisson	*The Boar's Head Theatre*, 1972
R. Tames	*Theatrical London*, 2006
R. Trumbach	*Sex and the Gender Revolution*, 1998
A. Williamson	*General Williamson's Diary, 1722-1747*, Royal Hist. Soc., Camden Third Series, vol. XXII, 1912
A. E. Wilson	*East End Entertainment*, 1954

Web Sites

http://www.londonlives.org

http://www.wiltons.org.uk   Wilton's Music Hall

9.   EDUCATION AND LITERACY

Introduction

Given the East End's subsequent reputation for poverty and ignorance, it may come as a surprise to learn that in the eighteenth century (C18), Whitechapel and nearby parishes were the home to a variety of well-educated men and women; including Daniel Fenning, a grammarian and prolific text book writer, two compilers of dictionaries, translators and Fellows of the Royal Society such as Samuel Jackson and Robert Shippen. Another aspect of local interests is revealed in wills, auction particulars, lists of book subscribers and insurance policies of Whitechapel residents that mention books and *philosophical instruments* [probably telescopes and microscopes].

For directors of the great trading houses, the dozen or so clergymen, dozens of schoolmasters and schoolmistresses, doctors, apothecaries, organists such as Samuel Manwearing, a blind organist at St Mary, Whitechapel, and clerks at the Bank of England, insurance companies, the Victualling Office and the Customs Office, a command of English and basic arithmetic was necessary. For some a knowledge of accounts and languages was essential. This chapter examines some aspects of adult literacy, and the opportunities for education and apprenticeships for the young men of Whitechapel.

Several examples illustrate the local demand for education. The *Daily Courant* for 25th March 1719 contained an advertisement from Joseph Swaffield at the Lion and Lamb in Whitechapel for:

> *Any man who is qualified for teaching Greek and Latin in a Writing School*

Some seventy years later a Mr. A. Henriques offered to teach French, Spanish and Dutch from his home at 51 Prescot Street. His knowledge was based on his travels through different countries, and his terms were said to be moderate. In 1790 we also find in Whitechapel, Jacob and David Grenada who were translators. These are good indications of the local demand for education and of need for fluency in the languages used by City traders with Europe and elsewhere. Dr Perry Gauci in discussing the skills of London's overseas merchants emphasised the admiration of C18 commentators for "Their faculty in languages and mathematics … and their understanding of double-entry accounting".[1] The *Daily Courant* for 1st May 1717 advertised the auction at the Church Row Coffee House near Aldgate, of Mr Benjamin Pratt's library, late curate of St Botolph, Aldgate, of *A choice collection of many valuable and scarce books in Divinity, History, Philosophy, Latin and English.*

Figure 10   DAVENANT'S SCHOOL

Literacy, Books and Newspapers

Between 1st April 1754 and 31st December 1756, 600 individuals who "were all of the parish" were married at St. Mary Whitechapel. Of these, sixty-three per cent were able to sign their names. This compares quite closely with the sixty-nine per cent of those married at St John church, Wapping, and seventy-six per cent at St Dunstan, Stepney, for the same period. These simple statistics hardly signify the full extent of adult literacy in the area. Equally, they hide the differences between the men, 77% of whom could sign, compared with only 49% of the women.[2]

At present we do not know how many of those married at St Mary had been educated in the area or were perhaps recent immigrants from the country. For the men of Whitechapel there were many clerical opportunities within walking distance, both locally and in the City, in a variety of offices; whilst many of the women would have been in more menial occupations as servants, cooks, washer women and silk winders.

Professor Peter Earle has examined this problem in London in relation to those who could sign depositions between 1660 and 1725. He noted "This can be only a very rough guide to literacy and hence by inference to education, but it is the only guide that is available on any scale for the early modern period". National studies indicate that by the 1750s sixty per cent of men and forty per cent of women could sign their names. So the figures from London's eastern parishes confirm Earle's conclusion, "that all Londoners, men and women, London-born and immigrants, were exceptionally literate by the standards of the age and were growing more so across the period studied."[3]

Several authors lived within a few hundred yards of the parish church. These included Captain Thomas Bowrey, who compiled a *Malay-English Dictionary* published in 1701; and the Reverend Andreas Bartelson of St George-in-the-East, who much later compiled a *Danish-English Dictionary*.

In 1765 the third edition of John Wright's *American Negotiator* was printed by J. Smith of Well Close Square and dedicated to Lord Samuel Sandys, Fifth Commissioner for Trade and Plantations. This very popular book consisted of a series of Tables that enabled a merchant to convert the varied currencies of the British Colonies in America as well as many islands in the West Indies such as Barbados and Jamaica.

Daniel Fenning [1714/5-1767] DNB, was a grammarian and text book writer, who moved to Whitechapel about 1747 or 1748, and lived in the High Street in a small house with a rent of £10. He seems to have given up school mastering at Bures school in Suffolk to work for the Royal Exchange Insurance Company in London. His earliest book of 1750 was *The Young Algebraist's Companion* and he wrote or contributed to some fourteen books on various subjects, including algebra, arithmetic and geography. He is best remembered for his textbooks on the English language. *The Royal Dictionary*, or *A Treasury of the English Language* (1761) was dedicated to George III and published by "his authority".

When he made his will he was living in Great Garden Street and was in business with Stanley Crowder, a bookseller in Paternoster Square. He held shares in sundry books viz[4]:

> One-sixteenth part of every impress of *The British Instructor*
> One-sixteenth part of every impress of *The Life of the Clerks*
> Also fifty books of every impression of the *Ready Book*
> 100 of every impression of *School Master's Companion*
> 100 of every impression of Purcell's *Dictionary*
> One-sixteenth part of a *Universal Spelling* Book

Wills sometimes reveal the ownership of books. John Samuel Thompson a surgeon in Whitechapel instructed his wife Belinda in 1777 *to keep all my books on surgery, physic for my sons.*[5] Samuel Perry owned 200 bound books and Richard Murrell, a surgeon and apothecary in Whitechapel, in 1776 left the following books:

> Rapin   *History of England and the reign of Queen Ann*
> Bishop Beveridge   *Private thoughts on religion, The life of Bishop Gridall*
> Carlyle   *Exposition on Job*

William Rogers. gentleman of Whitechapel in 1772, left all his books to his sons and all philosophical instruments and his son James was to have all his *drawings on paper* and his daughter Elizabeth all his bibles and religious books. Similarly David Lopez Pereira left his *Hebrew Library* to his sons.[6]

Whitechapel was not an area with any large-scale paper manufacturing or printing industries, though a Printing School was established in Gower's Walk in 1808. Insurance records have not been indexed for London before 1775 so there may be more stationers and booksellers than indicated in Table 15.

Table 15 STATIONERS AND BOOKSELLERS IN WHITECHAPEL

NAME	ABODE	REFERENCE
Galpin Baxter	Whitechapel	Ms 11936, vol. 136, 182862, 1761
Jacob Bunnett	139 Whitechapel	Ms 11936, vol. 328, 503956, 1785
William Demeza	75 Whitechapel	Ms 11936, vol. 292, 443366, 1782
Matthew Hesse	Goodman's Field	Ms 11936, vol. 260, 390527, 1777
Joseph Owen	Near Well Close Square	Ms 11936, vol. 176, 249194, 1767
Robert Scrutton	130 Whitechapel	Ms 11936, vol. 333, 512491, 1785
Thomas Smith	Ship Alley	Ms 11936, vol. 111, 146226, 1755
Ann Staples	Opposite the London Hospital	Ms 11936 vol. 133, 177061, 1760
Joseph Starling	139 Whitechapel	Ms 11936, vol. 257, 381913, 1777
Joseph Swaffield	High Street	Land tax 1740-1778
Thomas Wigg	30 Burr Street	Ms 11936, vol. 287, 435295

The insurance values declared by the booksellers in Whitechapel are low compared with the £1,000 or more of the major London booksellers such as Robinson and Roberts, who in 1769 insured stock, utensils and goods at 25 Paternoster Row for £5,500.[7]

For those in search of the news the proprietor, Anthony Wall of the new Coffee and Punch Room at the Angel and Crown in Whitechapel, advertised in 1746 that *the Daily Papers are regularly taken and Punches sold in small Quantities at reduced* rates.[8]

It is well recognised that circulating libraries were increasingly important in the C18, and between 1770 and 1780 there were nineteen or so such libraries in London with charges of between ten and twelve shillings per year.

It was a feature of eighteenth-century publishing that many books were launched with the opening of a subscription list. Amongst the men and women in Whitechapel and Well Close Square who supported such an approach can be found the following, though it is a far from complete listing.

W. Blackburne, 1786	*Picturesque Views* by Henry Boswell
Miss Mary Browne, 1742	*The Indulgent Father*, by Richard Mason
George Caffey, 1743	*The Schoolmaster's Assistant* by Thomas Dilworth
Revd. Dr Calvert, 1780	*The Ladies History of England*
John Foster, 1790	*A New and Complete History of the Bible*
Mrs Hammond, 1786	*The Fallen Cottage*, a poem by T. C. Rickman
William Mears, 1788	*Clavis Campanalogia* by William Jones and others
Arthur Powell, 1775	*The Complete English Peerage*
John Sweetsur, 1777	*The works of Flavius Josephus*
Mrs Windsor, 1795	*The Traditions; a legendary tale*, by Mary M. Sherwood

It is noticeable that none appear to have subscribed to books on travel and natural history compared with the men and women in Wapping and Mile End Old Town.[9]

Education and Apprenticeships

In the middle of the C18 several choices were available to parents and guardians in Whitechapel concerned with the education, and subsequent apprenticeships of their children or charges. A good introduction to the subject can be found in Helen Jewell's *Education in Early Modern England*. After considering the diversity of viewpoints on education in this period, she presented a very readable account of "her unashamedly selective analysis of education in early modern England".

Helen Jewell concluded that "Overall, English education may be considered to have been in a fairly healthy state in this evolutionary period. It was modernising, most obviously in its use of the more widely communicative vernacular. It embraced elements of both tradition and novelty, a fair number being combined in the dissenting academies. ... There was obviously a lack of overseeing direction: English education seems to have developed largely unsupervised, with no dominant planners, though plenty of theorists, and comparatively little government intervention."

Peter Earle concluded that "London was famous for its schools … and the quality of education available was yet another magnet drawing people into the metropolis."[10]

The concern of parents and guardians for the education of their charges is well shown by the will of Abraham Atkinson, a salesman of Whitechapel, who in 1762 left the residue of his estate in trust "for the sole use and benefit of my son Robert" who was to be apprenticed. More fortunate, in that a particular sum was stated in the will, were the three daughters of John Campbell, a brewer, who were left £1,900 in trust for their "maintenance and education".[11]

The wealthy employed tutors or sent their children to boarding schools before going on to public schools and the universities. Probably the best local private school was that of Michael Maittaire [1668-1747] DNB in MEOT. Maittaire had previously been Deputy Master at Westminster School and gave his students a good grounding in Latin, possibly Greek, and certainly an introduction to the classical literature. One of his pupils was Stephen Martin Leake, later to become Garter King of Arms. For the less wealthy there were a variety of small private schools in Whitechapel, MEOT, Bromley-by-Bow, Bethnal Green, Hackney and elsewhere. For some of the poor there was the possibility of entering Bancroft's School in Mile End Old Town. Other charity schools could be found such as that of the Lutheran church and the Middlesex Society for educating poor children in the Protestant Religion, which was established in 1761. Such a variety of schools could be found throughout Middlesex.[12]

Colm Kerrigan wrote that:

"In the eighteenth century several schools were founded by people associated with some of the East London's many industries, and city companies sometimes accepted responsibility for schools, usually when the will of one of their members requested them to act as Trustees".[13]

The main schools in the parishes and hamlets in and around Whitechapel, which were based on these principles, were:

> Coopers' School, established 1536 in Ratcliff
> Davenant's School, established in 1680 in Whitechapel
> Raine's Foundation, established 1719 in Charles Street, St George-in-the-East
> Parmiter's School, established 1722 in Bethnal Green

Rather further afield was Christ's Hospital School in Newgate Street, near the Old Bailey. Every year several boys and girls (often orphans) from Whitechapel would enter this famous school.

The registers show that in April 1740 Samuel, son of William Spraggs, Citizen and Leatherseller, entered the school, but was discharged in October 1747 and was apprenticed for seven years to serve the Honourable Chabert Penny, Attorney General of Jamaica.

In 1769 Thomas Strouts, son of Thomas deceased, Citizen and Tallow Chandler, of Whitechapel entered the school and discharged in 1774 by his mother Ann, who was living at The Gun in MEOT.

Similarly, in 1778 James, son of Alexander Alexander, who was born in Whitechapel entered the school in 1778 and was discharged December 1786 to Sarah Mills, his aunt who lived in Ratcliff.[14]

Popular with Whitechapel families was St Paul's School, which after the Great Fire of London was re-built just east of St Paul's Cathedral. The following boys were admitted to the school.[15]

Table 16   WHITECHAPEL BOYS AT ST PAUL'S SCHOOL

FATHER	SON	YEAR OF ENTRY	ABODE	UNIVERSITY
Parkinson	David	1746	Mansell Street	
Champante	William	1748	Whitechapel	
Robert Pritchard	Robert	1749	Red Lyon Street	Cambridge, BA 1757, MA 1760
Robert Ashby	Robert	1749	Well Close Square	
Joseph Mimms	William	1749	Whitechapel	
John Godfrey	John	1754	Against the London Hospital	
William Quick	William	1755	Prince of Orange's Head	
Joseph Bromhead	Joseph	1761	Whitechapel	Oxford, BA 1768, MA 1771
John Branson	John	1762	Cartwright Street	
William Inderby	Charles	1767	George Yard	
Simon Hide	Thomas	1771	Petticoat Lane	
Reay	Charles	1771	Ayliff Street	
Thomas Selby	Thomas	1774	Whitechapel	
Henry Layton	Thomas	1776	Cartwright Street	Cambridge, BA 1788, MA 1791
Robert Carter	Robert	1779	Rosemary Lane	
Samuel Goodeson	James	1783	18 Well Close Square	
James Richmond	Henry	1783	Ayliff Street	
William Denman	John George	1784	Mansell Street	
William Denman	Benjamin	1784	Mansell Street	

The only Whitechapel boy who appears to have entered Harrow School was Brian Jackson c. 1721, the son of James Jackson. He entered St John's College, Oxford in 1722, and was awarded his BA in 1726.[16]

Schooling in Whitechapel

The Reverend Daniel Noble's Academy in Leman Street offered the following curriculum:

> *Young gentlemen taught English, Latin, Greek, French, Writing, Drawing, Arithmetic, Merchants Accounts,, Elements of Geometry, Geography and the use of Globes, Navigation, Astronomy, Surveying, and Planning, and every branch of practical mathematics.*

This school would have been popular with young men preparing to be writers with the East India Company. More famous than any of these was Thomas Paine [1737-1809] DNB, who was employed as an usher for a few months in 1766. Subsequently, he wrote *The Rights of Man* in 1790 and *The Age of Reason* in 1793.[17] Mr Hart (1) in addition to proving opportunities to learn dances in 1754 also taught *Fencing, Languages and Mathematics at a Private Academy near the Golden Lion in Leman Street*.[18]

There are numerous references in the archives to schools and schoolmasters in Whitechapel and adjoining areas, excluding Raine's and Davenant's School, Table 17:

Table 17   SCHOOLS AND TEACHERS IN THE WHITECHAPEL AREA

NAME	LOCATION	NOTE	REFERENCE
Charity School	Whitechapel	Henry Southall	PROB 11/804, 1753
Charity School	Whitechapel	Henry Hinde	Essex R. O. D/DPX/T13 proved in 1778
George Caffey	Whitechapel	Schoolmaster	PROB 11/819, 1755
Mr Couchad	Academy Well Close Square	Thomas Munday's insurance on his household goods . at the Academy	Sun, vol. 171, 236630, 1766
Mr Coulthiet	Goodman's Fields Academy	Master	*London Evening Post*, 2-4 July 1761
Mr Tenand's Academy	Prescot Street		?
Noble's Academy	Mill Yard, Lemon Street	DNB Thomas Paine	*Gazetteer*, 25 December 1762
Free School	Nearly opposite the New Road	William Craswell's insurance	Sun, vol. 173, 240035, 1766
John Townsend	Goulston Square	Schoolmaster	PROB 11/920, 1766
Margaret Reynolds Margaret Brown	Church Row "Stepney"	School mistresses insured books for £10	Sun, vol. 263, 395118, 1778
Middlesex Society for educating poor children in the Protestant Religion	Cannon Street Road	Founded 1761	Court Henry Dirs, PROB 11/1538, 1812
German Charity School	Little Alie Street	Court Henry Dirs	PROB 11/1538, 1812

Inevitably the above descriptions may involve some duplication.

The Inns of Court

A number of the wealthier families in Whitechapel and Stepney sent their boys to the Inns of Court, in preparation for a legal career or as an alternative to university. As in the universities the courts neglected their educational functions, and an examination for a call to the Bar was said to be no more than a legal fiction. Verbal questions were put to students in stock words, and if an appropriate answer was received the candidate could be called to the Bar.

Admissions to Inner Temple:

Between 1600 and 1800 the following young men from Whitechapel, St George-in-the-East and neighbouring parishes were admitted to the Inner Temple, but few seem to have been subsequently called to the bar. The most successful was Albert Pell, the youngest son of Robert Pell of Well Close Square, who was called to the bar in 1795, and appointed Serjeant-at-Law in 1808. He retired in 1825, but in 1831 became a Judge of the Bankruptcy Court and was knighted.[19]

1604	Robert Dixon of Whitechapel was "specially admitted"
1631	John Dixon of Whitechapel
1651	Samuel, son of William Mellish of Stepney, called 1657, Bench in 1675
1685	Robert, son of Robert Waring of Whitechapel
1688	Stephen, youngest son of James Came of Whitechapel
1692	Maurice, son of Sir William Goulston of Whitechapel, "specially admitted"
1695	Squier, son of Reverend William Payne, Rector of Whitechapel
1698	Moses, son of Moses Lowman of Whitechapel
1718	William, son of James Herbert of Whitechapel, called 20 May 1726
1732	Richard, son of Thomas Spooner of Whitechapel, called 1737
1753	William, son of Boulton Mainwaring, of St George-in-the-East
1776	John, son of Maurice King of Great Alie Street
1783	Albert, son of Robert Pell of Well Close Square
1783	Robert, son of Robert Pell of Well Close Square
1788	William James, son of Rawson Aislabie of East Smithfield, called 1793
1800	John, son of John P. Batten, Ayliffe Street

Admissions to Middle Temple

1695	Squier, son of Reverend William Payne, Rector of Whitechapel
1718	William, son of James Herbert of Whitechapel, called 20 May 1726
1730	Andrew Osbourn, esq. J. P., Goulston Square, Whitechapel[20]

Admissions to Lincoln's Inn

23 January 1738	John Harrison, the son of Benjamin Harrison, an apothecary in MEOT
24 January 1753	William Mainwaring, son of Boulton Mainwaring, of St George-in-the-East
20 January 1776	John Watson Reed, eldest son of Joseph Reed, Shadwell

Boulton Mainwaring was the architect of the London Hospital and entered two sons to the Inner and Middle Temple.

Davenant's School, Whitechapel

The history of this famous school, which in 1965 moved from Whitechapel to Loughton, Essex, has been well told by one its former teachers Roland Reynolds in his 1996 book, on which the following is based.

Dr. John Johnson was Rector of St. Mary, Whitechapel, from 1626 until 1641, when he was deposed having become involved with Archbishop William Laud, [1573-1645] DNB. He was reinstated in 1660 after the death of Cromwell in 1658. His re-appointment was considered to be "ecclesiastical jobbery" and such was the local outcry that the majority of the congregation left to build their own church in Brick Lane, leaving Johnson presiding over a nearly empty church. Finally he was deposed in 1668 for bribery and corruption and ended his life a non-conformist minister.

Ralph Davenant married Mary, the daughter of Dr. John Johnson. He had matriculated from Oriel College, Oxford in 1655, and was an MA from Queens College, Cambridge, after the King had recommended this "ingenious young man". Eventually he was appointed Rector of St. Mary, Whitechapel in 1669 and still being a favourite of King Charles II he was appointed by royal writ, against the wishes of the patron of the living, the Rector of Stepney.

Davenant's first task was to re-build the church, which had fallen into a dilapidated condition and this work was completed by 1673. He then turned his attention to the education of the poor of the parish, but little happened until he made his will in 1682 six days before his death. In his will he left all his household goods and plate to his wife and decreed that on her death these were to be sold and the money raised to be used to build a school in Whitechapel. He also had other assets in the form of cash and lands in Southwark, and £100 was to be used to put twenty boys to apprenticeships. Davenant also had a farm near Great Baddow in Essex, which he left to his three daughters. In the event two daughters agreed that their share should be used to further the School project. Monies from the farm were also to be used to pay the schoolmaster's salary.

A meeting was held in June 1682 attended by Mary Davenant, her sister Sarah and several gentlemen and tradesmen from the parish, at which it was decided that a school should be built. It took some years before a site was identified on the site of old almshouses and a burying ground on the north side of the Whitechapel High Street. It was not until 1686 that the school was built on a site of one and a half acres. The school remained in its original condition until it was demolished in 1818 and a new building erected, which has survived to the present day.

The schoolmaster was given very precise instructions about his duties, which were to teach the boys "to read English and to write and Cypher … to teach them the catechism of the Church of England". There were to be forty poor boys, but the schoolmaster could not take additional paying pupils unless he paid for an Usher, and even then there were not to be more than thirty boys. It was also determined that twenty pound per year should be set aside towards "keeping a Skilful Woman of the Church of England to teach thirty poor girls born in the parish and chosen by the Trustees. One part of their day was to be spent reading "and at convenient times to learn without Book the Catechism of the Church of England" and the other part of the day to "Knit and sew plain work or to do any other Work when the Trustees will think needful".

Little is known about what precisely took place in the school, but it is thought that they were probably using the religious books produced by the Society for the Propagation of Christian Knowledge, founded in 1698 and later known as the SPCK; even if some of them were designed to make the children aware of the "insidious and harmful doctrines of the Roman Catholics". Perhaps use was also made of a *Guide to the English Tongue* published in 1710, by Thomas Dyche [d. 1722x7] DNB. This book consisted of pages and pages of words divided up according to the number of syllables. At some time after 1710 Dyche became master of the free school at Stratford-le-Bow and in 1723 published *A Dictionary of All Words Commonly Us'd in the English Language*.[21]

Like many other schools the trustees relied on legacies to provide funds for the school. A most useful and still remembered benefactor was an unknown lady, who left £1,000 to the school's trustees. This was used to buy farmland, which eventually became the site of Tilbury Fort; the profits were used for the benefit of the school. Another benefactor was the well-known local resident Luke Flood who late in the C18 left £1,000 to enable boys be given apprenticeships, as long as they had served their masters truly and faithfully and that they had regularly attended divine service.

There were also special collections four times a year at the Charity Sermons in the parish church. The views of the church towards its charity children was well shown by the Bishop of London's sermon in 1714 when he observed that it was:

> *Doubtless your intention that these objects of your charity be thus educated as that they may hereafter become useful in inferior stations* and he noted that the wearing of the school uniform *in constantly reminding them of their dependence it would teach them humility and their parents thankfulness.*

Clearly it was intended that the boys and girls were clothed from early in the school's history, but it is not until 1836 that we have a document showing the costs as follows:

Charge for clothing a boy

A Boy's suit	£0 – 14s – 00d
A shirt of dowlas cloth	£0 – 00s – 06d
A Knit cap with tuft of string	£0 – 00s – 10d
A band	£0 – 00s – 03d
A pair of shoes	£0 – 03s – 00d

Charge for clothing a girl

A Gown or Petticoat	£0 – 09s – 06d
A shift of dowlas cloth	£0 – 02s – 06d
Apron	£0 – 01s – 00d
A pair of leather bodice	£0 – 03s – 06d
A pair of woollen stockings	£0 – 00s – 10d
A pair of shoes	£0 – 02s – 06d

Precisely what colours were worn by the children is not known for certain, but one memory was of the girls wearing brown frocks and blue straw hats.

The Madras System of Schooling

Probably the most important impact of the Davenant School on British education arose from its involvement with the Madras System of Schooling. In 1806 the school invited the Reverend Andrew Bell, [1753-1832] DNB to visit them. He had returned from India in 1797, where he had been Superintendent of the Madras Orphanages for the Sons of Soldiers. Because of a shortage of teachers he had developed a system whereby the elder and more able boys were regarded as "monitors"; who taught groups of younger boys what they themselves had just been taught. Bell published in 1797 a pamphlet entitled *An Experiment in Education made at the Male Asylum of Madras*, but this appeared to have made little initial impact.

Bell stayed at the Whitechapel School for several weeks demonstrating his system and methods until September 1806. Within six months the trustees were expressing their general satisfaction with Bell's system of education, and included in their list of the benefits "the indolent are stimulated, the vicious reclaimed ... and it saves the expense of additional instructors". Many visitors came to the school to watch this experiment and the Bell system was subsequently greatly developed by Joseph Lancaster [1778-1838] DNB and became known as the "Lancaster" system.[22]

The Lutheran German Library

Following the establishment of the German Lutheran Chapel in Alie Street in 1762 and the growth of the German speaking community around the Whitechapel sugar refineries there was a need for a library at the chapel. It appears that the great majority of works translated from German into English or published in England during the C18 were in fact devotional and only a few hundred were translated in total. How many sugarbakers read such works must be a matter of some dispute.

The importance of the Alie Street library can be judged by its purchase in 1997 by the British Library.[23]

Apprenticeship

Apprenticeship was a well-established feature of life in eighteenth-century London, and has been much studied. The livery companies were all based in the City of London, and over the years had developed a variety of functions. Some tried to control the number of apprentices accepted by their freemen, and thus to restrict entry into their chosen trades. Some also tried to prevent non-members from working in the eastern suburbs, where they would be outside their control, but generally their searches did not penetrate as far as Whitechapel. However by 1700 wealthy companies such as the Ironmongers' had lost direct contact with their original trades. So a mercer might be a member of the Ironmongers', and an ironmonger a member of the Grocers' Company, and a grocer a member of the Mercers' Company.[24]

Hundreds of boys and and dozens of girls from Whitechapel at the age of about fourteen years were apprenticed to masters in the City of London or locally. Full lists can be found in the works of Cliff Webb. Usually the apprenticeships were for seven years, but eight years was normal for apothecaries. The lowest premiums paid were two or three pounds for children from the poorest families to be apprenticed to a weaver. As an example the Whitechapel Charity School contributed to the apprenticeship of John Pointer to William Waller of the Barber-Surgeons' Company in 1754.[25]

Of greater interest is that group of Whitechapel and St George-in-the-East merchants and traders who could afford premiums of £40 or more.

Table 18   APPRENTICESHIP PREMIUMS OF £ 40 OR MORE

FATHER	CHILD	PREMIUM £	LIVERY COMPANY	YEAR	NOTE
Flower Freeman	Joseph	525	Ironmongers'	1774	Ms 16982, vol. 2
John Redman	John	262-10-00	Fishmongers'	1768	Ms 5576, vol. 3
David Jennings	Joseph	80	Drapers'	1740	*Bindings. 1739-1793*
Roger Redman	James	80	Apothecaries	1744	Ms 8200, vol. 6
William Hamilton	William	52-10-00	Curriers'	1772	Ms 6112, vol. 3
John Meaves	John	50	Upholders'	1772	Ms 7142, vol. 10
Robert Pritchard	James	42	Stationers'	1746	D. F. McKenzie[26]
Benjamin Cope	Benjamin	40	Haberdashers'	1770	Ms 15860, vol. 9
John Forfurr	Anna	40	Upholders'	1766	Ms 7142, vol. 1
Stephen Horsford	John	40	Apothecaries	1743	Ms 5266, vol. 5

Of the men able to afford these large premiums we know most about Flower Freeman, a merchant, who lived in MEOT from 1765 until 1777. He was also a *senior clerk* at Sir James Creed's White Lead Works in Whitechapel; was a London Hospital governor for life from 1774 and elected Chairman in 1777. Dr Gauci emphasised that entry into the highest level of City merchants might require a family to raise over £1,000 for a premium, because "Despite the decline of the formal apprenticeship, the most important educational experience remained the tutelage of an experienced trader, from whom the mysteries of a specialist trade would be drawn".[27]

Stephen Horsford of Whitechapel sent his son John to Merchant Taylor's School in 1739 and he was subsequently apprenticed to Robert Pell, an apothecary of Well Close Square and a prominent member of the local community.

The family of John Horsford of Well Close Square is probably unique. Two of his sons went to Merchant Taylor's School: John in 1760 and James in 1766. John Horsford [1751-1817] DNB went on to Oxford University, but quickly left in 1771 to enrol in the East India Company's Army and rose to become Major General. He was knighted in 1815 and died in Cawnpore in 1817.[28]

Equally of interest were those Whitechapel merchants, who were recognised as leaders in their professions and could charge premiums of between £100 and £500, comparable to those charged by the leading City merchants.

Table 19   PREMIUMS PAID TO WHITECHAPEL MASTERS

MASTER	APPRENTICE	PREMIUM PAID £	TRADE	NOTE
Benjamin Kenton	David Pike Watts	500	Brewer	1776 Kenton, Master of the Vintners' Company.DNB
Luke Alder	Thomas White	105	Oilman	GL Ms 5523, vol. 3 Farriers' Company
Thomas Hedges	Benjamin Parsons	100	Cheesemonger	Clothworkers' Company, *Apprentices, 1755-1787*
Rice Davies	John Griffiths	80	Druggist	GL Ms 8200, vol. 8

David Pike Watts had wanted to marry the daughter of Benjamin Kenton, [1719-1800] DNB, a wealthy Whitechapel brewer, but Kenton refused permission. Instead he took Pike Watts into his office, a decision that led to considerable wealth; seemingly commensurate with the premium of £500. Pike Watts was a maternal uncle of John Constable, [1776–1837] DNB the famous painter.[29]

FURTHER READING

M. Dickson   *Teacher extraordinary: Joseph Lancaster, 1778-1838,* 1986
P. Earle   *The Making of the English Middle Class,* 1989
P. Gauci   *Emporium of the World: The Merchants of London 1660-1800,* 2007
M. Hilton and J. Sheffrin   *Educating the Child in Enlightenment Britain,* 2009
H. M. Jewell   *Education in Early Modern England,* 1998
C. Kerrigan   *A History of Tower Hamlets,* 1982
R. Reynolds   *The History of the Davenant Foundation Grammar School,* 1966

Web Sites

http://www.innertemple.org.uk/archive   Inner Temple
http://www.origins.net/help/aboutbo-lonapps.aspx   Cliff Webb's lists of apprentices and masters
http://www.origins.net/help/aboutbo-appgb.aspx   The index to the TNA series IR 1 of apprentices

10. CHURCHES, CHAPELS AND CHARITY

Introduction

Reflecting its larger and diverse population by the C18 Whitechapel contained a greater variety of religious houses than other parishes in East London. In addition to the parish church there was a Lutheran chapel, several Dissenting chapels and a few Catholic *mass* houses. Except for the Embassy chapels, most Catholic churches came into existence after the passing of the second Catholic Relief Act in 1791. This chapter, after a brief review of local churches and chapels including the Strict Baptists, looks at the involvement of a high church congregation in the political crisis of the 1710s; and provides examples of charity, both for individuals and for larger issues, such as the Palatinate refugees and the Sierra Leone project.

For the members of minority religions there was the need to travel outside the parish in order to worship. Members of the Jewish community such as Moses N. Brandon and Simon Israel probably preferred to live in Whitechapel rather than further east for their synagogues were in the City; in Bevis Marks and Dukes Place, Aldgate. Their burial ground was in MEOT. Similarly the Quakers of Whitechapel joined either the Meeting House in Ratcliff or worshipped in the City at Devonshire House. Men such as Andrew Knies worshipped at the German Evangelical Reformed St Paul's Church in Dutchy Lane off the Strand which moved in 1818 to their new church in Hooper Square, off Leman Street.[1]

The Dissenters had a variety of chapels locally. Two of particular interest were the Strict Baptist chapel in Wapping and the Independent Stepney Meeting in Mile End Old Town.

We can gain some idea of the life of a religious man from the diary of Elijah Goff, a coal merchant in St George-in-the-East, for he attended services of the Church of England and Dissenting chapels. He attended three church services most Sundays and was quite happy to travel some distance to listen to a good sermon. In the morning he generally went to the chapel of the Reverend Noah Hill in Old Gravel Lane. The afternoon service was often at St George-in-the-East especially if there was a *Charity Sermon* on behalf of one of the local institutions such as the London Hospital, the Magdalen Hospital or the Shakespeare Walk Society.

Figure 11   MEGG'S ALMSHOUSES

In the evenings he would often go to Salters' Hall in St Swithin's Lane in the City, which was the main Dissenting Chapel in London between 1689 and the 1820s when it was pulled down. About 1770 the Court of the Salters' Company was said to be composed wholly of Dissenters and C19 Salters *thanked heaven that those days of discord and bigotry have gone by*. Returning home from a service Goff would make a note in his diary of the text used by the preacher and then add a remark to the effect that *he hoped he could follow the guidance* or that it was a *very instructive sermon*. He also concluded every diary entry with thanks to God for his life and family, even when he was suffering from one of his regular attacks of gout.[2]

There were also a number of private burial grounds in Whitechapel, speculative ventures, "which took advantage of the fact that all the small parochial cemeteries were grossly overcrowded." One of these new burial grounds lay between Backchurch Lane (formerly Church Lane) and Gower's Walk, just south of the Commercial Road. The earliest reliable date for the existence of the burial ground is 1776 and it remained in use until it closed between 1854 and 1856.[3]

The Dissenters

The Dissenters were widely distributed throughout Stepney and had a variety of meeting houses. The VCH outlines nonconformists chapels before 1689. The most famous was the Independent Stepney Meeting, which was founded in 1644. Under the leadership of the Reverend Matthew Mead [1628/9-1699] DNB the congregation had grown to be the largest in London. Their Meeting House was built in 1674 in the garden of Worcester House in MEOT, just one hundred yards or so west of St Dunstan's church and facing on to Bull Lane. The physical closeness of these two major religious centres makes one wonder if there was any conflict on a Sunday morning between the two congregations. Certainly, Captain Stephen Martin Leake was recorded by his son *as having a strong disregard for dissenters*, and such feelings may have been common.[4]

Amongst the local chapels were:

* The Little Alie Baptist Church founded in 1754 following the schism with the Strict Baptists[5]
* The Great Alie Street (Zoar) Chapel (Strict Baptist)
* Mill Yard Baptist Chapel (Seventh Day Baptists)

Although a short walk east from Whitechapel it is likely that many would make their way into MEOT to listen to the young Samuel Brewer. He was appointed in 1747 and developed into a prominent and popular minister. His preaching style *evangelical, plain, pathetic, often enlivened by anecdote*, led to a rapid growth in the congregation, which grew to between two hundred and three hundred by the time of his death in 1796.[6]

Reverend Henry Mayo

Henry Mayo [1733-1793] DNB was the most prominent Dissenting minister in the Whitechapel area. He was known as the *literary anvil,* and had met Samuel Johnson and James Boswell. They enjoyed his firm expression of views even though these were diametrically opposed to those of Johnson.

Possibly born in Plymouth, Mayo applied in 1756 to a society of Christian men in London, who managed an academy for the education of young men for the Ministry among Independent Churches. An account of his faith and experience was read at a meeting in the October. He arrived in London in December 1756 "was examined, was approved as fit for a trial, and was admitted into the house of one of the Tutors, Dr John Conder, opposite Bancroft's Almshouses in the Mile End Road, London". Conder paid the land tax for two houses on the south side of the Mile End Road, which were made into one, and for which the rent was £17-10s.-0d..

In June 1757, Henry Mayo with two other students signed the articles of agreement, "having finished the time for trial of their abilities", received the consent of the Society to be supported by it during the course of their studies. Mayo lived in Well Close Square from the time of his marriage in 1764 until his death in 1793, owning two houses, numbers 50 and 51, and residing in the former. He was very hospitable and kept open house on Mondays when any friends were welcome. His first wife was Mrs Martin, the widow of a West India merchant [nee Jane Marder], but she died in 1764 shortly after the birth of their daughter Jane. His second wife was Elizabeth Belfour, with whom he had two more daughters; Elizabeth Belfour Mayo born in 1768 and Rebecca Holmes Mayo born in 1769. His second wife died soon after – before 1771 - and was interred in Alie Street burial ground, Whitechapel. In 1785 the Congregational Fund recommended that Dr Henry Mayo be asked to succeed Dr Gibbons at the Academy in Homerton.

During the riots to which many Dissenters were exposed, there were two attempts on his life by persons firing into his study at night and in one of the attacks he had a very narrow escape. He was a warm advocate of liberal principles and admired the struggle of the Americans for their rights, which issued in their independence. It is supposed he received his diploma of L.L.D from Harvard College, in New England, as he left a legacy to that college in his will of 1780. Mayo ventured into print early in his ministry with six letters in 1766 on Baptism. In 1768, he published an abridged edition of Dr Owen's valuable work on *Spiritual Mindedness*.[7]

The Strict and Particular Baptists

The third Baptist chapel in London was established in Wapping in 1656 and a Baptist meeting was also established in Boar's Head Yard in Whitechapel in 1684. It was here that John Bunyan [1628-1688] DNB preached his last sermon in 1688; the meeting finally closed in 1729.[8]

The Strict Baptists were founded in 1633 in Wapping-Stepney when John Spilsbury left the Particular Baptist church in Walthamstow to take charge of *a very great people which erected and enlarged a place in Meeting House Alley* in Wapping. In 1669 their Meeting House was "restored as in Cromwell's time". The origin of the Strict Baptists movement was in the belief that Christ in his death undertook to save particular individuals, usually referred to as the Elect. It was thought that no one could join this group – "Neither as any redeemed by Christ, or effectively, called, justified,or saved, but the Elect alone." This insistence on particular persons alone being chosen and saved, gave to the Calvinists, the obvious title of Particular Baptists. This group in Wapping attracted a large number of supporters and the church eventually moved from Wapping to Little Prescot Street, [LPS] then to Commercial Street in 1855 and finally in 1913/14 to Walthamstow.[9]

Stephen Williams is a little-known, but significant member of the church at Wapping and later at Little Prescot Street, Goodman's Fields. He was a prosperous glover, linen draper and textile printer, who became a Freeman of the City of London in 1742. In 1738 he "gave account of his dealings of God" and following his baptism he was accepted into full membership of the church. The subscription records for LPS show that between 1757 and his death in 1797, he donated 10 guineas annually, which represented over half of each year's total contributions. In 1756, he accepted the call to become a Deacon of the church and his name appears regularly in the minute books as one of those required to oversee and discipline unruly members.

Stephen Williams was influential in the appointment of two of the ministers at LPS. The first, being Samuel Burford, [c. 1726-1768] then Minister at Lyme Regis. The minutes show that James Fall had been proposed to take the deceased Samuel Wilson's place, but in a vote held in 1753, votes against his appointment narrowly outnumbered those in favour by four. The minutes show that Stephen Williams voted against Mr Fall's appointment. It is quite possible that Williams had Samuel Burford in mind for the post all along, his sister having married into the Burford family. However, despite doubts shown by some members of the congregation, which was to lead to Mr Fall setting up his own church at Little Alie Street and taking some of the members with him, the minutes state that on 27th April 1755 *The Church unanimously chose him [Burford] and thought proper to give him a call.*

Samuel Burford was assessed in the 1760 land tax on a small house with a rent of £10 in St George-in-the-East. He lived in Princes Square, just a few doors away from the Reverend David Jennings, D. D., the Pastor of the Independent Meeting in Old Gravel Lane. In 1758 he was probably one of the witnesses to the will of David Jennings.[10] Under the pastoral care of Samuel Burford, the church enjoyed considerable prosperity, both financially and in the growth of its congregation. After his unexpected death in 1768 he was buried at Bunhill Fields and on his headstone was recorded[11]:

> His virtues need no stone to show
> full well his friends his merits know;
> While living was by all beloved
> by all regretted when removed

In his 1811 *A History of the English Baptists*, Joseph Ivimey said of Samuel Burford "He possessed great humility of mind, and a sweetness and affability of temper ... His knowledge of divine truth was considerable and he explained the doctrines of grace in an experimental manner, whilst he urged the duties of religion by the most evangelical motives".

He was survived by a wife and eleven children. According to E. F. Kevan in his 1933 *London's Oldest Baptist Church,* the wider Burford family continued to support the Strict Baptists for a great many years. Between 1755 and 1838 no fewer than seventeen of Samuel Burford's own children and grandchildren became members of the church. It should be noted, however, that the minute books from the church at Old Gravel Lane, Wapping, show that both the Burford and Williams families had also been actively involved during the 17C.

Abraham Booth, [1734-1806] DNB, a provincial minister, was appointed to succeed Burford. This followed the recommendations of Stephen Williams and two other Deacons who had travelled to Nottinghamshire to assess his suitability for the role of leader of such a wealthy and educated congregation. He was to build upon the work of Samuel Burford and was remembered by his friend William Newman, the minister at Bow, as "a star of the first magnitude ... one of the brightest ornaments of the Baptist denomination".

Stephen Williams' religious devotion was not simply limited to his support of the church at Goodman's Fields. He gave generously of both his time and money to a number of charitable organisations, including The Society for Promoting Religious Knowledge Among the Poor; The Baptist College in Rhode Island; Dr Wheelock's Indian Charity School and The Orphans' Working School in City Road. In 1783 he became joint treasurer of the London Baptist Education Society. Such philanthropy was made possible by his successful businesses which included a substantial calico-printing works based at Stratford, Essex, and a wholesale linen-drapery at 27 Poultry, in the City of London. In 1793 he was named as one of the Deputies for the Civil Affairs of Dissenters for the following year.

The death of Stephen Williams, aged 86, was reported in the *Gentleman's Magazine's* Obituaries of Remarkable People in June 1797. Williams had accumulated considerable wealth and shortly before his death he was able to invest £10,000 in the Government's Loyalty Loan. His will details many family bequests totalling approximately £30,000 with freeholds and leases in the City of London and Stratford. The strength of his religious convictions is borne out by other bequests, including £2,000 to The Particular Baptist Fund in London; £100 to the Reverend Abraham Booth; £100 to the Deacons of the Congregation of Protestant Dissenters for use among the poorer members of the church; £200 to the Widows' Fund for the relief of the widows of poor Dissenting ministers; £100 to the Congregational or Independent Fund in London and £200 to the Orphan Charity School, City Road, Islington. He was buried at Bunhill on 17th June 1797, at a cost of £5. 5s. 6d, in the vault which already held the remains of his wife and children, who had predeceased him by several years.[12]

The succession of ministers of LPS from Samuel Wilson to Abraham Booth sought to educate and inspire their congregations by example and through their teachings of doctrine and biblical truths. In spite of such strong leadership and preaching there is considerable evidence within the LPS minute books that some members' conduct fell short of expectations. Deacons were authorised to admonish members of the congregation for such crimes as "disorderly and scandalous walking" and holding "heretical and shocking sentiments", along with equally serious issues such as bankruptcy and adultery for which they could be punished by suspension or even exclusion. Regular attendance at church was an essential requirement and "messengers" would visit the homes of those whose sense of duty to attend services did not match the exacting standards set by the church. Whilst some clearly fell short of the mark others thrived and built upon the strong foundations that had been instilled into them. Among those who took such inspiration were Thomas Pilley, the gifted preacher, who in 1769, was invited to become pastor of the church at Luton, a post he held for thirty years.

In 1782, Edward Burford, Peter Anstie and Ann Anstie sought permission to leave the congregation at LPS in order to establish a church at Preston where they had already begun to introduce new and high quality processes at the Mosney Print Works in Walton-le-Dale. In 1798 LPS gave leave to Thomas Burford and seven others to form a new church at Mare Street, Hackney. These and others went on to pass on those same strong principles to a new generation of believers, through their belief in God, the Gospels and the Baptist doctrine. They inspired countless others in the way they conducted themselves, their businesses and interacted with those less fortunate than themselves, both at home and abroad.[13]

St Mary, Whitechapel

John Stow wrote in 1603,

> *Now of Whitechapel church somewhat, and then back again to Aldgate. This church is as it were a chapel of ease to the parish of Stebineth, & the Parson of Stebineth hath the gift thereof: ... is now called St Mary Matfellon.*[14]

Guillery has described in great detail the important place that St Mary, rebuilt 1672-3, and St Matthias, Poplar, built 1642-54, had "at the heart of the post Reformation reshaping of England's ecclesiastical architecture". St Mary was rebuilt during the time of the Reverend Ralph Davenant; a period in which there was a "short-lived reversal of intolerant religious policy that followed the Declaration of Indulgence of March 1672, which was cancelled a year later." The red brick church was 90ft by 60 ft and joined to the fourteenth-century tower. An important aspect in designing the interior was the need to provide the worshippers with the opportunity to clearly see the preacher and hear the sermon; the interior was described as "very lightsome and spacious". The four stone columns were Corinthian and Composite rather than Tuscan. In 1810 Malcolm described the church as being nearly square, divided into three aisles with four round pillars and eight square pillars and with large Venetian windows and galleries. The parish church of St Mary was rebuilt in 1876. Its replacement was badly damaged in the Second World War and was eventually demolished in 1952.[15]

In 1708 Brasenose College, Oxford, purchased the advowson of Whitechapel and Stepney, which they held until 1864. The main reason for the acquisition of livings by colleges was to give employment to Fellows after leaving Oxford. Fellows were not permitted to be married or to hold livings above a certain amount; so the Rectors would resign their College fellowships when presented to a good living. Brasenose College had strong links with Cheshire and Lancashire, and many of the Rectors came from this area. During the C18 seven Rectors were appointed between 1708 and 1800, and their details are given in Appendix 7. The records of the time do not describe the help, comfort and leadership that the rectors gave their congregations, but concentrated instead on a variety of disputes. Many of the higher clergy in the C18 would have drawn their income from several benefices, and left pastoral care to their ill-paid curates. Thus it is difficult to judge how much affection the Rectors commanded locally. Certainly compared with the Rev'd Samuel Brewer at the Stepney Meeting, very few of the Rectors received any bequests from the parishioners, though some bequests to the poor were left to the churchwardens.

As was common elsewhere, Communion was only celebrated four times a year on Easter Day, Whit Sunday, Christmas Day and Good Friday.

The Succession Crisis

The Act of Succession of 1701 was passed to prevent a Jacobite re-claiming the throne. Thus when Queen Anne died in August 1714 she was followed by George I. However the Act did not qualm the debates and for several years the country was plunged into a series of crises. Dr Rogers has thrown light on the theatre of street politics of the time. The conflict over the succession was reflected in Whitechapel, where tensions rose high. In October 1714 a High Church congregation assaulted a visiting preacher who praised William III and the Duke of Marlborough, who had been the hero of Blenheim in 1704.

Further disturbances arose in Whitechapel in June 1715 where supporters of the Jacobite Pretender "sported white cockades in their hats" and the "rough music of marrow bones and cleavers ... called the Tory supporters to salute Oxford on his way to the Tower to await trial, the mob crying 'High Church and down with the Wiggs'". Disaffection continued to be rife throughout London and one man involved was Dr Richard Welton [1671/2-1726] DNB, who was Rector of Whitechapel from 1697 to 1715. He had neglected to take the Oath of Fidelity to the government and in consequence was ejected from his position. He was subsequently involved in a legal dispute with his successor Dr. Shippen.[16]

The *Weekly Packet* 9th November 1717 reported as follows:

> *On Sunday Morning last about 11 a Clock, Colonel Ellis, and three or four other Gentleman, the High Constable Wooster, and several Constables of the Liberty, with two Files of the Foot Guards, from the Tower, commanded by a Serjeant surrounded a house in Goodman's Fields, where Dr Welton the late Rector of Whitechapel keeps a non-juring*

Congregation, and demanded entrance, which being refused they immediately broke open the Door.

Then D'Oilie Mitchel, Tho. Sewell and J. Haynes and J. Hayns esq. three of the neighbouring Justices, rendered the Government Oaths to each of the Congregation (which consisted of about 300 persons) one by one. About 40 of them, whom Curiosity, not Conscience, had brought thither, readily took them: the rest absolutely refused; But were obliged upon Oath to give in their Names together with their Occupations and their places of Abode, which will be referred to the next Sessions at Hick's Hall in order to convict them of popish Recusancy, if they still persist in their Refusal to take Oaths.

The Doctor himself was examined first , and confessed he did not pray in his Congregation for the King and Royal Family as the Law requires; and he refused to take the Oaths. After the Congregation was dismissed, a Search was made for Arms, but none were found, though repeated Informations had been given upon Oath to several of his Majesty's Justices of the Peace, that Arms had been seen carried into the said house."

Watching these events with some trepidation was the Rector of Whitechapel, Robert Shippen, for his younger brother William [1673-1743] DNB, was a leading politician and Jacobite sympathiser. William Shippen was called to the Bar in 1699 and worked with a small band of sympathisers for a second Stuart Revolution. He was forthright in his opposition to the Militia Bill and was retained in the Tower of London in 1717 for a provocative speech he had made in the House of Commons. In 1721 he acted as the main channel of communication between English and Scottish Jacobites.[17]

Huguenots in Whitechapel

There were apparently few Huguenots in Whitechapel. However, some appear amongst the thousands that applied for entrance to the French Protestant Hospital. All applicants had to prove links with families that had escaped from Europe on religious grounds. From Whitechapel came in 1753 Daniel Delrome, who had lived with a plasterer in Catharine Wheel Alley, Whitechapel. Also from the Alley in 1779 came Elizabeth Grenier (Garnier) who was eighty years old and "tre infirme".[18]

The Quaker Meeting House and Burial Ground

Quaker life revolved around Weekly and Monthly Meetings in Ratcliff and Six Weekly and Yearly Meetings at the Gracechurch Street Friends Meeting House. The latter was concerned with broader issues, but also from time to time with providing finance to Ratcliff, which constantly struggled to raise funds. The Quakers purchased the land for a burial-ground in Whitechapel in 1687. The ground was in the Coverley's Fields north of the Whitechapel Road and in 1743 Lord Castlemaine, the proprietor, granted Friends a 500 years' lease, on payment of a 100 guineas, and the lease now extends to 2292.

The original ground was uneven, but eventually in 1698 a pond was filled in and the ground raised up and levelled. In 1690 twenty trees were planted. This burial-ground was under the particular care of Devonshire House in the City. A very large number of Friends who dwelt in the eastern parishes were buried there until it was closed for interment in 1857. Subsequently this ground became a recreation ground. "A curious circumstance occurred here in 1716. This was the stealing of the corpse from the ground by John Holmes (son of Michael Holmes, the gravedigger), and some of his companions. Michael Holmes was dismissed and ordered to quit his house by the gateway". This was not a unique event for body snatchers were also at work in MEOT in 1739, 1759 and 1786.[19]

St George, German Lutheran Chapel

Well worthy of a visit is the modest German Lutheran chapel which was built 1762-63, and "which preserves its atmospheric C18 galleried interior crowded with ox pews, pulpits and florid commandment boards". This chapel in Great Alie Street was built by the Hamburg merchants and sugar refiners who had settled Whitechapel. In an indenture of lease we find it involved:

1. Joel Johnson, Trinity, Minories, carpenter
2. Dederich Beckman, Aldgate, sugar refiner
3. Frederick Rider, Doctors' Common, sugar refiner

Dederich Beckmann, [c.1702-66] a prominent local German sugar refiner, was a major benefactor of the chapel with the large sum of £650, which was nearly one third of the total cost. He was also the father-in-law of the first Pastor, Dr Gustavus Anthony Wachsel [c. 1735-99]. Behind a two-door front to the street, the interior of the chapel is a large rectangular room with galleries above on either side. The box pews can still be seen in the chapel. A pulpit lies between the Tables of the Law. The chapel was restored by the Historic Churches Trust with additional finance from the Heritage Lottery Fund, English Heritage and others and reopened in 2004.

Wachsel published in 1766 *Entwürfe seiner Vormittags-Predigten* [drafts of his morning sermons]. The library of the chapel was purchased by the British Library in 1997. It has been shown that of the few hundred books translated from German in the C18 the majority were in fact devotional, (with Pietist works playing an important role at the beginning of the century).[20]

Individual Charity

It is a well-known problem for local historians that quite often a subject of broad national interest cannot be followed at the local level because of a lack of documentation. For Whitechapel there is a dearth of material concerning the operation of the Poor Law and the local workhouses, so a different approach was required. In the C18 there was a mixed economy of welfare in which the activities of state, church and voluntary organisations were often inextricably mixed. Thus the Poor Law was an example of state regulation and tax funding, but depended on unpaid volunteers at the local level for its operation.

Professor Hugh Cunningham in his introduction to *Charity, Philanthropy and Reform: From the 1690s to 1850*, pointed out that "a study of charity and philanthropy is drawn almost inevitably to the study of organizations. … Informal giving and private charity … receive little attention." The importance of volunteers in the charity sector was also examined by Dr Joanna Innes who emphasised in her essay that "voluntaristic practices and attitudes permeated the whole welfare field and were not peculiar to only part of it."[21]

These comments suggest that new insights on individual charity might be obtained from a detailed study of wills. For Whitechapel over one thousand PCC wills between 1740 and 1790 have been examined and they provide the basis for the following discussion and Appendix 8. These wills provide many examples of the range of benefactions given to poor individuals and to charities and institutions, both in England and overseas. There was, of course, some individual giving during a person's lifetime, not least to the numerous beggars. Other forms of support only appear to later observers when charities published lists of subscribers.

The first priority for the majority of will makers was to provide for their immediate families. William Noade in 1776 had other ideas, for he left only one shilling to his wife Martha *on account of her Baseness, Treachery and abominable wicked ways.* She was thus probably consigned to a life of poverty. Within family networks there are bequests to poorer members. For instance, John Samuel Thorogood left *£5 and her bed and furniture* to Sarah Moss as long as she remained a widow.[22]

When it came to servants there was a great range in the bequests, and probably the most fortunate were the servants of the wealthy James Spalding esquire. He left £100 to George Copestake and an annuity of £10 per annum to Susanna Hempstead. Such generosity would ensure that they did not drift into poverty. At a lower level, donations of between £5 and £20 to servants were quite common and ensured that the recipients could survive for at least a few months, in the event of being unable to obtain a new position.[23]

Amongst Whitechapel will makers the most popular institution was the London Hospital as a sizeable donation obtained several benefits and qualified the giver as a governor. Edward Cahill, Benjamin Goodwin and John Hammond, a sail cloth maker, all left £500, whilst Robert Summerhayes left £1,000.

The second most important recipient of charity were Megg's Almshouses, which was the special concern of the wealthy Benjamin Goodwin. In his 1767 will he left £700 in trust, which was to be used for the demolition of the old almshouses on the *south side of the road*. In its place were to be built *Six houses for the poor Alms people to dwell in according to the plan I have approved of.* The new almshouses were built on the north side of the Whitechapel Road near Dog Row. In addition he left £1,000 in bank annuities to the Rector and church wardens of St Mary Whitechapel; the interest to be dispersed on Christmas Day for the poor alms women. Donations of between £5 and £100 were also left to various charity schools in Whitechapel, Aldgate, St Katharine's, and further away in Newington Butts.[24]

It is also possible to identify some of the local merchants who made donations to national institutions. In 1754 Sir Joseph Hankey, an Alderman, and Sir George Colebrooke, Lord of the Manor of Stepney and Hackney, were stewards at a Charity Dinner at the Merchant Taylor's Hall for the Smallpox Hospital.

Another important institution was The Philanthropic Society established in September 1788 which[25]:

> *Had plans for bringing up Children of Vagrants and Criminals to Industry and Virtue to prevent both vice and misery and is calculated to increase the total amount of happiness and wealth.*

The society very quickly established itself with voluntary subscriptions and from time to time published lists of subscribers. In June 1790 the following well-known merchants and ladies from the area around Whitechapel subscribed one guinea each to the society:

P. Lock esq., Prescot Street	Erasmus Maddox, East Smithfield
Mrs Ord, Leman Street	Richard Parker esq., Well Close Square
William Quarrill, Whitechapel	Major Rhode, Leman Street

The Foundling Hospital

The granting of a Charter to the Foundling Hospital in October 1739 provided the opportunity for a number of local merchants to contribute to this important charity; which was established to provide care for illegitimate children, many found abandoned on the streets of London. Each child was given a new name [perhaps reflecting the place where they were found] with which to start their new life; examples include Sarah Tower, Molly Hamlets and Andrew Lymehouse together with the more fanciful Julius Caesar and Cloudesly Shovell, named after the famous Admiral.

Amongst the local merchants connected with the Foundling Hospital in its early days were[26]:

John Raymond esquire, Ratcliff Cross, signature on the Charter granted 17 October 1739

Adam Williamson at the Tower, signature on the Charter granted 17 October 1739

John Fell the younger of Red Lyon Street Wapping, elected 28 February 1739

John Collet, Well Close Square elected 2 October 1751

We now turn to two examples of the help provided by the residents of Whitechapel to assist large groups of displaced people in East London.

The Palatinate Camp at Whitechapel, October 1764

In 1764 a German adventurer called Stumple persuaded 800 persons from the German state of Palatinate to form a settlement on the islands of St. John and Le Croix in the Leeward Islands. As Britain controlled the sea routes to North America the Palatinates were first brought to London. Here they were abandoned by Stumple and they arrived in the Port of London in a most deplorable condition and in terrible want.

About 600 were allowed to come ashore and they retired to fields near Stepney and Bow. For days they existed on the verge of starvation till the minister of the German Lutheran Church in Great Alie Street pleaded their plight in the daily press. Immediately a fund was opened for their relief and a hundred tents were sent from the Tower. They were soon under cover and provided with food, and in a short time arrangements were made for their settlement in South Carolina. They were able to make this journey towards the end of the following year with everything necessary for their accommodation during the voyage and proper requisites for their support.[27]

The White Raven and the Sierra Leone Project

Whitechapel was also at the centre of another major project to help the poor in the 1780s; this time with the black community and a philanthropic project that eventually led to the founding of Sierra Leone.

The Reverend Hubert Mayo, Rector of St George-in-the-East "contributed to the appeal for money to fund the Sierra Leone project and was also a member of the Committee for the Abolition of Slavery. Mayo was particularly assiduous in converting and baptising Black people. As his obituary said 'I suppose no clergyman in England ever baptised so many Black men and Mulattoes [sic]'." Dr Kathleen Chater argues that in Mayo's parish "the entries relating to most of the Black people contain different information from those of the other parishioners, … and demonstrate that the majority of those baptised did not live in the parish." They came to Mayo to be baptised because it was a common but erroneous belief that this conferred freedom. Prior to 1770 there were only a few Black people baptised in every decade, but this changed and between 1780-9 the baptisms of Black people in St George-in-the-East numbered 69.[28]

Granville Sharp [1735-1813] DNB, is famous as a slavery abolitionist. In 1765 he "saw a poor Negro Boy about 16 or 17 years of age, standing at the door [of his brother's house in the Mincing Lane] with other sick people waiting for advice. The appearance of the Boy was so distressful (as he seemed ready to drop down) that Granville Sharp thought it right to go back and speak to his brother [William Sharp an eminent surgeon] that immediate relief might be given to him." The boy was a battered seventeen-year old African slave named Jonathan Strong. Eventually with help from the Sharps he "grew to be a stout good looking young man".[29]

Eventually after some years there were several major charitable attempts to relieve the position of the distressed black population. It was Jonas Hanway, [1712-1786] DNB "elderly benefactor of the down-and-out and abused in London" who in 1786 first noticed the plight of the black poor and commenced the concerted effort to aid them. Unofficially aided by Granville Sharp he launched an appeal to assist the 'Black Poor'. His initial concern had been for the East Indian seamen who were as destitute as the American and West India blacks; but it quickly became clear that the latter far outnumbered the former. Hanway gathered several of his colleagues in banking, business and philanthropy each week at Batson's Coffee House to assess the special problems the black poor encountered and to organise a solution. They collected £800 and what became known as the Committee for the Relief of the Black Poor distributed food each day at two public houses in London.[30]

One distribution point was the White Raven public house, just east of the London Hospital, nearly opposite the Blind Beggar of Bethnal Green public house. The other was the Yorkshire Stingo in Lisson Grove. We do not yet known why the White Raven was chosen, but perhaps it was because of the number of poor blacks in the area? "The Committee's agents began distributing six pence per person on 20th April 1786, giving the money to seventy-five black people. The next day they paid 119 people … until by 15th May they had given money to 1,943 destitute black people in London".

One considered solution to the numbers of black poor in London was that "they could leave Britain, individually or *en masse*" and this was clearly a situation "ripe for exploitation". Into this situation stepped Henry Smeathman, a business man and botanist, who proposed a "self-sufficient and lucrative colony in Sierra Leone".

Henry Smeathman [1742-86] DNB was born in Scarborough and his early enthusiasm for natural history had taken him in 1771 to Africa and the West Indies for about eight years. He had also been employed by Sir Joseph Banks, [1743-1820] DNB, President of the Royal Society, who funded numerous expeditions and maintained correspondence with plant collectors in many countries. "Styling himself a Gentleman", Smeathman sent a memorandum to the Lords Commissioners of His Majesty's Treasury.

This was couched in language which indicated that he had been called and was willing to serve; …

> *"being informed that a great number of Blacks and People of Colour, many of the Refugees from America and others had by land or sea been in his Majesty's service, were from the severity of the season in great distress …".*[31]

Smeathman proposed that for about £14 each, the black people would be carried to Sierra Leone, and supplied with three months of provisions, clothing, bedding, tools and medicine. Once there they would build housing and become self-sufficient, and quickly begin to supply Britain with various raw materials. He worked out the plan in enormous detail, tabulating how much bread, beef and pork, *pease* and *melapes*, oatmeal, flour, barley, suet, raisins, and "rum for grog" each person would need for the voyage and the subsequent three months.

He estimated that each man would need both a striped and a blue flannel jacket, a pair each of canvas and flannel trousers, a pair of shoes, four shirts, two knives, a razor and a hat. Similar provisions were made for women. He provided the names of the outfitters and agents who would assist him. In addition, and which the Committee later admitted should have alerted them, he meticulously listed the medicines he considered absolutely indispensable. Smeathman did not reveal to the Committee that he and his associates intended to use slave labour to establish a profit-making estate.

By 7th June 1786 the Committee had identified eight men who were thought to have leadership skills and could provide leadership in Sierra Leone. But some black people began to question the government's motives for sending them so far away and whether their liberty could be guaranteed. Hanway addressed the blacks at the White Raven, and was only partially successful in convincing them that the government's intentions were honourable. Smeathman died suddenly on 1st July thus throwing the whole Sierra Leone scheme into disarray. The Treasury then appointed Olaudah Equiano [c. 1745-1797] DNB as leader.[32] By 22nd November 1786 there were 105 blacks on board the *Belisarius* and 154 blacks on the *Atlantic*, numbers well above those being planned for. The full story has been told by Stephen Braidwood. In April 1787 three ships had reached Tenerife after a 13 day voyage from Plymouth, and by March 1788 only 130 black settlers were left; the rest had either died or run off. So was founded Sierra Leone.

FURTHER READING

C. Booth	*Life and Labour of the People in London, First Series, Poverty*, vol. 2, 1902
S. J. Braidwood	Initiatives and Organisation of the Black Poor, 1786-1787, *Slavery and Abolition*, 1989, 3, pp. 211-227
S. J. Braidwood	*Black Poor and White Philanthropists*, 1994
C. Chater	*Untold History,: black people in England and Wales during the period of the British Slave Trade, c. 1660-1837*, 2009
J. Cox	*Hatred Pursued Beyond the Grave: Tales of our Ancestors from the London Church Courts,* 1995
H. Cunningham and J. Innes, ed.	*Charity, Philanthropy and Reform: From the 1690s to 1850*, 1998
P. Edwards	*The Life of Olaudah Equiano*, 1989
C. Fyfe	*A History of Sierra Leone*, 1962
M. D. George	*London life in the eighteenth century*, 1951
G. Gerzina	*Black London: Life before Emancipation*, 1995
D. R. Green	*From Artisan to Paupers: Economic Change and Poverty in London, 1790-1870*, 1995
D. R. Green	*Pauper Capital: London and the Poor Law, 1790-1870*, 2010
T. Hitchcock	*Down and Out in Eighteenth Century London*, 2007

Web Sites

http://www.foundlingmuseum.org.uk	Foundling Museum
http://www.history.ac.uk/makinghistory/resources/articles/black_history	
http://pbfund.org.uk	Particular Baptist Fund
http://www.strictbaptisthistory.org.uk	Strict Baptist History
http://en.wikipedia.org/wiki/Strict_Baptists	Accessed 30 January 2011
http://www.workhouses.org.uk	Accessed 10 November 2010

11.   THE MERCHANTS, CRIME AND BANKRUPTCY

Introduction

This Chapter explores three important aspects of the eighteenth-century legal system that affected every merchant in Whitechapel, and indeed every man with a rent of £10 per annum.

- All men paying £10 or more in rent could be called to act as headboroughs and to attend as jurors at the Old Bailey, and, if of sufficient status, to act as Justices of the Peace

- A wide variety of crimes occurred in the area, but it was the victim of a crime that had to make a prosecution if the culprit was caught

- Probably more significant to a merchant than having some trifles stolen was the threat of bankruptcy in an age when trade was very unstable

The British in the C17 and C18 were very ambiguous about the need for a full-time police force. They relied greatly on the part-time services of headboroughs, constables and Justices of the Peace to tackle the problems of crime.

The London newspapers of the mid-eighteenth century regularly reported the activities of pickpockets, footpads, the keepers of disorderly houses, robbers and murderers, and it was thought that:

> "Throughout the [eighteenth] century Londoners lived in a world in which violence, disorder and brutal punishment (though decreasing) were still part of the normal background of life. Newgate, the gallows, the exploits of felons, figured largely in the press and in the current literature of the day. "[1]

What is amazing is that this turbulent background appeared to have little impact on the wealthy merchants who chose to live in the Whitechapel area. The prosperous merchants who lived in Well Close Square were only a few yards away from the notorious Rag Fair. Perhaps accompanied by a male servant and armed with a sword they felt safe in this environment for as Maureen Waller observed, "In London itself footpads roamed the ill-lit streets. It was said that no man might dine out unless armed to the teeth with swords, pistols, muskets and blunderbusses."[2]

Figure 12   HIGH LIFE AT MIDNIGHT

Constables, Headboroughs and Watchmen

In Whitechapel, as elsewhere, the detection and prevention of crime in the middle of the eighteenth century was the responsibility of locally elected constables and headboroughs. These were all men, whose rents were £10 or more per year, and who were elected on an annual basis.

Malcolm reports that about 1800 there were 16 headboroughs, one constable and four beadles in Whitechapel. Two of the beadles dealt with the removal of paupers and the other two took it in turns to attend at the Watch House. They were supported by watchmen, appointed by the vestry, and gatekeepers appointed by the Turnpike trustees. Watchmen were known in the parish as early as 1702 and an Act allowing Whitechapel to have paid night watchmen was passed in 1763.[3]

Typically, the headboroughs would walk around in pairs *to see if we could find any disorderly People*. When they found such a person, they would be taken to the Watch House until they could be brought before a Justice of the Peace. Clearly, such duties were not much liked by busy shopkeepers and other merchants so they would pay a fine or find a substitute. There was some risk in these duties and headboroughs would witness fights, house-breaking, and also have to confront men at night carrying suspicious sacks of probably stolen goods along the High Street.

In 1702 the Middlesex Sessions provided detailed instructions on the routes to be followed by the watchmen in Whitechapel. Three watchmen will go from the *Whitechapel Watch House into Goodman's Fields shall come together to the gate called Goodman Field Gate and then divide themselves* – one was to go only into Lambert Street, one to go into Rupert Street and one to go into Prescot Street.

The watchmen, who started their rounds from the Watch House in Rosemary Lane, were to go into Chamber Street, down Prescot Street and then to take their stand at the White Bear. In winter, which probably started on Michaelmas Day, the 29th September, the watchmen were on duty until 6 am and in summer until 4 am.[4]

Justices of the Peace and Jurors

The excellent Old Bailey online web site informs us that "The criteria for selecting members of grand and trial juries are not known, except that jurors were always men, had to meet a property qualification, and were supposed to be geographically representative. ... Research by John Beattie has shown that, during the C18, jurors were from the "broad middling ranks" of society; they were gentlemen, merchants, professionals and wealthier shopkeepers, tradesmen and artisans." But Burke thought otherwise.

Significantly, jurors tended to serve on more than one occasion, which meant that almost every jury included experienced members who were familiar with court procedure.[5]

Less serious offences were tried without juries by Justices of the Peace, later known as magistrates. They sat at Quarter Sessions, which were held four times a year. Justices of the Peace were unpaid and originally made money from court fees and fines that were levied on offenders, and often dealt with cases at their homes.

In the C18 many officers of the criminal justice system were considered corrupt. Beatrice and Sidney Webb in their monumental *The Parish and the County*, 1906, commented extensively on the breakdown of the Middlesex Bench in the C18. They wrote "The Justices of Middlesex, said Burke, without contradiction in 1780, were generally the scum of the earth – carpenters, brick makers and shoemakers; some of whom were notoriously men of such infamous characters that they were unworthy of any employ whatever, and others so ignorant that they could scarce write their names."

Their analysis of the situation led them to form a very poor opinion of Sir Samuel Gower and Boulton Mainwaring, both prominent local gentlemen. Mainwaring had held the salaried post of surveyor to the Tower Hamlets Court of Sewers. He was also closely connected with Raine's School and was the architect of the London Hospital. He first appeared as a Trustee of Raine's Foundation School in 1740 and was a regular attender at their monthly meetings. He became President in 1749 and was regularly in attendance until 1752, when his duties in planning the London Hospital became more demanding.

Mainwaring can be traced in the Middlesex Session Books from 1746 when he was asked to advise on repairs to Hicks Hall, the Court House in St John Street, Clerkenwell, the quality of the builder's work and the payment they should receive. In 1774 Mainwaring claimed payment from the Middlesex Bench for services he had provided over a period of ten years in superintending the alterations to the new House of Correction and the repairing of Hick's Hall. This claim was indignantly rejected on the ground that the county did not employ him as a surveyor. Indeed the Court informed him that *the services you have done the county were voluntarily, and in every sense of the word disinterested.*

Sir Samuel Gower [?-1755] was a prominent local dignitary who had a sailcloth manufactory a furlong south of St. Mary Church Whitechapel. He appears in Mill Yard in 1738 and in the following years acquired the nearby *Music House* of William Hallam and the New Exchange from Nicholas Gester. As described in Chapter 8 he was involved in an interesting conflict of interest over his licensing of notorious disorderly houses.[6]

Burford Camper [Camphire] from Shadwell, Robert Pell and John Shakespear were the local Justices who were most active in the persecution of the coal heavers and their leaders in the Spring of 1768. Camper was a leading coal "undertaker" and his house was attacked by a riotous mob. Later Camper was active in the crushing of the silk-weavers in late 1768 and 1769. In 1770 Camper with others were sitting at the Angel, Whitechapel, where they committed John Brannon and Hugh M'Mahon on suspicion of assaulting and murdering Mary Cuddy.[7]

Whilst Gower, Mainwaring and Robert Pell were three of the most important men in the area many of the local residents were appointed Justices of the Peace or appeared as Jurors at the Old Bailey.

The following men have so far been identified as Justices of the Peace in Whitechapel and St George-in-the-East from the Sun Fire Office's Middlesex fire claims[8]:

St George-in-the-East	Boulton Mainwaring 1748
	William Blackmore 1776-1787
Whitechapel	Charles Digby 1771
	William Quarrill 1788
	Robert Smith 1788

The duties of the Justices of the Peace sitting in Whitechapel were not confined to crimes occurring in the parish; they were also asked to adjudicate on crimes on the River Thames involving shipping and smuggling[9].

> *On 16 ult. was seized in the Thames a Brigantine called the Industry with 4,704 yards of Irish Camblets – laid on board her in 1754 in Cork in order to carry the same to some port beyond the seas, contrary to statute. On 21st two justices of the peace met in Whitechapel to proceed to the condemnation of the said Camblets and the vessel.*

Unlike today, a Justice's duties were not confined to the court house. As described in Chapter 4 bad meat had been taken to the door of Mr Justice Quarrill. After making enquiries he *ordered that the Beef seized at the house of Thomas Swan to be burnt near the place the same was seized and [he] directed a Number of Constables to Attend, which they did and the same was burnt.*

Jurors at the Old Bailey

Following the legal principle that Englishmen accused of crimes should be tried by their peers, separate grand and trial juries were appointed for the two superior legal jurisdictions covered by the Old Bailey: the City of London and the County of Middlesex. Fifty potential jurors were summoned by the Sheriff of London to attend the first day of the Guildhall Sessions in the City, out of which seventeen were chosen; after meeting for two days in the Guildhall, the London grand jury moved to the Old Bailey. The Middlesex grand jury was summoned by the Sheriff of Middlesex to sit at Hicks Hall.[10]

Trials at the Old Bailey were held before either the London Jury or the Middlesex Jury. The names of the jurors appear in the Proceedings and can now be found online. The lists of jurors do not provide their addresses so there must be some difficulty in identifying men with common names like John Smith or George Green. So Table 20 is a tentative tabulation:

Table 20   SOME WHITECHAPEL JURORS AT THE OLD BAILEY

NAME	YEAR	OCCUPATION	REFERENCE
Luke Alder	1775	Oilman	f17751018-1
Edward Brewer	1752	Brewer	f17520625-1
William Chapman	1772	Bell Founder	f17431012-1
Rice Davis	1775	Surgeon	f17750426-1
James Exeter	1770	Coach maker	f17751018-1
John Fellows	1774	Distiller	f17740413-1
William Foster	1763	Distiller	f17630223-1
John Long	1747	Sugar refiner	f17470116-1
Thomas Nash	1770	Sugar refiner	f17700221-1
Thomas Pack	1799	Bell Founder	f17990403-1
Jesse Russell	1791	Soap maker	f1791026-48
George Wyatt	1787	Soap maker	f17870221-1

Crime in East London

East London has long been associated in the public mind with a wide variety of criminals from John (Jack) Sheppard, [1702-1724] DNB, born in Stepney and executed at Tyburn, to Jack the Ripper murdering in 1888 and the Kray brothers active in the 20C. However, Dr Shoemaker in a detailed study of crime between c. 1660 and 1725 in London and rural Middlesex concluded:

> "all the west end parishes had higher prosecution rates than those found in the suburban parishes east of the City. Overall, per capita prosecutions in the eastern parishes … were only about one-third those in the western parishes, and indictment rates in the east end were not much higher than those in rural Middlesex."

He also found differences in the types of crime across the city, the eastern parishes having a greater extent of offences against the peace, whilst vice offences were rarely prosecuted. He concluded that the eastern parishes had fewer social tensions than the West End and though the population was increasing the "social composition remained stable and the eastern parishes were more socially homogeneous". Even so, we have shown wide disparities of wealth in Whitechapel, Wapping and Mile End Old Town, which have yet to be taken into account in this type of analysis.[11]

Rag Fair

From the seventeenth century until it was closed down in the beginning of the twentieth century Rag Fair and nearby areas such as Saltpetre Bank and Catharine Wheel Alley had a reputation for disorderly houses and robberies; and frequently appear in the records of the Old Bailey and the Middlesex Sessions. It has also been widely recognised that these were areas where the law officers were reluctant to go, but such considerations did not stop the land tax collectors penetrating into every dark alley. In 1700 the Middlesex Sessions ordered the high constable of the Tower Division to suppress the riotous and awful assemblies taking place around Rosemary Lane in Whitechapel. It was said that the crowds were buying and selling old clothes *and other things greatly suspected to be stolen*.[12]

Rag Fair has been described by Professor Tim Hitchcock as:

> "one of the most disorderly of London districts. It had an unsavoury connection with stolen goods … handkerchiefs and hatbands could be sold at the fair with impunity. The City authorities tried unsuccessfully to suppress it on several occasions. In 1737 the Lord Mayor, Thomas Barnard, proclaimed on behalf of the Common Council, 'in or near Little Tower-Hill, leading towards Rosemary Lane … continues a sort of market or fair for buying and selling of old rags and clothes … the ill got effects of thieves and robbers … this court to use their power and authority to remove this great and dangerous nuisance' …".[13]

Evidently any control was of a short-term nature for again in 1746 the Middlesex Sessions received detailed remonstrance from a Grand Jury sitting in Westminster. The Jury noted that *a great number of tumultuous people did in a riotous manner daily assembled themselves in great numbers, most part strangers and foreigners, as Scotch, Irish, French and many vagrant Jews, as well as English.* Because of the crowds the shopkeepers were forced to close their businesses and so "*greatly suffer in their trade.*[14]

In the latter decades of the C18 Francis Place warned that it was:

> "a dangerous place to be for any decent person to have gone into, he would
> assuredly have been robbed , and the fear of being robbed and otherwise
> ill-used would … prevent most people who knew the place … from venturing
> to go through it."

Drunkenness and fighting were common and amongst this "dirty and disorderly crew there were certainly ragged and homeless boys and girls, sleeping rough and picking pockets. There is some evidence that these children did develop a sense of self-identity, that they did see themselves as the City's Black Guard, with all its traditional and medieval implications of these words."

A local contemporary view of the area can be found in *The Times* on 28th March 1792. At that time a committee led by Francis Burton MP [1744-1832] had brought in a bill multiplying the metropolitan police courts and replacing trading justices by stipendiary magistrates. One aspect of the bill was the proposed location of offices in various parts of London, including Shoreditch and Whitechapel, where the public could quickly find a magistrate.

'W. H.' a ship owner from Wapping wrote to *The Times* regarding *the better regulating of Public Offices*. He argued that magistrates should be located about Tower Hill or East Smithfield. His reasons for recommending this course of action were:

First, in that neighbourhood there are some of the greatest receptacles for thieves of every description (viz) Saltpetre Bank, St Katharine's, Nightingale Lane, Gravel Lane and some parts of Wapping. I live in Wapping, and am in the habit of passing through all those places almost every day, and I know that were it not that a runner may be got in a few minutes, it would not be safe to pass through either of those places in the middle of the day much less at night.

Another reason is that some of the Runners are continually walking about the water-side, or are on the water to stop and apprehend lumpers, bum boat men and others, who make it their practice to plunder ships cargoes. I am myself in the shipping line, and have too often suffered by those plunderers. A short time since I had two ships robbed on one night. I applied to the Runners at the Office, in East Smithfield, and that in the night, three of whom went with me and apprehended the thieves, two of whom were convicted, and I recovered all my property.

Gentleman, I wish you to understand I have nothing to do with Magistrates, their Offices or Runners, And I submit this to the Committee merely for their information. I assure the Hon. Members, that it is the opinion of many respectable inhabitants, as well as myself, that did Mr Burton and the other Hon. Members know (or had they an idea) how much it would injure and leave this part of town open to plunder and riot, they would never think of leaving us without a Public Office or oblige us to go as far as Whitechapel, before we could procure the assistance of the police.

Crime in Whitechapel

One element in the situation was the Bloody Code, which McLynn described as "the product of a mentality that saw the gallows as the only deterrent to serious crime". As an example, if goods or money to the value of forty shillings or more were stolen from a dwelling house it was considered a capital offence. Mark Herber has provided a very readable pictorial history of *Criminal London* from medieval times to 1939, but provided no examples from Whitechapel in the C18; an omission that can be corrected from the Old Bailey online web site and newspapers that provide many examples of the variety of crime that might be encountered.[15]

In 1723 the Custom House officers seized *four bags of Coffee* at the White Hart Inn in Whitechapel together with a waggon and the horses. The coffee had been hidden inside a load of faggots. Horses stolen from farms and houses in Essex would often be brought into Whitechapel, where the Hay Market was an important centre for horse dealers, honest and dishonest. In 1723 an advertisement announced that a brown bay, seven years old of fourteen hands, had been stolen from Mr Thomas Newman's grounds in Barking and asking that any information should be given to Mr Swanson near the Nags Head.[16]

In 1698 a *Fellow was apprehended in Whitechapel who kidnapped or stole three children*. A similar case occurred in 1731 when a woman, who was begging door to door in Whitechapel, came to the home of a throwster, but instead of offering her money he kindly offered her work and took her in. Subsequently, she disappeared carrying away a child of five months. The mother was very distraught, but a few days later the child was found in the arms of a beggar woman, who was taken up and sent to Bridewell.[17]

In 1761 it was reported that a young woman was robbed in the New Road, Whitechapel, by two ruffians who broke her collar bone. She was rescued by *the Press Gang, who rendezvous at the Red Lyon opposite the Whitechapel Market*. Given the hatred usually generated by the Press Gangs this was an unusually generous act in the public interest.[18]

Pilfering from shops, workshops and warehouses was regularly reported across London. The merchants of Whitechapel found themselves as witnesses to thefts of sacks of flour, bushels of wheat and the theft of lead from a gutter at the top of a house. When a theft took place the owner might place an advertisement reporting the loss in the papers or send posters to the pawnbrokers or place them at taverns in the area in the hope that the goods would be recovered. A great deal depended on the honesty of pawnbrokers, those in Rag Fair, being well-known as fences.

Homosexuality

In eighteenth-century London there was the opportunity to engage in a wide variety of sexual practices as described by Dan Cruickshank and Netta Goldsmith, and Whitechapel had a certain reputation in these matters. The *County Journal* in October 1728 recorded that Isaac Milton was fined five Nobles and was ordered to stand in the pillory at Whitechapel Barrs. His crime as recorded in the Old Bailey Proceedings was that *at the Three Nuns in Whitechapel* he had lain with Jonathan Parrey *when the Prisoner would have had him commit Sodomy, but he refused it.* Parrey had first met Milton at Muff's House in Whitechapel and[19]:

> What strenthen'd this Evidence, was the Oath of Mr Willis, who depos'd, That when Parrey gave Information against Muff's House, he mentioned the Prisoner, as one of the filthy Wretches who resorted there to commit sodomitical Practices, and accordingly, when they went to search the House, they found the Prisoner amongst the ludicrous Company.

The Crowd and Crimes

At this time there were no full-time policemen. It was expected that the populace would try to stop a thief, and the streets would echo with cries of *Stop Thief* or *Murder, Murder* or *Watch, Watch*. One witness described how he *ran to hear the Noise, as you know country people do*. There are also examples of young men on horseback chasing thieves up Dog Row towards Bethnal Green, and of a mob of people who had *got a highwayman* in Whitechapel.

In another case, that probably attracted a large crowd, Paul Gotobed stepped out of an alehouse in Red Lion Street in Whitechapel and was knocked down and his pockets rifled. Then his *landlord took a piece of wood and I took the iron poker and we went out; they* [the prisoners, Lovley and others] *were come to the door ... and we were engaged* [in fighting] *for about fifteen minutes ... the watch came quickly to our assistance ... and knocked Lovley down*, who got up, but was *knocked down by a butcher ... this was within Whitechapel Barrs*.[20]

Robbed whilst Drunk

There were many cases of men being robbed whilst *cherry merry*, particularly late at night in Whitechapel High Street, Saltpetre Bank and Rag Fair. Thomas Hallum, a lighterman, in 1746 described at the Old Bailey how he *was coming from Mile End very much in Liquor and I was coming by the place where the prisoners live. They picked me up between ten o'clock and eleven o'clock at night and took me into a house, gave me a drink and asked me to stay the night. In a little time I fell asleep and stayed all night.* As Hallum could not remember what had been stolen the court was not very sympathetic, for it told him *If you have no other evidence you must reap the Fruit of your own Folly for going to such wicked Places.* Typically in such cases, the assailants, often women of low morals, would be found not guilty, as the men were drunk.[21]

Foot Pads

The side streets of Whitechapel were poorly lit, and one solution was to employ link-boys to light the way. They could not always be trusted for a "moon curser" led the unwary right into the path of those who would rob them. Typically in 1721 "Edward Giles and one John Dykes were committed to Newgate by Justice Ward for "several robberies on the Highway about Whitechapel, Stepney Fields and beyond". They were thought to been concerned in a recent robbery of Sir George Caswell, when he was returning from the country. In the robbery his coachman was shot at and wounded in the chin.[22]

Dick Turpin, Highwayman

Reports of coaches being held up on the highway between Aldgate and Stratford occur frequently in the C18, but it is Dick Turpin [1705-1739] DNB who is remembered as a great figure in the popular understanding of the highwaymen. Gillian Spraggs has written "Turpin was a most unpromising candidate for the role of legendary hero". Graham Seal has also dealt with "the legends and the history of certain highwaymen … who have become folk heroes", and Dick Turpin is certainly a leading English example of this genre. "Turpin's career of crime included some unpleasantly violent and distinctly unchivalrous actions against women. But Turpin's folkloric representation in song and story ignores these incidents". James Sharpe is another writer who has explored in great detail the criminal career, trial and execution of Dick Turpin.[23]

Dick Turpin, the son of an Essex innkeeper or farmer; became a butcher and had links to the Gregory gang who were stealing deer from Waltham and Epping Forests. In early 1735 he was living in Whitechapel and embarked on a career of crime, mostly around London, but also in Kent and Surrey. It is clear that at this time he was a member of the Essex gang who were "vicious criminals with no respect for property or for the right of people to enjoy the safety of their own homes" and now planned and executed robberies in and around London.

The Gregory gang with Turpin on 4th February brutally ransacked a house in Edgware. On the 8th February 1735 the Duke of Newcastle, Lord Lieutenant of Middlesex, offered a reward of £50 for information that led to the conviction of the gang. By the 1st March four of the gang had been caught and were all capitally convicted and their hangings scheduled for 10th March. Turpin and other members of the gang were still free and committing crimes. It was now that Turpin turned to highway robbery for which he became famous.

On 15th May 1735 the *Grub Street Journal* reported that *On Saturday night Turpin the butcher was with two men at an ale house in Whitechapel; a countryman, who knew him went secretly to see for a constable, but before he could get one they went off and left half a guinea upon the table in such haste, they could not stay for their change.*

In July, Turpin and Thomas Rowden held up travellers in the area of Barnes Common and robbed a man in Southwark. Gradually their activities were reduced especially after Rowden was caught in July 1736 and eventually transported in 1738 to America. Turpin probably made his way to Holland at the end of 1735 and disappears from public view until he re-appears in London. After the murder of Thomas Morris in Epping Forest in April 1737 Turpin escaped yet again and began to move north, eventually settling in Yorkshire.

In June 1737 a proclamation for Turpin's apprehension was issued with a £200 reward for his capture and it was from this time "that the Turpin legend originates". The legend of Turpin completing the ride to York in one day on Black Bess was an invention of around 1865 "and is a good example of subsequent media romanticisation of Turpin". Turpin made a living as a horse-stealer and dealer in Yorkshire, but was captured and went to the gallows in York on the 7th April 1739 and "died bravely in proper outlaw hero fashion".

Quite why Turpin became such a hero to subsequent generations is difficult to understand, not least because of some of his violent crimes and he was "not known to have been involved in any direct form of social protest or political action."[24]

However, not all encounters with highwaymen led to a complete loss of valuable goods. In September 1732 a Mr Birgin, an eminent wine merchant, was robbed by two highwaymen of his money, and a gold watch. However, he was apparently so keen to retrieve the watch that he said he would pay them more for it than they could obtain from a fence. So a few days later he sent his servant to The Moon in Whitechapel with ten guineas and the villains returned his watch safely.[25]

Local Courts and Prisons

The complexities of the English justice system have been examined in detail by Mark Herber, F. McLynn, J. A. Sharpe, R. B. Shoemaker and the Old Bailey online researchers and others, so we confine ourselves to aspects of the local scene and the range of courts and prisons in the parish.

One local man concerned with the conditions in Whitechapel prison was the Reverend Thomas Bray, [1658-1730] DNB, Minister of St Botolph, Aldgate, from 1708. After a time in Maryland he returned to England and set about amongst other things in procuring a Charter for the Society for the Propagation of the Gospel in Foreign Parts. Of his concerns it was said[26]:

> *To say no more he was a most compassionate Solicitor on Behalf of poor Prisoners, particularly those at Whitechapel and Marshalsea, where the prisoners being very numerous and exposed to great hardships, had for some Years past a plentiful Dinner was provided once a Week at the Expense of several Charitable Persons by the Doctor's Instigation, till the late Act for relieving all the Gaols in the Kingdom set them at Liberty.*

Courts of Pleas of Record and Rotation

One local problem was how to obtain redress for small debts without incurring great costs or the debtor languishing in prison for years and action was finally taken in 1781. An Act of 1781 recited that for *Time out of Mind* there had been a Court Baron in the manor of Stepney and Hackney for settling claims of less than 40 shillings.

Because so many men were away on the high seas, *it was necessary to create a Court of Pleas of Record* in the Manor of Stepney and Hackney. The Court was to be held every Thursday to determine cases before the Steward or his deputy, being a barrister of three years standing. It was recorded that the *present method of proceeding is dilatory and in most cases the Expenses exceeds the Debts to be rendered.*

So after the 1st July 1781 for sums above forty shillings and under £5 the Steward could issue a Summons for a debtor to appear at the Court House in the Whitechapel Road. A list of fees was included in the Act and *For entering every Complaint – One Shilling*, while the Jury were paid two shillings. The attorneys in 1781 included Major Wright from Well Close Square, Richard Cartwright, John Bexwell and Robert Wright.[27]

In 1781 the patentee of the Whitechapel Court obtained an Act reducing fees and limiting the term of imprisonment to one week for every pound of the total debt and costs (which were limited to 15 shillings). There was also in 1780 a Rotation Court in Whitechapel, which received complaints against victuallers and alehouse keepers.[28]

Cages and Prisons

For more serious cases of assault and robbery if a criminal was caught he might be left in the *cage* overnight before being taken before one of the local Justices of the Peace. They dealt with minor crime at quarter sessions and petty sessions; and were responsible for preserving public order, reading the Riot Act, calling in the military and issuing warrants, which were part of the process of initiating a prosecution.

For some crimes the punishment was one of public humiliation and *London Daily Post* mentioned that:

> *Yesterday two men were whipped from Whitechapel Bars to the Man in the Moon*
> *tavern and back again for stealing lead from a silk throwster, their master.*[29]

The choice of the Man in the Moon tavern was not unexpected. Earlier that year a newspaper report described how a Mr Hamerton of Lothbury ordered a coach to follow a man with two horses that he had recognised as being involved in an earlier robbery. The trail led to the Man in the Moon and when they confronted the owner of the horses, an Irishman called Cree, he "pulled out a pistol which he attempted to discharge at the Constable, but was at length secured".[30]

It is well-known that conditions in the prisons of London were very poor. They were also the centre for accusations of murder. The *Daily Journal* in 1730 reported the trial of William Acton, late Deputy Keeper of the Marshalsea Prison, at the Guildford Assizes for the murder of a baker from Whitechapel, *who was a Prisoner of Debt in his custody by overloading him with iron.*[31]

James Neild, [1744-1814] DNB, High Sheriff of the County of Bucks, a noted critic of the prison system at the end of the C18 wrote two comprehensive books on prisons and debtors. He notes that the prison for the liberties and manors of Stepney and Hackney was in Whitechapel and in it were confined those whose debts were above £2, but not exceeding £5.[32]

Neild was treasurer of the Society for the Relief of Persons Imprisoned under Small Debts, and was fully aware of the costs and hardships involved in such cases. He showed that in some courts the costs of a case could double the original debt as there was no pressure on an attorney to proceed quickly, and frequently a debtor could remain in prison for a year or more. He thus favoured the system he found in Whitechapel, whereby the length of time of imprisonment was fixed on the basis of one week in prison for every pound of the total debt and costs, and the latter could not exceed fifteen shillings in every suit. Neild showed that before the passing of an Act there had been thirty or forty prisoners in Whitechapel, but afterwards this dropped to three or four, a reflection of the time limits imposed on sentences.

The prison consisted of a two-storey building, with four rooms facing the road. The rooms were quite small being only 15 ft by 13 ft and 8 ft high. If a debtor wanted to sleep in one of these rooms he had to pay the Keeper, one shilling for the first night and sixpence for subsequent nights, a ready system for increasing his debt. Behind the building was a courtyard, 40ft by 20ft, in which was a small men's day room, and it was here that slept those who could not afford to be inside. From the courtyard a wooden staircase led up to a gallery in which were two sleeping rooms.

The gaoler, John Simpson, was a Sheriff's Officer and received no salary and no allowances.

Writing in about 1800 Malcolm referred to "A handsome new building, the Court of Requests for the Tower Hamlets, and in Court Street stands the Court House of the Manor of Stepney, to which is attached a prison for debtors under £5". Late in the C18 the Whitechapel Public Office was established following the Police Bill of the 1790s.[33]

Bankruptcy and Debtors

There is an extensive literature on the impact of crime on the residents of London. It is equally clear that the possibility of bankruptcy would involve a greater change in one's living conditions than being robbed of a few guineas and some silver buckles late at night in the High Street; or having soap, coffee and malt stolen in small quantities from a house or workshop.

Goods were always stolen in small quantities because there was a limit to how much a thief could carry without arising suspicion from the crowds and constables.

Dr Innes comments on the concentration "of prisoners for debt in the metropolis owed much to the special characteristics of the institutions operating there", which was not unexpected given the intensity of commercial activity in the metropolis. Dr Hoppit has examined the risks and failures in English business in his 1987 book and observed that in the early C18 the metropolis provided over half of all the nation's bankrupts; by the end of the century, about a third. Charles Dickens in *David Copperfield* has explored the impact of bankruptcy based on his family's experience.[34]

Dr Schwarz has analysed in detail the "long–run trends in the development of the capital's economy" and published a graph showing bankruptcies in London between 1710 and 1797. There were periods of high bankruptcies in 1726, "as well as periods with relatively high levels of bankruptcy during the early 1740s, the mid 1750s, the early and late 1770s". These reflect the fact that during the C18 incipient trade cycles "were so frequently interrupted by the outbreak of war as to be much more difficult to discern, while the national economy was less integrated".[35]

Chapter 5 provides further information on the vagaries of trade, especially amongst the sugar refiners, but the bell founders and soap makers also suffered from changing market forces. There was also, though difficult to demonstrate, incompetent management that sometimes led to bankruptcy.

The Bankrupts

Eighteenth-century newspapers regularly listed the men and women from all sections of society who had become bankrupt.

Sir George Colebrooke, Lord of the Manor of Stepney and Hackney, was bankrupted in 1773. He was a well-known financier, MP for Arundel between 1754 and 1774, Chairman of the EICo between 1769 and 1771, and a noted art collector. He had a house in fashionable Arlington Street, near to that of Sir Robert Walpole. After his bankruptcy he retired to France and lived there until 1786. In 1782 it was necessary to sell his undivided thirty-sixth share in the Mount Nesbitt Plantation in Grenada and "the third part of the negroes, stock and cattle". Also in the sale was a *moiety of £12,600 secured by mortgages in Antigua.*[36]

Less exalted in society was John Thorpe, a distiller and chapman of Whitechapel, who was listed bankrupt in February 1728. Such lists were, of course, useful for any of their creditors who were not aware of the change in trading conditions; and needed to ensure they were involved in subsequent legal proceedings.[37]

Whilst war and financial crashes were major causes of bankruptcies there were other reasons. One possible cause of bankruptcy is found in the comment by the appraisers of Henry Cooley, a member of the Merchant Taylors' Company, and described as a watchmaker near Whitechapel Church, who had a house with a rent of £15 in the High Street. It was noted that[38]:

> *The deceased's Books of Accounts were kept in a very irregular manner and the*
> *accounts therein are very much perplexed and confused so the appraisers were*
> *unable to state the amount of the debts.*

John Young, a tallow chandler in Whitechapel, was declared a bankrupt in 1759, and the procedures to be followed had been laid down by Parliament. At a meeting at the Guildhall the creditors, who had proved their debts of £10 and upwards, chose George Swanston, a butcher from Aldgate, and Phineas Pateshall, a tallow chandler from Fenchurch Street, as his 'Assignees'. His Assignees were instructed to *with all convenient speed [to] use their utmost means and endeavours to recover and get in the said debts and sums of money hereby assigned.*

John Young appears to have recovered from the bankruptcy for he was noted as a supplier to London Hospital, in 1762 and 1764. He was far from being the only bankrupt in Whitechapel as the frequent references in newspapers clearly demonstrate.[39] Other men and trades affected by bankruptcy included Thomas Sparrow and Edward Pary, brewers, William Peele a silkman late of London, and John Gardner, corn chandler.[40]

In 1720 a case was reported, which revealed one of the hazards of standing a bond on behalf of a friend or business associate. A Captain Silk, pewterer of Whitechapel, was bound for the greater part of a £1,600 debt to the Crown for custom dues on behalf of a Mr Penny, a tobacco merchant. When Penny defaulted on his debt, £136,000 in today's money, the unfortunate Silk was confined to Newgate for five or six years. It was said that Mr Penny had now returned from France and had compounded with the government for £1,200. Silk was due to be released in a day or two, but what he would say to Penny was not recorded.[41]

Debtors and Petitions

The *Evening Post* for 11th April 1723 contains a list of debtors in the prison in the Maze in Southwark, which identifies a dozen men and women from Whitechapel and Stepney. The list demonstrates the wide range of occupations from which this group was drawn.

> Edward Angell, a yeoman from Whitechapel
> Frances Colnett, a spinster from Whitechapel
> James Francis, a weaver from Whitechapel
> Thomas Hands, a brazier from Wapping
> William Miller, a turner in Black Horse Yard, Whitechapel
> Mary Valentine, a wool comber from Whitechapel
> John Witham, a glazier from Whitechapel

The *London Evening Post* in January 1729 noted a petition from the inhabitants of Wapping, Ratcliff and Whitechapel requesting "that the decision of all Debts up to or under 40 shillings may be determined by Justices of the Peace and so save the expense of going to law".

From June 1712 the *London Gazette* contains details of the application by numerous prisoners in Whitechapel Prison, who had petitioned one of the Justices of the Poor, *to bring them to a General Quarter Session at Hick's Hall to be discharged pursuant to an Act lately passed for the relief of insolvent debtors.*

Conclusions

This Chapter has demonstrated that the aspect of the legal system that had the greatest impact on those paying rent of £10 per year or more was the threat of bankruptcy.

Daniel Defoe in *The Complete English Tradesman* had much to say on the financial problems of tradesmen in the early 18C and had a Chapter entitled *Of the Tradesman in distress, and becoming Bankrupt*. He wrote:

"*The tradesman that buys warily, always pay surely, and every young beginner ought to buy cautiously; if he has money to pay, he never fear goods to be had; the merchants' warehouses are always open, and he may supply himself upon all occasions, as he wants, and as his customers call.*"

Equally, "*A tradesman ought to consider and measure well the extent of his own strength; his stock of money and credit, is properly his beginning for credit is stock as well as money. He that takes too much credit is really in as much danger as he that gives too much credit*".

He concluded "*Nor did you hear of so many commissions of bankrupt every week in the Gazette, as is now the case; in a word, whether you take the lower sort of tradesman, or the higher, where there were twenty that failed in those days, I believe I speak within compass if I say that five hundred turn insolvent now; it is, as I said above, an age of pleasure, and as the wise man said long ago, 'He that loves pleasure shall be a poor man', so it is now in an age of luxurious and expensive living.*"[42]

With regard to personal safety it is clear that many of the houses had shutters, padlocks and guard dogs, and that the residents took care to close windows and trap-doors leading to cellars, and that at least one set of night watchmen was armed. Many houses had servants, not all of whom could be trusted. The evidence is that cries for help were often heard and reacted to, and the crowds also played a part in controlling crime.

Finally, it should be noted that out of over 15,000 "ten pound" taxpayers and their families living in Whitechapel, Wapping and Mile End Old Town, only half a dozen appeared in the dock at the Old Bailey in thirty years - far more served in the Middlesex Jury. This may be due to gross under-recording of crime or it may reflect the particular conditions in the eastern parishes in the middle of the C18. More likely it is yet another confirmation of the concept of a *criminal class*, who lived in the rookeries, and certainly did not pay taxes.

So street-wise residents would avoid walking through Whitechapel late at night when under the influence of drink; this is shown by how few decent women were assaulted at night. More difficult to prevent was the theft of animals from the fields around the area and petty pilfering in shops and manufactories.

It appears that with sensible precautions about the security of their houses and shops, their choice of servants, and the avoidance of late-night travel, many families could lead a relatively stress-free life in these eastern parishes.

FURTHER READING

A. Ash. & J. E. Day	*Immortal Turpin: the history of England's most notorious highwayman*, 1948
D. Barlow	*Dick Turpin and the Gregory Gang*, 1973
J. Beattie	*Crime and the Courts in England, 1660-1800*, 1986
D. Cruickshank	*The Secret History of Georgian London, How the Wages of Sin Shaped the Capital*, 2009
Daniel Defoe	*The Complete English Tradesman*, 1726, 1987
N. M. Goldsmith	*The Worst of Crimes: Homosexuality and the Law in Eighteenth-century London*, 1998
A. G. Griffiths	*The chronicles of Newgate*, 1884, 1987
P. Haining	*The English Highwayman*, 1991
D. Hay, et al	*Albion's Fatal Tree: Crime and Society in Eighteenth-Century England*, 1975
M. Herber	*Criminal London: A Pictorial History from Medieval Times to 1939*, 2002
J. Hoppit	*Risk and Failure in English Business, 1700-1800*, 1987
F. McLynn	*Crime and Punishment in Eighteenth-Century England*, 1991
J. Neild	*State of Prisons in England, Scotland and Wales, extending to various places therein assigned not for Debtors only, but for felons also, and other criminal offenders*, 1812
G. J. Prenderghast	Stand and Delivery, *Ancestors*, March 2006, pp. 35-40
E. A. Reynolds	*Before the Bobbies: The Night Watch and Police Reform in Metropolitan London, 1720-1830*, 1998
L. D. Schwarz	*London in the age of industrialisation: entrepreneurs, labour force and living conditions, 1700-1850*, 1993
G. Seal	*The Outlaw Legend, A cultural Tradition in Britain, America and Australia*, 1996
J. A. Sharpe	*Crime in Early Modern England, 1550-1750*, 1999
J. A. Sharpe	*Dick Turpin:The myth of the English Highwayman*, 2004
W. J. Shelton	*English Hunger and Industrial Disputes: A study of social conflict during the first decade of George III's reign*, 1973
R. B. Shoemaker	*Prosecution and Punishment, Petty crime and the law in London and rural Middlesex, c. 1660-1725*, 1991
G. Spraggs	*Outlaws and Highwaymen: The Cult of the Robber in England from the Middle Ages to the Nineteenth Century*, 2001
M. Waller	*1700, Scenes from London Life*, 2000
B. and S. Webb	*The Parish and the County*, 1906

Web Sites

http://www.exclassics.com/newgate/ngintro.htm	Newgate Calendar
http://www.oldbaileyonline.org	Old Bailey Online
http://www.justis.ac.uk	Acts of Parliament
http://www.londonlives.org/static/Project	London Lives 1690 to 1800, Crime, Poverty, Social Policy

12.   THE TOWER HAMLETS MILITIA

Introduction

In addition to my own research the background to this Chapter relies on the studies of the late Professor John Western and the latest book of Professor Malcolm Wanklyn, but to date no one has apparently studied the Tower Hamlets Militia in detail.

For the residents of Whitechapel and surrounding areas the militia was the source of opportunities, threats and entertainment.

- Opportunities, particular for the wealthier merchants, who aspired to be officers in the militia or suppliers of arms, bread, meat, hay, straw and uniforms.

- A threat to those able-bodied men, who were liable to be called up by ballot, but could not afford to pay for a substitute.

- Entertainment for the *flaneurs* because the parades and exercises of the Tower Militia with colours flying might involve nearly 2,000 horses with accompanying drums and trumpets.

It may also have provided feelings of local pride given that the Tower Hamlets regiment played an important role in the Civil War in 1644; and that the two regiments of the Tower Militia established in 1647 came under the control of the Constable of the Tower of London.

As Dr. Western observed "Many civilians seem to have been fascinated by the spectacle of the military. The movement of the army attracted much interest, and its camps were regularly visited".[1]

To understand the militia it is necessary to realise that in the eighteenth century (C18) the defence of the realm relied on the Royal Navy, a small standing army and the militia; and each came with a range of political, financial and strategic problems.

Figure 13   THE WHITECHAPEL MILITIA

The naval problem for politicians was that it might take four years or more between the ordering of a first-rate warship and its arrival into service. Such a long lead-time did not fit easily into the short-term strategic and financial considerations of governments. Equally, the navy had problems in recruiting and retaining seamen.

The problem with the army was that two years after the death in 1658 of Oliver Cromwell the nation "had a deep hatred of military rule and a permanent distrust and loathing of standing armies". Following the Restoration a small standing army was established, but "it was not held in high esteem". Officers bought their commissions, and Colonels were the proprietors of their regiments and Captains were proprietors of their companies.[2]

In addition, a large standing army was perceived to be expensive and undisciplined, especially during times of peace. But perhaps more important was the envy and hostility raised by those who controlled the army and enjoyed greater access to patronage; an important aspect of life in the C18. An even more serious issue was the possibility of army interference in affairs of state.[3]

So the British in the C17 and C18 were very ambivalent about the need for a large, permanent standing army and the role of the militia. Was the militia there to support the army at all times, or might it be used to replace the army in some difficult situations or oppose them if the army became rebellious?[4]

The Origins of the Tower Militia

There was a long-standing tradition, that can be traced back to at least the C13 of citizens, who possessed arms, forming part-time bands to defend their property and resist invaders. "These had a double origin. From the ancient obligation on each man to keep arms according to his social rank had evolved an obligation on all property owners to supply and equip soldiers (or to serve in person) for home defence. At the same time the practice grew up of selecting a proportion of the able-bodied manhood of each county to receive a certain amount of military training for some days each year at the common expense".[5]

There are many examples of the citizens of London setting forth with their arms, pikes and swords in support of the King and government. From the time of Elizabeth I, local defence forces made up of part-time soldiers were known as Trained Bands. As an example, at the time of the Spanish Armada in 1587 "London was organised for defence, with the City's Trained Bands mustered and increased to 10,000 men".[6]

The best-known London based groups of Volunteers were the Honourable Artillery Company [HAC] and the six regiments of the City Militia; but our concern is with the Tower Militia, later known as the Tower Hamlets Militia. Before the Civil War, the Trained Bands of the Tower Hamlets comprised 600 men in several independent companies under the control of the Lieutenant of the Tower. By 1643 the House of Commons had determined that the seven Hamlet companies should be formed into a separate regiment. In September 1643 the Tower Hamlets Trained Bands paraded with 849 muskets and 385 pikes together with seventy officers.[7]

The Tower Militia in the early 1640s consisted of the prestigious Red Trained Band and the Yellow Auxiliaries, and played an important role in the Civil War. In June 1644 they were involved in an operation at Cropredy Bridge, just north of Banbury, as described by Professor Wanklyn:

> "At the end of June [1644] the two armies were manoeuvring for position in the Upper Cherwell valley to the north of the royalist stronghold of Banbury. Sir William Waller sent two parties across the Cherwell, one at Great Bourton to attack the [royalist] rearguard and prevent it returning to Banbury, and the other a mile to the north of Cropredy to stop the main body coming to the rescue. However, according to Lieutenant Colonel Birch, Sir William chose the wrong troops for the job. Instead of employing his own rearguard, made up of his best musketeers supported by horse, he gave the task first to cavalry alone which did not have the requisite fire power. … In reserve were the Tower Hamlets regiment which should have been in the van."

In the resulting mêlée "the royalists captured or killed several hundred foot and took eight artillery pieces". "The Tower Hamlets regiment prevented further disaster. Taking up a position covering the approach to Cropredy bridge, it put up a strong barrage of covering fire, which stopped the royalists in their tracks and permitted what was left of the support group to reach safety. At nightfall on 30th June the royalists marched back towards Banbury."[8]

The origins of the Tower Hamlets Militia can be traced back to the months preceding the outbreak of the second Civil War when London became a prime centre of royalist conspiracy and insurrection. As described by Dr Ian Gentles:[9]

> "On 13 December 1647 an elaborate plot by cavaliers to seize the Tower of London was uncovered. The Earl of Cleveland and Sir Marmaduke Langdale were reported to have enlisted 40 officers, 1,800 horse and a large number of foot to storm the Tower and take it for the king. It was evident that the existing six regiments of Trained Bands in London were inadequate for the defence of the City and the army had to brought in to quell the conspiracy."

> "Security around the Tower was increased by an ordinance constituting a separate committee for the Tower Hamlets militia. The committee members included such pro-army stalwarts as Colonel Robert Tichborne, Maurice Thompson, Martin Noell and Samuel Moyer. Sir Thomas Fairfax, as Constable of the Tower, was given immediate power and command over the Trained Bands and auxiliaries within the said Hamlets".

Two regiments were formed, the Colonels being respectively the Constable and Lieutenant of the Tower; two very important positions with deep historical origins. The post of Constable of the Tower was "one of the oldest in England, dating back to within a few years of the Conquest and has always been one of great honour and dignity".

The Tower Militia was called out a week after Easter Sunday 1648 to attend a large crowd of apprentices that had gathered in Moorfields to challenge the magistrates. The militia was led by the radical Captain Gage, a silk throwster and "tub preacher". As the crowd refused to disperse the militia fired at the apprentices, but were overpowered and the company's colours were seized. Some of the apprentices marched in to Whitechapel, but the main body set off down Fleet Street shouting *now for Prince Charles*.[10]

The Militia Act of August 1651 mentions Tower Hamlets and in March 1659/1660 an Act was passed for *Settling the Militia*, and amongst the men listed was the unusually named Fowlke Wormlayton. Subsequent Acts of Parliament defined how the militia was to be raised, paid and organised. Over the next two hundred years the militia was involved in a wide range of duties including the provision of guards at the Tower and participation in ceremonial duties. It was not until 1686 that a long-standing dispute was resolved over the exact boundaries of the Tower Liberties, which included Well Close Square, and thus defined part of the area from which men could be balloted for the Tower Hamlets Militia.[11]

A problem perceived by the HAC was that at the beginning of the reign of William III in 1689 "the influx of new members rarely came up to expectations. This was particularly the case with regard to the officers of the six Trained Bands of the City and Tower Hamlets, many of whom failed to comply with the ancient custom that they should undergo their military training in the ranks of the Company."[12]

The Militia between 1730 and 1757

The militia was sometimes described as a "decayed and little used force", but the newspapers recorded many examples of parades and drills carried out by various Volunteer Troops in the eastern parishes. In 1728 the Cripplegate Grenadiers applied to Colonel Williamson in the Tower for permission to *March and perform in Exercise at Hackney* and to march through Tower Hamlets beating drums.[13]

The *Daily Advertiser*, 6th September 1731 reported a *fine exercise in arms* by the Grenadiers from Whitechapel, Cripplegate, Southwark and St Clements. The *Daily Courant*, 11th September 1733 reported that four companies of Grenadiers including one from Whitechapel *will perform a fine Exercise at Arms in the Fields under Sir George Whitmore.*

London's militia was often involved on ceremonial occasions and were recorded in the diary of Lt. General Adam Williamson, [1733/4-1798] DNB, Deputy Lieutenant of the Tower. In 1741 the Lord Mayor elect demanded the liberty of being proceeded by the HAC as he made his way to the swearing-in at the Tower. It was thought however that when the procession entered the Tower Hill Ground that *the militia of the Hamlets of the Tower or the Warders were sufficient to guard his Lordship.*

When the procession arrived at the steps to the Court the HAC wheeled to their right and marched through an opening of the militia and drew up behind them stretching into Tower Street. Before leaving, the Lord Mayor inspected the militia; the two regiments making a street for this purpose, but they *should have opened it wider, for the officers had scarce room to drop the spears of their Pikes.*

In more traditional mode, Williamson was proud to accompany Lord Leicester, Constable of the Tower, 1732-37, in his coach to review two regiments of the Militia of Tower Hamlets on Tower Hill. As a military man he was critical of the marching, for *by allowing large gaps to exist between one company and another, the mob was able to break between them.*

In March 1746 the king authorised the raising of a regiment of Volunteers within the precincts of the Tower and more than 10,000 men in ten companies were to form the Gentlemen Volunteers of the Regiment of the Foot raised in Tower Hamlets under the command of Colonel Richard Offarell. The Tower Hamlets Militia has been traced until the 1890s in Bethnal Green; by 1912 they were known as the 1st Division, London Division of the Royal Engineers.[14]

In 1755 John Chamberlayne listed the seventy-four Honourable Deputy Lieutenants of Tower Hamlets, and this included several prominent local merchants:

> Richard Burford, merchant of Wapping
> Sir Samuel Gower, sail cloth maker, Whitechapel
> Sir Joseph Hankey, Alderman, brother-in-law of Sir James Creed
> Edward Lee, apothecary, Mile End Old Town
> Stephen Martin Leake, Garter King of Arms, Mile End Old Town
> Ebenezer Mussell, property developer, Bethnal Green
> Thomas Quarrill, oil and colourman, Whitechapel
> Richard Ricards, glass maker, St George-in-the-East

Samuel Gower also held the probably more active position of Lieutenant Colonel of the First Regiment. Chamberlayne also lists the officers and men of the two regiments of the Tower Hamlets Militia including Lynell Lee, esquire of Ratcliff, who was the Third Captain of the Second Regiment.[15]

Under the 1757 Act the Tower Militia was left with the privilege of a separate lieutenancy under the Constable of the Tower of London rather than under Thomas Pelham-Holles, Duke of Newcastle. He had strenuously opposed the militia bill and possibly thought that if he could not stop the bill then he as Lord Lieutenant of Middlesex could at least ensure that his friends would gain by being nominated officers with the additional benefit of making profits on supply contracts.[16] A typical bureaucratic problem arose in 1760 with the death of George II; for it was realised [probably by the Duke and his friends] that the Constable of the Tower had been granted his position by the late King. The question was raised of whether the Constable still had authority to appoint his Deputy Lieutenant as colonel of the First Regiment? The legal answer was "Yes", which probably upset the Duke of Newcastle and his supporters.

The records for 1763 show that *The Divisions or Districts in the Tower Liberties are ordinarily (regarding the Militia) called Roles or Beats and the Companies are raised out of these Beats, each Captain having his particular Beat.* It was calculated that the Beats of the regiments contained a total of 5,053 men potentially liable to serve. After deducting the men *under arms, paupers* and the *incapable* there remained 3,496 men, whose names would go into the annual ballot. Unfortunately the names of these men appear not to have survived.[17]

A printed form survives from 1749, which is a *summons to appear in the second regiment.* Those summoned could, however, send as a replacement *an able-bodied man, completely equipped, to List and Serve therein, with such Arms as the Law directs, viz. Each man with a Firelock Musket, a Bayonet to fix on the Muzzle, a Cartouche Box, a two-edged sword, half a pound of powder and half a pound of bullets.* The summons to arms might be a beat of drums, or a notice on the church door and the men who responded were instructed to come *clean dressed.*[18]

The Riot Act

The Justices of the Peace could call out the militia when they thought that they and the elected headboroughs and constables were unable to maintain control. Such disorders invoked the reading of the Riot Act, a process associated with much misunderstanding and fear. There had long been a common law offence of riot committed when three or more assembled together to achieve a common purpose by violence or tumult. In the wake of serious rioting following the succession of George I, the Riot Act was passed in June 1715. This Act made it a felony for 12 or more persons riotously to assemble, and not to disperse within an hour if so ordered.[19]

The Act allowed for the militia to be dispatched into areas when riots and major disorders were imminent. One such call on the Militia occurred in July 1736 when:[20]

> *About half an hour after eleven o'clock a Troop of Horse Guards was sent through Whitechapel to Bow to disperse a mob that was gathering near Whitechapel Mount and in the adjoining streets. It was said that the 'Populace, though kept under by the Trained Volunteers, seemed so much incensed against the Irish'.*

A large crowd had assembled in Shoreditch on the 26th July with cries of 'Down with the Irish'. The Riot Act was read on the 27th July. The next day large crowds continued to assemble and were only dispersed when the Tower Hamlets Militia was called out against them. "Melting away through the alleys and courts of the East End, they escaped the soldiers and attacked Irish houses in Whitechapel."[21]

The Jacobite Rebellion, 1745

Stephen Martin Leake, Garter King of Arms, and a resident of MEOT, claimed to have played a major part in the defence of London in 1745; probably because of his position as one of the Honourable Deputy Lieutenants of Tower Hamlets, but as there were over seventy such men it is difficult to find exactly what he precisely achieved.

As Prince Charles and his Highland levies marched towards London, George II raised his standard on Finchley Common and reviewed the Trained Bands and Volunteers. In the City the alarm signal was seven cannons to be fired at intervals of half a minute from the Tower. "On hearing this every officer and soldier of the six regiments of Trained Bands without waiting for the beat of drums ... was to repair, with the usual quantity of powder and ball, to the usual rendezvous of his regiment."[22]

For the Tower Hamlets Militia their nightly post was a theatre. In October 1745 advertisements for performances of *The Massacre of Paris* at *The Late Wells Theatre*, Goodmans Fields, announced that the Concert would be concluded at 9.30pm *the Wells being appointed (after the Entertainment is over) for the main Guard of the Militia of the Tower Hamlets.*[23]

Members of the militia had to take the following oath, demonstrating one of the ways in which the government was attempting to increase opposition to Prince Charles and his followers:[24]

> *I do sincerely promise and swear, that I will be faithful, and bear true Allegiance, to His Majesty King George, So help me God.*

> *I swear, that I do from my heart, abhor, detest, and abjure, as impious and heretical, that Damnable Doctrine and Position, That Princes excommunicated or deprived by the Pope, or any authority of the See of Rome, may be deposed or murther'd by their Subjects, or any other whatsoever.*

> *And I do declare, that no Foreign Prince, Person, Prelate, State or Potentate, hath, or ought to have, any Jurisdiction, Power, Superiority, Pre-eminence, or Authority, Ecclesiastical or Civil, within this Realm, So help me God.*

An indication of how these events were treated in the City was recorded in an address to the King by the Lord Mayor and citizens of London, who were *filled with a just detestation and Abhorrence of this daring and execrable attempt* at a wicked and unnatural rebellion.[25]

The Militia Act of 1757

In the 1750s the memory of the Jacobite Rebellion of 1745-6, together with the threat of invasion by the French, determined Parliament to re-establish the militia as a local defence force. An Act of 1757 passed under the pressure of the Seven Years War, remodelled its organisation and recruiting procedures. A force of 60,000 men was envisaged ... and each County was to take a census of able-bodied men between eighteen and fifty years of age (later reduced to forty-five) and select a portion of them from each parish by drawing lots.[26]

Militia service was for three years, when the procedure was repeated to refill the ranks. Service involved training each Sunday between February and October in the locality; and a few days drill at Whitweek. From 1786 a lengthening list of the men who were exempt included the clergy, dissenting teachers and preachers, apprentices, seafaring men, and Thames watermen. The parish list was affixed to the door of the parish church on the appointed Sunday and the selected men were given seven days notice at their homes to appear for training.[27] It was widely recognised that the militia raised in 1757 had little military training, and in 1760 it was reported that *Several of the old Sergeants who were ordered to instruct the Militia that were first raised having completed them in Exercise are now going to instruct those who are last recruited'*.[28]

The basic elements of training were the manual exercises (i.e. arms drill), the firings and the practice of marching and evolutions – the rapid alteration of a unit's formation from line to column or square and back. These parade-ground movements were then hopefully the basis of the actual motions made on the battlefield. Bernard Cornwell's *Sharpe's Escape* brilliantly describes the movements led by Captain Richard Sharpe during the Bussaco Campaign in Portugal in 1811; when Sharpe was in charge of the light company of the South Essex Regiment fighting the French.

There would also be some target practice, and for the more ambitious there were mock battles and practice in scouting. Although many drill books were published privately it was not until 1792 that there was an official army drill book; each regiment had its own rules. From 1762 the embodied militia received twenty-eight days continuous drill a year. To save money only two-thirds of the force was trained each year from 1786 and this economy was only removed in 1802 by reducing the period of training to twenty-one days.[29]

Whilst there may have been some pride in the association with the Tower of London, this was not reflected in the pay. For "The army rates of pay which applied to the embodied militia did not change for a century after the Revolution. Officers and men alike had normally to pay for their food and lodging." There were a variety of allowances available to the militia to cover clothing, increases in the cost of bread and meat, and forage for the horses that carried tents and the surgeon's medical chest from place to place. But, as revealed later, corrupt officers had many ways of depriving the militiamen of honestly earned allowances.[30]

In the 1790s there was much criticism in parliament at the profits made by colonels, which were not spent on their battalions. It was only from 1781 that the militia was liable even to be regularly mustered by Commissaries of Militia, to ensure that fictitious men were not borne on the books. But when a lieutenant of militia was cashiered for doing this in 1781, Lt. Gen. Parker remarked that the militia did not see this offence in the same light as the army. He pointed out that it was the practice of the militia to draw pay for the full establishment of a corps, however incomplete it was.[31]

The War with the French 1756-1762

The increasing tension between England and its neighbour was revealed in the *Public Advertiser* 24th April 1755 which expressed anxiety when reporting that *last week a small French vessel put into Plymouth Harbour under pretence of Distress but most probably to observe what is doing there*. Britain went to war with the French in May 1756, but it was not until June 1758 that a bill was passed and finance became available for a militia of 32,000 men. When tension with France increased in 1759 William Pitt on the 5th June politely wrote to the Governor of the Tower (and all the Lord Lieutenants) regarding *Intelligence of the Actual Preparations making in the French Ports to invade the Kingdom*. He demanded an exact Return of the actual state and condition of the Militia in the Tower Division. The role of the Tower Hamlets Militia during the war is still uncertain, but was probably confined to guarding the Tower and watching over prisoners.[32]

Militia Societies, 1762-1800

Not many men, especially tradesmen and skilled craftsmen, wanted to spend time with the militia; and this led to the practice of allowing substitutes. If a fine of £10 was paid then the "principal" was automatically appointed to serve again next time. So for the most part the militiamen were neither persons of substance nor joining out of patriotic enthusiasm. It was probably easier to find substitutes locally in parishes like Whitechapel with its larger proportion of the poor than in the West End, but there was another alternative.

One response to the problem of providing substitutes to serve in the militia occurred in 1762 when *A Society of Gentlemen of Great Property* in Surrey set up an insurance scheme. With a fund of £5,000 they inviting premiums of 10s. 6d., that would indemnify the subscriber for three years.[33]

Within London the first initiative appeared in November 1779 when a Militia Society was set up within Westminster. By the 1790s its area of operation had extended to *Persons living within 30 miles of the Bills of Mortality*. A premium of 7s. 6d. ensured that the subscriber *If drawn they will make the oath that they are not worth £500 (as in such is the case* [when] *the parish pays something towards the expense of a substitute*). For a higher premium of 10s. 6d. a subscriber could avoid the problems and cost of attending the Society's offices, which were then at 1 York Street, Covent Garden.[34]

In 1797 the Society was quoting premiums for the Tower Hamlets Militia of 18 shillings and 21 shillings respectively, which were lower than those for the Supplementary Militia.[35]

The Militia between 1760 and 1797

From 1760 onwards the new King George III and his favourite, the Earl of Bute, supported the continuance of the militia thus reversing previous policies. "The increasing wars and revolutions in the last quarter of the C18 led to the nation became more willing to support the militia and the reliance of the government on it steadily increased … increasingly they sought to enlarge the militia and to turn it into something more like an army of reserve, from which the regular troops could be recruited."[36]

The Officers

To qualify as a militia officer it was necessary to meet both property and religious criteria. Legally, militia officers were required to be members of the Church of England, but Catholics and Dissenters are to be found as officers. The property qualifications of militia officers were laid down as follows for *Cities with their own Lieutenancy*:

Table 21   QUALIFICATIONS FOR MILITIA OFFICERS IN 1757

POSITION	POSSESSOR OF LAND WORTH £	POSSESSOR OF PERSONAL ESTATE WORTH £
Field Officers	300	5,000
Captain	150	2,500
Lieutenant	50	750
Ensign	50	750

Many men in Whitechapel and surrounding areas qualified to be militia officers, as shown below.

The Tower Hamlets Militia Bill 1797

In December 1796 the House of Commons began discussion of the Tower Hamlets Militia Bill, which received the Royal Assent in June 1797; by which Act *1,120 Men were to be raised in the Hamlets*. They were to be formed into two regiments; one *to remain within the Hamlet for the Defence and Preservation thereof*, and the other *to be put under the command of such General Officer as the King should appoint … and could go beyond twelve miles from the Tower of London*.[37]

On 25th February 1797 the *London Chronicle* listed the men who had received commissions in the Tower Hamlets Militia [THM]. What military experience the following local dignitaries had is uncertain:

> Joseph Merceron [c. 1764-1839] DNB, the notorious trading justice from Bethnal Green, who in 1797 was appointed a Captain of the Second Regiment.

> William Clapperson, Captain, 1797 Second Regiment, Tower Hamlets Militia. He had been a Raines School Steward between 1781 and 1784.

> Major Wright, an Ensign in 1997, Lieutenant in 1798 Second Regiment, who resigned in October 1800.

Major Wright had begun his career in Whitechapel and became the leading attorney in Wapping (Major being his forename). He prospered greatly for, as his 1818 will reveals, he was then living in Wanstead and also had property in Sandgate, Kent, and Upton Place, Essex. The originally surprising discovery that his executor was the corrupt Joseph Merceron, can now be explained by their membership of the THM.[38]

In April 1797 Elijah Goff junior was commissioned as a Captain in the Tower Hamlets Provisional Cavalry. Goff was a surveyor who in 1796 worked for the Merchant Taylors' Company. He was the son of Elijah Goff, a prominent coal merchant who lived in St George-in-the-East.[39]

It was not long before the THM were receiving the attention of the press. In 1797 it was noted that *The Military Gentleman who behaved indecorously at Vauxhall Gardens on Saturday evening did not belong to the East India Volunteers but to the THM*. This produced a reply from Alexander Tuack, a captain in the First Regiment, writing from Haggerstone Castle, south of Berwick-upon-Tweed. He stated that he was a member of the THM at the Vauxhall Gardens on the night in question with a young ensign, and earnestly protested that the young man was not capable of behaving in a disorderly manner.[40]

Along with other militia the THM experienced men deserting, and in at least two cases this resulted in press coverage. William Sagger with other deserters was hunted down in 1797 by Sergeant Joseph Pearce and Corporal Daniel Webb. Sagger was accused of several highway and footpad robberies and shots were fired during his arrest in Cow Cross Gate.[41]

For John Clarke, a private in the First Regiment, the punishment for desertion was 1,000 lashes: the first 525 being administered in Hackney. The *Oracle*, 8th January 1798 sententiously proclaimed he was *A young man, well-known about town in a class of life, which depressing him of character, occasioned the severity of the sentence*. Whether he received the full punishment is uncertain.

Promotions and announcements re officers can be found on the *London Gazette* web site and short details of their parades, meetings with the King and dinners, often appeared in the Newspapers.

In May 1798 the Duke of York and several General Officers reviewed the two Regiments of the Tower Hamlets Militia in the London Fields, Hackney Road, at which the THM *went through their evolutions with the greatest exactness*.[42]

In June 1799 Captain William Brodie and Major Matthew Smith of the THM were introduced to the King, another event which indicated the social standing of the THM at Court.[43]

The colours of both Regiments were blessed in services at St Mary, Whitechapel; it was also stated that the Second Regiment attended the divine service every Sunday. There was also time for social events. Colonel Mark Beaufoy, of the First Regiment, in November 1798 *gave an excellent Dinner to the Corps ... at the Freemasons Tavern, the Entertainment was marked by Loyalty, good humour and festivity*. Beaufoy [1764-1827] DNB, an astronomer and physicist, had been taught by and was a good friend of William Bayly [1737-1810] DNB, who had been an astronomer on Cook's third voyage.[44]

In 1798 a great honour was bestowed on the Tower Hamlets Militia when General Vernon confirmed that in future they were to be known as the Royal Regiment of Militia. In 1799 Thomas Rowlandson recorded in fine detail and colour the *Loyal Volunteers of London and surrounding areas*. His splendidly illustrated book provides brief details of the foundation and the officers in each Regiment. In London's eastern parishes the majority of these Militia consisted of a company with between 70 and 90 privates led by a captain and sometimes a lieutenant. The following were established:

Mile End Volunteers	First Company, Captain John Liptrap
	Second Company, Captain Tompson
Poplar and Blackwall	Commander, John Perry (2)
Ratcliff	Captain, Joseph Brown
Tower Ward Association	Commandant, Lt. Colonel William Curtis
	First Captain, Thomas Dawson
	Second Captain, George Mackenzie

For the defence of Wapping, St George-in-the-East and Shadwell the Union Volunteers were formed in 1798 under the Presidency of Peter Mellish esquire. Their Commandant was his brother William Mellish. They met at the Dundee Lodge in Wapping, the centre for local freemasons.

For the defence of St Mary Whitechapel there were two companies:[45]

First Company	Captain, Carsten Rhode
Second Company	Captain, Matthew Craven

Britain and France at War, 1793-1815

As tension between Great Britain and France increased and war was declared in February 1793; the Deputy Lieutenants of the Tower met the appointed officers of the respective regiments to discuss the situation. A further meeting in May 1794 recognising the *State of Affairs rendered it expedient for the Security of the Metropolis to increase the Militia Force ... and to raise Volunteer Companies within the Hamlets*. It was estimated that it would cost £4,000 to raise three companies.[46]

It was at the end of 1796 that the government embarked on a much more ambitious programme to treble the size of the militia. The quota for Middlesex was raised to 5,830 and in the eastern parishes the following local militia was formed.[47]

Table 22   REGULAR MILITIA

MILITIA	DATES	TNA
East London	1796-1820	WO 13/1353-70
1st East Middlesex	1780-1876	WO 13/1419-44
1st Tower Hamlets	1797-1876	WO 13/2143-68
2nd Tower Hamlets	1797-1876	WO 13/2169-93

Table 23   SUPPLEMENTARY MILITIA

MILITIA	DATES	TNA
East London	1805-1814	WO.13/2525
East Middlesex	1799-1816	WO.13/2528
1st Tower Hamlets	1805-1815	WO.13/2561
2nd Tower Hamlets	1805-1816	WO.13/2562

The lists of men discharged from the local militia indicate that they were born in places as distant as Scotland, Tipperary, Durham and Somerset; which possibly reflects both the diversity of the local community and the need to find any substitutes prepared to accept such onerous positions. One advantage of serving in these Volunteer Corps and armed associations was that it carried exemption from militia service. It is also clear that an army life appealed to some men such as James Tuffnell. He enlisted in 1778 and served in the 17th, 60th, 41st and 84th Foot Regiments before being discharged aged fifty after 32 years of service. He subsequently became a Chelsea pensioner.[48]

Voluntary Subscriptions

National excitement grew following France's declaration of war on 7th March 1793, but there was the usual problem of raising finance. Much later on the 26th January 1798 the Bank of England announced that it had opened Books at the Chief Cashier's Office for the collection of Voluntary Subscriptions as a "Contribution to the Prosecution of the War". In February 1798 the Committee of Merchants, Bankers, Traders and other inhabitants of the Metropolis also announced that books were open at the Mansion House for the collection of Voluntary Subscriptions.[49]

By the 17th February 1798 over £80,000 [over £2,500,00 in today's money] had been raised. From Whitechapel, John and Joseph Coope, and John Coope junior, of Osborne Street, together with William Watson at 32 Burr Street, had each given £100. John Coope senior was a member of the Salters' Company and a director of the Phoenix Fire Office. Also contributing to the fund were "The Field Officers, Captains, Subaltern Officers. Non-commissioned officers, drummers and privates of the First Regiment Tower Hamlets Militia" who raised £100. Later that year Admiral Nelson defeated the French fleet at the Battle of the Nile, which was a cause for great national celebration.[50]

The Irish Problem

Given the large numbers of Irishmen working for the coal merchants along the Thames in Wapping and Ratcliff there is an interesting link between the Tower Hamlets Militia and the problems the British government faced in Ireland in the late C18. These problems were many and varied and were exacerbated by the excitement generated by both the American War of Independence and the French Revolution. During 1785 and 1786 there had been much trouble in Munster, which was only put down by the employment of a large force. One problem for the British commanders in Ireland was that the four regiments quartered in Ireland, had become known as "The Irish Horse" and "were absolutely useless and untrustworthy".[51]

The problem after February 1793 was the threat of a French invasion of Ireland – a possibility compounded because of the well-known trade for many years established between Irish ports and the French. In the same month it was decided to call out another 19,000 additional militiamen, but the majority of men were poorly regarded substitutes. In the north of Ireland the Society of United Irishmen, founded by Theobald Wolfe Tone (1763-1798) DNB was pressing for parliamentary reform. Then in 1795 the Orange Society was created following a fight in Armagh between the "Defenders" and the "Peep-of-Day-Boys".

By 1796 the government felt it necessary to pass several Acts of Insurrection to cope with the state of anarchy in Ireland. From June onwards the government was sending thousand of militiamen to Ireland. On 15th June a royal message informed the Commons that the officers and men of certain militia regiments had offered to serve in Ireland and asked for legislation to make this possible for a limited time.[52]

In December 1797 Napoleon arrived in Paris and in May 1798 the rebellion "which had been for so long been simmering in Ireland broke out at last into flames." In June 1798 it was again necessary to call upon the English Militia to volunteer for duty in Ireland and an Act was passed that enabled them and other Militia to carry out this duty.[53]

On the 22 August 1798 the French landed at Lillale Bay in County Mayo and for a couple of weeks battled with the British army before surrendering on 9th September.[54]

The Second Regiment of the Tower Hamlets Militia had been serving in Ireland for an initial tour of six months from June 1798. In January 1799, Henry Dundas, the Secretary of State for War, writing from Downing Street, politely enquired if the regiment would continue to serve there. He then exerted additional pressure by stating that *the safety of Ireland might be very much exposed if any part of this valuable force should be withdrawn.*[55]

We have yet to discover the role of the Second Regiment of the Tower Hamlets Militia in Ireland.

The Militia between 1799 and 1807

The numbers required for the militia were raised in 1796 to a theoretical total of over 100,000, but after a drastic reduction in 1799-1801 the militia in Great Britain was fixed in 1802 at 51,489, of which 9,000 were in Scotland.

For September 1802 we have a statement concerning the status of the Tower Hamlets Volunteers.

Table 24   TOWER HAMLETS VOLUNTEERS

VOLUNTEERS	SERJEANT SPEARS	MUSQUETS
Mile End	16	300
Whitechapel	18	500
Shadwell & Wapping	-	500
Limehouse	9	239
St George-in-the-East	-	300
Ratcliff	16	300
Shoreditch	18	400
Bromley	6	180
Poplar and Blackwall	10	260
Totals	93	2379

A Spear in this context refers to a pike that was only of ceremonial use by this time.

A letter from Downing Street in August 1803 to the Constable of the Tower confirms that the clothing allowance for a man was twenty shillings, and this sum had to last three years. The per diem for exercising twenty days a year was just one shilling a day, which doesn't sound very attractive.

In 1805 we have an example of cooperation between the local militia when members of the Hackney Association lent horses, drivers, carts, wagons and coaches to the Tower Hamlets Militia. "These men and materials were made available to them in the event of an invasion by the French".[56]

In 1807 the Loyal Whitechapel Infantry was commanded by Lt. Colonel William Hardy who lived at 89 Cheapside. In that year they carried out 26 days of Exercise and 26 days of Permanent Duty.

The Loyal Whitechapel Infantry at this time consisted of the following companies:

Grenadiers	Captain Henderson's Company
Rifle	Captain James Wilcox's Company
Light Infantry	Captain Evitt's Company
First Battalion	Captain John Wildman's Company
Second Battalion	Captain Richard Dames's Company
Third Battalion	Captain John Smith's Company
Fourth Battalion	Captain Edward Maxfield's Company
Fifth Battalion	Captain Gabriel Hesse's Company

Courts Martial

The Tower Hamlets Militia was not without its problems as revealed by a series of courts martial between 1800 and 1813.

In October 1800 Thomas Hartley, the paymaster of the First Regiment of the THM, was found guilty of receiving illegal gratuities from two of the regiment's suppliers; Thomas Dalby a butcher from Moorfields and William Carter, a baker from Edmonton. It was suggested that the proceeds were due to be given to Lt. Scott the regimental Quarter Master.

In September 1801 Lt. John Stanton, the Second Regiment's surgeon faced a courts martial for neglect of his duties. Amongst the allegations were his failure to have rooms in the regimental hospital white-washed after a period with infectious disease; and failure to provide an "Ointment for the cure of the Itch". There were several other accusations including his acceptance of money from Joshua Howard in Captain Merceron's company and giving him a sickness certificate so that he was discharged. As he was only found guilty of the white-washing failure, he was initially sentenced to three months without pay, but this was subsequently reduced to one month after considering the duration of his arrest.

But all was not well for he appeared at a second courts martial at Chelsea in December 1806 "for conduct unbecoming of an officer and a gentleman". Again there were a number of charges including that of receiving £40 that he demanded of James Young in exchange for "providing him with the situation of assistant surgeon together with a commission as an ensign in Royal East London Regiment of Militia". This was a serious charge and Stanton was found guilty and dismissed from the service.

The most serious courts martial involved a large number of accusations made against Colonel Mark Beaufoy of the First Regiment in 1813.

> Recruiting soldiers outside the county in Shropshire, Somerset and elsewhere
> Depriving the recruits for the past 3 years of part of their bounty, due to be paid on enrolment
> Imposing a series of illegal charges on soldiers such as charging them for coach hire on the way to parades and guard duties
> Making illegal deductions from the pay and allowances of the soldiers. Such as 4½d per month for providing pipe-clay and whiting for cleaning, when for part of the time the regimental store could not supply these materials

Beaufoy was accused of allowing the regimental pay sergeants to operate from a public house in Bethnal Green. One unfortunate result was that the soldiers "subsequently engaged in insobriety". One wonders if such practices had grown up under the corrupting influence of Captain Joseph Merceron [c. 1764-1839] DNB, the notorious trading justice from Bethnal Green?

In the event Beaufoy was found not guilty of the majority of the charges and mildly reprimanded for his neglect on other charges and his improper language when addressing his fellow officers. In the event no sentence was passed - the court having received favourable reports and considering his twenty years of service, but he was relieved of his command in 1814.[57]

FURTHER READING

S. Conway	*War, State And Society in Mid-Eighteenth-Century Britain and Ireland*, 2006
B. Cornwell	*Sharpe's Escape*, 2004
J. Fortescue	The Army, *Johnson's England: An account of the Life and Manners of his Age*, ed. A. S. Turberville, 1952, pp. 66-87
I. Gentles	The Struggle for London in the Second Civil War, *The Historical Journal*, 1983, 26, pp. 277-305
J. S. W. Gibson & M. Medlycott	*Militia Lists and Musters, 1757-1876*, 2004
G. Goold Walker	*The Honourable Artillery Company, 1537-1987*, 1986
J. Gregory & J. Stevenson	*Britain in the Eighteenth Century, 1688-1820*, 2007
C. James	*A collection of the charges, opinions and sentences of general courts marshal: as published by authority from, the year 1795 to the present time ..*, 1820
T. Rowlandson	*The Loyal Volunteers of London and the Environs, Infantry and Cavalry and their respective uniforms*, 1799
W. Spences	*Records of the Militia and Volunteer Forces from 1757 to 1945*, 1997
J. Stevenson	*Popular Disturbances in England, 1700-1832*, 1992
A. F. Tytler	*A collection of the charges, opinions and sentences of general courts martial*, 1824 Third edition
M. Wanklyn	*The Warrior Generals: Winning the British Civil Wars, 1642-1652*, 2010
J. R. Western	*The English Militia in the Eighteenth Century: the Story of a Political Issue, 1660-1802*, 1965
A. Williamson	*Diary, 1722-1747*, ed. J. C. Fox 1912
D. Wilson	*The Tower: 1078-1978*, 1978
Lord A. F. Tytler Woodhouselee	*An Essay on Military Law and the practice of courts martial*, 1814
G. J. Younghusband	*A short history of the Tower of London*, 1926

Web Site

http://www.londongazette.org.uk	*London Gazette*
http://www.armymuseum.org.uk	National Army Museum, Ogilby Trust

13. MEDICAL SERVICES AND HOSPITALS

Introduction

It is very clear that in the eighteenth century (C18) "there were certainly plenty of sick people to be cared for. Epidemic diseases, such as smallpox and measles, and endemic ones, such as the ubiquitous 'fever', were part of everyone's experience. Crippling chronic diseases, consumption and rickets for example, were common." Such experiences were to be found across London so Whitechapel was not unique in this matter. The big difference from today was that medical services in London were provided by charitable institutions and individuals with no government assistance.[1]

When considering the need for medical help the residents of Whitechapel had a wide range of options from homespun remedies for colds and fevers, to quacks selling marvellous cures, midwives (male and female), and bone setters; in addition to the professionally trained and locally well-established apothecaries, surgeons, dentists and doctors together with two hospitals. After 1782 the Eastern Dispensary in Leman Street provided free health care to the poor of the adjacent area.

Many wills were made by *poorly*, *weak* and *sick* men and women who quite often recognised the nursing help they had received from family and friends. Sacheverall Dangerfield a *coal meter* left to *My nurse Elizabeth Lewis of Whitechapel, which hath six children, £100 for the Great Care for my wife and likewise myself*. Similarly, but perhaps from a different motive, Nicholas Leonard, vintner, left one shilling to his wife, but all his estate to his housekeeper Ann Cartwright *for her faithful service and tender care of me*.[2]

There were also available numerous pedlars of quack medicines. *The Cephalick and Pulmonick Species, a little of which smoked with Tobacco wonderfully comforts the Brain and Nerves and removes Pain and Noise in the Head ... Apoplexies and Vertigo* was for sale at the Golden Half Moon in Leman Street.[3]

Another quack was Joanna Stephens, who had been awarded by the government £5,000 for her cure of the stone, "when in reality her powders consisted of nothing more than egg shells and garden snails."[4]

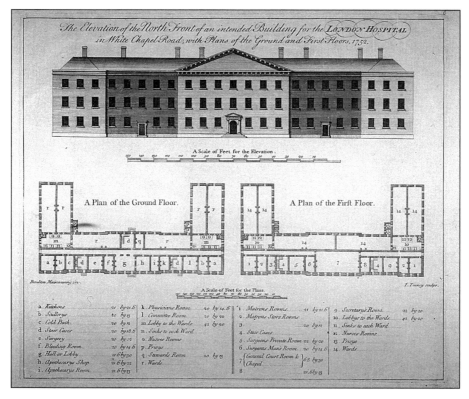

Figure 14   THE LONDON HOSPITAL

The late Professor Roy Porter in his exploration of the role of Quacks in 18th century medicine refers to Mrs Sarah/Sally Mapp, a well-known bone setter from Epsom, who enjoyed a good press and "One set of verses exploits her success to ridicule the regular [medical practitioners]".[5]

> *YOU Surgeons of London, who puzzle your Pates,*
> *To ride in your Coaches and purchase Estates,*
> *Give over for Shame, for your Pride has a Fall,*
> *And Doctress of Epsom has out-done you all*

Her famed skill naturally attracted impersonators and in August 1736:[6]

> *Several Persons who had the Misfortune of Lameness, in different Degrees,*
> *crowded to the White Hart Inn in Whitechapel, on hearing Mrs Mapp, the famous*
> *Bonesetter was there, some of them were admitted to her, and were relieved as they*
> *apprehended; but a Gentleman who happened to come by, declared Mrs Mapp was at*
> *Epsom, and that this must be some Imposter, upon which the Woman thought proper*
> *to move off, to avoid the Insults of the Populace.*

In the *Weekly Journal* for 4th November 1721 an advertisement appeared for *"a Perfect and Speedy Cure for Scurvy,* which *was only to be found at Mr Spooner's next door to the Black Horse Inn, Leman Street at one shilling and sixpence per bottle.*

Accidents and Diseases

The residents of Whitechapel suffered from a variety of accidents and diseases, as did other residents of London. Accidents, which were reported in the newspapers, covered a great range such as:

> Scalded in a malt pan, *Weekly Packet*, 3rd December 1715

> Hit by a wheel of a cart, *Weekly Journal*, 27th August 1720

> Fall from the top of a house, *Weekly Packet,* 3rd September 1720

> Drowned in a tub of water, *British Journal*, 27th August 1726

> Killed by *glasshouse shears falling on him, London Evening Post*, 9th January 1728

> Mr Tidd was seized by a mastiff dog who tore his breast, *Penny London Post*, 3-5 April 1751

> Drowned whilst bathing in a gravel pit in Stepney Fields, *Public Advertiser*, 15th July 1761

> In August 1761 a coach was over-turned by a *quantity of rubbish* in the street.
> *Public Advertiser*, 19th August 1761

The *County Journal* 20th April 1728 recorded that two gentlemen being in liquor and riding full speed up Dog Row *jostled against each other and fell down.* One died on the spot and the other broke his arm.

The *Daily Journal* 16th July 1736 reported that a *Coach with three women in it over-turned near Whitechapel Church by which accident a Woman with Child was delivered of a fine Boy, though she was in a miserable condition, the other women falling upon her.*

A more bizarre accident occurred during the execution of Simon, Lord Lovat, a leader of the Jacobean Rebellion, on Tower Hill in 1745.

Such was the public interest in this execution that thousands gathered on Tower Hill to watch. Indeed 400 or so clambered on to the stage scaffolding in order to get a closer view – something to boast about to your grand children in years to come? Inevitably, the stage collapsed and the newspapers reported between 12 and 15 dead and many injured, and this included Mr Gordon of Prescot Street, who broke a leg.[7]

For more serious illnesses it was useful to know a governor of the London Hospital; for they were allowed one patient in the hospital at a time and had the right to recommend any number on an outpatient basis. Fortunately many local men took advantage of these privileges, and the EICo sent an annual donation in recognition of the services rendered by the hospital to their seamen.

The London dealt with a range of accidents and diseases and Clark-Kennedy details the problems of deciding who should be admitted to the hospital. Those suffering from accidents or acute cases were admitted at all hours of the day or night, but all other patients had to present themselves at one of the weekly committee days, armed with a governor's letter. Children under the age of seven years of age were not admitted unless they had a fracture, needed an amputation or for "cutting of the stone". Mental patients were sent to the Bethlem Hospital.

Amongst the diseases and complaints for which cures were sought were hernias, venereal diseases, smallpox, epilepsy, varicose ulcers, malaria (ague), carbuncles and cysts, dysentery, typhoid and typhus. But it must be remembered that in the 1750s "there were still no anaesthetics, no antiseptics and no vaccinations". Treatments involved blood-letting, purgation, sweating, and cupping, and the supply of quinine. Equally, doctors had few accurate ways of diagnosing the cause of a fever.[8]

Causes of Death

Leonard Schwarz observed that "To reach adulthood in London one needed a large supply of antibodies". As we do not know the exact size of London's population nor the number of deaths it is difficult to estimate death rates, but "It is clear that London's death rates were extremely high in the eighteenth century, particularly in its second quarter." Stephen Inwood quotes the suggestion that the annual mortality rate was between 40 and 45 per 1000 between 1725 and 1750 compared with a national rate of 28 per 1000.[9]

Deaths amongst children were very high and "To judge from the Bills of Mortality, nearly 40% of deaths in London between 1700 and 1750, and about a third thereafter, were due to deaths among children under two years old and fully half of all London burials throughout the century were of children. These heavy losses were not confined to the poor and the gin-sodden".

Many years ago Dr Dorothy George studied the causes of death in London and for 1780 recorded the number of annual deaths from certain diseases according to the London Bills of Mortality. Out of 100,000 living in the ten years ending with 1780 she showed the following:

Apoplexy	55
Asthma	85
Child-bed and miscarriages	47
Consumption [tuberculosis]	1,120
Dropsy	225
Fevers	621
Gout	15
Measles	48
Palsy	17
Small pox	502
Old age	324

However, the Bills of Mortality, which were weekly returns of baptisms and death recorded from the 16th century onwards by the Company of Parish Clerks representing 109 parishes in and near London, were notoriously inaccurate. The Bills probably indicate the range of the causes of death, even if the numbers are unreliable. The classification of disease was also thoroughly unscientific and defective so that convulsions was "a popular catch-all diagnosis which could cover all the early stages of smallpox and perhaps other childhood diseases such as measles".[10]

J. Marshall in 1832 published a monumental examination of the Bills of Mortality and found for diseases of infancy that between 1740 and 1780 seventy-three per cent died from convulsions and nearly twelve per cent from teething. He also recorded the incidence of *Head mould shot, Horse Shoe Head* and *Water in the Head.*

The latest researchers into this topic are Boulton and Schwarz who in 2010 published "Yet another enquiry into the trustworthiness" of the Bills. They concluded:

> "That while they remain tolerably accurate in aggregate, particularly when considered over a number of years, they are liable to be very misleading if particular localities and parishes are considered."

> "Crucially, they are most misleading guides for those who had died in one parish but whose family chose to have them buried in another."

Another well-known problem described by Appelby was that the *searchers* were often old women who would "visit the house of the deceased, view the body, and perhaps discuss the cause of death with relatives or whoever might offer an opinion as to why the person had died."

An example of the short-term variability in the supposed causes of deaths amongst adults in Whitechapel occurred in the 1770s. In 1775, 107 died from *consumption* and 47 from *decline*; whilst in 1780 only six died from *consumption* and 175 died from *decline*. Do these changes represent the true position or merely a change in the views and experience of the *searchers*?

Another recent study, which also scaled the heights of statistical demography, is the work of Dr John Landers in *Death and the Metropolis*. Table 25 provides Landers's examination of the causes of death between 1700 and 1799, also based on the Bills of Mortality.

Table 25   CONTRIBUTION OF CAUSES OF DEATH TO TOTAL BURIALS IN BILLS OF MORTALITY (in percentages)

	1700-24	1725-49	1750-74	1775-99
Consumption	12.6	15.7	19.5	24.5
Fevers	14.9	15.3	13.9	11.3
Infancy	39.2	37.6	35	32.2
Smallpox	7.3	7.8	10	9.3
All other	26.0	26.0	21.6	22.7

Within London for the period 1750-9 Landers placed Whitechapel in the group of parishes with "high mortality" because the burials of children were 4,483 and those of adults 4,939, whilst baptisms were some 2,000 lower at 7,232. What is well-established is that in the mid-1750s the deaths in London greatly exceeded births and that the expectation of life for a child born in London was only about 37 years, due to the high mortality amongst children under the age of five years. However, if a child survived to six or seven years or more it had a reasonable chance of living a long life.[11]

With the proviso that we are not certain of the ability of the *searchers*, who were sent out to record deaths, to correctly identify the cause of death, Tables 26 and 27 record the causes of death for those under one year of age and those who were one, two, three or four years of age in Whitechapel.

Table 26   MAIN CAUSES OF DEATH IN INFANTS UNDER ONE YEAR OF AGE

YEAR	NUMBER OF DEATHS	CONVULSIONS %	SMALLPOX %	TEETH %
1743	123	46.3	5.7	6.5
1760	162	89.5	2.5	0.01
1770	161	77.0	3.7	4.4
1775	133	69.2	19.6	6.8
1780	118	76.3	3.4	3.4

Clearly, as elsewhere in London, "convulsions" were the main cause of death for children under one year of age. It is not yet clear why "convulsions" were so low in 1743 compared with later years. In 1743 fifteen children were stillborn and another six were overlain; higher numbers than in later years.

In 1743 the *searchers* used twenty-one different terms to describe a cause of death. These included seven children who died from *Horse Shoe Head* [Encephalitis], and two who died from *Itch* and *Mortification*; categories dropped in later years. Given the lack of the necessary knowledge needed to identify specific diseases only the numbers for smallpox can be considered reasonably reliable.[12]

Table 27   MAIN CAUSES OF DEATH IN CHILDREN FROM ONE TO FOUR YEARS OF AGE

YEAR	NUMBER OF DEATHS	CONVULSIONS %	SMALLPOX %	TEETH %
1743	69	7.7	37.7	24.1
1760	231	10.4	26.0	48.1
1770	153	11.1	12.4	34.0
1775	115	13.9	55.6	13.9
1780	111	36.0	8.1	8.1

Smallpox

Smallpox was endemic in London and particularly affected immigrant families, who had yet to build up the necessary resistance. It is estimated that in English epidemics between 1721 and 1783 slightly more than one case in six was fatal. For those that survived "Smallpox was loathsome to experience and could be continuingly unpleasant in its after-effects for survivors, in the form of pitting, scarring or impaired vision".[13]

So it is interesting to look at the records for Whitechapel. The results of an examination of the variation in deaths due to smallpox over the period 1743-1812 are presented in Tables 28 and 29; 1743 being the first year that the causes of death were noted in the registers for St. Mary, Whitechapel. The causes of death are not recorded every year so Table 28 represents just a selection and further work is required. The Tables confirm that in Whitechapel smallpox was predominantly a disease of childhood; defined as children under five years of age.

Table 28 demonstrates a peak of deaths from smallpox in 1775. Earlier peaks in smallpox deaths in London had occurred in 1746 and the great epidemic of 1751-53. In 1775 it is noticeable that between January and June fifty-seven children under the age of fifteen years and five adults died from smallpox; higher numbers for this time of year than normal.

Table 28   SMALLPOX DEATHS AMONGST CHILDREN AND ADULTS, 1743-1780 IN WHITECHAPEL

YEAR	Number of Child Smallpox Deaths	Number of Adult Smallpox Deaths	Proportion of Child Smallpox Deaths %
1743	54	9	85.7
1760	89	11	89.0
1765	81	10	89.0
1770	26	3	89.6
1775	90	5	94.7
1780	19	2	89.5

Detailed research is continuing on these excellent registers, but several points may be noted. The ratio of child deaths from smallpox to adults is some 10% lower than Manchester 1769-74 with 99%, but much higher than parishes in rural areas of southern England. The curate recording the deaths in 1743-1744 also noted that 18.8% of the children who died from smallpox were *poor*. We do not know his criteria for making this judgement, but it is noticeable that a number of the children came from the poor and crowded conditions of Salt Petre Bank.

Given the large population of Whitechapel the number of adults dying from smallpox seems very small but perhaps many adults had suffered from smallpox in childhood. Another point of interest is that November 1743 saw the death of five adults from smallpox, the largest monthly total in two years. At present we do not know if these adults were long-time residents of Whitechapel or were recent immigrants from more rural areas.

An important discussion on the history of smallpox in eighteenth-century London will be conducted in *Economic History Review* later in 2011 by leading experts on the subject. Davenport, Schwarz and Boulton have analysed smallpox deaths in the parishes of St Martin-in-the-Fields and St Dunstan Stepney in an attempt to understand changes over the eighteenth century.

Peter Razzell has contributed to the discussion with his analysis of deaths in St Mary, Whitechapel for the periods 1743-8 and 1760-1812 and the importance of inoculation.[14]

Table 29   SMALLPOX MORTALITY IN ST MARY WHITECHAPEL, 1760-1812

PERIOD	NUMBER OF SMALLPOX DEATHS UNDER 10	NUMBER OF BAPTISMS	CHILD MORTALITY RATE FROM SMALLPOX PER 1000 BAPTISMS
1760-69	803	7401	108
1770-79	492	7977	62
1780-89	517	7724	67
1790-99	462	7915	58
1800-09	448	7267	62
1810-12	116	2235	52

The pioneers of inoculation in Britain were Robert Sutton [bap. 1708-1788] DNB and his son Daniel [1735-1819] DNB. Robert opened his first inoculation house in 1757 in Suffolk. Subsequently, his son aggressively developed forty-seven authorized partnerships by 1768 in England, Ireland, Wales and overseas. In 1769 he had inoculation houses in Kensington Gore and Brentford, both far from Whitechapel. In addition his charges of 20, 10 or 5 guineas meant that the service would not have been available to the poor in Whitechapel.[15]

Inevitably, doctors appeared who were prepared to charge more reasonable prices than Daniel Sutton; who boosted his profits by insisting on a preparatory period with a residential regime of diet, purging and exercise before inoculation. In 1770 a Dr Perry of Fleet Street advertised his inoculation service with subscribers paying three guineas with a reduced charge of ten guineas for a party of twelve people. In addition he was willing to inoculate any number of the poor without charge if supported by the recommendations of parish officers as *Objects of Pity.*[16]

But where did young children in Whitechapel get inoculated against smallpox? Some were undoubtedly inoculated by local doctors and nurses, but as yet we have no evidence for this. There were also unqualified practioners some of whom were thought to be gypsies.

The policy of the London Hospital was not to treat children under the age of seven years, and not to admit "Persons suspected of smallpox". Instead they made arrangements with the Smallpox Hospital, established in 1746, "to receive such sick Persons under this Complaint as shall be recommended by this Charity".

The Smallpox Hospital was specifically *for the relief of poor distressed housekeepers, labourers, servants, and strangers, seized with this unhappy distemper, who will here be immediately relieved in the best manner without expense.*[17] The Smallpox Hospital maintained a house for inoculation in Islington and in 1752 opened a new building in Cold Bath Fields on the site of the present-day Kings Cross station. It also had an out-patient service and this may have involved doctors in Whitechapel.

Immunity to Disease

It was accepted in the C18 that illness might affect one family, but not their neighbours; even within a family one person might be immune to common diseases. These patterns of disease have been revealed in the near-by, semi-rural hamlet of MEOT. Living within a few hundred yards of each other were the families of Reuben Harding, a corn dealer, Nathaniel Mines, a poor cordwainer, Dr. Samuel Pye, one of the local doctors, and Captain James Cook. All these families lost young children, but the family of Stephen Martin Leake [1702-73] DNB, the Garter King of Arms, was remarkable in that his wife, six sons and three daughters all lived in MEOT and survived his death. Leake and his children had all been born in or near MEOT and his wife came from a Hertfordshire family. Clearly they came from robust stock.[18]

The wife of Captain James Cook [1728-1779] DNB, Elizabeth nee Batts [1741-1835], lived most of her life in the riverside parishes and then in MEOT from 1765 until about 1786 when she moved to Clapham, south of the river. She lived to the grand age of ninety-four years presumably reflecting her family's long-term inherited resistance to the locally prevalent pathogens and diseases. Similar cases will be found in Whitechapel.[19]

There may also have been individuals living locally like "Typhoid Mary", otherwise Mary Mallon [1869-1938], who was born in county Tyrone in northern Ireland. She moved to the United States in 1884, and subsequently was found to be a healthy carrier of the pathogen associated with typhoid fever. Over the course of her career as a cook in New York she was presumed to have infected some 53 people, three of whom died.[20]

It was not until the 1840s that the reports of William Farr of the General Register Office "cast a great deal of light on urban conditions, consistently pointing to the inescapable conclusion that mortality increased directly in proportion to density of habitation".[21]

Medical Services

Over fifty apothecaries, surgeons and chemists, were to be found in the area with many servicing the local community while others worked in the Royal Navy or in the Merchant Service. A short walk to the east, along the Great Essex Road in MEOT could be found the home and shop first of Joseph Woodward (-1741), then Dr. William Connop (1742-65). Also in MEOT was the home and shop of Dr. Samuel Pye (1732-72), graduate of Glasgow university, and a member of the Royal College of Physicians. Nearby were the homes of Edward Lee, Snr. (1741-56) and Edward Lee, Jnr. (1756-65), both apothecaries and surgeons. By the 1770s there were four druggists and apothecaries in MEOT.[22]

Appendix 9 lists many of the medical practitioners that were working in the area, but must not be regarded as a complete listing; especially as it was only in the 1780s that the newspapers began to contain more information on these men. Most is known about John Harris (1), an eminent apothecary *one of the oldest in the profession with a worth of £10,000*, worth nearly £700,000 in today's money, who died in 1743. In his will he left much property to his son John (2), his daughter Anna Maria and to his grandsons John and Archdall Harris. He also left them *all my shop goods, drugs, medicines, still, utensils and materials belonging to the Art and Mystery of Surgery and Pharmacy and also my pharmacy and laboratory share at Apothecary Hall together with goods and furniture in the surgery*.[23]

At the end of the C18 there was a group of surgeons based around Old Gravel Lane. At the centre of the group was Thomas Hawes, formerly of Old Gravel Lane, but later of Patriot Square in Bethnal Green. He was planning to join the *Benjamin* sailing to West Africa and the West Indies, presumably as part of the slave trade, and appointed his mother as guardian. He owned property in St. George-in-the-East, Bermondsey and Plaistow. The good friends mentioned in his will were George Morgan, surgeon in Ratcliff Highway, and Abraham Toulmin, surgeon in Old Gravel Lane. The will also reveals that he had been widowed with three young children. To his friend George Morgan he left his set of Bell's *Surgery elegantly bound in calf and gilt in seven volumes*; his set of Alblone's *Anatomical Plates* in large folio, Cowper's *Anatomy*, two syringes and pipes, his anatomical preparations, and all his surgical books and instruments that he had with him at sea. William Cowper [1666-1709] surgeon and anatomist, had published his *Anatomy of the Human Body* in 1698, and it had been reprinted several times.

To his friend Captain John Harris (3), captain of the *Benjamin*, which he shipped on from Liverpool; Hawes left his *yellow metal mounted cutlass* and in *the event that I should not have sold it during the voyage* otherwise my *Fusee and Bayonet*. His will contained a long list of silverware including two silver salts, one pair of plated candlesticks, and details of those left to him by his father. Unfortunately for his young family he died only three months after sailing for Africa.[24]

The most distinguished local surgeon was Samuel Jackson, M.R.C.S., FSA, FRS, who lived in St George-in-the-East between 1795 and 1820. He is remembered because of the Jacksonian Prize, the most coveted prize awarded by the Royal College of Surgeons. Samuel Orange was baptised on 20th April 1766 at the Threadneedle Street, French Huguenot church, and was apprenticed to William Blizard, surgeon, in 1782. He changed his name to Jackson in 1793. This may have coincided with his marriage to the daughter of a wealthy ship broker in Wapping, whose name he assumed, but the marriage has not yet been traced. The wealth he gained from this marriage and the rents from the property he owned locally enabled him to free himself from the medical profession. He enlisted in the Second Regiment of the Tower Hamlets militia in 1797, and rose to Lt. Colonel in 1810. In summary he "brought a very gay life to a very usual end".

The *Calendar* of the Royal College of Surgeons states "In the year 1880 [sic 1800] Mr Samuel Jackson, FRS, a Member of the College, announced his intention of giving a sum of £10 annually as a Prize to the Author of the best Dissertation on a practical subject in surgery. In order to make the donation perpetual, he subsequently gave to the College a sum … which he vested in the name of those members of the Court of Assistants under a Deed of Trust, dated 13th April 1806".

Samuel Jackson, was made a Fellow of the Royal Society in November 1798. He was proposed by Buisck Haward; the other signatures were those of important surgeons; William Blizard, and John Abernethy, surgeon at St Bartholomew's Hospital. William Blizard [1743-1835] DNB was accepted at the London soon after it opened. He was appointed as a surgeon at the Magdalen, and a surgeon and governor of the London, which he served for fifty-four years, and was knighted in 1802. It was Blizard that suggested to his former pupil that he should provide the money for the prize.[25]

Josiah Cole, an apothecary living in Whitechapel High Street, was one of the original subscribers to the London Infirmary in 1740. He fitted out the apothecary's shop that the Infirmary bought from Mr Harris of Ayliff Street in 1741.

The Royal London and Magdalen Hospitals

Whitechapel was home to two important hospitals; the London and the Magdalen, both based on the philanthropic ideas developed in the early C18. Each required a great deal of fund raising and attracted the support of many people of the highest quality, including Queen Charlotte and the Duke of Gloucester. In addition there were Lord Mayors of London and many merchants with connections with the East India Company, the Bank of England, the Russia Company, and the Office of Ordnance at the Tower.

The London Hospital

On the 23rd September 1740 seven gentlemen gathered at the Feathers Tavern in Cheapside in the City of London. They were the first subscribers to an "intended new Infirmary", which eventually became the Royal London Hospital in the Whitechapel Road. The minutes of this first meeting confirmed their intention to have weekly meetings to discuss the new infirmary; and their aim was to raise one hundred guineas by their next meeting on the 30th. In seeking subscriptions they were following the pattern established for Guy's, Westminster and St. George's hospitals at the beginning of the C18; but differed in that the man leading the campaign for a new infirmary was the professionally trained John Harrison [1718-1753], who had just gained the freedom of the Barber-Surgeons' Company. Harrison was only twenty-two years old, but became the formative influence on the development of the hospital over the next thirteen years.

The first location for the infirmary was a house in Featherstone Street, north of Moorgate, which accepted its first patients on 3rd November 1740. The search for subscriptions was successful and, in addition to attracting funds from the nobility, there were also subscribers who paid five guineas a year. Within a few months the house in Featherstone Street, which only had thirty beds, was found to be inadequate for the demand, and the hospital moved to a house in Prescot Street in Whitechapel in May 1741. By now the charity was properly constituted and all subscribers paying five guineas a year became "governors"; subscribers of thirty guineas in a lump sum became "life governors". In May 1742 the subscriptions totalled £594 and there were twenty-nine patients in the house and 311 outpatients. As the hospital was clearly meeting a strong demand it became necessary to lease three adjacent houses. In the 1750s in Prescot Street there were no properties with rents of £20 or more and the only large group of buildings was the London Infirmary, which moved there in May 1741. John Harrison was assessed on the rent of £60 on four houses and a lobby in 1750, and "was undoubtedly the moving spirit in its foundation".[26]

One feature of many charities at this time was the annual festival, which featured a sermon preached by some eminent churchman in one of the city churches, a procession through the City led by two beadles in their livery, followed by the president in his coach;, the directors carrying their staves and wearing their badge, and the medical staff. This would be followed by a feast at one of the livery halls in the City. Such a festival might attract over four hundred men and women, who paid four shillings a head, plus gatecrashers, and raised money for the charity. It displayed to others the status and importance of its supporters, and also enabled important policy issues to be raised.

Two related problems at this time were that the demand for the hospital continued to grow, and the houses in Prescot Street were proving expensive to maintain. In his sermon to the annual festival in 1744 the Bishop of Worcester urged the governors to start the process of looking for a site where a new hospital could be built. This task was given to Boulton Mainwaring, the hospital's surveyor, who lived locally in Wapping Street. By June 1748 he had identified a site in the Whitechapel Road, next to the Mount, a remnant of the defences erected around London, at the outbreak of the civil war in 1642. Initially, the governors rejected this site, as perhaps being too expensive. Then they rejected another site in Bethnal Green as "too far from Town for the Physicians and Surgeons"; for the surgeons had their private practices in Harley Street to attend to. Eventually in September 1749 a deal was made with Mr. Worrall, the owner of the site in the Whitechapel Road, who, of course, had in the meantime realised the value of his land and increased his price by £300.

Legal negotiations were very prolonged and it was not until May 1751 that the building committee asked Boulton Mainwaring "to prepare a plan or plans of a Building fit for the reception of two hundred Patients for the present with Proper Offices and with a Reserve to increase that building as circumstances may require". In December 1751 the final plan was approved of a central block with two wings spreading out to the south and capacity for 350 patients. The hospital was to be set back seventy feet from the Whitechapel Road, and it was thought that all the wards would have a southerly aspect, "which in the opinion of the Physicians and surgeons was most desirable for the Patients". Broadly, this is the building, which has been the core of the London to the present day.

There was great excitement at the annual festival in 1752 and considerable amounts of money were raised, but always the court of governors were careful to lay down rules for the correct negotiation of the many building and suppliers' contracts, to avoid charges of favouritism or corruption.

The decision to site such a large building in Whitechapel was a considerable boost to the local economy. The first local men to obtain contracts were John Mann, a carpenter, and Thomas Andrews a builder and the foundations were laid on 11th June 1752. Thomas Andrews can be traced from 1741 until his death in 1785, in the adjoining hamlet of MEOT, where he built and owned a number of houses. It was necessary to suspend the building work during the winter, and also care had to be taken to prevent frost damage. It was also necessary to provide watchmen to prevent the theft of materials.

Completing the Building

Whilst building continued into 1754 there was considerable concern at the expense of continuing to keep patients in the rapidly decaying houses in Prescot Street; and a dropping off in subscriptions, when a further £2,566 was needed to complete the London Hospital. In 1754 the governors, insured the partly-built hospital for £4,000.[27] It was necessary to stop building for a while, but fortunately funds continued to flow in. Building work was resumed in 1756, the first patients being admitted in September 1757. By December 1759 the central block of the hospital was "completely finished", but only the foundations of the two wings had been built.[28]

Hydrotherapy

Captain Richard Johnson at the Royal Bagnio in Leman Street was advertising in 1729 that:

> *At the same Place is the best Cold Bath in London, as can be made appear, by its relieving a greater Number of People (that have been afflicted with various Disorders) than any other Bath in or about London has done, in the same Space of Time, that it hath been in Use.*

This new departure was no mere gimmick. Following the establishment of the London in Prescot Street, "John Harrison was desired to wait on Captain Johnson to ask his Leave to make use of his Cold Bath and, in case of Refusal, to make the best Bargain he could for such of those Patients in the House whose case required such Relief". The London made use of the bagnio's facilities for hydrotherapy until they built baths of their own in 1757. The presumably sunken cold bath was in a small room of only about 20 ft by 12 ft and continued in use until 1824.[29]

John Andree [1697/8-1785] DNB, was the physician at the London, who took the most interest in the advantages of bathing. During his life he was best-known as the physician who extolled the medicinal properties of the alternative water derived from a particular well in the village of West Tilbury, Essex.

His account of the benefits of Tilbury water remained in print for half a century, reflecting its popularity; the water was promoted as a *true specifick* for diarrhoeas and all kind of fluxes and was considered to be *fitted by nature to absorb and correct the acrimonious contents of the stomach and bowels.*[30]

The Tilbury Waters were distributed around London by John Ellison, a Whitechapel druggist and chemist; and also from his warehouse in Pall Mall. Ellison can be traced in the London Directories from 1759 until 1772 and his rent of £50 in Whitechapel indicates a property of some size and status.[31]

Suppliers to the London

Food and Drink

Once the hospital opened there was a need for a wide range of food and drink. As early as June 1754 the London advertised for suppliers of *Good Ox, Beef, Mutton, Grass Lamb, Country Pork and Suet* and for *Good Cambridge Butter, Cheshire, Gloucester and New Cheese and Hog's Lard.* The diet appears to modern eyes to be very green and organic and was, of course, locally resourced.[32]

On the 29th December 1756 a waggon from the Waistfield and Moss brewery in MEOT rumbled down the Mile End Road with six barrels of beer for which they charged forty-eight shillings. The demand for beer at the London was considerable for on the 1st January 1757 there was an order for another five barrels, and again on the 8th, and again on the 12th. Such was the need that Waistfield and Moss supplied 116 barrels between 26th March and 18th June in 1757. Quite whom the beer was for is not clear as the London did not officially open until September 1757; perhaps it was a bribe to keep the workmen on site? Subsequently the main supplier was the more famous John Charrington, who by the 1770s had complete control of the Mile End brewery.

More basic materials were supplied by Henry Bampton & Co, vinegar makers; John Esam supplied oatmeal and bran, Peter Lefevre provided flour, Thomas Lewis a butcher supplied *1,026 stone of meat at two shillings and twopence per stone*, and casks of honey came from Sam Bodington a grocer. Peter Lindsay regularly delivered milk between 1756 and 1761 and charged one shilling and three pence a quart. In 1757 Thomas Hunt, a cheesemonger, provided 280lbs of butter at sixpence per pound. Another prominent supplier was Rawlinson Davison, grocer, who provided sugar, cinnamon, treacle, prunes, sago, nuts, pepper and pimento.

Medical Supplies

Thomas Wrigglesworth supplied in 1758 an *Amputing Saw, Set and cleaned*; and John Adams a cooper in the High Street provided twelve pairs of crutches for nine shillings in 1757. Sylvanius Bevan and Timothy Bevan, both governors, supplied drugs from their shop in Lombard Street, and Charles Lewis charged three shillings *for a parcel of herbs* in addition to *400 Poppy heads* for a modest four shillings.

Soaps and Oils

Thomas and William Quarrill were well-known men in the local community, being Justices of the Peace, and prominent in the Paving Commission. They were also life governors of the London, as well as supplying soap and in 1757 a *bushel of Fullers Earth*. Another oilman Richard Grundy supplied *sweet oil, lamp oil, hard soap* and *Castille soap*, and there was also a need for starch, stone blue and cotton for the lamps.

Bibles and Coffins

For the betterment of their patients it was decided in 1758 to order six Quarto Bibles to be supplied by William Meadows the booksellers. There was also a need in 1759 for William Hamilton and Son, the undertakers in Whitechapel High Street, to supply six large coffins at a cost of £1-4s-0d.

Miscellaneous Services

In the C18 the London Hospital required a great variety of services. From the famous Whitechapel Bell Foundary they purchased *a bell for the front gate* in 1762 for a very precise five shillings and four pence; and from Thomas Lawton came *eight dozen chamber pots*. Messrs Coles and Fenton, smiths, mended the locks in Sarah's Ward; Gilbert Ford a copper smith supplied two warming pans and a tin kettle, and Thomas Sabe provided *two large Kettles with covers* for six shillings. Abraham North in Gracechurch Street supplied mops, brooms and brushes. Robert Phipps an upholsterer *goose feathers to fill pillows*, which suggests more comfort than might have been expected, and Ann Waters coal and charcoal. Joel Johnson from Whitechapel carted sand from Old Ford and Josiah Cannon; a tallow chandler supplied *three dozen candles at five shillings and eight pence a dozen*.[33]

The Governors

In 1774 there were over 1,800 governors; both "life" and "annual" and contributors. They ranged from His Royal Highness, William Duke of Gloucester, who was President, to the Principal Officers of Ordnance in the Tower of London; who presumably had on occasion to send men to the hospital after an accident in their workshops. The East India Company and the Rt. Hon. John Earl of Sandwich, at the Admiralty, were also active supporters of the hospital. Governors and supporters came from all over the south-east of England from Norwich down to Hampshire, west to Bath, and north to Lichfield and North Wales, but the majority were based in and around London.

Many local merchants became governors of the London, partly to display their wealth, but also to take advantage of the privileges. These included the unwritten right to recommend patients for treatment, and then to get them into hospital. This might enable their servants or employees to gain early access to treatment, but could also be used to help out a friend or colleague, with the hope of some reciprocal gift in the future. A number of governors lived in Whitechapel and Well Close Square and Table 30 shows the number of patients they recommended to the London between July 1778 and and January 1784:

**TABLE 30   SOME WHITECHAPEL GOVERNORS OF THE LONDON HOSPITAL
AND THE NUMBER OF RECOMMENDED PATIENTS**

NAME	NOTES	NUMBER
William Blackmore	Surgeon, apothecary. Trustee Raine's School.	25
Robert Bullock	Brewer. TNA PROB 11/1304, 1798	20
William Clarence	Grocer	28
Isaac Colnett	Blacksmith	20
Isaac Lermitte	Tailor. Trustee Raine's School.	21
Samuel Davy Liptrap	Distiller. 1788 Master of Distillers' Company	21
Redbourn Tomkins	Butchers' Company	22

Although we do not fully understand the way in which diseases were described we have as examples the men and women recommended by governors to the London for treatment in January 1791:[34]

> Elijah Goff, recommended Edward Watson, a tailor from Wapping, suffering from *Arthrody*.

> Samuel Liptrap recommended Walter Probart, a labourer from Whitechapel, suffering from catarrh.

> Robert Maden recommended Ann Rines, a servant from Whitechapel, who was *vomiting*.

> Redman Tomkins recommended Peter Taylor, a bricklayer from Whitechapel, with catarrh.

Amongst the local governors were Flower Freeman, esq. from Buckle Street, who was a governor for life in 1774 and elected Chairman in 1777. Other governors included Isaac Lefevre, a distiller, whose successful enterprise at Bromley-by-Bow, led to the creation of the Glyn Mills Bank. He lived on Stepney Green. Another governor in 1788-89 was Samuel Davy Liptrap, a distiller, who lived in the Fitzhugh House in MEOT with a rack rent of £80 and was Chairman of the London Hospital in 1785.

Three prominent local churchmen were also governors; the Rev'd Dr. Herbert Mayo, Rector of St. George, Ratcliff Highway, who lived in Well Close Square; the Rev'd Dr Robert Markham, Rector of Whitechapel, and the Rev'd Dr Ralph Crawley, Rector of St. Dunstan, Stepney. Other local governors were Carston Dirs, Abiall Horne and Crichton-Francis Horne, John Koe, Jens Pedersen, Robert Pell, a Justice of the Peace, Theophilus Pritzler, Major Rhode a sugar refiner, and George Wollf, all of Well Close Square. Another governor was Laurence Sulivan, a prominent governor of the East India Company, who lived for some years in Stepney Green.

The Magdalen Hospital

Introduction

Amongst the many issues of concern raised in the social discussions of the C17 and C18 was the plight of women who had contravened the moral code. In the 1690s the Society for the Reformation of Manners was established and by 1710 there were said to be forty-two such societies in London. This enthusiasm for a stricter moral code diminished with time until the creation by Thomas Coram [c. 1668-1751] DNB in 1739 of the Foundling Hospital; and attention again turned to the plight of single mothers.

Inevitably, as today, there were differences of opinion on why women turned to prostitution. Dingley and Hanway portrayed them as "genteel victims of aristocratic libertinism", while the more practical John Fielding with his experience as a magistrate "asserted the majority of harlots were labouring-class women, driven into whoredom by economic need". Fielding suggested building a public laundry staffed by "Girls of the Poor". A discussion in the *Gentlemen's Magazine* in 1751 made proposals that such women could be helped by placing them in institutions, where they may have a better life and learn some useful skills, such as knitting and spinning.[35]

It was in March 1758 that Robert Dingley, [bpt. 1710-1781] FRS, DNB, a well-known philanthropist, submitted detailed plans in a pamphlet entitled *Proposals for Establishing a Public Place of Reception for Penitent Prostitutes*. His plans covered the *Government, Establishment and the Domestic Oeconomy* of such an institution. They were so quickly supported that within a few weeks he had taken the lease of the Infirmary in Prescot Street, Whitechapel, vacated by the London Hospital, and within three months raised over £3,500.[36]

By June 1758 there had been called a General Meeting of subscribers when a detailed constitution was agreed and within weeks all the staff had been appointed. Quite quickly news of the new institution spread around London and the first six women were admitted in August 1758. The background to these women is not well-known, but in 1759 it was said that *out of one hundred girls in the Infirmary above a seventh part have not yet seen their fifteenth birthday, several are under fourteen years and a third of the whole have been betrayed before that age*. Great emphasis was placed in the constitution on the need to exert the *utmost, Care and Delicacy, Humanity and Tenderness* in caring for the penitents. This was to continue to be their policy for over two-hundred years.

The Infirmary in Prescot Street

Dingley's committee leased for seven years and six months a house on the south side of Goodman's Fields at an annual rent of £48. The house was planned to take fifty women, but such was the demand that by November 1758 they had taken on two adjoining houses and the numbers had expanded to about 130. However, they should have been aware that one of the London's complaints about the house was the high cost of maintenance; and in 1760 they spent £255 on repairs. In addition to the bedrooms and workrooms the Infirmary had a chapel, a brewery and kitchens.

Having over one hundred former prostitutes in one place was bound to excite passers-by; even in an area notorious for its loose women, so one feature of the front of the house was that *to prevent the prying curiosity of the public, there is not only a close gate and a porter but the windows next the street are concealed by wooden blinds sloping from the bottom of each, so as to admit the light only from the top.*

With no funds being made available by the government the success of the Hospital depended on the ability of the governors and committee to continue to attract donations and gifts. In this they were successful and in a single year received over £5,000. The *Book of Wills* between 1757 and 1778 records donations from as far afield as Barbados and India.

A Visit to the Magdalen in 1760

As an indication of the social support for the Magdalen the writer Horace Walpole [1717-1790] DNB described a visit to Prescot Street in 1760.[37]

> "We met at Northumberland House at five, and set out in four coaches; Prince Edward, colonel Brudnell, his groom, Lady Northumberland, Lady Mary Coke, Lady Carlisle, Miss Pelham, Lady Hertford and, Lord Beauchamp, Lord Huntingdon, old Bowman and I. This new convent is beyond Goodman's Fields, and I assure you, would content any Catholic alive. We were received by a vast mob, for princes are not so common at that end of town. Lord Hertford, at the head of the governors with their white staves, met us at the door, and led the Prince directly into the chapel, where, before the altar, was an armchair for him with a blue damask cushion … and a footstool of black cloth with gold nails. The chapel is small and low, but neat, hung with Gothic paper, and tablets of benefactions. At the west end were enclosed the sisterhood, above an hundred and thirty, all in greyish brown stuffs, broad handkerchiefs, and flat straw hats, with a blue ribbon, pulled quite over their faces."

After the service they retired for tea in the refectory where *all the nuns, without their hats were ranged at long tables, ready for supper. … We were shown their work, which is making linen, and bead work and they earn £10 per week.*

Care for the Penitents

In the 1760s once a woman was admitted and clothed she immediately benefited from a much improved diet as follows:

Breakfast	Milk porridge or bread and butter	
Dinner	Sundays:	Roast beef and puddings
	Mondays:	Boiled mutton and greens
	Tuesday:	Mutton broth with rice, herbs, roots and bread
	Wednesday	Roast veal and puddings
	Thursday:	Boiled beef and greens
	Friday:	Beef broth with rice, bread, etc
	Saturday:	Apple puddings till the apples are gone, and then stock or neat's [Ox] feet.
Supper		Bread and cheese

Not surprisingly the famous Captain Jonas Hanway wrote in 1761, that *most of the women in the house grow fat with a diet so much more regular, as well as simpler, than they have been accustomed to.* However, for several years Hanway would not allow the staff and patients to drink tea, so they maintained their own brewery on the premises. Each woman was entitled to 2½ pints of beer per day, but if they worked in the washroom or bakery this was increased to two quarts. It was not until 1770 that Hanway and committee finally agreed that everyone could enjoy tea. The cheese allowance for every one was two ounces per day, but in 1762 Cheshire cheese was replaced by Gloucester as *better for women.*

Walpole had commented on the work of the penitents and in 1760 the hospital raised about £282 by selling that done by the women in *making fine and slop skirts, various sorts of milliners and household linen.* The hope was that by giving the young women new skills they could return to work after a few months or more of the hospital's care and training.

Initially there was no sick ward, but the hospital retained the services of several doctors; such as Dr James Grieve, FRS, [bpt 1703-1763] DNB who had connections with St. Thomas's hospital, and Dr William Saunders [1743-1817] DNB who had a distinguished career at Guy's hospital.[38]

The Infirmary remained in Prescot Street until 1769, when it moved to a new building in St. George's Fields in Southwark, where it continued its work with prostitutes. Later in the twentieth century they worked with young women being assessed before sentencing by magistrates. The success of the hospital can be judged by the fact that probably over 15,000 women had been admitted to the Magdalen before its closure in the 1990s.

The Eastern Dispensary

The late C18 was the period when the dispensary movement grew in London. It had been realised that there was a need for charitable institutions; that would operate in the area between hospitals and the workhouses in providing medical services, especially to the poor. Their supporters emphasised that such services could be delivered more economically than in hospitals. For surgeons and doctors it also provided an alternative career to that of being a staff member in a hospital, where opportunities to join were limited by the long-term stability of hospital staff, who were appointed for life.

A score of such dispensaries opened between 1769 and 1810; half of them being built after 1790 and they mainly catered for the poor. The General Dispensary was opened in 1770 and the Eastern Dispensary in 1782. By 1802 John Feltham wrote enthusiastically about London dispensaries and perhaps with some exaggeration that "About 50,000 persons are supplied with medicine and advice gratis, one third of whom at least are attended in their own habitation".[39]

The principal of the dispensary "was the establishment of a centre at which the poor might attend for advice and free medicine, while those who could not attend were visited in their homes." The area covered by the Eastern Dispensary extended from London Bridge to Limehouse and northwards to include all of Whitechapel and as far as Bishopsgate Street. As a result of their visits the dispensary doctors were said to know a great deal about conditions amongst the poor, and the resulting publications enabled their experiences to be shared with others. One service provided in some homes was that of inoculation against smallpox.[40]

Funding for the Eastern Dispensary came from annual subscribers. Those paying one guinea a year were entitled to have one patient on the medicine list at a time and one lying-in patient in the year. Those paying two guineas had double the number of patients and so on. Those paying ten guineas a year became governors for life. Several officials at the Dispensary came from the local merchant networks as shown in Table 31.

In order to receive medical help a potential patient had to obtain a letter of recommendation from a subscriber. Patients were received between 9 am and 10 am from Monday to Saturday at the dispensary in Alie Street and provided with advice and medicines. Those patients unable to get to Alie Street sent their letters to the dispensary before 10 am and would receive a home visit.

These home visits "introduced a significant group of London physicians to the problems of poverty and disease amongst the city's ordinary people. Unlike hospital or private practice, dispensary service actually took the doctors into the homes of the poor, and they were shocked by what they saw."[41]

Table 31   OFFICIALS OF THE EASTERN DISPENSARY

NAME	POSITION	NOTES
Norrison Coverdale	Steward, 1785	Ship owner and merchant
Sir Thomas Coxhead	Vice-President, 1785	Wapping Timber merchant
Rice Davis		Surgeon, Burr Street, 1791-94, and Little Alie Street, 1796-1811
Robert Haden	Steward, 1785	1770, 1775 Directory, Philip and, Robert Haden cheesemongers, 361 Wapping.
Richard Maddock	Steward, 1785	Maddock family's fine tapered sarcophagus in SE corner of Altab Ali Park [1770-1801] with armorial panel on the west end.
Samuel Wegener	Secretary 1782-88	Wapping attorney and Secretary of Dundee Arms Lodge, 1783
James Wegener	Secretary 1789	
George Wolff	Received subscriptions, 1785	Well Close Square, Norwegian timber merchant
Robert Wright		41 Well Close Square, attorney

One interesting aspect of the relationship between the dispensary and its patients was that if the latter did not write a letter of thanks for the help they had received they were excluded from *the future favour of the charity*.

The *Morning Post* for 11th March 1789 reported that since its founding in 1782 the Eastern Dispensary had treated the following:

10,854 have been admitted

9,665 have been cured and relieved

253 have been discharged for non-attendance

407 have died

529 are now under care

Of the above 2,025 had been attended in their homes and 1,108 women had had children delivered.

As with other major charities of the time the Eastern Dispensary held annual sermons and dinners. The sermons were preached at St John, Wapping in 1784, St Dunstan, Stepney in 1786 and St Paul, Shadwell in 1789; whilst the dinners were at the London Tavern in Bishopsgate. Newspaper advertisements reveal that subscriptions could be received in the City by Sir James Esdaile at Esdaile, Hammett and Esdaile, bankers, and the Treasurer John Wills esq. in Mark Lane, and locally by eminent merchants such as James Shepherd esq of Wapping, a well-known Quaker.

FURTHER READING

A. B. Appelby	Nutrition and Disease: The Case of London, 1550-1750, *Journal of Interdisciplinary History*, vol. VI, I, Summer 1975, pp. 1-22
J. Boulton and J. Schwarz	Yet another enquiry into the trustworthiness of eighteenth-century London Bills of Mortality, *Local Population Studies*, 85, Autumn 2010, pp. 28-45
J. A. I. Champion, ed.	*Epidemic Disease in London*, 1993
A. E. Clark-Kennedy	*The London: A study in the Voluntary Hospital System,* vol. 1, 1740-1840, 1962
H. F. B. Compston	*The Magdalen Hospital: The story of a great charity*, 1917
R. Dingley Doyle	A Georgian Spa in Essex, *Country Life*, 23 October 1969
M. D. George	*London Life in the Eighteenth Century*, 1965
A. Hardy	The medical response to epidemic disease during the long eighteenth century, *Epidemic Disease in London*, J. A. I. Champion ed. 1993
S. Inwood	*A History of London*, 1998
J. Landers	*Death and the Metropolis: Studies in the demographic history of London, 1670-1830*, 1993
R. A. Lewis	*Edwin Chadwick and the public health movement, 1832-54*, 1952
J. Marshall	*Mortality of the Metropolis*, 1832
S. B. P. Pearce	*An ideal in the working: The story of the Magdalen Hospital, 1758–1958*, 1958
R. Porter	*Quacks, Fakers and Charlatans in English Medicine*, 2000
P. Razzell	*The Conquest of Smallpox*, 1997
P. Razzell	*Population and Disease: Transforming English Society, 1550-1850*, 2007
G. F. E. Rudé	*Hanovarian London: 1714-1808*, 1971
L. D. Schwarz	London 1700-1840, *The Cambridge Urban History of Britain, vol. II, 1540-1840*, 2000, pp. 649-655
F. H. W. Sheppard	*London 1808-1870: The Infernal Wen*, 1971
J. R. Smith	*The Speckled Monster: smallpox in England, 1670-1970, with particular reference to Essex*, 1987
D. W. Wright	*Index of London Surgical and Scientific Instrument Makers, 1736-1811*, 1988, Guildhall
D. W. Wright	*Index of London Surgical Practitioners, 1736-1811*, 1988, Guildhall

Web Sites

http://www.bartsandthelondon.nhs.uk
http://www.royalcollegeofphysicians.org.uk

14. CONCLUSIONS

Derek Morris and Ken Cozens

Introduction

With the completion of the first phase of our research on Whitechapel, Wapping and Mile End Old Town, it is now possible to ignore the restrictions imposed by parish boundaries and to begin drawing conclusions about the nature of society in these areas in the eighteenth century. For too long historians have relied on a series of stereotypes with the emphasis on poverty, crime and "dirty industries", to portray these eastern parishes, when in fact the emphasis should be on the important role played by local entrepreneurs in London's growing economy and world-wide trading networks. Our work provides many examples that reinforce Leonard Schwarz's view that "London merchants had a different geography [from the aristocrats in Westminster]: that of the City and the East End".

Our first conclusion is that the methodology outlined in Chapter 1 provides a robust framework for more detailed sectoral studies. The identification in the land tax records of the "ten pound householders"; and the linking of hundreds of these men and women to many other records such as wills, insurance policies and deeds, essentially compensates for the lack of census data before 1841. The value of our approach to urban history was first noted by Professor Michael Port, University of London, who described the *Mile End Old Town* book as presenting "a markedly different picture from that traditional one of East London still presented in a dismissive paragraph even in well-reputed histories".

In the eighteenth century, towns developed in the Midlands and the north of England that benefited from the availability of raw materials such as coal and iron, or had the advantage of fast-flowing streams to provide power to mills and factories. Other towns developed because they were located at the focus of the expanding road and canal systems, or had good access to the sea.

Whitechapel in 1750 in contrast clearly lacked any of these advantages, yet with a population of about 25,000 was double the size of Hull and Sheffield and similar in size to Birmingham, Glasgow and Liverpool. So how did the economy of Whitechapel develop to employ so many workers? The answer lies in the development by entrepreneurs of the service and processing industries along the two major linear transportation features that dominated Whitechapel, Wapping and MEOT.

- The north bank of the Thames which had developed over the years as a major location for businesses linked to the shipping industries and the import and export trades.

- The Great Essex Road, which led from Aldgate east towards Stratford and East Anglia, was the location for industries meeting both the needs of travellers and Londoners' need for hay and the produce of local nursery gardens and more distant farms.

Between these two important centres of economic growth were located the processing industries. These transformed a variety of raw materials into the finished products that were much in demand by Londoners; beer, candles, gin, glass, oils, soap, sugar and textiles. There were also the more specialist suppliers of artificial stone, church bells, clay pipes, guns, ropes and sailcloth.

The four main factors that enabled these industries to flourish were:

- London's growing demand for a wide range of services and products
- The availability of finance to fund the capital needs of industries, especially sugar refining, brewing and shipping
- A succession of men with the energy and managerial skills to take advantage of the growing markets and financial expertise available in the City
- A plentiful supply of labour as men and women moved into London from Essex and East Anglia

In each of London's eastern parishes can be identified men and families who in the eighteenth century were significant in their chosen professions and trades. That family-based business partnerships were an essential part of the fabric of City of London in the eighteenth-century has been explored by writers, such as Dr Peter Earle and Dr Perry Gauci.

Our work on Whitechapel, Wapping and Mile End Old Town shows in greater detail than previously available that many business partnerships existed across London's eastern parishes, and that their trade connections were worldwide.

In Whitechapel and St George-in-the-East were the Scandinavian timber merchants and dozens of sugar-refiners, tallow chandlers, soap and glass manufacturers, and an important distillery. In the High Street were many taverns together with stable keepers catering for travellers and the important Hay Market, together with wholesale butchers and cheesemongers. Wealthy merchants such as Samuel Perry lived in Goodman's Fields, and hundreds of the "middling sort" employed servants and owned carriages and silver.

In Wapping were the important Henley family with major interests in shipping. The Hennikers, celebrated by a town of that name in New Hampshire, were the largest suppliers of timber to the Royal Navy; and the Camden, Calvert and King group traded internationally. Our research has shown for the first time the importance of Wapping to the wealth of London. Because of its unique maritime character it attracted many trades associated with the sea, and in the eighteenth century acted as a major centre for the provisioning of a mighty British maritime nation.

Mile End Old Town, with a smaller population than Whitechapel and Wapping, evolved in a very different manner. In the middle of the eighteenth century it was home for a dominantly "middling sort" of person, many of whom had made their homes and fortunes in the river-side parishes. This hamlet of just a few hundred houses, had seven different functions, and although several of them can be found in other villages around London, the combination is one that further study may show to be unique.

Mile End Old Town was a convenient and attractive centre for merchants involved with shipping and overseas trade to live and work; convenient both for the shipping industries along the Thames and for the insurance and financial services available in the City. Interestingly many of the merchant families were of long-standing locally, such as the Jones, Fitzhughs, Slaters and Winters. It was very popular with directors of the East India Company, such as Laurence Sulivan, and sea captains, such as the Slater family. Later it was the home for David Ricardo, the famous broker and economist, who lived at the New Grove, from about 1803 until 1812, in a house he insured for £3,000.

Mile End Old Town also serviced the passing traffic down the Great Essex Road between London and the towns and ports of East Anglia, and was a centre for brewing and ropemaking, and home for corn merchants, meal men, and corn factors. It was a centre for extensive market gardens and nurseries, and was famous for being the home of James Gordon, the leading nurseryman in London, if not England. For London-based parishes and livery companies it was a suitable area in which to establish almshouses and schools, and for others it was a centre for the education of Dissenting Ministers and for a variety of small schools. Finally, it was a centre for both pleasure and for retirement.

These findings challenge many modern views concerning "suburbs" and the stability of family businesses in the eighteenth century.

It is thus clear that the character and economy in these eastern parishes changed very quickly over distances as small as a few hundred yards. This agrees with the mosaic depiction of London provided by Evans in 1980, but we now have a better understanding of the economic factors that produced this structure.

Local sources of finance

Peter Earle emphasised for the period 1660-1730 "that London's industries offered a very wide variety of opportunities to the middle-class entrepreneur and that the size of the business and their rewards varied accordingly". He also noted that "to get rich you had to start rich or at least comfortably well off". A large starting capital of several hundred pounds was required in many industries. Investment in industry was not to everyone's liking. Henry Bampton a vinegar maker advised his sisters to vest their monies in government securities and "by no means to accept Personal or Land securities for any part of the monies they may be possessed of".[1]

It is now clear from the wills of the wealthier merchants in Whitechapel that they followed the system of "partible inheritance"; a "system whereby all children, or in some cases all sons, received a share of an estate, in contrast to the system of 'primogeniture". Thus in 1749 Robert Wheatle a merchant left £1,000 to all his children at the age of twenty one.[2]

Henry Dodson left £500 to his son for he was *better able to shift in the world than his sister.*[3]

In some cases the father had already advanced or lent money to a son. The wealthy surgeon John Harris (1) left £1,000 of Bank of England stock to his son John *besides the fortune he has already had from me.* Similarly, Thomas Munday lent £800 at 3% to his son, also Thomas.[4]

There are dozens of other examples from which it is clear that funds were available to the sons of Whitechapel merchants that enabled them to set up in business. We have yet to examine where these businesses were established; were they local, in the City, in the provinces or overseas?

The Career Paths

Peter Earle's observations also led us to conclude that it would be of interest to examine the origin of the many men who came into the eastern parishes and played a major part in the development of the local industries. There appear to have been two major career paths.

In the processing industries, young men supported by family and finance came to east London from the provinces. They did not have technical expertise but made up for this with their energy and entrepreneurial skills. Jesse Russell came from Newcastle-under-Lyme and established a major position in London's soap industry. John Charrington came from a Hertfordshire family and was looking "about him for a business, which, while essentially sound, was yet in a state of health uncertain enough to be willing to take a partner who had only a modest sum to invest". From his share in the Waistfield and Moss brewery in MEOT grew a major enterprise that continued brewing locally until 1975.

The sugar industry relied on finance from the City and the expertise of many German refiners and labourers.

One example of a local man who established a fortune in the brewing industry is Benjamin Kenton a victualler. His bequests in 1800 totalled £63,550, equivalent to over £2,000,000 in today's money; and many went to local churches and charity schools, as he was a man of lowly origins. His prominent monument can be found in St Dunstan, Stepney.

To establish oneself in the maritime industries it was necessary to have spent years at sea acquiring skills, knowledge and contacts. Then with some capital it was possible to join one of the local trading groups or join the elite "shipping interest" supplying ships to the East India Company. In adjacent parishes can be found a range of important merchants who followed this career path. In Wapping were the Camden, Calvert and King network, the Hennikers, and the Henleys. Further east in MEOT, Ratcliff and Shadwell there were hundreds of families who for generations had developed strong links with the East India Company such as the Slaters and Larkins.

The Slater family had its origins in Kirkwall, Orkney, and Gilbert Slater (I) arrived in London about 1706 aged twenty years. He forged close connections with the thriving maritime world of East London, which continued over three generations until at least 1793. Gilbert Slater (II) advanced the family fortunes from their grand house just south of St Dunstan, Stepney, from where he also played a role in civic affairs. The third generation of the family moved to Knotts Green, Leyton in Essex, where Gilbert Slater (III) died an extremely wealthy man. This can be gauged from both his lifestyle and the fact that he left his wife an annual income of £1,300. Each of his children was to receive £5,000 upon reaching the age of twenty-one and each daughter was to receive an additional £3,000.

Three generations of the Larkin family served the EICo between 1746 and 1834 as described in Jean Sutton's enthralling book *The East India Company's Maritime Service, 1746-1834*. Like many mariners they originated at one of the coastal ports. William Larkins came from Dover and his family established themselves from 1755 in Poplar. They were but one family from Stepney that benefited from "The customs of the 'hereditary bottom' and the 'perpetual command' which established in effect, a monopoly of the supply of ships and commanders within the Company's overall monopoly."

An example of a young man from the provinces who became prominent in the banking industry is the young William Alers. He had taken the mail coach from Alnwick to London a "raw youth, in my 18th year, with the wide world before me, & utterly ignorant in what part of the world, or in what position in life, my peregrination, then begun would end". His patron was Stephen Hall, a partner in Hankey's bank, who lived in MEOT at the end of the eighteenth century, and took the young William Alers into his house. Alers joined Hankey and Co. in 1790 and became the senior partner in 1830.

The networks

There is increasing realisation of the importance to merchants of both commercial and social networks. Trinity House held an important position with regard to many aspects of the maritime industries; and men throughout the eastern parishes were elected to the prestigious position of Elder Brethren. Social networks were established through families, churches and chapels, livery companies and the Freemason Lodges. Also important were the Royal Society, and the Royal Society of Arts, Manufacture, and Commerce; whose title reveals its orientation towards solving eighteenth-century problems of industry, trade and agriculture. There were also more local groups such as the Spitalfields Mathematical Society.

In the seventeenth century one of the most important networks in Whitechapel revolved around the Meggs family and the rectors of St Mary, Whitechapel. William Meggs (1616-1678), was a wealthy merchant who lived in a large *Mansion House* with fifteen hearths. Meggs financed both the rebuilding of St Mary church and the establishment of Megg's Almshouses. His brother Dr James Meggs DD was rector of Theydon Garner, Essex.[5]

Judith Meggs had married in 1627 Dr. John Johnson, who was Rector of St. Mary, Whitechapel, from 1626 until 1641, and again from 1660 until 1668. Their daughter Mary in turn married Ralph Davenant, who was rector of St Mary between 1669 and 1682, and she was left £120 by William Meggs.

In 1637 William's sister Alice married into the wealthy Goulston family of Barkway, Hertfordshire. The marriage settlement of his nephew William Goulston to Frediswood Morris involved over £13,000. Sir William Goulston's bequests of 1675 led to the establishment of Goulston Street. In addition to property in Whitechapel he owned land in Kent and Norfolk.[6]

Throughout the eastern parishes in the eighteenth century there developed widespread networks of communication between families that often entered into partnerships to develop an enterprise. Recent work has highlighted many previously unconsidered and important linkages on both a local and global scale. There were networks extending to North America, the West Indies, the Levant, Russia, Africa and the Far East. More local networks developed between local wholesale butchers such as the Mellish and Kilbinton families, and hay salesmen dealt with farmers and dealers in Essex, Hertfordshire and Suffolk. There were few contacts with Kent or Surrey. Indeed it would seem that there were more connections between MEOT and the West Indies than with Kent.

Here lies the importance of our studies, which have illustrated how certain influential merchants created a vibrant maritime area with strong connections to the sea, but one also that could trade internationally. Merchants in areas such as Wapping created wealth for the British State through foreign trade, and provided tax revenue that supported a massive and powerful maritime infrastructure.

They also helped finance a lasting British maritime supremacy, one that would allow for the growth of a global British Empire.

Banking and Investments

Whilst a merchant would initially concentrate his financial resources on his main line of business such as brewing or shipping; it was essential at some point to invest more widely to ensure some safety in the rapidly changing markets and political situations of the eighteenth century.

For the "shipping interest" of the East India Company the spreading of risk by investing in a number of ships at the same time was widely practised. As a general merchant's wealth increased he might invest in local property or shipping. Many bought shares in the East India Company and the South Sea Company, or lent money out in mortgages at four or five per cent. For some, investment in the West

India Dock Company in the 1790s provided further opportunities for wealth creation. Merchants with investments in West Indian plantations included Purser Dowers and Robert Wheatle in Whitechapel, Nathaniel Phillips in MEOT, and John and William Camden in Wapping.

There are many examples of successful East London merchants and traders establishing themselves on estates and farms in Essex and surrounding counties but rarely south of the river. This was a process observed especially after 1660 and also noted by Daniel Defoe in the early eighteenth century. The debate on emulation has continued to the present day, with an academic emphasis on the "big bourgeoisie" who purchased landed estates. Our evidence shows that an interest in such investments could be found in men with a wide range of backgrounds who were certainly not members of the "big bourgeoisie".

Daniel Defoe had commented on the propensity of successful businessmen to establish estates in the countryside around towns and cities. Defoe had two concerns: one was that *the rising tradesmen swells into the gentry, and the declining gentry sinks into trade* and that *the declining gentry in the ebb of their fortunes frequently push their sons into trade and they ... often restore the fortunes of their family. Thus tradesmen become gentry and gentlemen becoming tradesmen.*

The wealth created in Stepney, Whitechapel and surrounding parishes in the late-eighteenth century by the brewing, distilling, ship-owning and naval contracts industries led to several merchants becoming involved in the formation of private banks, as a suitable investment route for their profits. Local men such as Sir William Curtis, William Currie, Stephen Hall and Isaac and John Lefevre were leaders in these important commercial developments, as the British economy grew after the 1750s.

Sir William Curtis MP was a successful biscuit baker from Wapping. He was elected Lord Mayor in 1795-6, and established the bank known as Robarts, Curtis, Were, Hornyold, Berwick and Co. with offices in Cornhill.

William Currie [1720-1781] was born at Duns in Berwickshire, but was determined to make his fortune by moving to London. This he achieved by first investing in a distillery in Poplar, and then by marrying Madeline, the daughter of Isaac Lefevre, another successful distillery owner, who lived at 37 Stepney Green from 1764 until after 1793. His move into banking took place in 1773, when Curries and Co., was established. The Currie family were eminent in City banking for many years until the famous Glyn, Mills Bank took them over in 1864. Curries Bank was known by various names as the partners changed, but in 1785 was trading as Lefevre, Curries, James and Yallowby, which reflected the involvement of John Lefevre, a wealthy distiller and banker from Old Ford.

One local and very successful supplier of timber and other services to both the Army and the Navy was John Henniker, from Wapping and then Stratford; whose partnership also included Edward Wheler in 1776 and William Mills, of Glyn, Mills Bank, in 1787. He was a subscriber to government loans and a director of London Assurance and close to the Bank of England. He was thus an important influence in financial circles, through the partnership of Henniker, Devaynes and Wombell, although not a banker himself. Originally goldsmiths, the Hankey bank was established before 1685 and thus was one of the oldest banking houses in the city. A local man involved with the bank was Stephen Hall from MEOT, who joined Hankeys as a partner in 1768.

Urban Developments

Broadly, our research has confirmed the views of Dr Leonard Schwarz and Professors Ball and Sunderland, and challenges the so-called "East-West Model" of London's development.

A traditional model of London is to contrast the West End versus the East End, as described by Power and called by Peter Guillery a "hierarchical construct". In 2001 Ball and Sunderland also challenged this "misleading geographical metaphor" as it "did not make much economic sense". In their view the close proximity of markets and institutions gives cities their economic rationale, but there is also another important element because of the competition for scarce urban resources. These ideas are well shown along Whitechapel High Street with its service industries and in Wapping in which a narrow strip of land immediately adjacent to the Thames was the location for a large number of "middling order" merchants. The decisions involved in locating businesses along these two major lines of transportation deserve further study.

Dr. Leonard Schwarz's analysis of the 1798 assessed taxes showed that in London the middling order with average incomes between £80 and £130, formed 16-21 per cent of London's adult male population. He also noted that the members of tax class III, whose median incomes were a little over £80 a year … spread themselves remarkably evenly across London, forming about a tenth of the population everywhere, irrespective of the wealth or poverty of their parish. In the Tower Division householders of class III formed 31% of all those householders liable to pay assessed taxes.

This valuable snapshot of London in 1798 leaves unanswered the question of whether this pattern can be traced earlier in the eighteenth century. We also need to know how long a middling-order family stayed in London's eastern parishes, before moving to Hampstead or Chelsea or their estates in the home counties.

We have been able to identify the men and women of the "middling order" in the sixty years before 1798 by using the land tax, lists of housekeepers and many other archives. These were the people who provided the energy and finance that ensured development of the local economy of Whitechapel and Wapping. They also filled the many posts appointed by the Vestry; churchwardens and overseers of the poor, and served as Justices of the Peace and collectors of tax. Their philanthropic activities supported a wide range of charities both in England and Scandinavia.

It is possible to identify many families that retained their connections in the area for fifty years or more.

In Wapping the family of Michael Henley were active from before 1770 until about 1830 before purchasing an estate at Waterperry House near Oxford. In St George-in-the-East, the Pell family of surgeons and attorneys can be traced locally from the 1730s to the 1780s. The most successful member of this family was Sir Albert Pell, who was called to the bar in 1795, and in 1831 became a Judge of the Bankruptcy Court.

In Whitechapel the Liptrap family ran their distillery from 1767 until 1789. In MEOT the family of Thomas Fitzhugh, with close connections to the East India Company, can be traced from as early as 1714 until 1849, by which time they were established on their estate near Wrexham in Denbighshire. Clearly, the families that invested in the economy of eighteenth-century Whitechapel found it convenient, and indeed necessary, to live close to their shops and factories. The more successful families then purchased or leased small estates in Essex and Hertfordshire; mainly as havens away from the smoke of London but also to indicate their wealth and status. We have so far traced over 300 such estates.

Our work also agrees with the ideas of Professor Doreen Massey and others that developed the view "that cities are essentially open, mobile, mixed places". But such broad theories appear to have little capacity to predict the role of any specific part of a city and its surroundings, hence the need for detailed local studies.

The Future

We are well aware that our research has not covered all aspects of life in these eastern parishes. Partly this is because of lack of surviving archives, partly a matter of time and partly our emphasis on looking at subjects which have been neglected by earlier researchers. We have yet to fully explore the archives of the freemasons and the private water companies. Women are mentioned throughout our books but we have yet to focus on their education, their contribution to the success of their husbands or their contribution to maintaining social networks. Nor have we examined Dr Leonara's Davidoff perception, based on studies of Essex, Suffolk and Birmingham, that towards the end of the eighteenth century that women were central to a new pattern of family life that was developing. We also need to explore the careers of the men who had the technical expertise essential to the processing industries. Were they local men from families with a tradition of working in these industries?

An outstanding problem is to examine the evolution of the eastern parishes after 1800. Truman attempted to describe the transformation of the area before the arrival of the railways in 1830s and the "eternal slums" of Victorian times.

There is now an urgent need to update Truman's work and to explore the transition of the area from the eighteenth to the nineteenth century.

The future of local history in the state-funded academy has been examined by George and Yanina Sheeran of Bradford University. What is clear is that it is only through detailed studies of London's eastern parishes that their complex nature has been revealed and many traditional stereotypes have been challenged. It is now essential that future generations are inspired to continue research of the fascinating maritime and industrial history of London's eastern parishes in a more inter-disciplinary way, and are encouraged to exchange and publish their findings.

Increasing use is being made of the internet[7] but it must be realised that it will be many years before the insurance records before 1775 and the Middlesex Deeds Registers from 1709 to 1938 will be online. There is a need for greater spirit of co-operation among historical researchers, whether it be those working on local or family history, or professionals such as museum curators and academics with responsibility to raise awareness of a need for the digital archiving of more localized history archives. Whitechapel, Mile End Old Town, Wapping and other London riverside parishes provided wealth and opportunity for a great British maritime and trading nation. Let us not forget this fascinating heritage.

FURTHER READING

M. Ball and D. Sunderland	*An Economic History of London, 1800-1904*, 2001
M. Beerbühl, and J. Vögele	*Spinning the Commercial web: international trade, merchants and commercial cities, c. 1640-1939*, 2004
P. J. Corfield	*The Impact of English Towns, 1700-1800*, 1989
L. Davidoff and C. Hall	*Family Fortunes: Men and women of the English Middle class, 1780-1850*, 1987, 2002
N. Draper	The City of London and slavery: evidence from the first dock companies, 1795-1800, *Economic History Review*, 61, 2, 2008 pp. 432-466
P. Earle	*The Making of the English Middle Class: Business, society and family life in London, 1660-1730,* 1989
P. Gauci	*Emporium of the World: The Merchants of London 1660-1800*, 2007
M. Haunton	Discovering Archives: what's on the web?, *Local History News*, no. 100, Summer 2011 pp. 8-10
M. Hilton and J. Sheffrin	*Educating the Child in Enlightenment Britain*, 2009
H. Horwitz	'The mess of the middle class' revisited: the case of the 'big bourgeoisie' of Augustan London, *Continuity and Change*, II 1987, pp 263-96
E. Jones	London in the early Seventeenth Century: An Ecological Approach, *The London Journal*, vol. 6, No. 2, 1980
G. McGilvary	*Guardian of the East India Company; The Life of Laurence Sulivan*, 2006
D. Morris	*Mile End Old Town, 1740-1780; a Social History of an Early Modern London Suburb,* 2007
D. Morris and K. Cozens	*Wapping 1600-1800, A social history of an Early Modern London Maritime Suburb,* 2009
D. Morris	A Critical Review of London's Eastern suburbs in the Eighteenth-Century, First Annual London Studies Conference, July 2011
M. Port	*Newsletter* no. 58, London Topographical Society, May 2004
M. J. Power	The East and West in early modern London, *Wealth and power in Tudor England*, ed. I. W. Ives and others, 1978, pp. 167-185
L. D. Schwarz	Social class and social geography: the middle classes in London at the end of the eighteenth century, *The Eighteenth-Century Town: A reader in English Urban History, 1680-1820*, 1990, ed. P. Borsay
L. D. Schwarz	*London in the Age of Industrialisation: entrepreneurs, labour force and living conditions, 1700-1850*, 1992
L. D. Schwarz	London 1700-1840, *The Cambridge Urban History of Britain, vol. II, 1540-1840*, 2000
G. & Y. Sheeran	Opinion: 'No longer the 1948 show' – local history in the 21st century, *The Local Historian*, vol. 39, 4, November 2009, pp. 314-323
L. A. G. Strong	*A brewer's progress, 1757-1957, A survey of Charrington's brewery*, 1957
J. Sutton	*The East India Company's Maritime Service, 1746-1834: Masters of the Eastern Seas,* 2010
C. S. Truman	*Mile End Green: its romance and history: famous residents and their association with historic events*, East London History Group, 1968
J. White	*London in the Eighteenth Century: A Great and Monstrous Thing*, tbp 2012

Acknowledgements

My first great debt is to the many dedicated archivists, who have managed to preserve many thousands of documents for such a long period of time.

My second great debt is to those modern archivists, historians, librarians and friends who have encouraged my studies, suggested new lines of research and generally urged me to get on with writing. In particular Ken Cozens, Greenwich Maritime Institute, University of Greenwich, for constant advice and help on London's merchant networks and the use of the Internet.

Alison Botterill for constant help on a variety of questions, and with Fiona Duxbury and David Woodruff, Librarian, Strict Baptist Historical Society, for sharing their research on Stephen Williams and the Strict Baptists, Graham Davies, Lyme Regis Museum Research Team for information on Baptists in Lyme Regis. Dr Kathleen Chater for valuable assistance on the Sierra Leone project. Stan Cook for assistance with gunmakers. Michael Elliston for help with the streets of Whitechapel over the past 300 years. Stephen Freeth, Jeremy Smith, Howard Doble, Richard Wiltshire, Charlie Turpie and their staff at Guildhall Library and LMA. Georgina Green for help with the records of Essex and particularly Valentine House, Ilford, Mr. Peter Guillery, English Heritage, and Dr Andrew Wareham, British Academy Hearth Tax Project, Roehampton University, for their advice on the Hearth Tax. James Gunn for help with the Henry Mayo and his family, Malcolm Barr Hamilton, Christopher Lloyd and Sally Jacobs of the Tower Hamlets Local History Library, Alan Hughes, Whitechapel Bell Foundry Ltd, Dr. Margaret Makepeace, Lead Curator, East India Company Records, British Library, Bryan Mawer for help with sugarbakers, Michael Noble for sharing his knowledge of glass makers, Michael Readman for sharing his deep knowledge of the Hermitage and Delft ware, Derek Stimpson of the Gunmakers' Company for advice on the Proof House and gunmaking. Cliff Thornton, President of the Captain Cook Society, R. Warren for help re the sugar industry, Brian Hardyman for sharing his research on the Russell-Watts family, Dr Perry Gauci, Lincoln College Oxford University, Professor Derek Keene, Dr Matthew Davies, Dr Jim Galloway, Dr Mark Latham and Olwen Myhill at the Centre for Metropolitan History, the contributors to the seminar on Metropolitan History, and Mr. Richard Palmer, all of the University of London, Dr. L. Schwarz, University of Birmingham, Dr Elizabeth McKellar of the Open University, Professor Peter Razzell for sharing his deep knowledge of smallpox in eighteenth-century London, Ms Susan Snell, Archivist and Records Manager, Library and Museum of Freemasonry, London, Dr. Elizabeth Williamson, Executive Editor and Ms J. Davies of the VCH.

I am very grateful for the support and critical views of David Ayres, Sonia Ayres, Alison Botterill, Stephen Freeth, former Keeper of Manuscripts, Guildhall, London, Ian Hemmin, Dr Eileen Henderson, Madeline Morris, Charles O'Brien of the Pevsner Guides, Richard Palmer and Dr Michael Scott. Dr Richard Morris supplied valuable IT expertise.

Front cover by W. H. Pyne from The Graham Watson Collection, Emmanuel College, Cambridge, reproduced by courtesy of The Master and Fellows of Emmanuel College, Cambridge. Figure I was reproduced from *A History of the County of Middlesex*, Volume XI, (Oxford University Press, 1998) page 4, by permission of the Executive Editor. Figures 2, 3, 4, 5, 6, 7, 8, 9, 10, 11, 12, 13, 14 are copyright the Guildhall Library, City of London. The back cover reproduced by permission of the Guildhall Art Gallery.

Permission to quote from my articles in their publications has been given by The East London History Society, The East of London Family History Society, the London Topographical Society and the Society of Genealogists. Permission to quote from their archives and publications has been given by Aviva Group Archive, AXA Insurance UK plc, Essex County Council Heritage Services, Guildhall Library, London, Hertfordshire Archives and Local Studies, London Metropolitan Archive, Norfolk Archives, Royal and Sun Insurance Group plc, Tower Hamlets Local History Library. The lists of members of Lodges are copyright and reproduced by permission of the United Grand Lodge of England. Permission has been granted by the Worshipful Company of Distillers' Company for the use of their records. Every effort has been made to establish contact with the copyright holders and I welcome up to date information on any I have failed so far to find.

Finally, my grateful thanks to Philip Mernick, Chairman, East London History Society, and to our friends who shared an interest in Whitechapel: Michael Elliston, Jean Haynes, Colm Kerrigan, Tom Ridge, Tony Saint and Isobel Watson, and for long term support and to the many correspondents worldwide who freely shared the results of their own research.

GLOSSARY

Many of the terms used in this book have more detailed descriptions in David Hey's *The Oxford Companion to Local and Family History*, 2010.

Where available the definition is taken from Dr. Samuel Johnson's *Dictionary of the English Language*, using the 1843 edition of the 1756 abridgement. For definitions of London streets, buildings and institutions see the *London Encyclopaedia*, ed. B. Weinreb and C. Hibbert, 1995 and *The London Encyclopaedia*, John and Julia Keay, 2008.

admission	The act of admitting to some position, standing or privilege
Assistants	Senior posts in a livery company
bagnio	A house for bathing, sweating, and otherwise cleansing the body
Baumé	Specific gravity scale
The Bloody Code	The name traditionally given to the English system of criminal law during the period 1688-1815, when a huge number of felonies punished by death were added to the statute book
cage	A small prison cell in Watch House, the village lock-up
Calvinists	Followers of the French theologian John Calvin died 1564
camelet	Dr Johnson A stuff originally made of silk and camel's hair but now of with wool and silk
cartouche	A cartridge belt
carroon	Small open carriage
chaldron	Dr. Johnson *A dry English measure of coals, consisting of thirty-six bushels heaped up, according to the sealed bushel kept at the Guildhall.* Across England a chaldron varied from 32 to 36 bushels.
Cholic	The intensely bitter tonic and stomachic root of the star grass, *Aletris fariocosa*
city of London	The entire built up area of London
City of London	The area controlled by the City of London Corporation, formerly the Corporation of London
clysters	See enemas
cordwainer	Dr. Johnson *a shoemaker*. From Cordovan*: cordwain* - goat-skin leather originally from Cordova in Spain
Corporation of London	From the 3rd January 2006 known as the City of London Corporation
counting house	Dr. Johnson *The room appropriated to books and accounts*
Court of Assistants	An official body in a livery company
Dates Old Style	The calendar was reformed in 1752
	All dates before 1752 are given in the Old Style, though in the text the year is taken to have begun on 1 January, e.g. the 23 February 1750 (OS) is shown as 23 February 1751
Dates New Style	From medieval times until 1752 the New Year was held to begin on Lady Day, 25 March. England moved to the New Style in 1752 with the New Year beginning on 1 January.
deal	Dr. Johnson, *Firwood, or the wood of pines*
Devonshire House	Quaker Meeting House in London
Elder Brethren	The Trinity House of Deptford Strond had 30 Elder Brethren
embodied	A term describing a militia regiment embodied within the regular army
enemas	Liquid preparations, often water and soap, or oil, which were injected into the rectum through a syringe
Fencibles	A traditional Scottish term for regiments raised by noblemen
fire engine	(i) Dr. Johnson, *A machine for extinguishing accidental fires by a stream or jet of water*
	(ii) In the 18th century also the name given to an engine powered by steam
Freemen of a livery company	
	Dr. Johnson *One partaking of rights, privileges, communities*
	A Freeman was entitled to practice his trade within the City of London
fustian	Thick twilled cotton cloth
Goodman's Fields	An area in the south of the parish of Whitechapel developed in the early eighteenth century, except for an open rectangular area known as the Tenter Ground. Lies between the Minories and Leman Street
Guildhall	The centre of civic government for the City of London
Hand-in-Hand	Fire and Life Insurance Company established in 1696
headborough	Unpaid official elected by the vestry; originally a manorial office
Hearth Tax	A tax levied twice a year between 1662 and 1688, TNA E 179
journeymen	In a livery company men who had served an apprenticeship but were not yet free
Lady Day	The 25th March, the official start of the year until 1752
Light infantry	Men intended to fight in irregular formation as skirmishers, especially in rough country
link	A torch carried by a link boy
liveryman	A freeman promoted within a livery company; originally wore the distinctive livery
lumpers	Men who unload ships, stevedores
mace	Dr. Johnson, *A kind of [nutmeg] spice*
manufactory	Dr Johnson "The place where a manufactory is carried on" and "The practice of making any piece of workmanship", a factory or workshop.
Michaelmas	The 29th September, the feast of St. Michael the Archangel, the time when half-yearly rents were due
Middlesex Sessions	The court for the justices of the peace for the county of Middlesex which included Stepney. The sessions had the power to deal with cases of murder, riot, theft, assault, poaching, etc, and also dealt with many administrative matters such as the operation of the Poor Law.
Middling sort	People with incomes of between £60 and £200 pa in the eighteenth century
Noble	A former English gold coin first issued 1351
NADFAS	National Association of Decorative and Fine Arts Societies
organzine silk	The elaborately processed silk thread necessary for the warp
overseer of the poor	An unpaid official elected by the vestry to levy a poor rate and supervise its distribution
Oyer	Dr. Johnson, *A court of oyer and terminer is a judicature where causes are heard and determined.* They dealt with the more serious crimes of murder, treason and rebellion

peck	A measure of capacity for dry goods equal to 2 gallons
Petition	(i) A request or supplication; particularly for a placement in government or a private company
	(ii) Also a request to sessions and local authorities
porter	(i) One who carries burdens for hire
	(ii) A dark brown bitter beer brewed from charred or malted malt
premium	Amount paid for an apprentice to a master typically between £4 for a weaver to over £1000 for a wealthy merchant
Proof house	The house of the Gunmakers' Company in the Commercial Road, where small fire-arms were tested by firing a large charge or by hydraulic pressure
proprietors	In the land tax from 1780 are shown separately from tenants
quaggy	Dr Johnson *boggy; soft; not solid*
rack rents	Dr. Johnson *Rents raised to the maximum.* Occur in land tax registers in 1727 and from 1766
Rag Fair	(i) A market in Rosemary Lane, Whitechapel
	(ii) Also used to describe a notorious area for thieves and corrupt pawnbrokers and fences
rod, pole or perch	Measurement of 5 1/2 yards; forty rods equal one furlong, 220 yards
rookery, rookeries	Slum areas in London, e.g. St. Giles off Tottenham Court Road
Searches	Were undertaken by officials from livery companies to look for traders and workmen operating without being free of the appropriate livery company
Sewer rate	A rate paid to Commissioners for Sewers
shrub	A beverage of sweetened fruit juices, sometimes with spirit
slop seller	One who sells ready made clothes
Small beer	Weak beer
specie	Coin as opposed to paper money
Stepney	(i) A large parish in the eastern suburbs of London
	(ii) A small village centred on St. Dunstan's church
Stepney Causeway	A street just south west of St. Dunstan's church, favoured by merchants and mariners
stone	A unit of weight equal to 14lbs (6.35kg)
Supercargo	Dr. Johnson, *An officer in the ship whose business is to manage the trade.*
tenter fields	An area where cloth was stretched and dried
Tithe	The tenth part assigned to the maintenance of the ministry
Trinity House	The Corporation of Trinity House of Deptford Strond. Charter renewed in 1547
two-pair of stairs window	Second floor
undertaker	Dr Johnson *One who engages to build for another at a certain price.*
Vestry	(i) Dr. Johnson, *A parochial assembly, commonly convened in the vestry*
	(ii) A room or part of a church, in which vestments, vessels and records are kept, also used for parochial meetings
wainscotted	Panel work of oak or other wood, used to line the walls of an apartment
warp	The threads stretched lengthwise in a loom to be crossed by the weft
weft	The threads woven across a warp to make fabric
Watch house	Dr. Johnson *A place where the watch is set*
	The building from which the night watch operated from and the forerunner of the police station
writers	(i) A clerk in the service of the East India Company
	(ii) More generally a professional scribe or clerk
Yeoman	(i) A farmer, often owning land
	(ii) Yeoman of the Guard at the Tower of London, In the 18th century the position could be purchased for a sum of £200 or so.

APPENDIX 1

THE STREETS OF WHITECHAPEL AND ADJACENT PARISHES

A to Z of GEORGIAN LONDON J. Rocque, 1747	A to Z of REGENCY LONDON R. Horwood/ W. Faden, 1813	MODERN A to Z
Ayliff Street	Great and Little Ayliff Street	Alie Street/Goodman's Stile
Buckle Street	Duncan Street, Little Buckle Street	
Butcher Row	Butcher Row	Now within St Katherine Dock
Cable Street	Cable Street	Cable Street
Chambers Street	Chambers Street	Chamber Street
Church Lane, Whitechapel	Church Lane	Whitechapel Lane/Gowers Walk
Colchester Street	Colchester Street	Colchester Street
East Smithfield	East Smithfield	East Smithfield
Glasshouse Yard, Goodman's Yard	Glasshouse Yard	
Goodman's Fields	*An open space on map*	Tenter Street, Mark Street, etc
Goodman's Yard	Goodman's Yard	Goodman's Yard
Goulston Square	Goulston Square	Goulston Street
Goulston Street	Goulston Street	Goulston Street
Heydon Yard, Minories	Haydon Yard	
Heydon Square, Minories	Haydon Square	
Whitechapel High Street	High Street	Whitechapel Road
Lambert Street, Ayliff Street	Lambeth Street	Near Gower's Walk
Lemon Street, Ayliff Street	Leman Street	Leman Street/Colchester Street
Mansel Street	Mansel Street	Mansell Street
Minories	Minories	Minories
Petticoat Lane, Whitechapel	Petticoat Lane	Middlesex Street
Plow Street, Whitechapel	Plough Street	Plough Street
Prescot Street, Goodman's Fields	Great Prescott Street	Prescot Street
Red Lion Street, Whitechapel	Red Lion Street	
Rosemary Lane, Minories	Rosemary Lane	Royal Mint Street
Rupert Street, Ayliff Street	Rupert Street	Between Leman Street and Gower's Walk, Royal Bank of Scotland
Saltpetre Bank, East Smithfield	Dock Street	Dock Street
Somerset Street, Whitechapel	Somerset Street	Somerset Street
Well Close Square, Rosemary Lane	Well Close Square	Wellclose Square
Well Street, East Smithfield	Well Street	Ensign Street
White Lion Street	White Lion Street	Leman Street (south)

APPENDIX 2

VOTERS FROM WHITECHAPEL IN 1768

NAME	ADDRESS	NOTES	LIVERY COMPANY	PERSONAL ESTATE £	RENT £
Thomas Ackland			Grocers'		
Moses Adams	Petticoat Lane		Bricklayers		
John Adams	High Street	Cooper	Coopers'	33	25
Edward Akerman	Goodman's Fields		Needlemans'		
Luke Alder	High Street	Oil and colourman	Farriers'	50	30
Henry Aldred			Sadlers'		
Eugene Allen	High Street	SUN	Innholders'	75	36
Richard Arnold	Tongue's Yard		Farriers'		12
Phillip Baker	High Street	Cheesemonger, will	Leathersellers'		14
John Basden			Joiners'		
William Bayzand	Goodman's Fields		Cutlers'		
Daniel Beale	Goodman's Fields		Bakers'		
Thomas Boardman	Great Alie Street	Pewterer, supplier London Hospital	Pewterers'	13	
William Bond	High Street		Grocers'	75	32
Joseph Boone	Aldgate High Street		Turners'		
Isaac Boquet	Without Aldgate		Apothecaries'		
Charles Boyce,	Rosemary Lane		Feltmakers'		12
Richard Bridgeman	Aldgate High Street		Grocers'		
James Brock	Brick Lane		Joiners'		
Joseph Bromehead			Skinners'		

NAME	ADDRESS	NOTES	LIVERY COMPANY	PERSONAL ESTATE £	RENT £
James Butcher	Prescott Street		Coopers'		
Henry Butler jnr.	Rosemary Lane		Feltmakers'		
Edward Cahill	Goodman's Fields		Scriveners'		
Nathaniel Clarkson	Goodman Street		Merchant Taylors'		
James Coates	Aldgate High Street		Tallow Chandlers'		
Isaac Collnett	High Street	Blacksmith, tyresmith	Blacksmiths'		32
John Cook	Aldgate High Street		Butchers'		
Peter Cook	High Street		Tin-plate Workers'		10
John Coope	Rupert Street		Salters'		30
Henry Crane			Turners'		
George Crosby	Buckle Street	Sugar refiner	Fishmongers'	90	25
Joshua Crowden	High Street		Cordwainers'	50	18
Thomas Denning	High Street	Cooper, will.	Coopers'		25
William Denman	Mansell Street		Joiners'		15
Richard Dewshurst			Coopers'		
Joseph Dizington	St George		Merchant Taylors'		
Richard Dodd	Near Whitechapel Road		Bakers'		
William Draper	High Street	Cheesemonger, Victualler	Vintners'		60
John Everard	Goodman's Fields		Skinners'		15
Thomas Farrow			Cordwainers'		
William Fillingham	Tongue's Yard	Livery keeper	Ironmongers'	50	70
Joseph Fisher	Prescott Street		Tallow Chandlers'	75	15
William Fleming			Glovers'		
John George	Well Close Square		Glovers'		
William Gill	Court Street		Dyers'		
Joseph Gwyn	High Street	Carpenter	Bricklayers'		12
Abell Hall	Well Close Square		Glassmakers'		
William Hamilton jnr	High Street	Upholsterer, undertaker	Clothworkers'	50	25
Thomas Hawes	High Street	Probate	Grocers'		21
Samuel Hawkins	Leman Street	Builder	Carpenters'	25	30
Humphery Haydon	High Street	Sailmaker. Supplier of canvas to Royal Navy	Blacksmiths'	75	22
Nevill Henson			Innholders'		
Simon Hilliolt	Aldgate High Street		Butchers'		
Charles Holdsworth	High Street		Patten-makers'	25	25
William Hollamby, jnr	Leman Street		Innholders'		20
James Jackson			Weavers'		
Joel Johnson	Church Lane	Carter	Carpenters'		25
John Jones	Prince's Square		Glovers'		
Isaac Kelso	Chambers Street Goodman's Fields	Victualler, brewer	Fletchers'		
Thomas Langley			Carpenters'		
William Lindus	High Street	Gentleman	Butchers'		28
John Marchant	Aldgate High Street		Feltmakers'		
Thomas Matson	Aldgate High Street		Haberdashers'		
Joseph Mayo	Goodman's Yard	?The Anvil	Loriners'		
John Miller	Aldgate High Street		Innholders'		
Robert Newcombe	Mansell Street		Glass-sellers'		15
Richard Palmer			Barbers'		
Allens Parsons	High Street	Hay salesman	Tallow Chandlers'	25	12
Thomas Pearson			Joiners'		
Joseph Pettitt	High Street	? James	Coachmakers'		22
John Poole	High Street		Bowyers'		12
Thomas Price	High Street	Cheesemonger	Clothworkers'		30
William Read	High Street	Distiller	Embroiderers'	75	22
John Rex	High Street Goodman's Fields	Distiller	Distillers'	45	25
Noble Reynolds	Whitechapel Road	Victualler, London Hospital	Barbers'		
Jacob Richardson	Aldgate High Street		Musicians'		
William Rogers	Aldgate High Street		Haberdashers'		
William Scott	High Street		Barbers'		30
William Scullard	Goodman's Fields	? Merchant, broker	Vintners'	100	18
James Shaw	Well Close Square		Needlemakers'		6?

NAME	ADDRESS	NOTES	LIVERY COMPANY	PERSONAL ESTATE £	RENT £
William Shaw	Well Close Square		Goldsmiths'		
Joseph Short	High Street	Factor	Bakers'		15
Joseph Skinner	Goodman's Fields		Distiller's		
James Spalding	High Street	Grocer	Grocers'	75	45
William Stone			Armourers' and Brasiers'		
William Taylor	Goodman's Fields		Carriers'		12
Peter Thorne			Innholders'		
John Thoytes	Whitechapel Road		Armourers' and Brasiers'		
William Thoytes			Armourers' and Brasiers'	300	50
Redman Tomkins	High Street	Butcher, governor, London Hospital	Butchers'	75	16
Andrew Touse	Goodman's Fields		Joiners'		
Arnold Tuesman			Bakers'		
George Waddington	Aldgate High Street		Innholders'		
John Waine	High Street		Butchers'		12
Peter Walkers	Goodman's Fields		Ironmongers'		
Cecil Waring	Great Alie Street		Skinners'	25	12
John Watts			Pewterers'		
Samuel Weddell	Aldgate High Street		Drapers'		
George Wellings	Somerset Street		Plaisterers'		
Richard Weston	High Street		Butchers'		12
Daniel Whalley			Clothworkers'		
Richard Whiteshead	Tongue's Yard	Coach maker	Coachmakers'		30
Peter Whitwell			Distillers'		
Edward Wildman	Whitechapel Road		Leathersellers'		
John Williams	Well Close Square		Drapers'		
James Wrench			Coachmakers'		

APPENDIX 3

HOLDERS OF 300 OUNCES OF SILVER OR MORE IN EAST LONDON, 1757-1762

NAME	OUNCES T 47/5	YEARS	OCCUPATION
John Barker	800	1759-62	
Edward Boddicott	300	1757-61	
Captain Pinson Bonham	400	1757	EIC captain?
Robert Bridgeman	400	1757-61	
Alexander Champion	500	1757-62	
Martha Cole	300	1757-58	
John Coles	400	1757-61	
John Collett	700	1757-59	
Thomas Corner	300	1757-58	
John Dumbleton	300	1757-59	
Ann Edwards	600	1757-58	
William Forster	400	1757-58	
Benjamin Goodwin	400	1757-62	
Abigail Harris	300	1757-60	
George Hayley	1100	1757-58	
Claus Heide	700	1760-62	Sugar refiner
John Hutchinson	1000	1759-62	
Francis Laurson	500	1757	Scrivener
Joseph T. Lockyer	800	1760-62	
John Marriott	400	1757-62	
Elizabeth Massa	400	1758-62	
Diana Neale	400	1757-62	
Sarah Nicholson	500	1757-62	
Ann Ord	500	1757-62	
John Pelly	400	1757-61	Captain. ? Trinity House.
John Player	400	1757-62	
William Reynolds	400	1757-62	Captain
Elizabeth Tolson	800	1757-59	
Jacob Treve	600	1757, 58	
George Willson	400	1757	Governor L. Hospital, corn factor

APPENDIX 4

1780 SOME HOUSEHOLDS TAXED ON MALE SERVANTS

NAME	STREET	SERVANTS	OCCUPATION
Thomas Bullock	High Street	3	
John Baker	Mansell Street	3	
Charles Bowles	Glasshouse Yard	3	
Samuel Charlett	Brick Lane	2	
John Coope	Whitechapel, Rupert Street	2	Sugar refiner
William Chapman	Road side	1	Bell founder
George Crosby	Road side	2	Sugar refiner
De Daniel Castroo	Great Ayliffe Street	2	
William Complin	Mansell Street	1	Surgeon
Richard Davis	Burr Street	1	
James Fisher	Whitechapel	1	Attorney, Protestant Association
Creed, Farr and Co.	Whitechapel	1	White Lead Works
Dr. Georgslenner	Mansell Street	2	
Elizabeth Horrocks	Prescot Street	1	Widow ?
George Hayley	Great Ayliff Street	3	Alderman
Samuel Hawkins	Great Ayliff Street	1	Building developer
Dudley Hyatt	Great Ayliff Street	2	
Edward Hawkins	Great Ayliff Street	2	Building developer
Thomas Jordan	Great Ayliff Street	3	Brewer
William Loft	Goodman's Fields	1	Dancing master
Robert Markham, DD.	Whitechapel	1	Rector
Dr Mayo	Well Close Square	1	Minister
William Midford	Burr Street	1	
James Montgomery	Prescott Street	1	
Thomas Pack	Road side	1	Bell Founder
George Prior	Prescott Street	1	
Patience Parker	Mansell Street	1	
Robert Pitt	Well Close Square	1	
Theophilus Pritzler	Well Close Square	1	Sugar refiner
Thomas Proctor	Graces Alley	1	
John Rahn	Burr Street	1	Surgeon
Carsten Rhode	Well Close Square	1	Sugar refiner
Major Rhode	Great Ayliff Street	1	Attorney
John Rix	High Street	1	
James Spalding	Whitechapel	1	Wealthy merchant
William Scullard	Mansell Street	2	Merchant
Claude Scott	Great Ayliff Street	2	Merchant
David Samuda	Great Ayliff Street	1	African merchant
William Toulmin	Prescott Street	1	Surgeon
Robert Wilson	Great Ayliff Street	2	Corn factor
Diderich Wackerbath	Well Close Square	1	Sugar refiner
William Wright	Well Close Square	1	Victualler
George Woolf	Well Close Square	2	Sugar refiner

APPENDIX 5

SOME SUGAR REFINERIES IN EAST LONDON
IN THE EIGHTEENTH CENTURY

Based on Appendix 3 *Directory of Sugar Refineries* in Bryan Mawer's *Sugarbakers: From sweat to sweetness*, 2007, 2011

LOCATION	FIRST YEAR	LAST YEAR	SUGAR BAKERS	NOTES
Alie Street	1773	1868		
Angel Alley	1719	1830		
Betts Street	1758	1841	Wackerbath	
Breezers Hill	1758	1868	Holtzmeyer	
Brewhouse Lane	1761	1817		
Brick Lane	1757	1821	T. Pritzler, 1777	
Broad Street	1728	1794		
Buckle Street	1723	1799		
Cable Street	1766	1841		
Charlotte Street	1798	1829	Holzmeyer	
Church Lane	1761	1868	John Turquand 1776-77	
Coal Stairs	1753	1780		
Dock Street	1722	1868	G. Hesse 1752	Salt Petre Bank
East Smithfield	1727	1799	J. Krietmayer	
Fieldgate Street	1736	1868	J. Brissault, 1760-63	
Goodman's Stile	1799	1868	Gregory Trapp & Co. 1794	
Goodman's Yard	1777	1830		
Gowers Walk	1794	1868		
Great Garden Street	1747	1865	G. Lear1789-1799	
Great Prescott Street	1798	1846		
King James's Stairs	1746	1752		
Lambeth Street	1734	1868	Buckley Schulerman 1763	
Leman Street	1724	1868		
Mansell Street	1739	1848	Spalding, Slack and Hawes, 1771	
Milk Yard	1747	1762		
Narrow Street	1772	1817		
New Road	1789	1833	John Detmar, 1796-98	
Osborn Street	1732	1868	J. Coope 1777	
Parsons Street	1748	1840	J Wackerbarth 1771	
Pell Street	1783	1868	George Detmar	
Pennington Street	1763	1846	Court Dirs	
Princes Place	1772	1851	D. Wackerbarth 1772-76	
Rosemary Lane	1742	1830	Dederick Wackerbath 1798-99	
Rupert Street	1723	1868	Otto Drost 1770	
Shorter Street	1777	1824	Carsten Dirs 1777	
St George Street	1748	1851	Christopher Ludekin 1766-1785	Ratcliff highway
Well Street	1739	1836	Diederick Wackerbarth 1789	
Well Close Square	1724	1868	Peter Rhode 1747-61	
Wentworth Street	1756	1832	Egnar and Lear 1766	
Whitechapel Road	1754	1836	J. L. Turquand 1777-78	

APPENDIX 6

SILK THROWSTERS IN WHITECHAPEL

The rent column shows first the rent, and, if available the personal estate, e.g. £24/50

NAME	OCCUPATION	ABODE	RENT £	INSURANCE	NOTES
Francis Benson	Silk manufacturer	Mansell Street	24/50		1770 Directory.
John Dutch	Silk throwster	Catherine Wheel Alley	1779 £500		SUN Ms 11936, 276/471145, 1779
George Fothergill	Silk throwster	Catherine Wheel Alley	1743, £1000	SUN	Ms 11936, 64/93375
Thomas Fothergill	Silk throwster	Catherine Wheel Alley	22/75	1750, £300	SUN Ms 11936, 88/119440 Insured stock in Stamford, and Southampton.
Jonathan Fuller	Silk throwster	High Street		1756	1756 PROB 11/826
Daniel Garnault	Silk throwster	High Street	20/100	£2,000	Catherine Wheel Alley
John Harris	Silk throwster	Leman Street	30/100		1760 and 1770 Directories.
Thomas Harris	Silk throwster	Leman Street	30		PROB 11/778 18 April 1750. Followed by John Harris.
Samuel Hawkins jnr	Silk throwster	Leman Street	30	1760	SUN Ms 11936, 133/177549, Sept 1760. Link to Hereford.
John Kendrick	Silk throwster				PROB 11/842 1758 link to Cheshunt
Elizabeth Newman	Silk throwster	Windmill Alley	15	1758	SUN Ms 11936, 125/165353, 1758, £800
Samuel Petty	Silk throwster	Little Alie Street	20		PROB 11/711 1741
David & Joseph Phillimore	Silk throwsters	Goodman's Fields	40/200	1763, £1,000	HAND Ms 8674, 98/81752, 1763
James Plantier	Silk throwster	Mason's Court		1748, £1,200	PROB 11/775, 1749.
Thomas Reason	Silk throwster	Leman Street			
John Sharrard	Silk throwster	Goodman's Fields		1748, £500	Old Bailey
Daniel Sharrer	Silk throwster	Little Alie Street	28		
Susannah Sharrer	Silk throwster	Little Alie Street	20		1770 Directory.
John Shower	Silk throwster	Leman Street		1747, £500	
Samuel Skinner	Silk throwster	Whitechapel		Died 1732 worth £8,000	*Daily Post*, 6 February 1730
Samuel Spragg	Silk throwster	Mason's Court		1758, £800	IOR L/AG/1/1/11 f. 152, 1704
John Weld	Silk throwster	Church Lane	10/50	1740	PROB 11/750 1746

APPENDIX 7

RECTORS OF St MARY's WHITECHAPEL 1697 to 1800

The rectors from 1697 until 1800 were:

Dr Richard Welton [1671/2-1717] DNB, who was Rector of Whitechapel from 1697 to 1715. He admitted on 3 March 1688 to Gonville and Caius College, Cambridge, at the age of sixteen. He graduated BA (1692), MA (1695) and DD (1708) or 1697 ref Malcolm.

From 1708 the advowson of St. Dunstan's, Stepney was held by Brasenose College, Oxford, and the Rector had jurisdiction over St.Mary's, Whitechapel. As for Stepney and Wapping the majority of the Rectors were not from London or Middlesex but came from Lancashire and Cheshire, reflecting the strong links of the college with these counties.

Dr Robert Shippen, DD, [1675-1745] DNB received his BA. in 1696. Typically in an age of pluralism he became Rector of Stepney in 1710, was instituted in 1716 as Rector of Whitechapel and Rector of Amersham in 1744. He became a Fellow of the Royal Society in 1706, and had been Professor of Music at Gresham's College, although he lacked qualifications in music, was Vice-Chancellor of the university in 1720. In spite of his position in society he was described by a contemporary critic as "sly, lecherous, corrupt, covetous, unscrupulous, selfish, immoral and could be relied upon to give a support where he saw his own advantage". Similar views were held by one of his Whitechapel parishioners, who in a pamphlet of 1716 accused Shippen of "too fond and Over-weaning Indulgence of your ambition and covetousness … You have Committed a Theft and A Violence".

Edward Traherne received his BA. in 1726 and was Vice Principal 1740-1 and 1743-4 and became Rector from 1746 until his death in 1749.

John Davie was the son of the Reverend Samuel Davie, Rector of Tattenhall in Cheshire. He attended Westminster School from November 1719, entered Brasenose College and received his BA. in 1731 and MA. in 1734. He was Rector of Whitechapel from January 1750 until he died in August 1756.

Dr Roger Mather, DD., received his BA. in 1739. He became Rector of Whitechapel in 1757 and died in 1768. He had been given dispensation to simultaneously also hold the Rectorship at Penn in Bucks. RSA member 1757-64.

Dr. Robert Markham, DD., received his BA. from St Johns, Cambridge, in 1748, and became Rector from 1757 until his death in 1786 at the age of 59. He had been chaplain in Ordinary to the King. In 1780 he was taxed on one male servant.

Dr John Holmes, DD., received his BA. in 1766 and was Rector of Whitechapel from 1786 until his death in 1795. In 1792 elected to the Paving Commissioners. Will TNA PROB 11/1265 proved 1795 shows that he wished to be buried Haslingden parish of Whalley in Lancashire where his parents were buried. He left £100 to Brasenose College for books and £100 to the London Hospital and £10 to his curate Revd Edward Robson. John Marks was the sexton. Every thing in the parsonage was to be buried including a "stock of wine" in the cellar. He also held estates in Yorkshire and Lancashire.

Thomas Wright received his BA. in 1779, and was Rector of Whitechapel from 1796 until 1805.

Edward Robson was first a curate and in 1816, he was also a Middlesex Magistrate.

References

J. P. Malcolm, *Anecdotes of the manners and customs of London during the 18th century*, 1810, vol. 4, pp. 446-447

Brasenose College, Oxford Monographs

APPENDIX 8

CHARITABLE BEQUESTS

NAME	WILL TNA PROB 11	BEQUESTS	OCCUPATION
John Adams	1180	£10 for poor of Stepney meeting.	Cooper
Matthew Bateman	869	£100 to London Hospital	Esquire with estate in Essex
Henry Batley	960	£100 to St Luke's Hospital for lunatics	Gentleman
Revd. John Brittan	1250	£20 to poor of Baptist church.	Minister
Edward Cahill	1044	£500 to London Hospital	Broker
George Capadose	1240	£30 to Jewish synagogue, Amsterdam. £20 to a synagogue in London.	Portuguese merchant
John Compton	921	5 guineas to Whitechapel Free School	Tallow chandler
John Coverley	909	5 guineas for poor	Scrivener
Abraham Elias	959	£50 to poor of Synagogue at Hoxton	
Charles Foster	1052	£10 to three charity schools in Whitechapel, Aldgate and St. Catherine's.	Gentleman
Benjamin Goodwin	930	£700 to re-build Meggs Almshouses and interest on £400 to provide coal to the almshouses. £30 to Whitechapel Charity School. Dividends on £200 for '4 poor ancient inhabitants'.	Gentleman
John Hammond	1320	£500 London Hospital. £1000 Foundling Hospital. £100 Marine Society. £200 for widows and sons of the clergy.	Sail cloth manufacturer
Revd. John Holmes, D.D.	1265	£100 London Hospital.	Minister
Peter Hue	860	3 guineas to 6 poor families in Whitechapel £50 to London Hospital. £50 to French Hospital.	
Andrew Knies	1509	£100 plus interest to the poor of Reformed church of Savoy	Sugar distiller
Thomas Lewis	1283	£50 to Charity School, Whitechapel £500 to Mile End Chapel Charity. £50 to St George's-in-the-East Charity School.	
Joseph I. Levy	1134	£25 to Jewish poor.	
Thomas Massa	1094	£5 to poor of Brentwood and South Weald, Essex. Monthly bequests of 1 shilling to 12 widows.	Baker
Lazarus Myers	1344	Numerous bequests to Jewish charities in London and Germany.	
Thomas Pack	1074	£100 to Lying in charity for delivering poor women.	
James Paon	754	£5 to Ministers and Elders of French church, Spitalfields.	
Daniel Peacock	1304	Interest on £100 for Megg's Almshouses.	Gentleman
Charles Povey	726	50 guineas to Charity School, Newington Butts.	Gentleman
James Spalding	1064	£50 to London Hospital £20 for poor of Whitechapel £20 to poor of Whitechapel. £5 to poor of Sudbury.	Esquire
John Spieker	1007	£500 London Hospital £200 to Lunatic's Hospital £100 to Foundling's Hospital £500 to Swedish church, Princes Square, Ratcliff £1000 to a merchant's widows charity Stockholm £1500 for poor of Abo, Finland.	Merchant

NAME	WILL TNA PROB 11	BEQUESTS	OCCUPATION
Robert Summerhayes	1140	£1000 London Hospital. £1500 to Devon and Exeter Hospital. £500 to charity for relief of Dissenting Clergymen. £500 St Luke's hospital for Lunatics.	Gentleman
Christian Tielhen	862	German Lutheran church, Savoy	Sugar refiner
David Walker	1095	£1000 for poor of Quaker Meeting, Devonshire Street. £1000 for Quaker poor of Cumberland.	Linen weaver

APPENDIX 9

MEDICAL PRACTIONERS IN WHITECHAPEL BEFORE 1800

NAME	OCCUPATION	NOTES
Joseph Ager	Surgeon	1794-1811, Whitechapel
Thomas Ager	Surgeon	1784, Mansel Street
Richard Barton	Surgeon	PROB 11/710 proved 1741 surgeon White Horse Street Stepney freehold estate Southampton.
Nicholas Birch	Surgeon	1784-1811, 38 Mansel Street.1802 Surgeon extra to the Prince of Wales. Complin and Birch, 1784-1805
William Blackmore	Surgeon and apothecary	Sun 1769 Well Close Square. Treasurer, Raines Charity School LMA ACC/1811/2/1/2.
Josiah Cole	Apothecary	He lived in Whitechapel High Street and was one of the original subscribers to the London Infirmary in 1740. He fitted out the apothecary's shop bought from Mr Harris of Ayliff Street in 1741. Clark-Kennedy p. 22,
John Cox	Surgeon	1796 New Road Whitechapel.
Benjamin Da Costa	Surgeon	1794-1811 Whitechapel Road
Darkin & Son	Dentists	1789-1799, 71 Whitechapel
Darkin & Campbell	Dentists	1802-1811, 71 Whitechapel
Rice Davies	Surgeon	1791-94, Burr Street Little Alie Street, 1796-1811
John Devall	Apothecary	MDR 1761/1, 176, MDR 1758/2, 96
John Eckley	Apothecary, London Hospital	PROB 11/896 proved 1764
Nicholas Edwards	Surgeon	PROB 11/828 1757 John Field refers to his friend a surgeon in Whitechapel. 1763 Whitechapel.
John Ellison	Druggist	Paving Commissioner in 1772 PROB 11/1189 proved 1790 with link to Yorkshire.
John Gilson	Surgeon	1784-1799, 141 Whitechapel 1799-1802, Gilson & Ager
Ambrose Hallett	Surgeon, Apothecary	1791-1805, Whitechapel Hallett & Read, 1809, 92 Whitechapel Road
John Harris	Surgeon	PROB 11/725 proved 1743 *Daily Post* 1 April 1743 reports the death of Mr Harris 'an eminent apothecary 'one of the oldest in the profession with a worth of £10,000.'
Swift Heckford	Surgeon?	PROB 11/922 proved 1766, property in manor of Water Belchamp or Belchamp Mortliain Essex.
Samuel Jackson	Surgeon	St George-in-the-East, 1796-1811
Stephen Leach	Chemist and druggist	Sun 1754 at Glambers Head, Whitechapel HHG stock £900 and a small house in Hackney.
John Lyons	Chemist apothecary and haberdasher	Sun 1754, Rosemary Lane. Household goods, and stock in his three adjoining houses £700.
William Massa	Apothecary	MDR 1748/1, 10
Caleb Miller	Surgeon	1791, Leman Street
Francis Moseley	Surgeon	1799-1802, Great Alie Street
Richard Murrell	Surgeon apothecary	PROB 11/1017, 1776
William Newman	Chemist	Sun 1742, 1749, near The Mount, Whitechapel Road insured his laboratory for £300.

NAME	OCCUPATION	NOTES
John Parkinson (I)	Dentist	1781-86, Church Lane, Whitechapel.
Robert Pell	Surgeon	1763, Well Close Square
William Salter (I)	Dentist, Apothecary	1789-90, 64 High Street Whitechapel
Joseph Sandford	Surgeon	PROB 11/765 1748, buried Whitechapel; shop with medicines, stills, mortars and pestles
George Sayer	Surgeon, apothecary	Lived in High Street appeared in 1760 re will of George Smith PROB 11/854 1760.
John Solley	Apothecary	PROB 11/813 proved 1755. Property in Suffolk and Essex.
Samuel Staines	Surgeon, Apothecary	1765-67, Mansell Street
Stephen Smith Ward	General practioner	His son Nathaniel Bagshaw Ward FRS [1791-1868] DNB was a botanist who invented the Wardian case which enabled plants to be transferred around the world.
James Woodward	Surgeon	1796-1811, Whitechapel Road.
James Woolsey	Surgeon	Sun 1762 of Well Close Square insured household goods, books etc for £500. In 1759 he was executor to the will of John Herring of Ratcliff Highway. 1791 Well Close Square.
Thomas Woolsey	Surgeon	PROB 11/849 5 Sept 1759

FAMOUS AND NOTABLE PEOPLE

The majority of the following have entries in the 2011 online edition of the Dictionary of National Biography.

INDEX TO 16th - 17th CENTURIES

INDEX TO 18th CENTURY

INDEX TO PLACES OVERSEAS

INDEX TO PLACES IN UK AND IRELAND

LONDON AND MIDDLESEX

The creators of archives were never certain of which parish a street may have been in. Given that street names change with time and that streets may cross several parishes for the precise location of streets in London please use J. Rocque *The A to Z of Georgian London*, 1981.

INDEX TO SUBJECTS

End Notes to Chapters 1 to 14

Abbreviations

Barnett,	D. Barnett, *London, Hub of the Industrial Revolution: A Revisionary History, 1775-1825*, 1998
Clark,	P. Clark & R. Gillespie, eds. *Two Capitals: London and Dublin: 1500-1840*, 2001
George,	M. D. George, *London Life in the Eighteenth Century*, 1965
Guillery,	P. Guillery, *The Small House in eighteenth-century London, A Social and Architectural History*, 2004
HAND,	LMA, Ms 8674, Hand-in-Hand
Malcolm,	J. P. Malcolm, *Londinium Redivivum or an ancient history and modern description of London*, 1803-7
Morris, *MEOT*,	D. Morris, *Mile End Old Town, 1740–1780; A social history of an Early Modern London Suburb*, 2007
Morris, *Wapping*,	D. Morris and K. Cozens, *Wapping 1600-1800, A social history of an Early Modern London Maritime Suburb*, 2009
OLD BAILEY,	Old Bailey online Reference Number
Pevsner *East*,	B. Cherry, C. O'Brien and N. Pevsner, *London 5: East*, in *The Buildings of England* series, 2005
Pevsner *City*,	S. Bradley & N. Pevsner, *London 1: The City of London*, 1997
Schwarz,	L. D. Schwarz, *London in the age of industrialisation: entrepreneurs, labour force and living conditions, 1700-1850*, 1993
Spence,	C. Spence, *Atlas of London in the 1690s*, 2000
Stow,	J. Stow, *A Survey of London*, 1603 reprinted 1971
SUN,	LMA, Ms 11936, Sun Fire Office
VCH,	*Middlesex, Middlesex*, vol. XI, *Early Stepney and Bethnal Green*, 1998, ed. C. R. J. Currie
Western,	J. R. Western, *The English Militia in the Eighteenth Century: the Story of a Political Issue, 1660-1802*, 1965

Notes to Chapter 1....Introduction

1. J. Gregory & J. Stevenson, *Britain in the Eighteenth Century, 1688-1820*, 2007, p. 245
2. Guillery, p. 21; J. Noorthouck, *A new history of London including Westminster and Southwark*, 1773, p. 769
3. S. Porter, *Shakespeare's London: Everyday Life in London, 1580-1616*, 2009, pp. 210-213; H. T. Stephenson, *Shakespeare's London*, 1905, p. 287
4. Stow; Malcolm, vol. 4, p. 9
5. Stow, I, pp. 72, 126, 127
6. M. J. Power, *The urban development of East London, 1500-1700*, London University Ph. D. 1971
7. P. Guillery, Houses in London, in C. Ferguson and W. Wareham, *London and Middlesex Hearth Tax*, BRS Hearth Tax Series (forthcoming 2012); P. Guillery, London's Suburbs, House Size and the Hearth Tax, in P. S. Barnwell and M. Airs, eds. *Houses and the Hearth Tax: the later Stuart house and society*, 2006, pp. 35-40
8. P. Guillery, Suburban Models, or Calvinism and Continuity in London's Seventeenth century Church Architecture, *Architectural History*, vol. 48, 2005, p. 89, PROB 11/356 William Meggs, 1678
9. Spence, pp. 68, 177, Appendix III
10. LMA, CLC/525/Ms06015 land tax Whitechapel
11. E. McKellar, *The birth of modern London: The development and design of the city, 1660-1720*, 1999, pp. 29, 182, 219-223; L. D. Schwarz, London 1700-1840, in *The Cambridge Urban History of Britain, vol. II, 1540-1840* 2000, p. 657; Pevsner *East*, pp. 22-35; D. Defoe, A *Tour through the whole Island of Great Britain*, 1734-36, p. 287
12. George, pp. 75, 82
13. H. Phillips, *Mid-Georgian London: a topographical and social survey of central and western London about 1750*, 1964; F. H. W. Sheppard, Sources and Methods used for the Survey of London, *The Study of Urban History*, ed. H. J. Dyos, 1968, pp. 131-145; D. Morris, The Land Tax Assessments for Mile End Old Town, 1741-1790, *Newsletter* No. 51, November 2000, London, Topographical Society; D. Morris and K. Cozens, Huguenots and Housing: Insurance and Land Tax 1740-1840, *Huguenot Families*, No. 18 June 2008
14. J. Gibson, et al, *Land and Window Tax Assessments*, 2004; E. Baigent, Economy and Society in eighteenth-century English towns: Bristol in the 1770s, in D. Denecke and G. Shaw, *Urban Historical Geography, Recent Progress in Britain and Germany*, 1988; LMA, MJ/SB/ Freeholders lists for the Ossulstone Hundred [Film X066/...]
15. D. T. Hawkins, *Fire Insurance Records for family and local historians, 1696 to 1929*, 2003
16. LMA, MR/LV Licensed Victuallers Records
17. Morris, *Wapping*, pp. 145-150
18. Personal communication from Michael Elliston

Notes to Chapter 2   Governing Whitechapel

1. VCH, *Middlesex*, vol. XI, pp. 20-22, 63-70; Stow, II, p. 136
2. P. J. Corfield, *The Impact of English Towns, 1700-1800*, 1989, p. 81
3. J. Innes, Managing the Metropolis: London's Social Problems and their Control, c.1660-1830, in Clark, pp. 53-79
4. *Journal of House of Commons* vol XXII, 1733-37, pp. 270-1
5. J. L. & B. Hammond, Poverty, Crime and Philanthropy, in *Johnson's England*, ed. A. S. Turberville, 1952, vol. 1, pp. 300-335
6. D. R. Green, *From Artisan to Paupers: Economic Change and Poverty in London, 1790-1870*, 1995; D. R. Green, *Pauper Capital: London and the Poor Law, 1790-1870*, 2010
7. D. Hey, *Oxford Encyclopaedia of Local History*, 2010, p. 540
8. *Weekly Journal*, 1 August 1724; *Daily Courant*, 19 November 1724; *Daily Courant*, 28 May 1725
9. http://www.workhouses.org.uk accessed 17 November 2010
10. SUN, vol. 176, 246747
11. P. Langford, *A Polite and Commercial Period: England 1727-1783*, 1992, pp. 63, 152
12. T. Hitchcock, *Down and Out in Eighteenth-Century London*, 2007, pp. 138, 139, 142
13. Malcolm, vol. 4, pp. 455-456
14. All Hallows by the Tower *Vestry minutes*
15. LMA, P 93/GEO1/90 Trustees minutes for St George-in-the-East, 1790-1793
16. *Daily Gazetteer*, 18 January 1740, 30 January 1740; *General Evening Post*, 8-10 January 1740
17. Guildhall, GL Ms 6207/1A, Distillers' Company, *Court Minutes 1730-1756*
18. *Daily Journal*, 28 April 1733, http://en.wikipedia.org/wiki/John_Harris accessed 8 August 2011
19. Hanway's Act 7 Geo. III c.39

20. T. Hitchcock et al, eds. *Chronicling Poverty - The Voices and Strategies of the English Poor, 1640-1840*, 1997
21. LMA, Middlesex Session Books, April 1692, J. Innes & N. Rogers, Politics and governments, 1700-1840, *The Cambridge Urban History of Britain, vol. II, 1540-1840*, 2000, p. 536
22. THLHL Ste/230 *Whitechapel Paving Commission Rough Minutes, 1771-1775*; THLHL Ste/241 *Minutes of the Commissioners for paving the High Street in Whitechapel*
23. BL Add. Ms 30869, *John Wilkes Correspondence*, vol. III, 1766-67
24. J. Innes, Managing the Metropolis: London's Social Problems and their Control, *c.*1660-1830, in Clark, pp. 68, 73
25. LMA P 93/MRY1/218, *Acts of Parliament, 1727-1837*, Whitechapel Union
26. *Public Advertiser*, 6 July 1770
27. F. O'Gormon *Voters, Patrons, Politics: The Unreformed Electoral System of Hanoverian England, 1724-1832*, 1989
28. *The Middlesex Journal*, 22-24 February 1770; G. F. E. Rudé, *Hanovarian London: 1714-1808*, 1971, pp. 162-182; DNB John Wilkes MP, accessed 26 May 2011 OBIN 101029410
29. LMA, CLC/525/Ms06015 land tax for Whitechapel
30. LMA, Ms 24178 Index to papers of Thomas Bowrey, LMA, CLC/427/Ms03041 Bowrey Papers
31. LMA, CLC/525/Ms06015/31 Whitechapel land tax 1764

Notes to Chapter 3   Living in Whitechapel

1. Pevsner *City*, pp. 66-70; Guillery, p. 54
2. Pevsner *East*, pp. 426-428
3. Guildhall Collage, record 22182 Robert Schnebbellie; Pevsner *East,* p. 400
4. Guillery, pp. 3, 34, 40
5. George, p. 100
6. LMA Information Leaflet No. 9, *Land Tax Assessments for London and Middlesex*, 2010
7. Spence, pp. 67-74, 177, Appendix III
8. LMA Information Leaflet No. 48, *Fire Insurance Records*, 2010
9. Morris, *MEOT*, pp. 11-24, 119
10. HAND, vol. 106, 85630
11. HAND, vol. 93, 79358
12. HAND, vol. 96, 80695
13. D. Morris, Fitzhugh House, Mile End Old Town, Stepney, 1738 - 1849, *Newsletter*, No. 48, May 1999, London Topographical Society, pp. 10-11; Guillery, pp. 165-6
14. TNA PROB 31/468/592 John Creed 1762
15. TNA PROB 31/433/633 Thomas Sibley 1756; TNA PROB 31/433/634 Elizabeth Sibley 1759
16. George, pp. 75-83
17. HAND, vol. 87, 71689
18. Guillery, p. 52; LMA, CLC/525/Ms06009/47 land tax Shadwell
19. http://www.british-history.ac.uk, Whitechapel 'Four Shillings in the Pound Aid, 1693-94'
20. LMA, CLC/525/Ms06015, Whitechapel land tax returns
21. HAND, vol. 72, 70706
22. HAND, vol. 90, 78393
23. HAND, vol. 74, 71709
24. Pevsner *East*, pp. 432, 435
25. SUN, vol. 287, 433988; HAND, vol. 76, 67213
26. *Public Advertiser*, 22 May 1760
27. HAND, vol. 83, 75330
28. TNA PROB 11/774, Avery Taylor 1749
29. HAND, vol. 97, 81088
30. C. Shammas, *The Pre-Industrial Consumer in England and America*, 1990, p. 302
31. DNB John Perry accessed 28 April 2011 OBIN 101021997; http://www.british-history.ac.uk, Portsoken Ward, Barrs Precinct, 'Four Shillings in the Pound Aid, 1693-94'; TNA PROB 3/23/4 Samuel Perry, 1724; TNA PROB 11/595, Samuel Perry, 1724; *Weekly Journal,* 23 November 1723
32. L. Weatherill, *Consumer behaviour and social status in England, 1660-1760*, 1988, pp. 28, 184, Table 8.2
33. LMA, DL/C/005/Ms09184/004 Box 1 1731 Commissary Court
34. C. Clutton, *Britten's Old Clocks and Watches and their makers: A history of styles in clocks and their mechanisms*, 1982, p. 499
35. Morris, *MEOT,* pp. 117-128
36. TNA PROB 31/672/548, Thomas Jarvis 1778
37. TNA PROB 31/120/534, George Mussell 1733
38. TNA PROB 31/574/52, Henry Cooley 1772
39. TNA PROB 11/726, Charles Povey 1743
40. 29 Geo.2 cap. XIV Duties on silver, D. Morris, Silver and Carriage Duties; 1757-1766, *Genealogists' Magazine*, vol. 30, no. 5, March 2011, pp. 147-151; TNA T 47/5 Tax on silver
41. L. Weatherill, *Consumer behaviour and social status in England, 1660-1760*, 1988, p. 29
42. TNA PROB 31/487/322 Sarah Sparke 1764
43. TNA T 47/7 List of people ... as have not regularly paid the duty, 1776
44. H. W. Dickinson, *Water Supply of Greater London*, 1954, pp. 8, 9, 14, 30, 31, 118, 119
45. D. Defoe, *The Complete English Tradesman*, 1726, 1987, p. 84
46. P. Earle, *The Making of the English Middle Class,* 1989, pp. 218-229; George, pp. 119-120
47. P. Earle, *The Making of the English Middle Class,* 1989, p. 162
48. Schwarz, p. 45; L. Schwarz, English servants and their employers during the eighteenth and nineteenth centuries, *Economic History Review*, 52, 1999, pp. 236-56; Society of Genealogists SP/TAX. An index of names, abodes and number of servants; TNA T 47/8 1780 Tax on Male Servants
49. TNA PROB 11/1137, Susannah Jones 1786
50. TNA PROB 11/1213, William Scullard 1792
51. *General Evening Post*, 22-24 September 1761; *Whitehall Evening Post*, 12-15 December 1761
52. *A. Williamson's Diary, 1722-1747*, ed. J. C. Fox 1912; J. Allen, *Leaves from the Past; the diary of John Allen, sometime a brewer of Wapping*, 1905; THLHL, TH 8383, Goff, E. *Diaries, 1778-1796*; British Library Eg MSS 3814 Letters of Eliza Hawkins nee Rhode

53. L. D. Schwarz, London 1700-1840, in *The Cambridge Urban History of Britain, vol. II, 1540-1840*, 2000, p. 657; *Daily Post Boy*, 30 March 1733; *English Post*, 25-27 May 1702
54. *Public Advertiser*, 15 August 1754
55. SUN, vol. 273, 411453
56. *Daily Courant*, 6 February 1720
57. George, pp. 41-51; L. D. Schwarz, London 1700-1840, in *The Cambridge Urban History of Britain, vol. II, 1540-1840*, 2000, p. 652
58. *St James Chronicle*, 24-26 March 1768
59. *Gazetteer and London Daily Advertiser*, 11 October 1762
60. *Daily Post*, 29 August 1727
61. LMA, M/93/38, 17 July 1769 Stepney Manorial Records
62. Morris *Wapping*, pp. 127-129
63. W. J. Songhurst, *Quator Coronatorum Antigrapha, Masonic Reprints of the Quatuor Lodge, No. 2076, London*, vol. X The Minutes of the Grand, Lodge of Freemasons of England, 1723-1739, 1913; LMA, CLC/525/Ms06015, Whitechapel land tax, MR/LV/7/49, MR/LV/8/68 Licensed Victuallers
64. The Library and Museum of Freemasonry, SN 759 Lodge of Unity No. 376 D, Whitechapel, The Library and Museum of Freemasonry, GBR 1991 HC 12/D/7a Prospectus entitled *Masonic Charity for Clothing and Educating the Sons of Indigent Freemasons*, 1808

Notes to Chapter 4   The Service Industries

1. *Reading Weekly Journal*, 7 April 1739
2. L. Schwarz, Hanovarian London: The Making of a Service Town, in Clark, pp. 93-110
3. Stow, I, p. 126
4. *Daily* Advertiser, 1 January 1774; P. Jennings, Liquor licensing and the local historian: the Victorian public house, *The Local Historian*, vol. 41, 2, May 2011, pp. 121-137
5. TNA PROB 31/714/400, John Nixon 1782
6. D. B. Morris, Drinking in Mile End, 1750, *East London Record*, vol. XIX, 1998, pp. 37-40
7. HAND, vol. 106, 74650; SUN, vol. 55, 52402
8. SUN, vol. 64, 93910; SUN, vol. 83, 111959
9. SUN, vol. 85, 116055; TNA PROB 3/24/6 John Barnes; TNA PROB 31/329/159 and 186 Joseph Prick 1751
10. Daniel Defoe, *Moll Flanders,* 1722, p. 237
11. S. R. Hovland, The Gardens of Later Medieval London, *The London Gardener*, 2006-7, Appendix
12. Survey of London, *Spitalfields*, vol. XXVII, 1957, pp. 278-80; DNB Leonard Gurle accessed 30 March 2011 OBIN 101037496; C. Driver & M. Berriedale-Johnson, *Pepys at Table*, 1984, p. 10
13. J. H. Harvey, Leonard Gurle's Nurseries and some others, *Garden History*, vol. 3, 3, Summer, 1975, pp. 42-49
14. J. Cox, *London's East End: Life and Traditions*, 1994, p. 47; J. Harvey, *Early Nurserymen*, 1974, p. 46
15. TNA PROB 11/909 John Coverly 1765; TNA PROB 11/1600 Major Wright 1818
16. C. Hibbert, *King Mob: The story of Lord George Gordon and the Riots of 1780*, 2004, p. 39
17. A. Forshaw & T. Bergström, *Smithfield, Past and Present*, 1990; K. J. Bonser, *The drovers, who they were and how they went, an epic of the English countryside*, 1970; Spence, p. 118
18. Guildhall GL, Ms 6443, vol. 8, Butchers' Company Court Minutes, 1762-1774, 4 November 1762
19. R. Porter, *London: A Social History*, 1994, p. 135
20. Spence, p. 34, Fig. 2.6
21. *General Advertiser*, 29 April 1746, *Public Advertiser*, 18 March 1755
22. C. G. Harper, *The Norwich Road*, 1903
23. *London Evening Post*, 27-29 January 1761
24. J. P. Bowen, The Carriers of Lancaster, 1824-1912, *The Local Historian*, August 2010, vol. 43, 3, pp. 178-190; D. Morris, Silver and Carriage Duties; 1757-1766, *Genealogists' Magazine*, vol. 30, no. 5, March 2011, pp. 147-151
25. TNA T/47/2, T 47/3, Duties on Coaches and other Carriages, T 47/4, Duties on silver and carriages; THLHL, S. Martin Leake *Account Books*, Microfilm 474
26. *London Gazette*, 25 August 1744
27. TNA PROB 11/1088 Robert Boston 1782
28. TNA PROB 11//824 Thomas Sibley 1756; TNA PROB 31/433/633, 634 Thomas and Elizabeth Sibley 1756
29. TNA PROB 31/173/162, 163 John Fothergill 1738
30. Guildhall GL Ms 5384 Saddlers' Company, Wardens' Accounts 1555-1822; *London Evening Post*, 30 September-2 October 1760
31. HAND, vol. 83, 75330
32. HAND, vol. 97, 81088

Notes to Chapter 5   The Manufacturing Industries

1. Barnett, p. 1; VCH, *Middlesex*, vol. 2, Industries; R. Porter, *London: A Social History*, 2000, pp. 168-170; Morris, *Wapping*, pp. 140-141
2. J. Summerson, *Georgian London*, 1978, pp. 130-1; *Common Sense or The Englishmens Journal*, 16 June 1739; A. Kelly, *Mrs Coade's Stone*, 1990, pp. 31-45; *Monthly Chronicle*, May 1730; *Champion or Evening Advertiser*, 6 March 1732; *Gazette and New Daily Advertiser*, 27 October 1770; *Lloyd's Evening Post*, 28-30 January 1767; *London Evening Post*, 10-12 December 1767
3. *Public Advertiser*, 13 February 1770
4. *Public Advertiser*, 17 September 1771
5. DNB Eleanor Coade, accessed 25 February 2011 OBIN 101037296, J. Havill, *Eleanor Coade*, 1986; B. Weinreb & C. Hibbert, *The London Encyclopedia*, 1995, p 101
6. Spence, pp. 117-8
7. SUN, vol. 176, 246992; SUN, vol. 183, 259090; HAND, vol. 109, 86736; SUN, vol. 194, 279625; TNA, ADM/112/162, Pork contracts, 1776; SUN, vol. 290, 439821
8. Essex Record Office D/DC/27/820-824, 1 September 1780; Guildhall GL Ms 6453, vol. 3, 13 July 1776 Butchers' Company
9. P. Mathias, *The brewing industry in England 1700-1830*, 1959; D. B. Morris, Two Early Breweries in Mile End Old Town, Stepney, 1700-1780, *Brewery History*, No. 102, Winter 200; L. A. G. Strong, *A brewer's progress, 1757-1957, A survey of Charrington's brewery*, 1957; Trueman, Hanbury, Buxton and Company, *Trumans, the brewers: the story of Truman, Hanbury Buxton and Company,* 1966

10. LMA, ACC 1811/2/1, Minute Book Raine's Foundation School
11. LMA, MR/LV/7/49 1760 The London Hospital; A. E. Clark-Kennedy, *The London: A study in the Voluntary Hospital System,* vol. 1, 1740-1840, 1962 p. 72
12. H. H. Janes, *Albion brewery, 1808-1958: the story of Mann, Cross and Paulin Ltd,* 1959
13. J. Allen, *Leaves from the Past; the diary of John Allen, sometime a brewer of Wapping,* 1905
14. Whitechapel Bell Foundry, *The Whitechapel Bell Foundry,* 1977; VCH, *Middlesex,* vol. 2, pp. 165-168; G. Dodds, *Church Bells of Hertfordshire,* 1994; A. D. Tyssen, The History of the Whitechapel Bell Foundry, LAMAS *Transactions,* New Series, 5, (1924-26) 1929, pp. 195-220
15. D. J. McGill, *Ballycastle's Heritage and Town Guide,* 2008
16. TNA PROB 11/952, Thomas Lester 1769; TNA PROB 11/1074 Thomas Pack 1781
17. TNA PROB 11/1123, William Chapman 1784
18. Essex Record Office D/P 18/6/2, Personal communication from Alan Hughes, Whitechapel Bell Foundry
19. P. Razzell, The role of Personal. Domestic, and Public Hygiene in shaping English mortality patterns, 1500-1899, *Population and Disease: Transforming English Society, 1550-1850,* 2007; SUN, vol. 202, 290909; Barnett, p. 92
20. Philip Mottram personal communication, 2005
21. P. Deane & W. A. Cole, *British Economic Growth, 1688-1959,* 1964, p. 72
22. OLD BAILEY, t1791026-48 accessed 13 March 2011; OLD BAILEY, t17961026-6 accessed 13 March 2011
23. Anon, Elizabethan plaster ceiling, from an old house in Goodman's Yard, *The Builder,* 23 September 1848
24. P. Earle, *The Making of the English Middle Class,* 1989, p. 107
25. J. Rule, *The Vital Centre: England's Developing Economy, 1714-1815,* 1992, p. 150; George, pp. 202, 203; R. Campbell *London Tradesman,* 1747, pp.103-4
26. *Daily Post,* 6 June 1720
27. LMA, MDR 1727/5/164
28. LMA, MDR 1728/3/124
29. IOR/L/AG/1/1/15 f.191, IOR/L/AG/1/1/17 f.143
30. TNA PROB 11/872 James Creed 1762
31. TNA SP 36/56 June 1741, Geoffrey Saul personal communication, Michael Elliston personal communication
32. D. J. Rowe, *Lead Manufactory in Britain: a History,* 1983, pp. 1-14, 141, 191
33. LMA, Ms 8674, vol. 77, 63939, 1751 HAND, LMA, CLC/525/Ms06015/28 and 35, Whitechapel land tax, TNA T 47/8 male servant tax
34. Barnett, pp. 168-9, P. Earle, *The Making of the English Middle Class,* 1989, p. 107
35. LMA, Ms 11936, vol. 202, 292293, 1770 SUN
36. *Whitehall Evening Post,* 10 May 1755, LMA, Ms 11936, vol. 141, 187409, 1762 SUN, TNA PROB 11/1305 William Quarrill 1798, London Hospital suppliers LH/F/8/5, LMA, Ms 8674, vol. 96, 80880, 1761, HAND, TNA PROB 11/1015 John Jones 1776
37. TNA PROB 11/1536, Luke Alder, 1812, LMA, Ms 11936, vol. 125, 164527, 1758 SUN
38. Morris, *MEOT,* p. 31
39. R. Pares, The London Sugar Market, 1740-1769, *Econ. History Review.* 2nd Series, IX, 1956-57, pp. 254-270
40. Morris, *MEOT,* p. 56
41. Morris, *Wapping,* pp. 52-55
42. P. Earle, *The Making of the English Middle Class,* 1989, p. 107, LMA, Ms 8674, vol. 74, 51462, 52220, 1749 HAND, LMA, Ms 11936, vol. 254, 381252, vol. 258, 385370, vol. 259, 387519, 1777 SUN, D. Barnett, pp. 45-46
43. Norfolk Record Office, FEL 705
44. VCH, *Middlesex,* vol. 2, 1970, ed. W. Page, Industries, C. Welch, p. 131
45. G. Dodd, A Day in a Sugar Refinery, Chapter V of *Days at the Factories,* 1843
46. G. Hurren, *Phoenix renascent: a history of the Phoenix Assurance Company Ltd, 1782-1968,* 1973
47. LMA, Ms 11936, vol. 149, 201412 1763 SUN
48. H. Rössler, Die Zuckerbäcker waren vornehmlich Hannoveraner, *Jahrbuch* der Männer vom Morgenstern, Bd 81, 2002, H. Rössler, H. & M. Schulte Beerbühl, Auf ins gelobte Land – Aspekte der deutschen Englandwanderung im 18. und 19. Jahrhundert, in *Archiv für Familienforschung,* 6, 3, 2002
49. TNA PROB 11/936 Paul Johnson 1768, LMA, Ms 11936, vol. 173, 240089, 1766 SUN, LMA, Ms 11936, vol. 186, 263302, 1768 SUN Trapp
50. LMA Ms 8674, vol. 72, 53730, HAND, 1748, Gower, TNA PROB 11/832 Samuel Gower 1757
51. TNA PROB 11/1320 John Hammond 1799, TNA ADM 106/3608, LMA, Ms 11936, vol. 148, 200952, SUN, Phillip Splidt junior 1763, LMA, Ms 8674, vol. 98 , 81602, Philip Splidt LMA, Ms 11936, vol. 118, 156226 SUN, Humphery Haydon 1757
52. htpp://www.genuki.org.uk for details of Cook's *Gunmakers and Allied Trades Index,* email gunmakers-family@yahoo.com
53. Spence, p. 118, Morris, *Wapping,* pp. 15, 139
54. LMA Ms 5226/2-6 Gunmakers' Company, Masters and Wardens List
55. R. Beaumont, *Purdey's: The guns and their makers,* 1984
56. 1760 Directory Waller & Son. James Waller, gunmaker in 1770 Directory. TNA PROB 11/925 James Waller 1767
57. TNA PROB 11/1249 James Reynolds 1794
58. TNA PROB 11/1118 William Pursell 1784
59. TNA PROB 11/1043 Thomas Sherwood 1778
60. TNA PROB 11/1189 Joseph Knock 1790
61. TNA PROB 11/1347 Joseph Green 1800

Notes to Chapter 6   The Silk Industry

1. E. A. Wrigley, *Poverty, Progress, and Population,* 2004, p. 283
2. R. D. Gwynne, *Huguenot Heritage,* 2001, pp. 83-87
3. D. C. Coleman, *Courtaulds: an economic and social history,* 1969, vol. 1, p. 33; George, pp. 179 -191
4. M. Cox, *Life and Death in Spitalfields: 1700-1850,* 1996, p. 62
5. George, p. 179; Morris, *Wapping,* p. 86
6. British Library OIOC E/3/105 East India Company Letter Book December 1731 p. 191,
7. Robins, *The Corporation that changed the World,* 2006, pp. 46-7, 63
8. British Library OIOC L/AG/1/6/11 *Commercial Journal,* July 1735 – June 1742; G. Green, Sir Charles Raymond, *Essex Journal,* 2008, vol. 43, no.1, pp. 38-43

9. K. N. Chaudhuri, *The Trading World of Asia and the English East India Company 1660-1760*, 1978, Chapter 15 Raw Silk, pp. 343-358, Appendix 5 Statistical Tables, Table C.18 Total imports of raw silk from Asia, 1664-1760
10. IOR L/AG/1/1/10. f.455, 1701
11. *Daily Post*, 16 January 1742
12. *General Advertiser*, 24 April 1751; *London Evening Post*, 24 September 1751
13. George, pp. 183-186; Schwarz, pp. 36-37
14. D. C. Coleman, *Courtaulds: an economic and social history*, vol. 1, 1969, pp. 11, 32
15. OLD BAILEY, t17650417-43 accessed 6 March 2011
16. TNA, PROB 31/450/226 Daniel Cook 1761, N. Rothstein, Canterbury and London: The silk industry in the late Seventeenth Century, *Textile History*, 1989, 1, vol. 20, 1, pp. 33-47
17. HAND, vol. 59, 23910
18. VCH, *Middlesex*, vol. XI, pp. 92-95
19. SUN, vol. 88, 119440
20. *Gazetteer and Daily Advertiser*, 14 March 1765
21. N. Rothstein, The successful and the unsuccessful Huguenot, another look at the London silk industry in the 18th and early 19th centuries, *Proc. of the Huguenot Society*, vol. XXV, 1989-1993, pp. 439-450, TNA PROB 11/826 Jonathan Fuller 1756
22. S. R. H. Jones, Technology, Transaction Costs, and the Transition to Factory Production in the British Silk Industry, 1700-1870, *Journal of Economic History*, vol. XLVII, no. 1 March 1987, pp. 71-96
23. George, p. 186
24. S. M. Hill, *Sherborne House and its People*, 1996, p. 47
25. Barnett, p. 57
26. S. Bryer, *Whitchurch Silk Mill, A brief guide*, 2009

Notes to Chapter 7   The Hay Market, Carts and Carriages

1. C. Davies, Whitechapel Haymarket, East London History Society *Bulletin*, no. 13, 1970
2. R. Perren, Markets and Marketing, *The agrarian history of England and Wales*, vol. 6, 1750-1850, ed. G. E. Mingay, 1989, p. 194
3. THLHL, Minutes of the Paving Commissioners for High Street, Whitechapel, 1778-1800; STE/241, DNB George Colebrooke accessed 7 May 2011 OBIN 101037301
4. P. Deane & W. A. Cole, *British Economic Growth, 1688-1959*, 1964, pp. 48, 65; R. Perren, Markets and Marketing, *The agrarian history of England and Wales*, vol. 6, 1750-1850, ed. G. E. Mingay, 1989, pp. 232, 234
5. G. E. Mingay, ed. *The agrarian history of England and Wales*, vol. 6, 1750-1850, 1989, Statistical Appendix, p. 1137
6. Personal communications Paul Poulton and Tony Saint
7. *Gazetteer and New Daily Advertiser*, 8 September 1778
8. H. H. Lamb, *Climate, present, past and future*, 1977, vol. 2 Climatic history and the future, Appendix V, Tables V. 10 and V. 33; *Whitehall Evening Post*, 22-24 January 1760; *St James Chronicle*, 25-28 July 1760; *Whitehall Evening Post*, 16-19 and 21-23 February 1760; *London Chronicle*, 16-19 and 23-26 February 1760; *Public Advertiser*, 1 August 1760; Lloyds Evening Post, 24-26 September 1760; VCH, *A History of Hertfordshire*, 1902, 1971, p. 40, ed. W. Pope, Climate by J. Hopkinson
9. J. Kington, *The Weather Journals of a Rutland Squire: Thomas Barker of Lyndon Hall*, 1980, pp. 19, 119
10. A. Young, *General View of the Agriculture of Hertfordshire*, 1804, 1971, pp. 86, 133
11. *London Gazette*, 15 March 1803
12. Western, pp. 386, 389
13. THLHL *Minutes of the Paving Commissioners for High Street, Whitechapel, 1778-1800*, STE/241
14. Act 36 Geo III, c 88
15. Hertfordshire Archives and Local Studies, D/EAS 4358, 4359, Mary Gingell and Son and Cruickshank vs. Abraham Wackett
16. D. Morris, Silver and Carriage Duties; 1757-1766, *Genealogists' Magazine*, vol. 30, no. 5, March 2011, pp. 147-151; TNA, T 47/2, T 47/3, Duties on Coaches and other Carriages; T 47/4, Duties on silver and carriages; T 47/6 Late duties, actual and suspected defaulters, 1757-1768; T 47/7 Late duties, actual and suspected defaulters, 1776
17. H. Adler, The Baal Shem of London, *Trans. of the Jewish Historical Society*, vol. 5, 1902-1905, pp. 148-173
18. D. Parry, *English Horse Drawn Vehicles*, 1979
19. Act of Parliament, 13 Geo. III c. 84
20. TNA PROB 11/1481, Allen Parsons 1808; TNA PROB 11/767, Joseph Auslow 1749

Notes to Chapter 8   The Theatres, Bagnios and Swimming Pools

1. http://www.wiltons.org.uk, re Wilton's Music Hall
2. George, p. 280, A. E. Wilson, *East End Entertainment*, 1954, p. 36
3. DNB Thomas Odell accessed 25 March 2011 OBIN 101020536
4. *Daily Post*, 18 October 1735
5. DNB Henry Fielding accessed 25 March 2011, OBIN 101009400
6. George, pp. 279-280
7. A. E. Wilson, *East End Entertainment*, 1954, p. 31
8. C. B. Hogan, The New Wells, Goodman's Fields, 1739-1752, *Theatre Notebook*, 3, 1949, pp. 67-72; S. Rosenfeld, Theatres in Goodman's Fields, *Theatre Notebook*, 1, 1946, pp. 48-50
9. DNB Edward Shepherd, accessed 21 May 2011 OBIN 101049341
10. A. Williamson, *General Williamson's Diary, 1722-1747*, Royal Hist. Soc., Camden Third Series, vol. XXII, 1912
11. *Daily Post*, 14 July 1732
12. DNB David Garrick accessed 7 May 201, OBIN 101010408
13. *Daily Courant*, 17 February 1725; *Daily Courant*, 5 January 1730, TNA PROB 11/832 Samuel Gower 1757
14. *General Advertiser*, 29 October 1745
15. George, p. 280
16. LMA, MJ/SP/1750/05/001, May 1750 *Report on New Wells Playhouse*
17. *General Advertiser*, 22 October 1752
18. George, p. 387
19. DNB William Charles Macready accessed 21 May 2011 OBIN 101017741
20. J. Chamberlayne, ed. *Magnæ Britanniæ notitia: or the present state of Great Britain,*, 1736-1745
21. HAND, vol. 29, 48606
22. Somerset Archive and Record Service, DD\HW/201727, Marriage settlement of William Collier and Ann Carpenter of Whitechapel

23. A. E. Clark-Kennedy, *The London Hospital* 1963, vol. 1, p. 44, London Hospital Archive; LH/S/2/17/1 London Hospital front block plan of proposed alteration, drawing no. 4, Rowland Plumbe, 1899
24. DNB John Andree accessed 29 January 2011 OBIN 101000514
25. R. Dingley Doyle, A Georgian Spa in Essex, *Country Life*, 23 October 1969; D. Gibbs, "Dr Andree, MD (Rheims), LRCP, founding physician of the London Hospital, *Journal of Medical Biography*, 2003, 11, pp. 87-94
26. SUN, vol. 84, 115692
27. An Act for confirming a Partition between John Leman, Esquire, and Elizabeth Newnham, and John Newnham, Esquire, of several Estates in the City of London and Counties of Middlesex and Huntingdon. 1756
28. LMA, Middlesex Sessions Papers – Justices' Working Documents, 16 October 1750, *London Lives, 1690-1800* (www.londonlives.org), LMS, MPS 504090049
29. TNA PROB 11/951 Richard Johnson 1769
30. Dr. Southwood Smith, *Reports on the sanitary state of the labouring classes ...in and about the metropolis* London, 1839, p. 42
31. *The Daily Advertiser*, 4 June 1777
32. J. Black, *Eighteenth-Century Britain, 1688-1783*, 2008, p. 149

Notes to Chapter 9   Literacy and Education

1. *The Oracle*, 11 May 1791; SUN, vol. 367, 566810; P. Gauci, *Emporium of the World: The Merchants of London 1660-1800*, 2007, pp. 99-100
2. Morris, *MEOT*, p. 81; Morris, *Wapping*, p. 85
3. P. Earle, *A City Full of People: Men and Women in London, 1650-1750*, 1994, pp. 35-38
4. TNA PROB 11/932 David Fenning 1767; DNB David Fenning accessed 20 February 2011 OBIN 101069580
5. TNA PROB 3/23/4 Samuel Perry 1724; TNA PROB 11/1017 Richard Murrell 1776; TNA PROB 11/1030, John Samuel Thompson 1777
6. TNA PROB 11/975 William Rogers 1772, TNA PROB 11/821 David Lopez Pereira 1756
7. Barnett, p. 172
8. *General Advertiser*, 29 April 1746
9. http://www.bl.uk/eresources/dbstptitles/eresourcesb.htm
10. H. M. Jewell, *Education in Early Modern England*, 1998 p. 194, P. Earle, *The Making of the English Middle Class,* 1989, p. 65
11. TNA PROB 11/892 Abraham Atkinson 1763; TNA PROB 11/946 John Campbell 1769
12. DNB Michael Maittaire accessed 10 May 2011 OBIN 101017841
13. C. Kerrigan, *A History of Tower Hamlets,* 1982, p. 56
14. LMA, Ms 12818, *Christ's Hospital School, Children's Register*
15. R. G. Gardiner, *The Admission Registers of St Paul's School from 1748 to 1876*, 1884
16. W. T. T. Gunn, *The Harrow School Register, 1571-1800*, 1934
17. DNB Thomas Paine accessed 7 May 2011 OBIN 101021133
18. *Public Advertiser*, 15 August 1754
19. http://www.innertemple.org.uk/archive, accessed 10 February 2011
20. H. A. C. Sturgess, ed. *Register of Admissions to the Honourable Society of the Middle Temple, From the Fifteenth Century to 1975*, 1975
21. DNB Thomas Dyche accessed 6 April 2011 OBIN 101008345
22. DNB Andrew Bell, accessed 10 February 2011 OBIN 101001995; DNB Joseph Lancaster accessed 6 April 2011 OBIN 1010515963
23. G. Jefcoate, German Printing and Bookselling in Eighteenth Century London: Evidence and Interpretation, *Archiv für Geschichte des Buchwesens*, Band 57, 2003
24. L. Davidoff, The family in Britain, *The Cambridge Social History of Britain, 1750-1950*, vol. 2, People and Their Environment, ed. F. M. L. Thompson, 1990, pp. 86-88
25. Guildhall, GL Ms 5266, vol. 5, Apprentice Bindings, John Pointer, 1754 Barber-Surgeons' Company
26. D. F. McKenzie, *Stationers' Company Apprentices, 1701-1800*, 1978
27. P. Gauci, *Emporium of the World: The Merchants of London 1660*-1800, 2007, p. 114
28. DNB John Horsford accessed 6 March 2011 OBIN 101013817
29. DNB John Constable accessed 7 May 2011 OBIN 101006107; DNB Benjamin Kenton accessed 7 May 2011 OBIN 101015428

Notes to Chapter 10   Churches, Chapels and Charity

1. A. Rottmann, *London Catholic Churches*, 1926;, VCH, *Middlesex*, vol. XI, pp. 70-86; Morris, *MEOT*, pp. 67, 68, 72; H. Deike, *A Short History of the German Evangelical Reformed St Paul's Church*, 1907, LMA P54.9 DEI, TNA PROB 11/1509 Andrew Knies 1810
2. THLHL, TH 8383, *The Diary of Elijah Goff, Coal Merchant 1788-1796*
3. B. Watson, The Burial Grounds of Backchurch Lane, Whitechapel, *East London Record*, 17, 1994-1995
4. VCH, *Middlesex*, vol. XI, pp. 81-83; DNB Matthew Mead accessed 7 May 2011 OBIN 101018466
5. THLHL TH W/LAS, Little Alie Street Baptist Church Registers
6. Morris, *MEOT,* pp. 67, 68
7. DNB Henry Mayo accessed 7 May 2011 OBIN 101018456; H. M. Gunn, *The Family Memorials*, 1900, the life of the Reverend Henry Mayo.
8. W. T. Whitley, *The Baptists of London: 1612-1924*, 1928, pp. 103, 295; DNB John Bunyan accessed 7 May 2011 OBIN 101003949
9. http://en.wikipedia.org/wiki/Strict_Baptists accessed 30 January 2011
10. LMA, CLC/525/Ms06016, St George-in-the-East land tax; TNA PROB 11/879, David Jennings 1762
11. A. W. Light, *Bunhill*, 1915, 1933
12. TNA PROB 11/1294, Stephen Williams 1797
13. Personal communications from Alison Botterill, Fiona Duxbury and David Woodruff
14. Stow, II, p. 72
15. P. Guillery, Suburban Models, or Calvinism and Continuity in London's Seventeenth century Church Architecture, *Architectural History*, vol. 48, 2005, pp. 69-106; Guillery, p. 163; Malcolm, vol. 4, pp. 446-447
16. N. Rogers, Popular protest in early Hanovarian London, *Past and Present*, 1978, 79, pp. 70-100; N. Rogers, Popular